Elusive Alliance

ELUSIVE ALLIANCE

The German Occupation of Poland in World War I

JESSE KAUFFMAN

Harvard University Press

Cambridge, Massachusetts
London, England
2015

First printing

Library of Congress Cataloging-in-Publication Data

Kauffman, Jesse, 1974–
Elusive alliance : the German occupation of Poland in World War I /
Jesse Kauffman.
pages   cm
Includes bibliographical references and index.
ISBN 978-0-674-28601-6 (alk. paper)
1. Poland—History—German occupation, 1914–1918.
2. World War, 1914–1918—Poland.   I. Title.
DK4390.K38   2015
940.3'438—dc23   2014049891

For Lena

Contents

Occupied central Europe, 1915–1917

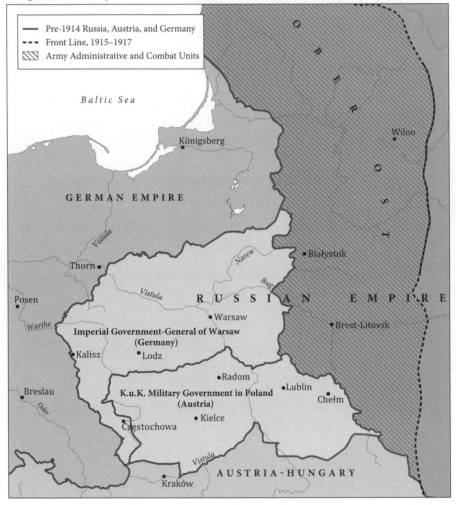

Legend:
— Pre-1914 Russia, Austria, and Germany
--- Front Line, 1915–1917
▨ Army Administrative and Combat Units

Baltic Sea

O B E R O S T

Königsberg

Wilno

GERMAN EMPIRE

Vistula

Thorn

Narew

Białystok

Bug

Posen

Vistula

R U S S I A N   E M P I R E

Warthe

Warsaw

Imperial Government-General of Warsaw (Germany)

Brest-Litovsk

Kalisz

Lodz

Breslau

Radom

Lublin

Oder

K.u.K. Military Government in Poland (Austria)

Chełm

Częstochowa

Kielce

Vistula

AUSTRIA-HUNGARY

Kraków

Ethnolinguistic distribution of Polish populations in central Europe, c. 1900

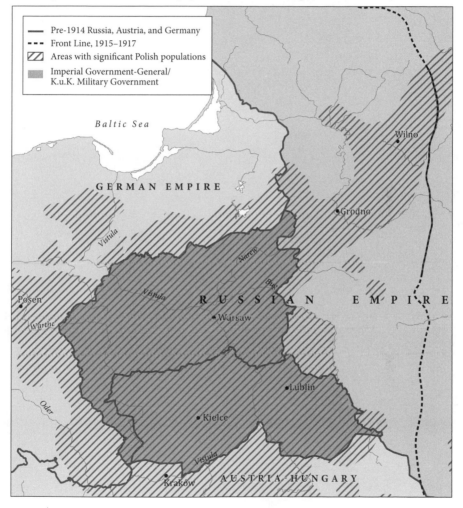

Legend:
— Pre-1914 Russia, Austria, and Germany
- - - Front Line, 1915–1917
▨ Areas with significant Polish populations
▨ Imperial Government-General/
K.u.K. Military Government

Baltic Sea

GERMAN EMPIRE

RUSSIAN EMPIRE

AUSTRIA-HUNGARY

Vistula
Narew
Bug
Oder
Warthe

Posen
Warsaw
Wilno
Grodno
Lublin
Kielce
Kraków

The peace of Europe rests on a poorly sealed tomb—the tomb of Poland.

—JEAN HERBETTE, *L' Echo de Paris*, 16 August 1914

Introduction

The Unknown War and Its Forgotten Occupation

German troops entered Warsaw for the first time in the twentieth century on 5 August 1915, near the end of a series of offensives that Austro-German forces had launched across the entire eastern front that spring. "I eyed them with curiosity," wrote one Varsovian, a thirty-six-year-old economist named Mieczysław Jankowski, "with their green-gray uniforms and their . . . 'pickelhaub' helmets." The German soldiers were "neatly dressed and well-equipped," Jankowski noted, "and their gear, despite the lengthy fighting, [was] in impeccable order."[1] The troops' long fight was not over yet. German soldiers continued their drive eastward, and by the following month, when the attacks finally ground to a halt, the Central Powers had succeeded in driving the armies of Tsar Nicholas II completely out of central Europe. The front now extended from the Baltic coast just west of Riga, south around Pinsk, in the Pripet Marshes east of Brest-Litovsk, all the way down to the Habsburg city of Czernowitz in the foothills of the Carpathian mountains.

The victors were immediately faced with the problem of securing their conquests and filling the administrative void left in the wake of the retreating Russian armies, who, in addition to destroying bridges, deporting civilians, and setting fires as they fled, had also taken the resources of the Russian state with them. In the north and east, in what is today Lithuania, Latvia, and Byelorussia, the newly conquered territory was placed under the control of the German army's eastern command. It came to be known as OberOst, a name derived from the title Oberbefehlshaber Ost, or Supreme Commander in the East, who was the territory's highest authority. In the south, in what had been part of Russia's Polish territories, the Austrians created the Military Government-General, with its administrative center in Lublin.[2] Between them, comprising the remainder of Russian Poland, the Germans established the Imperial Government-General of Warsaw, a sprawling occupation regime staffed by bureaucrats and military officers and presided over by a career army officer named Hans Hartwig von Beseler. The regime was to endure until the end of the war more than three years later.

What did the Germans do while in control of this fractious, restive, and strategically crucial territory at the center of Europe? Did the Government-General's leaders harbor any long-term plans for the Polish lands that had passed under their rule? Did these plans find concrete institutional expression of any kind? To what degree were the politics of the Government-General linked with domestic politics in Prussia, where an ugly and heated Polish-German nationality conflict simmered? How did native tensions and conflicts shape the course of the occupation? What can the occupation government's actions tell us about Germany during the Great War, and about the Great War in general? What can the conduct of the Imperial Government-General tell us about the continuities of German history? These questions have been given surprisingly little attention by historians. The standard work on the German occupation of Poland during the Great War remains German historian Werner Conze's *Polnische Nation und deutsche Politik im Ersten Weltkrieg* (The Polish Nation and German Policy in the First World War), published more than fifty years ago.[3] There are some signs of change: in recent years, a handful of Polish and German scholars have turned their attention to this neglected episode in the history of the Great War.[4] Among French, British, and American scholars, however, it generally remains—as one German historian has called it—a "forgotten occupation."[5]

Whatever the reasons for this, it is at least in part rooted in a much broader and long-standing neglect of the Great War's eastern theater. For nearly a century, the western front has exercised a powerful allure on the imaginations of scholars and the general public alike. The images most readily associated with the First World War—the horrific, bloody stalemate of the trenches, the slaughter of infantrymen charging into machine guns, the first clashes of fighter aces above the battlefield, the disillusionment and despair of the young innocents caught up in the maelstrom—were primarily generated by the war in the west (and the superb poets and novelists who fought there). Likewise, the scholarly conversation about the Great War has long centered on the western front, even as research agendas have shifted from the analysis of high politics and military operations to questions rooted in the methodologies of cultural and social history.[6] As Vejas Liulevicius has noted, the title of Winston Churchill's book on the eastern front, *The Unknown War,* was as apt in the year 2000 as it was in 1931, the year of its publication.[7] Thus the fact that a German military regime spent more than three years of the war ruling in Poland—an area that seethed with political and social tensions; that linked Germany, Austria, and Russia together in complex ways; that was inhabited by a people whose co-nationals in the Reich were engaged in a bitter struggle with the state over assimilation; that, because of this, posed peculiar political problems for Germany; and that, a little over twenty years later, would be brutalized by the Nazis in a horrific campaign of enslavement and murder—has somehow fallen through the historical cracks. This book aims to remedy this by exploring this regime and its policies, an exploration that pays rich analytical dividends for our understanding of many key questions in the fields of German, Polish, and Jewish history, as well as, more broadly, the history of the Great War, of empires and nationalism, and of central Europe in the tumultuous first half of the twentieth century.

The Germans arrived in Poland in 1915 having given little thought to what they might do with these territories should the course of the war bring them under their control. This failure of strategic imagination, however, was remedied by the intelligent and ambitious German officer who ruled occupied Poland as Governor-General, Hans Hartwig von Beseler. Over the course of his tenure in Poland, General Beseler became convinced that it was in Germany's interests to sponsor (and thus control) the restoration of a Polish state in central Europe. The satellite state that Beseler had in mind was to be a constitutional monarchy, subordinate to Germany in matters of foreign and military policy but autonomous in matters of culture and domestic politics. Over the course of the occupation, this ambition became translated into a set of institutions intended to realize this project of what would today be called "nation building." A Polish university was reestablished in Warsaw, decades after the Russians had transformed the erstwhile Polish capital's main institution of higher learning into an outpost of the Russian state and Russian culture; public elementary schools taught their students about Polish history and literature in the Polish language, celebrated the great events and personalities of the heroic version of Polish history, and staged plays by patriotic Polish writers, all forbidden under the Tsar; a nascent central state was created, along with an embryonic army; and cities were administered by elected city councils, a practice introduced by the German occupiers. These institutions evolved over the course of time. They were frequently created to serve some short-term goal, such as garnering the Germans good publicity abroad, or shifting some of the administrative burden of occupation to the locals. As Beseler's vision of Poland's place in the postwar political order crystallized, however, these institutions became the centerpieces of the German state-building enterprise in Poland. In general, they were to serve two purposes. One was the training—the "education" *(Erziehung)*, as Beseler liked to put it—of the Congress Kingdom's Poles in the practice of self-government. The other was the creation of an institutional foundation during the war for the state that would be built on it afterward.

This project ultimately failed, for reasons that will be analyzed throughout this book. Nonetheless, an examination of this occupation—of its ideologies and institutions, its interactions with the natives, and its relationship between the nature of the ends sought by the Germans and the means employed to achieve them—enriches and complicates the view of several key historical questions. Perhaps foremost among them is the degree of continuity between Nazi Germany and previous eras of German history.

Special Paths, Drives to the East, and Colonial Turns

The Great War has long played a central role in reinforcing and supporting the idea that German history was locked into a *Sonderweg*—a "special path"— leading inexorably to ruin and murder. This is due in part to the long shadow cast by Fritz Fischer's enormously influential 1961 work, *Griff nach der Weltmacht: Die Kriegszielpolitik des kaiserlichen Deutschland, 1914–18* (which appeared in English as *Germany's Aims in the First World War*).[8] In it, Fischer argues that Germany—motivated primarily by domestic political concerns— bore the bulk of the responsibility for launching the conflict, which it hoped to use to conquer and annex large amounts of territory. Fischer was not the first historian to document that such "expansionist" war aims existed within

Germany. What was unique, however, was the sweeping nature of Fischer's indictment. Drawing on an overwhelming amount of archival material, Fischer argued that no segment of imperial society had been immune to the lure of conquest. Organizations and individuals of virtually every political stripe, representing the whole of the Wilhelmine world, were tainted by annexationism. One of Fischer's chief targets was Chancellor Bethmann Hollweg, posited by some historians, such as Gerhard Ritter, as a moderate, but accused by Fischer of eager, greedy collusion in this imperial project.[9] Drawing Bethmann into the (supposed) German struggle to establish itself as a world imperial power made Fischer's argument one that was about much more than the First World War: Bethmann Hollweg now took his place firmly in the bleak pantheon of greedy German conquerors, a pantheon that included Bismarck and, of course, Hitler. By thus seamlessly joining the Second World War with the First, and Imperial Germany with Nazi Germany, *Griff nach der Weltmacht* played a major role in establishing the idea of a *Sonderweg* as the driving force in German history, and of the two wars as nearly indistinguishable variations on a shared theme.[10] Fischer's view that the Germans deliberately schemed and plotted to launch the war is no longer widely shared, but the ideas at the heart of his argument—that Germany was responsible for the war, that Germany lusted after colonial-style annexations within Europe, and that the First World War is best understood as a kind of restrained rehearsal for the Second—have assumed the status of consensus.[11]

This enduring influence is due, in part, to the powerful and understandable resonance given to these arguments by the Second World War. However, it is also due to the numerous works published by Fischer's students and intellectual heirs in support of his thesis. Of these, by far the most important, particularly with regard to Germany's putative ambitions in the east, has been his pupil Imanuel Geiss's *Der polnische Grenzstreifen, 1914–1918* (The Polish Border Strip, 1914–1918).[12] In it, Geiss documents various plans made in Germany during the war—implicating, as Fischer does, both military commanders and civilian elites—to annex a stretch of frontier territory between Germany and what was, at the time of the war, Russia's Polish lands. In many of these visions, this border strip was to be Germanized by moving out its Polish and Jewish inhabitants and moving German settlers in. Both the loss of the war and the enduring cultural restraints of the period prevented the plan from being realized. Yet the very existence of the *idea* of the Germanized border strip constitutes, for Geiss, an important chapter in the "prehistory of National Socialism," a prehistory that would find its fulfillment only a short time later in the brutal Nazi occupation of Poland.[13] Like Fischer's, Geiss's arguments have, over the decades, taken on the quality of a truth universally acknowledged, and his work has played its own crucially important role in linking together Nazi and Imperial Germany.[14]

Geiss's arguments, in addition to reflecting an enduringly influential interpretation of Germany in the First World War, are also representative of another master narrative of German history that sometimes intersects with, and sometimes runs parallel to, the Sonderweg vision of a Germany propelled by internal pathologies toward its inevitable destiny of National Socialist barbarism. The eastern-focused variant of this metanarrative posits long-festering cultural or institutional hostility in Germany toward eastern Europe that finally found its fullest expression under the Nazis.[15] An early variant of this argument—that eastern Europe was the victim of a centuries-old German "Drive to the East" (Drang nach Osten) that was brought to murderous fulfillment under Hitler—has been exposed as the work of febrile propagandists and discredited.[16] More recent work on the German–eastern European relationship has tended to focus on subtle cultural factors such as ideologies and mentalities.[17] A related strand of argumentation has posited that Germany's relationship with eastern Europe, and especially the horrors visited upon it by the Nazis, can be explained with recourse to the broader history of European colonialism. In this reading, generally known as the "colonial turn," the lands of the east played the role for Germany that places such as India or the Congo did for other European nations, though, in keeping with the trend toward the history of mentalities and ideologies, the emphasis is on the way the Germans thought about the east.[18] Finally, a third variant of the historical literature on Germany and the east has focused primarily on Prussia's eastern provinces and the state's bitter demographic and cultural conflict with the significant Polish minority living there. Here too methodologies and research agendas have changed over the decades, but the general emphasis of the scholarship has tended to fall on the antagonism and festering hatreds brewing in places like Posen and West Prussia that, in this reading, ultimately fed like a toxic stream into the larger torrent of Nazi Germany's brutality.[19]

Occupations and the Great War in European History

The idea of festering eastern-focused pathologies linking Wilhelmine and Nazi Germany has been reinforced by recent work on German occupations during the Great War. Long a topic neglected by historians (in marked contrast to the occupations of the Second World War), these occupations are beginning to emerge as an area of interest to scholars.[20] While most scholarly attention has focused on the west, arguably the most influential book about occupations during the Great War has been Vejas Liulevicius's *War Land on the Eastern Front: Culture, National Identity and German Occupation in World War I,* a study of the institutions and policies of Erich Ludendorff and the OberOst regime.[21] While Liulevicius detects in the occupation government's policies and its treatment of the civilians under its control the first stirrings of the Nazi occupation of eastern Europe, this is not the book's main concern. Liulevicius's real focus is on what can broadly be termed the Germans' "perceptions" of the territory they were occupying and the way this perception ultimately resulted in the horrors of the Second World War. Out of the way the soldiers formed opinions about and tried to make sense of the unfamiliar world around them, Liulevicius argues, emerged a virulently pathological German view of "the east." "Viewing dirty, chaotic lands of war," he writes, "produced a volatile and explosive mixture of associations in those who looked" at them. "Desire for possession contended with revulsion, a tension expressing itself in urges for violent transformation and cleaning."[22] Like the *Grenzstreifen,* this vision merely needed a short incubation period back in Germany before it was forcibly transported back across the frontier to wreak murderous havoc in the east. Owing in part to the influence of Liulevicius's pathbreaking book, scholarship on occupations during the Great War is beginning to show tentative signs of a shift in interest toward the east, and several new works have appeared on eastern occupations to complement *War Land.* The most important of these, by Christian Westerhoff, divides its attention between OberOst and the Imperial Government-General and is narrowly concerned with the role of forced labor in these occupations. Westerhoff is more conflicted about how closely linked the occupations of the First and Second World Wars are, and he does not fail to note the differences between the two. Like Liulevicius, however, he sees latently poisonous forces at work, and he judges the First World War to be important mainly in terms of how it helped facilitate, even if in some subtle way, the brutality of the Nazis.[23]

Studies of Germany's western occupations have likewise helped create the sense of a seamless segue between the First World War and the Second. The most important book of these works has been John Horne and Alan Kramer's *German Atrocities 1914: A History of Denial*.[24] Horne and Kramer conclusively establish that atrocities—including the widespread shooting of civilians—did indeed occur during the initial western invasions of 1914 and were often sanctioned by German commanders. While the continuities of German history are not, perhaps, their main concern—and while Horne and Kramer's book is properly seen as a study of an invasion rather than an occupation—*German Atrocities* has done much to cement the connection between the two world wars and the two occupations.[25] While not ruling out factors such as fear and confusion when analyzing and explaining the events they so thoroughly document, the authors locate their ultimate cause in certain peculiarities of German military culture, including a deep hatred of irregular warfare and a dismissive contempt for generally accepted laws and customs of war. This too, they argue, would find full expression in the Nazi occupation of Europe, as reflected in the way that the National Socialists treated both civilians under their rule as well as irregular resistance fighters. Other works on the western occupations have tended in the same direction, a trend made clear in their titles, of which *Rehearsals* and *The Red Scars* are two noteworthy examples.[26]

Poland's Forgotten Great War

In marked contrast to the clear role played by the Great War in German history and historiography, as well as the enduring hold the war has on both scholars and the public alike in France, Germany, and Britain, the war's place in Polish history and memory has long been far more complex and ambiguous. Polish interest in the war was lively in the years immediately after it ended, for the obvious reason that it had resulted in the reestablishment of a Polish state. However, much of the history written in this period was highly politicized and polemical in nature, and continued, by other means, the competition for influence waged by the two major Polish political figures of the period, Józef Piłsudski and Roman Dmowski. The longtime rivals had each played a prominent and highly visible role in the struggle to return a Polish state to the map of Europe, so partisans of each filled journals, newspapers, and bookshelves with arguments meant to demonstrate that "their" political leader deserved most of the credit for Poland's liberation. Interest in the First World War, however, evaporated after the unparalleled catastrophe and trauma of the Second. The Great War was virtually obliterated from scholarly and popular attention, with very little written about it in the decades after 1945. The work that was done, meanwhile, was subjected to the political and ideological constraints of Communism. The reestablishment of Polish statehood continued to be a main theme of Communist-era Polish histories of the Great War, but in the Marxist reading it was the revolutions in Austria, Germany, and—above all—Russia that undermined the imperialist powers and led to Polish independence. Much of this work thus focuses on the wartime activities of obscure and marginal socialist political movements and activists, who thereby became improbable pioneers in the struggle for Polish independence.[27] German concessions made during the war are dismissed in these works as a sham meant only to secure German control over Poland, which was to serve "as an area of . . . exploitation, a source of labor and cannon fodder, [and] a deployment point and defensive barrier against Russia," all serving the "economic, military, and political motives, interests, and aims of German imperialism in central and eastern Europe."[28] The fall of Communism did not lead to renewed Polish interest in the Great War, though several Polish historians have recently written excellent books that may signal a new era of scholarly engagement with it.[29] The war's centenary may also generate a wave of popular interest. Still, in Poland the Great War remains thoroughly overshadowed by the Second World War, as well as inextricably linked with the establishment of Polish independence, which lends it a positive quality that it has long since ceased to have in any of the major belligerent countries.[30]

This book engages in a renewed exploration of this "forgotten" war and occupation in Poland, offering a broad view of the complex interactions between Polish society and the institutions and forces called into being by the war, as well as a renewed evaluation of its place in modern Polish history. At the same time, it mounts a challenge to many of the established arguments and interpretations concerning Germany and the currents of latent National Socialist brutality that supposedly course through its history. To begin with, the Imperial German occupation of Poland was in no way comparable with the grotesque barbarity of the Nazis. It is certainly true that the occupied population suffered numerous and serious hardships under the Germans during the First World War. However, these were primarily economic in nature; the wanton, unrestrained, and chaotic violence and murder that were the essence of the experience of occupation in Poland during the Second World War were largely absent during the First. The differences, however, run deeper than this. The two occupations were fundamentally different in both the political ends they wanted to achieve and the means employed to achieve them. Imperial Germany wanted to create a client state based, to some degree, on the consent of the clients. Toward this end the occupiers liberalized many of the harsher restrictions on Polish cultural and political life that had been enforced by the Russians; although the Germans did not hesitate to assert their authority when challenged or threatened, and while they did much that alienated and angered the occupied population, they always remained conscious of the fact that their political ambitions would come to naught if their authority rested on force alone. The result was that, at its heart, Germany's occupation during the Great War was marked by a constant attempt to recalibrate the balance between consent and coercion. To act too harshly would mean to stir up hatreds that could potentially endure; to act too leniently could threaten the stability of the regime and possibly the German war effort. In contrast, the Nazis had no such worries. In their vision, Poland was to become a kind of slave colony, its subhuman Slavic inhabitants slated for cultural—and, maybe, physical—annihilation. Polish political life under the Nazis was completely extinguished, and those who could be expected to keep the hope of its return alive were murdered or imprisoned. Cultural life suffered a similar fate, with transgressions punishable by death. Warsaw University and its fate is emblematic of the difference between the two occupations and the two political imaginations that guided them: in the First World War, the Germans established and supported the school. In the Second World War, the Nazis closed it, threatening with imprisonment and murder anyone who dared try to circumvent their restrictions on Polish education. Some of the professors who had gotten their faculty jobs during the first German occupation died in Nazi camps.

The relatively accommodating attitude adopted by the Imperial Government-General also calls into question the degree to which the nationality conflict in Prussia's Polish territories provided the ideological fuel for the brutality of the Nazis. If, by 1914, the Polish-Prussian relationship was so poisoned that it hovered on the very brink of genocide, why did the pressures of war and the erosion of restraints that such pressures bring not lead to greater violence in occupied Poland? Without denying that the conflicts of the late nineteenth century played a role in shaping Nazi hostility to Poland, this book argues that much of Nazi Germany's hatred of Poland was generated by the First World War and its aftermath—not only by the loss of territory to the new Polish state but also by the fact that Germany's occupation army in Poland mutinied and handed its weapons over to the Poles.[31] Wars, it was been pointed out, generate hate-filled "war cultures" that must be demobilized as surely as armies.[32] The hatreds generated by wartime and postwar events in Poland were never demobilized in Germany, with fateful consequences.

The Search for Order in Central Europe, 1905–1947

In addition to offering an expanded explanation for the sources of National Socialist barbarism in Poland, this book offers several new arguments about how the German occupation in Poland should be interpreted. Two key ideas are at the heart of these arguments: one is that the occupation must be situated within the context of the political and social tensions and upheavals that roiled central Europe in the first half of the twentieth century; the other is that the occupation occurred in a peculiar twilight period—a period that was neither wartime nor peacetime—in which the sense that the old order had been irrevocably destroyed was pervasive, but profound uncertainty existed about what should replace it.[33]

A number of prominent scholars have recently begun to suggest that the First World War must be placed within a history of early twentieth-century violence and instability that is both chronologically and geographically expansive. John Horne, for example, suggests embedding the war in a narrative that begins with the First Balkan War in 1912 and ends in 1923, with events such as the turn to "Socialism in One Country" in Russia and the conclusion of the Turkish War of Independence.[34] For making sense of Germany's occupation of Poland, this book suggests an even broader chronological and geographical context. Chronologically, the necessary starting point is the Russian Revolution of 1905. That upheaval unleashed a startling amount of violence in Russia's border territories, including places, such as the Baltic lands and Poland, that the Germans would occupy ten years later.[35] The stability created at the end of the revolution was deceptive and better thought of as a temporary suspension of hostilities; central Europe continued to seethe with latent conflicts involving social, national, and religious tensions that frequently overlapped in complex ways. (When, for example, a Bolshevik Latvian peasant in 1905 murdered his noble German landlord, was that an expression of nationalist hatreds, social resentments, or revolutionary fervor? This dismal question is difficult, if not impossible, to answer, but it lies at the heart of much of the tragic history of Europe's "bloodlands."[36]) Anti-Semites; socialists (reform-minded moderates as well as militant revolutionaries); nationalists advancing claims on behalf of real or imagined Polish, Ukrainian, German, Russian, Byelorussian, Latvian, and Estonian nations (claims that were not only irreconcilable with each other but also frequently with competing visions within the same nationalist movements); Zionists of a bewildering variety; Orthodox and Catholic (Roman and Greek) Christians; dissatisfied and militant industrial workers; peasant political activists—all of these groups and more harbored visions of how the political and social order in central Europe could be rearranged. Existing alongside them, of course, were conservative loyalists who hoped to maintain the status quo, or at least a recognizable version of it. These tensions, which had burst to the surface in 1905, were given free rein, and in many ways accelerated, when the Great War destroyed the central European political order. Examining the way that the Germans' institutions of occupation interacted with these wholly native tensions and ambitions illustrates the degree to which the course of the occupation must be understood within the broader context of not only German but central European history. The occupation, this book argues, marks a crucially important chapter in a story that, after beginning in 1905, finds a temporary, deceptive stability in 1921, with the signing of the Peace of Riga, and ultimately ends with the expulsions and forcible settling of borders in 1947. This was the long twilight of centuries of imperial rule in the region, when internal and external forces caused the collapse of the reigning powers, and various ideologies and political movements offered their own visions of what should replace them. Illustrating the role played by these native actors in shaping the course of the occupation also serves as a corrective to a German-centered approach to this epoch in the history of the region. As Tara Zahra has astutely noted, scholarship on the Germans in central Europe tends to unwittingly replicate aspects of German nationalist thinking about the east: by casting the inhabitants of central Europe as passive victims of the Germans (or as figments of the German ideological imagination), the argument is implicitly made that the only people who really mattered in the region were, in the final analysis, the Germans.[37]

This book also argues that Germany's state-building project in Poland occurred at a peculiar moment in the history of the war in the east. Michael Geyer, writing about Germany between the armistice of November 1918 and the signing of the Treaty of Versailles the following year, characterizes this time as falling somewhere "between war and postwar."[38] This perfectly captures the odd quality of the years from 1915 to 1918 in occupied Poland. Of course, the war was still raging on many fronts, but the fighting on the territory of the Government-General was mostly over by August 1915. (There is a surreal quality to the fact that the Germans in Poland were holding contentious discussions with teachers over the language to be used in schools, for example, or discussing the complexities of Polish politics with local elites and notables in the elegant halls of Warsaw's Royal Castle, while the raging battles elsewhere on the eastern, Italian, and western fronts consumed hundreds of thousands of lives.) This helps explain an important quality of the Germans' project in Poland. While certain of the Germans' policies, especially the economic ones, were intended to help the German war effort, much of their effort and the most important of the institutions they created were meant to contribute to the political shape of central Europe *after* the war. The Germans' policies were not merely aimed at winning the war; they were also part of a conscious program of postwar reconstruction, and thus meant to win the peace as well.[39] These competing pressures led German policy in two very different and antagonistic directions. The impossibility of harmonizing them was one of the most important reasons why the alliance the Germans sought with Poland was destined to remain elusive.

Geyer further notes that this liminal period was characterized by a distinct and widespread sense that the old order was gone forever, destroyed beyond repair on the battlefields and in the trenches of the war. Yet the question of what might replace it was wide open; the old certainties had vanished in clouds of artillery smoke and poison gas, but new norms and values to replace them had not yet crystallized into a shared vision of the postwar world.[40] Crucially, this includes the acceptance of the sovereign nation-state, whose emergence from the political wreckage of the war as the fundamental organizational unit of both domestic and foreign politics has long been seen as a given. As Alfred Cobban pointed out decades ago, however, the division of Europe into sovereign nation-states after the war was a development largely unforeseen by most contemporary actors—even those, such as Woodrow Wilson, most closely identified with the triumph of national self-determination at the war's end.[41] This idea will be developed at length in this book's conclusion; for now, it is important to note that Germany's state-building project in Poland took place within this period of uncertainty and experimentation. Focusing on Germany's project as an attempt at postwar reconstruction, and situating it within a *global* cultural context of how the postwar world was imagined, reveal the Germans' occupation to be simply one of many ways in which contemporary actors sought to restore order and advance their own interests in the new, uncertain world. Dismissals (or condemnations) by historians of Germany's attempts to create a satellite state in Poland often conceal within them a tacit acceptance of the nation-state as an analytical (and moral) norm that is ahistorical; buffer zones, client states, federations, and various forms of imperial domination were all part of the way that the belligerent nations on all sides imagined the world after the war (not to mention the visions of radical transformation harbored by the Bolsheviks and Woodrow Wilson). Acknowledging this provides a far richer understanding of the international cultural and political context within which the Germans conducted their state-building experiment. It also provides a helpful starting point for transnational comparisons of Germany's so-called war aims (which were really postwar aims) with those of other states that does not degenerate into a sterile and fruitless exercise in comparative villainy and greed (though it is worth mentioning here that Germany's aims in Poland compare favorably in many ways to the shabby squabbling between Russia, France, and Britain over imperial spoils in the Near East—conducted while their soldiers died together by the tens of thousands in an ostensibly shared—and ostensibly noble—cause.[42])

Finally, wars and their conclusions do not mark neat historical caesurae; historical forces at work before a war are often accelerated, or changed in some other way, by the war itself, and then continue to influence events once the war has ended.[43] Seen broadly, this is true of the general upheavals of the region that began in 1905, as noted above. But the more specific historical phenomenon that intertwined with the war and the German occupation, and that would be utterly changed by the war, with profound consequences not only for central Europe but for the region as a whole, was the long-simmering "Polish Question."

The "Polish Question" from the Congress of Vienna to the Eve of the Great War

Central Europe had once been home to a formidable and geographically extensive Polish state, the Polish-Lithuanian Rzeczpospolita (Republic or Commonwealth).[44] In the course of the eighteenth century, the Rzeczpospolita was removed from the map of Europe by its neighbors in a series of annexations. If there was any hope of restoring Polish statehood to central Europe after that, however, it was definitively extinguished at the Congress of Vienna, where, as part of the victors' distribution of spoils, Austria, Russia, and Prussia once again divided up the territory of the vanished Rzeczpospolita among themselves. This was a fateful act with enormous consequences, not only for the inhabitants of the newly annexed Polish territories but for the partitioning powers as well.[45]

Throughout the nineteenth century, the policy of each partitioning power veered between relatively benign tolerance and harsh repression. The swing was most dramatic in Russia. After the Congress of Vienna, Tsar Alexander I had granted a remarkably liberal constitution to his Polish territories, officially called the Kingdom of Poland. In November 1830, however, a group of Polish elites staged an armed uprising in an attempt to win back Polish independence. Russian victory was followed by a crackdown on Polish liberties and restrictions on Polish cultural life. More extensive liberalization followed in the 1860s, under the leadership of the Tsar's administrator in

Poland, Aleksander Wielopolski. A conservative Polish aristocrat, Wielopolski believed that the loyalty of the Tsar's Polish subjects would be solidified, rather than endangered, by granting concessions to Polish wishes for a measure of cultural and political autonomy. More uncompromising Polish nationalists, however, took advantage of the resulting relaxation of Russia's tight control to organize another uprising, which began in January 1863.[46] Russian victory was once again followed by a wave of repression, this one much harsher than the last. Polish institutions were closed and some revolutionaries were executed, with thousands more marched to Siberia and other points east. Thus began a period of intense "Russification" in the erstwhile Polish Kingdom, whose name was discarded. In the "Vistula region" *(Privilinskij kraj)*, as the Kingdom was now called, Russian became the language of instruction in public schools, and public displays of Polish patriotism, such as the celebration of Polish national heroes, were strictly forbidden, among other measures meant to erase any Polish sense of particularity. This failed, and the "Congress Kingdom" was host to a variety of nationalist movements by the turn of the twentieth century. Once again, in 1905, Polish discontent (both national and, in this case, social) erupted into violence and revolution. Hoping to save his Polish territories, Nicholas II promised renewed concessions, though not much came of these. Thus Russia's Polish territories on the eve of the war festered with social and political grievances, grievances that were nurtured and inflamed by long historical (and lived) memories of oppression and thwarted ambitions.

In Austria, mutual hostility reigned in the decades after the Congress of Vienna, but later in the nineteenth century the Habsburgs granted Galicia (their share of the partitions) wide-ranging political and social autonomy. Galicia was politically dominated by its Polish nobles, while Polish culture flourished at the universities at Kraków and Lwów and among the educated Polish elites. The Habsburg attempt to found Polish loyalty on toleration seemed to have been a great success; the Habsburg partition was remarkably stable after a failed 1846 uprising of Polish nobles and their subsequent slaughter by peasants, and the Galician Polish elite were reliably loyal to the Emperor. Nonetheless, by the eve of the war trouble also stirred in this peaceable outpost of Polish Europe, as new political movements, such as National Democracy, challenged the traditional system of Galician loyalty, while rising nationalism and peasant discontent led to simmering tensions between

Ukrainians, Poles, and Jews. In 1908, Galician viceroy Andrzej Potocki was assassinated by a young Ukrainian nationalist, a symptom of the decay of the nineteenth-century order in the Austrian partition.

The history of the Poles in the Prussian partition is crucial to an understanding of how the Germans fared in occupied Poland, since their reputation (and the reputations of the other two powers) preceded them. For most of the nineteenth century, Prussia's Polish territories were relatively quiet, with Prussia spared the kinds of spectacular uprisings that periodically erupted across the frontier in Russian Poland. From the founding of the Reich to 1914, however, relations between the Prussian state and its Polish subjects were steadily poisoned by decades of Prussian hostility to the Poles, both official and unofficial. The Kulturkampf was responsible for initiating this steady decline of Prussian-Polish relations. Whether the Poles were a calculated target of the Kulturkampf is still a matter of some debate, but Bismarck's postunification assault on the Catholic Church was undeniably accompanied by a steady stream of anti-Polish measures, including new legal restrictions on Polish associations and educational institutions. In addition, the anti-Catholic heart of the Kulturkampf was bound to translate into policies that were viewed by the Poles as an attack on their nationality. The May Laws, for example, with their tightening of state control over the clergy, acquired an extra layer of significance in Prussia's Polish territories. If one of the Kulturkampf's aims was in fact the weakening of Polish national sentiment, it failed miserably. In the end, its net result was to spread, for the first time, a sense of collective grievance among Prussia's Poles that crossed ideological, social, and geographic boundaries.[47]

Prussia evidently failed to heed the lessons of the Kulturkampf's failure, as the state's official hostility to the Poles only increased in the following decade. Under the guidance of Kultusminister Gustav von Gossler, the state moved further to restrict Polish-language education in Prussian Poland while German schools in the east were marked for special state support. In addition, in 1886 Prussia passed the notorious Settlement Law, which created a special Colonization Commission charged with buying Polish land and resettling it with Germans. At about the same time, the conviction began to spread among some Germans that a desperate nationality struggle was brewing in Prussian Poland, a struggle the Germans were losing. Statistics suggested that the Polish population was increasing vis-à-vis the Germans there, provoking concerns that the provinces were in danger of being lost to a "Slavic flood."[48]

The Prussian state's assault on its Polish subjects eased somewhat under the chancellorship of Leo von Caprivi, but the very moderate concessions of his government gave rise to a new political organization that dedicated itself to the struggle for German supremacy in the east, the German Eastern Marches Association (Deutscher Ostmarkenverein), its official name as of 1899. Founded in 1894 by Adolf Hansemann, Hermann Kennemann, and Heinrich von Tiedemann, the society's members saw themselves as the frontline foot soldiers in the struggle against the "Polish Peril." Its members not only lobbied the Prussian state to maintain an aggressive anti-Polish stance in the east but they worked to spread concern about the "Polish Peril" among the German population beyond Prussia, which they thought insufficiently alarmed.[49] This helps explain why one of the society's most famous members, Max Weber, devoted most of his 1895 inauguration speech in Freiburg, far distant from the nationality struggle in the east, to dire warnings about the demographic gains being made by Prussia's Poles, whom he labeled an "inferior race."[50] The society's numbers were never particularly large, but the zeal with which they pursued their aims helped make "Hakatism" (after the founders' initials) synonymous with chauvinistic, anti-Polish German hostility.[51]

Caprivi's fall ended the "Era of Reconciliation" between the state and the Poles, and Prussia's hostile Polenpolitik reached its height in the years between his political demise and the outbreak of the Great War. Official antagonism toward Poles was readopted as state policy under Hohenlohe, but it was during the chancellorship of Bernhard von Bülow that Prussia's anti-Polish policies reached their crescendo. A war, Bülow had remarked in the 1880s, would provide Prussia with a most welcome chance "to expel *en masse* the Poles from our Polish territories." It is therefore not surprising that it was under his government that the state began to eradicate the last vestiges of Polish education in Prussian Poland by slowly but inexorably ending religious instruction in the language, precipitating a wave of Polish school strikes at the beginning of the twentieth century.[52] The year after the strikes ended, the Prussians passed the most egregiously oppressive piece of anti-Polish legislation in the state's history: the Expropriation Act. A reaction to the dismal failure of the Colonization Commission, the act empowered the Prussian state forcibly to confiscate Polish land. The passage of the act created an uproar both in Prussia and abroad, and gained Prussia little more than ill-will; it was applied only once, in 1912, against four Polish estates totaling around 1,700 hectares (the landlords thus deprived were paid for their property).[53] Given the spectacular failures of Germany's policies in Polish Prussia over the decades and the intensity of the hostility they had inflamed, it is difficult to see what could have led to a mutually acceptable resolution of the deadlock in which Germany and its Polish subjects found themselves by the time war broke out. When it did, some Polish newspapers rather obviously declared their sympathies for the Entente, with one journalist writing in October 1914 that "the heroic defense of Antwerp will remain for ever one of history's most beautiful pages, a testimony of the exceptional strength of a people . . . who also struggle with an overpowering opponent for their independence."[54]

The cluster of ideas, interests, and pressures that drove Polish policy in each partitioning power was different. There was, however, one aspect of each state's relations with its Polish minority that was the same; that was, moreover, unique to the Polish Question in this period; and that is absolutely essential for making sense of the vicissitudes of Polish history in the nineteenth and early twentieth centuries. Poland was a classic imperial "shatterzone" in the sense formulated by Eric Weitz—a place where foreign and domestic policy are deeply and inextricably intertwined.[55] Because the partitions resulted in each empire becoming home to a sizable Polish population, each power's domestic Polish policies were thereafter inextricably linked with its relations to the other two powers. This seems to have been realized clearly at the time only by the British representative at Vienna, Viscount Castlereagh, the most far-sighted and astute observer of the Polish Question at the Congress (it is surely no coincidence that he hailed from the ranks of the Anglo-Irish nobility). "I am convinced," Castlereagh wrote in January 1815,

> that the only hope of tranquility now in Poland . . . and especially of preserving to Austria and Prussia their portions of that Kingdom, is for the two latter states to adopt a Polish system of administration as a defense against the inroads of the [relatively accommodating] Russian policy.

Castlereagh's recommendation succinctly captures all that would become most vexing to the partitioning powers about the Polish Question, as it is a prescription for domestic policy that acknowledges its profound foreign political implications.[56] An all-Polish rising could have led to a violent catastrophe in central Europe, with a civil war and foreign wars blending into bewildering and unrestrained violence of the sort associated with the Wars of Religion. Conversely, hostilities between two or more of the powers could have led to the temptation to use the discontent of the other's Polish minority as a weapon by stirring up internal discontent while posing as the champion of Polish liberation. (Of course, this would lead to the necessity of recalibrating one's own Polish policies, a potentially dangerous course of action. Bismarck summed this up brilliantly: "Poland," he once remarked, "is a weapon which we shall seize against our wishes because we have nothing better available. It is like a hot iron which we shall use to defend ourselves."[57]) The temptation to instrumentalize Polish nationalism in the event of war was not limited to the partitioning empires alone. Any state that wished to could try to harness Polish discontent for its own foreign political purposes. Thus international tensions that involved Austria, Prussia, or Russia in any way tended to provoke renewed interest in the Polish Question by both Polish activists as well as other powers, such as France and Britain. (In 1831, Carl von Clausewitz had irritably noted that few of his countrymen seemed to appreciate that any increase in Polish power would *inevitably* mean a concomitant influence in French power vis-à-vis Germany.[58]) Napoleon III, for example, wanted to fight the Crimean War in part by supporting a Polish uprising against Russia. The British were not as enthusiastic, warning of unforeseen complications and the potential spread of uncontrollable civil and foreign wars throughout Europe—reinforcing the argument that the fault lines of the European state system ran through, and were perceived by contemporaries to run through, Poland.[59]

This intertwining of the foreign with the domestic in the Polish "shatter-zone" is key to understanding much of how and why the partitioning powers treated their Polish minorities as they did. The Polish policies of the empires can almost be read like a thermometer gauging the health of the European society of states in the late nineteenth century, with repression indicating normalcy, and stability and tolerance akin to a fever indicating serious ill health. To Bismarck, harsh policies against the Poles were important to the maintenance of peace in central Europe, particularly with Russia, and good German-Russian relations meant repression in Prussian Poland.[60] The Caprivi government's inauguration of the "Era of Reconciliation," however, was conversely due in part to the lapse of the Reinsurance Treaty and the renewed possibility of war with Russia.[61] "Our concession of a few hours a week of Polish instruction in the schools," Caprivi told the cabinet in 1893, "is a price worth paying to hold [the Poles] on our side."[62] Likewise symptomatic of rising international tensions was the 1914 request of Nicholas II's foreign minister, Sergei Sazonov, to reconsider Russia's harsh policies toward its Polish territories. Convinced that war was approaching, Sazonov thought that Russia's enemies would have little trouble rallying the Poles against the Tsarist empire. It was in Russia's best interests, he argued (fruitlessly), to reverse the tables and take the lead in winning Polish loyalty.[63] Austrian Galicia, meanwhile, proved to be a tolerant and congenial host in the years before the First World War to a flourishing and lively array of armed anti-Russian Polish nationalist groups. These included legally sanctioned organizations like the Riflemen's Associations (Związki Strzeleckie) as well as the Union of Active Struggle (Związek Walki Czynnej). The Union was an organization of murky official status that was founded to coordinate the organization and training of Polish fighters in Galicia. Eventually linking together the riflemen's clubs, the Union was directly connected with the Polish nationalist leader Józef Piłsudski and his Polish Socialist Party (PPS).[64]

Piłsudski and the PPS represented one of the Polish political movements that was vying for the loyalties of Poles and seeking a new political answer to the Polish Question in the early twentieth century. Another was National Democracy, led by Piłsudski's rival Roman Dmowski. There were, of course, other political movements in Polish Europe, such as the peasant parties, the radical socialists of the far left, and the Russian loyalists of the Realist party; by 1907, even the PPS had split into two factions. But the National Democrats and the nationalist Piłsudskite wing of the PPS were well organized and determined. Their influence, meanwhile, could not be contained by the borders that divided one part of partitioned Poland from another. National Democracy was extremely popular among urban Polish elites throughout Polish Europe, while intellectuals and students, especially in Galicia and Russian Poland, had constructed an intense cult of personality around the formidable Piłsudski. Just like the Polish policies of the partitioning powers, the ambitions of the two movements combined foreign and domestic political elements. That is, each offered competing visions not only for how domestic Polish politics might be constituted but also for how international political space in central Europe might be ordered. Dmowski and his movement were characterized by their integral nationalism and virulent anti-Semitism. Internationally, National Democracy sought a solution to the Polish Question under Russian auspices. Its hostility was mostly directed westward, against the hated *Hakatismus* of Germany, whose relatively wealthy and well-developed Polish territories it coveted. The PPS, on the other hand, rejected racially defined nationalism and was utterly devoted to the cause of Polish independence. Its geographic ambitions were the precise opposite of National Democracy's, as it hoped to regain for Polish rule the eastern lands of the vanished Polish-Lithuanian union. To Piłsudski and his followers, each of the partitioning powers was an enemy that would, in time, have to be dealt with. But it was the Russians who were the most hated foe. The end of Russian rule in Congress Poland was, to the PPS, the sine qua non of their political plans.[65]

Such was the state of the Polish Question on the eve of the Great War. When violence erupted in 1914, both of the main Polish political parties as well as the partitioning Great Powers struggled to impose their answer to the question amid the destruction of the old European political order. For the winner of this struggle was the possibility of stability, or freedom; for the loser, perhaps, a "Polish Serbia,"[66] backed by one Great Power and exercising an intractable irredentist allure on the Polish subjects of the others. It was against this background of competing and mutually exclusive political ambitions, of a highly complicated national question violently loosed of its restraints, that Beseler first formulated and then worked to implement an answer of his own.

1

Prometheus Bound

The German Conquest and Occupation of Poland

In August 1914, the restraints keeping the Polish Question in check became one of the First World War's earliest casualties. From the conflict's opening days, the central European Great Powers worked to mobilize Polish discontent in the service of their respective war efforts, sending promises of a bright future for Polish national aspirations ahead of their armies as they marched into battle. Virtually overnight, Polish nationalism was transformed from a source of potential international instability into a weapon in the struggle for military and political mastery on the eastern front. Germany, despite its history of hostility to Polish nationalism, took an active role in this initial drive for Polish sympathies, but it gave little serious thought to what it might actually do if the "fortunes of war" brought German armies into Russia's Polish territories. When these came under German occupation in 1915, this failure of strategic imagination was remedied by the ambitious German Governor-General, Hans Hartwig von Beseler. Over the course of his tenure in Poland, Beseler became convinced that it would be in Germany's best interests to support—and thereby control—the creation of a new Polish state in central Europe. A dependent Polish state, he reasoned, would be a useful ally in a potential future war with Russia—or Austria. Beseler also believed that there neither could nor should be a return to the era of the partitions; the constant upheavals of that era had shown that a different answer to the Polish Question was essential to the stability of central Europe. Moreover, the war—by simultaneously smashing restraints and encouraging aspirations—had destroyed the possibility of reestablishing the status quo ante bellum. Some state or movement was going to seize the momentum in Polish Europe and direct it toward its own ends. Germany could not afford to be indifferent to the outcome of this contest for mastery of the Polish Question.

While the specific details of what, exactly, the new Kingdom of Poland was to look like (and where, exactly, it was going to be located) fluctuated somewhat over the course of the war, in its general outlines, Beseler's vision remained quite consistent. The newly reconstituted Kingdom of Poland was to be created from the territory of the Congress Kingdom, with possible border expansions eastward, and was to be a constitutional monarchy with full autonomy in matters of cultural and domestic politics. A series of treaties and agreements would bring this Polish satellite firmly within the orbit of the German economy, as well as provide German control over what was, to Beseler, the most important aspects of this new polity: its foreign policy and its military affairs. Despite moments of doubt and despair, Beseler would maintain a resolute devotion to this vision throughout the war.

Because of Beseler's extensive authority as Governor-General, it did not have to remain just a vision. From 1916 to 1918, Beseler's ambitions for Poland were translated into a series of policies and institutions meant to bring it to realization (a process he came to believe would take decades, at the very least). His authority beyond the Government-General, however, was limited, and Beseler had to work hard to convince the numerous skeptics in the army and the government that his course was the wisest one—not ideal, perhaps, but the least bad of a series of unpleasant and risky (from the German point of view) options. Beseler met with mixed success in his attempts to swing the full weight of the German state behind his ambitions, and he often felt stymied by politicians and military commanders that he thought shortsighted and foolish. These figures were just some of the many obstacles that Beseler believed blocked the path toward full realization of a policy to which he had committed himself, obstacles that produced a revealing burst of exasperation from Beseler when, in a moment of frustration, he referred to himself as "Prometheus bound," persecuted for valiantly trying to bring light to a benighted land. He did not, however, take careful enough note of the myth's warnings about the dangers of hubris.

The Outbreak of the War and the Mobilization of Polish Opinion

In both Germany and Russia, the beginning of the war was marked by clumsy attempts to rally Polish opinion, both at home and abroad, to their respective causes. In Germany, the attempt to mollify some of the Polish enmity that its policies had created actually began before it had formally gone to war, a sign that the Germans had never lost sight of the fact that Polish opinion would be of importance in any central European war. In the last days of July 1914, the Kaiser asked the Vatican to appoint a conservative Prussian Pole, Edward Likowski, to the archbishopric of Posen-Gnesen, a post that had been vacant since 1906. (The Vatican obliged, and Likowski was formally installed in late August.[1]) Once the fighting began, the Poles across the frontier in Russia became the targets of German propaganda. A hastily improvised German appeal calling for the Tsar's Polish subjects to rise and fight for "freedom and independence" against the "Muscovite yoke" was delivered by air over the front lines into Russia between 7 and 8 August. Germany's transparently self-interested appeals were shrugged off by most of Russia's Polish subjects. Germany's reputation as an implacable enemy of Polish aspirations, generated by the decades of the Polish-Prussian nationality conflict, was simply too well entrenched to be overcome by crude propaganda. In addition, Polish hostility to Germany was further inflamed by the German military's conduct in the border city of Kalisz in August 1914, when, for reasons that remain obscure, the Germans bombarded and burned the town and engaged in summary executions of civilians. As the war accelerated the contest for Polish loyalties, the Russians ensured that the memory of the brutal events of Kalisz remained fresh, not least because it helped deflect Polish attention away from Russian outrages. In part because of Russian propaganda, the Germans' actions in Kalisz continued to feed popular Polish anger against them for months, and even years, afterward.[2]

In Russian Poland, the mobilization of the military at the outbreak of the war went far more smoothly than many had expected. Given the severity of the instability that occurred during and after the Revolution of 1905, the fear was widespread that the Poles would resist, or even rebel, when mobilization was declared. But the Tsar's Polish subjects not only mobilized without incident; Russian units—including Cossacks—were cheered in the streets of Warsaw.[3] The Russians followed mobilization with their own public appeal to Polish sentiment, hoping, like the Germans, to harness Polish discontent to its war effort. After a great deal of internal political wrangling, the appeal was issued by Grand Duke Nicholas on 15 August 1914 (and lacked, as in the German case, the imperial signature). "Poles!" it began,

> The hour has sounded when the sacred dream of your fathers and fore-fathers can come true. A century and a half has passed since the living flesh of Poland was torn in pieces but her soul is not dead. It lives in the hope that the hour will come in which resuscitated Poland will recon-cile herself fraternally with Great Russia. The Russian troops bring to you the happy message of reconciliation. May the frontiers disappear that divide the Polish nation, thus making of them a unity under the sceptre of the Emperor of Russia! Under that sceptre Poland will be reborn, free in religion, in language and in self-government . . . Great Russia comes to meet you with open heart and brotherly hand. She is convinced that the sword which struck the enemy at Grunwald is not yet rusted.[4]

The Grand Duke's extraordinary manifesto (extraordinary because it ne-glects to acknowledge the leading role played by Russia in tearing the "living flesh of Poland" into pieces) was better received in Russian Poland than the Germans' clumsy appeal, though not everyone was convinced. "Poland re-membered well Mickiewicz's prayer for a 'war of peoples,'" noted Włodzimierz Gałecki, a schoolteacher, referring to the poet's plea in his "Pilgrim's Litany" ("For a general war for the liberation of peoples! We beseech thee, Lord . . . For a happy death on the field of battle. We beseech thee, Lord").[5] "Now that war had arrived," Gałecki continues, Poland "was not interested in autonomy granted by the grace of the Tsar."[6] Whatever its impact on Polish opinion, however, the Russian manifesto was a highly significant development. By ex-plicitly targeting the Poles of both Germany and Austria and staking a claim to their territory, Russia had taken a step that would inevitably make the ne-gotiation of peace between the two sides far more difficult, a fact widely re-alized at the time. In London, *The Times* noted on 17 August that "the Tsar's offer, if it is effective, makes the quarrel between Russia and the two Central dynasties inexpiable. It is the most signal proof which Russia could give that she means her war with her great neighbors to be war to the knife." Likewise, the French writer Emile Faguet noted that the manifesto meant that Russia would be "*for ever* . . . in a state of hostility towards Prussia and Austria." In addition, the manifesto encouraged Polish ambitions while simultaneously eroding the political and mental restraints keeping those ambitions constrained. The prewar order was thus already destroyed, perhaps irrevocably, by August 1914.[7] A fundamentally new answer to the Polish Question was becoming conceivable at the same time that it was becoming not only possible, but inevitable.

The Poles were not only the targets of mobilization from above; the outbreak of the war also saw an upsurge in Polish political mobilization from below. Throughout Russian Poland, elites organized themselves into "Civic Committees" (*Komitety Obywatelskie*) that eventually expanded their reach into Austrian Galicia, refusing to respect "boundaries established by conquerors." Originally founded to ameliorate the hardships imposed on society by the mobilization for war, the local committees, linked to a Central Civic Committee in Warsaw, quickly took on the role of state administrators. In general, the committees were dominated by conservatives and National Democrats. The president of the Warsaw Civic Committee, for example, was Prince Zdzisław Lubomirski, who had worked to promote Polish culture within the boundaries of the Tsarist state, while the vice president of the Central Civic Committee was Stanisław Grabski, a National Democrat who would go on to play an important role in the Government of the Second Polish Republic.[8] While the generally loyalist and pro-Russian committees were the most immediately visible aspect of Polish self-mobilization, opposition organizations were spurred to activity as well, though they remained concealed from official view. The socialist nationalists of the PPS, for example, organized the Polish Military Organization (POW) to serve as a clandestine military organization loyal to Piłsudski. The revolutionary socialist parties of the far left, such as the PPS-Left, the SDKPiL (Social Democracy of the Kingdom of Poland and Lithuania), and the Jewish socialists of the Bund, meanwhile, formed an Interparty Workers' Council (Międzypartyjna Rada Robotnicza).[9] Of course, not everyone jumped into politics; vacationing with his family in

Austrian territory, the teacher Gałecki found himself stranded in a state now at war with his own and, moreover, one in which the rail system had been commandeered by the army. His main concern was getting himself and his family home, which he finally managed to do, via a series of chaotic and excruciatingly uncomfortable train rides.[10] Nonetheless, the political energies released by the outbreak of the war in Poland meant that, by the time the Germans arrived in August 1915, powerful forces had been set in motion with which the occupation regime would have to come to terms.

In Galicia, home to numerous semi-clandestine Polish political organizations and long-established traditions of organized Polish politics, the upsurge of Polish political activity was simultaneously more chaotic and more organized than in Prussia or Russia. On 6 August, Piłsudski led a contingent of guerrillas loyal to him north into Russian Poland's Kielce Province. In addition to his rifles, he was armed with a manifesto calling on the Poles of the Kingdom to follow him in an uprising against Russia and naming him commander of the Polish army. The manifesto was issued in the name of a Warsaw-based Polish national government that was wholly fabricated. Neither the manifesto nor the presence of Piłsudski and his adventurers in the Congress Kingdom sparked the uprising that Piłsudski hoped would greet his entry into Russian territory, and he was pressured to return to Austria. Piłsudski's adventure was followed ten days later by the establishment of the Supreme National Committee (Naczelny Komitet Narodowy/NKN) in Kraków. Dominated by the conservative Galician elite but including a broad spectrum of Austrian Polish political movements, including, at least initially, National Democracy, it was viewed by Austrian loyalists as an institutional base from which to work for the solution to the "Polish Question" that was favored by the Galician loyalist elite: a union of Galicia with Russia's Polish lands (usually known as the "Austro-Polish" solution.) The NKN included a military department headed by the future Prime Minister and Commander-in-Chief, Władysław Sikorski. The institutional base for the establishment of more regular Polish participation in the war was thus created; the NKN and the Austrian central government agreed to work together to establish Polish military units, called the Polish Legions. Piłsudski and his paramilitaries were absorbed into them, with Piłsudski given command of the First Brigade, from whence comes the famous Polish anthem of the era, "We of the First Brigade" (My, Pierwsza Brygada).[11]

The Creation of the Imperial Government-General of Warsaw

It is possible that political energies mobilized in Poland would simply have dissipated had the fighting ended in 1914 or the first half of 1915. In mid-1915, however, the fortunes of war transpired to push the rupture with the prewar order in Poland, already begun in August 1914, past the point of no return. On 1 May, an artillery bombardment announced the beginning of the so-called Gorlice-Tarnów offensive, a joint Austro-German attack that would result in one of the most stunning battlefield victories of the Great War. Led by the German XI Army under August von Mackensen, the ground attack was launched the following day from a line southeast of Kraków. Throughout the spring and summer and into the early fall, the main thrust of the assault, combined with complementary attacks in the northern and central areas of the Russian front, steadily drove the Russian army out of central Europe.[12] In early August, Varsovians waited in a state of "anxiety" as the raging battle drew audibly and visibly closer to them. On 4 August, Russian troops evacuated across the Vistula bridges to Praga, on the river's east bank. They destroyed the bridges the following day as German forces entered the city.[13] The Germans ultimately succeeded in driving the Russians from Praga, and the eastern offensive continued into the fall, when it finally ground to a halt.

The defeat was a humiliating catastrophe for the Russian military, but the real losers were the poor unfortunates who found themselves in the path of the Russian withdrawal. The Russians, in addition to evacuating official personnel from Poland as the Germans drove eastward, embarked on a scorched earth retreat, destroying and burning whatever they could not take with them. According to the Polish historian J. Dąbrowski, "everything that could be removed from Warsaw was, beginning with military supplies and concluding with the furnishings of the Royal and Łazienki Castles. Particular care was taken to remove bank deposits and factory equipment."[14] People were removed as well, with thousands of "suspect" Jews and Germans throughout Poland brutally rounded up and deported eastward.[15]

For the Germans, the victories provided a major boost to morale. One German participant in the fighting who went on to become an eminent historian, Gerhard Ritter, later recalled "the enormous lift" the victories "gave

to German spirits."[16] This included the spirits of the more radical annexationists, whose fevered hopes for conquest and subjugation were inflamed by the
great victory.[17] It is not quite clear, however, if the stunning successes of Germany's armies on the battlefield translated into much of a net strategic gain
for the Germans, particularly since Russia had not been knocked out of the
war. Indeed, the primary effect of the conquests may have been the freeing
up of troops to be slaughtered in great numbers the following year at Verdun.[18]
In addition, Germany now had to administer a large stretch of territory that
was fraught with political complications, devastated by the fighting and the
brutal Russian retreat, and stripped of its government institutions. To administer this land, the Germans established the Imperial Government-General
of Warsaw in August 1915.

From the outset, the Government-General was marked by a peculiar du-
ality in its structure. It consisted of both military and civilian elements whose
relationship to each other was juridically murky. When it was created, an
army officer, General Hans Hartwig von Beseler, was appointed to serve as
Governor-General (Generalgouverneur). In addition to being supreme commander of the occupation forces, Beseler answered only to the Emperor,
giving him a degree of autonomy rare for military officers. At the same time,
however, a civilian Chief Administrator (Verwaltungschef), Wolfgang von
Kries, was appointed head of the civilian branch of the Government-General.
As a civilian administrator, Kries was formally subordinate to the Imperial
Ministry of the Interior, whose head, Clemens Delbrück, believed that the
civilian arm of the occupation regime should maintain its independence
vis-à-vis the military. (In many respects, this reflected the administrative
confusion and chaos in Germany itself, where the State of Siege [Belager-
ungszustand] implemented at the beginning of the war had created a new
government of military rulers, the Deputy Commanding Generals, that par-
alleled and overlapped with the established state and federal institutions.
These military officers were supposed to rule over the regular peacetime civilian authorities, yet they could not have functioned without them, leading
to confusion and uncertainty about the precise responsibilities of each arm.
In both Germany and the Government-General, confusion was exacerbated
by the fact that the jurisdictional boundaries of the military administrators
frequently overlapped with multiple civilian boundaries.[19]) Remarkably, however, this civil-military confusion was not paralyzing to the workings of the

occupation regime. This was due in part to the fact that Beseler and Kries managed to forge an efficient working relationship, and in part to the fact that Beseler and the military were effective in asserting their will and becoming the de facto, if never quite de jure, supreme authorities in the Government-General.[20]

The dual authority at the head of the Government-General was replicated in its broader structure. Beseler commanded the occupation troops. In 1915, these numbered just over forty-one battalions (down to thirty-five in mid-1918), in addition to cavalry, artillery, and engineering units. Between 1915 and 1916, these forces were augmented by additional units that were sent to occupied Poland to complete a portion of their infantry training. Additional training facilities were maintained for German aircrews, artillery forces, and officer candidates.[21] Immediately below Beseler in the chain of command stood eleven military governors, who formally received their appointments from the Emperor and ruled over areas of command known as Militärgouvernements. Their duties were supposedly restricted to "military tasks," but they were also granted authority to deal with *polizeilich* matters (i.e., matters related to public security and order), a broad category in a land under military occupation. Beseler noted that, just as in Germany, this had the potential to cause some overlap with the duties of the top layer of administrators of Kries' *Zivilverwaltung,* the district chiefs (Kreischefs). The Government-General was divided into about thirty districts, with Warsaw and Lodz constituting their own special districts headed by Chiefs of Police.[22]

The relations between the civil and military elements of the occupation regime were not the only source of friction and uncertainty in the Government-General's early days. The Germans also had to determine what role their erstwhile enemy and current ally, Austria, would play in the occupation. Like the Germans, the Poles, and the Russians, the Austrians realized that the Polish Question had been given new vitality by the outbreak of the war; and they, like everyone else, feared the repercussions if they did not assert mastery over the Polish situation. This conflict of interests had shown itself to be a potential source of trouble as early as August 1914, when the Austrians had informed Berlin that, in the event that the Congress Kingdom were conquered, it would be best to place it under the rule of a Warsaw-based Austrian Governor-General. Once the Kingdom was occupied, the allies began to squabble over how to rule it; the Austrians wanted to create a condominium (joint rule with shared sovereignty), a plan the Germans rejected. In September, at a meeting in Teschen, the Germans and Austrians finally agreed to split Russian Poland into two occupation zones. The borders of Germany's 62,000-square-kilometer zone stretched from Kalisz in the west to Siedlce in the southeast and nearly to Białystok in the northeast, taking in the major urban centers of Warsaw, which became the Government-General's administrative seat, and Lodz, the "Polish Manchester." In the north, it shared a frontier with East Prussia and the conquered Russian province of Suwałki, which was under the control of OberOst.[23] The population over which the Imperial Government-General ruled (about 6 million people) was extraordinarily diverse in terms of language, religion, and ethnicity. The majority were Polish-speaking Catholics, but there were sizable minority populations, including Germans and a large Yiddish-speaking and Orthodox Jewish community, which comprised up to 15 percent of prewar Poland's population and lived primarily in towns and cities, where they sometimes constituted over half of the residents.[24] The Austrian zone to the south, which was ruled from Lublin, was similar in physical size (43,000 square kilometers) but was overwhelmingly rural and home to only about 3.5 million people.[25] The Austrians were granted the right to a special representative in Warsaw, though the question of whether Austrian newspapers would be allowed to circulate in the German zone was left unresolved (see Maps 1 and 2).[26]

The Foundations of Beseler's *Polenpolitik*

As head of the Imperial Government-General, Hans Hartwig von Beseler was entrusted with an enormous amount of responsibility and power and faced with numerous complicated administrative and political questions. It was not the sort of job for which his successful military career had provided much preparation, though his sharp and imaginative mind, nurtured by his upbringing in the milieu of the Berlin Bildungsbürgertum, would help him grapple with the demands of his new appointment. Von Beseler had been born into a distinguished middle-class family in 1850 in Greifswald. His father, Georg Beseler, was a prominent Berlin law professor and a veteran of the constitutional parliament of 1848, while Hans Hartwig's brother, Max, became Prussian minister of justice in 1905. The future General Beseler received a traditional education at a Gymnasium, where he excelled at mathematics and nurtured a keen interest in German literature. As both a child and a young man, he was immersed in the spirit of northern Germany's meteoric rise to central European dominance. He was filled with enthusiasm at the military victories of the 1860s, while his mind and character were further shaped by the distinguished visitors who came to call on his parents. The list of the Beselers' houseguests reads like a who's who of the northern German intellectual elite: Treitschke, Mommsen, Ranke, Sybel, Duncker. Beseler entered the army as an engineer after finishing his *Abitur* in 1868 (he had wanted to join the navy, but his father dissuaded him). After fighting as a lieutenant in the Franco-Prussian War, he rose steadily through the ranks (1882 Hauptmann, 1897 Oberst, 1907 General der Infanterie) while passing through a variety of staff and command positions. His postings included two stints at the Kriegsakademie (War Academy)—once in the late 1870s as a student and once, a decade later, as an instructor—and two tours at the General Staff. Beseler very nearly achieved the pinnacle of military success when the Chief of the Military Cabinet, Dietrich Graf von Hülsen-Haeseler, recommended him to the Kaiser as Schlieffen's successor as Chief of the General Staff. The Emperor initially supported Beseler's candidacy, but his support was always lukewarm and he eventually changed his mind.[27] The highest position Beseler achieved was head of the Engineer and Pioneer Corps and Inspector-General of Fortresses before his career was seemingly ended by a bitterly resented forced retirement at the end of 1910. At the outbreak of the war, however, Beseler was returned to duty as the head of the III Reserve Corps. He distinguished himself and gained a measure of popular renown in the first years of the war owing to his capture of the fortresses of Antwerp (October 1914) and Modlin/Novogeorgievsk (August 1915).[28]

When he was appointed Governor-General, Beseler installed himself in the elegant Belvedere palace, on the edge of Warsaw's Łazienki Park. Among some locals, he established a reputation as a reserved, scholarly sort who kept to himself and enjoyed "solitary walks in [the Belvedere's] garden."[29] But Beseler was a military man, and his appointment caused him "mixed feelings." The position carried with it great responsibility, but it ended his active participation in the war and did not seem quite a soldierly sort of job.[30] "For the moment," he wrote to his wife, Clara, on 4 September 1915, "I've completely forgotten that I'm a soldier, and I dream only of policies and administration—dreams from which

I hope to awake soon, since my heart is with the troops." (He seemed particularly troubled by the number of letters that arrived for him: "Dear God! If I had to answer them all myself!"[31]) Yet the army, though the focus of Beseler's life, was not his only interest. Beseler had long nursed a keen interest in politics but, because of his military career, he had had to remain a spectator. "If I have any objection to my position," Beseler confided to a friend in 1875, "it is that I will likely never be able to participate in politics, and I regret that, as I have the liveliest interest in it and would, I believe . . . make a quite passable deputy."[32] After his retirement Beseler devoted most of his time to writing about military subjects, but he was given some opportunity to sample political life when he became, in 1912, a member of the Prussian House of Lords. With his appointment as Governor-General, he sensed his chance finally to test his political mettle. "Now we will really see," Beseler wrote to Clara in September, "if there is anything of the statesman and politician in me."[33] It was an opportunity of which he would make full use, throwing himself headlong into the task of first formulating and then carrying out an occupation policy whose success, he became convinced, was utterly essential to Germany's national security.

Beseler arrived at his post knowing very little of Poland, and evidence for his prewar attitudes and thoughts on the subject is nonexistent. Certainly his interest and participation in Prussian politics would have inclined him against cooperation with the Poles at best, and nurtured a deep-seated loathing in him at worst.[34] Most of the evidence from his first few months as Governor-General suggests that he did not harbor any particularly warm sentiments for the people now under his rule. In August 1915, the month he was appointed, Beseler discovered that Bethmann Hollweg had told Falkenhayn that Germany would be better off treating the Poles as "good friends" in order to present a unified front against the "Russian Slavic flood." The Governor-General privately noted that any Polish-German cooperation would be better founded on the far more reliable cement of fear.[35] In addition, Beseler complained to Clara in mid-September 1915 that

> the gentlemen of Poland, who we are supposed to treat as friends (!) [sic], are getting uppity and busying themselves with political foolishness, but

they've made a mistake if they think they're going to get one over on me; they forget that their country is a theater of war, and, for the time being, a conquered Russ[ian] province.[36]

Nor was the Imperial Government-General's mission likely to encourage political experiments or extended reflections on the future of central Europe. In October 1915, Beseler was still describing his "main task" as "maintain[ing] calm and order with severity and fairness." Political activity of any sort, he believed, had no place in occupied Poland, since no decisions had been made regarding what might happen to it after the war.[37] In keeping with this, Beseler's first actions as Governor-General had been largely negative. He disbanded several Polish political and social organizations, for example, and instituted strict censorship.[38]

The patronizing, mistrustful tone that marked Beseler's early thoughts about occupied Poland never fully vanished, and it would resurface often in his public and private correspondence. However, he was not long into his tenure when he began to express more favorable opinions of the conquered people, even if these opinions were frequently qualified in some way. This shift seems to have occurred as Beseler got to know Poland better in his first few months as Governor-General. He worked quickly to remedy his initial ignorance, receiving briefings from Bogdan Graf von Hutten-Czapski, a prominent Prussian Polish nobleman assigned to the occupation government, reading extensively in Polish history and literature, and traveling throughout the lands placed under his control.[39] In the fall of 1915, Beseler wrote a letter to his wife, Clara, that reveals a view of the Poles and Poland different from the hostile one expressed earlier. Having spent some time traveling through the Government-General, Beseler told Clara that it was "beautiful beyond all expectations and favored by nature." However, Poland was also

lacking good government and the superior intelligence of an intellectually distinguished people. The Poles have been repressed by the Russians, they don't know what they want and the cleavage amongst the inhabitants, especially as well the unfortunate Jews, hinders the growth of progress. It's a pity about this land, but about its people too, who are certainly gifted . . . What will one day become of all this is still <u>completely</u> unclear.[40]

This mix of condescension and fondness became characteristic of Beseler's recorded thoughts on Poland, although the balance between the positive and the negative elements was constantly shifting (the very next month he told Clara that the Poles were "presumptuous and arrogant"[41]) and was often dependent on the degree to which those over whom he ruled did what he wanted them to do. Still, this admiration probably made him more amenable to working with and listening to Polish elites than he might otherwise have been.

The above letter to Clara reveals another recurring theme in Beseler's wartime correspondence about Poland, one that would play a profound role in shaping the Governor-General's sense of his mission in occupied Poland, the institutions created to realize it, and even the language used to describe and justify it: namely, that the Poles were, collectively speaking, not ready to rule their own state. Beseler expressed this idea by repeatedly referring to the Poles as "immature" *(unreif)*. The word abounds in Beseler's correspondence, official and private, from his years as Governor-General. This "immaturity" had, Beseler believed, several telltale symptoms. Polish demands that the reestablishment of a Polish state take place immediately, for example, were foremost among them. ("If they were left to their own devices," Beseler wrote to Clara in October 1915, "they would soon eat each other up."[42]) Polish unhappiness with the hard burdens of war and occupation were another sign of it. In 1917, Beseler noted that, in the eyes of the Poles, the Germans had replaced the Russians as "the oppressors." He concluded, however, that he could not "after all, blame the childishly ignorant and inexperienced Poles" for tiring of the occupation and its attendant hardships.[43] As the occupation developed, Beseler would use other language that reflected this belief in Polish "immaturity." In 1916, for example, in a meeting of the Prussian cabinet (Staatsministerium), Beseler argued that the Poles "[had] to be trained to run their own government" ("Das Land müsse zur eigenen Regierung erzogen werden"). The word chosen by Beseler to describe this enterprise, in which his regime by this time was already deeply enmeshed, is highly revealing. "Erziehen"—to bring up, educate, or train—is a word commonly applied to the raising of children, and it implies the careful inculcation of a set of values and habits in the young and malleable.[44]

It would be easy, and not entirely inaccurate, to dismiss this crass condescension as racism. However, labeling the Poles as "immature" suggests a certain flexibility that the essentialism of vulgar, pseudoscientific racialist thinking, of the sort that so deeply infused European culture at this time, does not. Full of subtle meanings that are lost in translation (*unreif* can also mean unripe), it implies that time and care can produce change. This is reflective of the fact that Beseler believed Poland's political shortcomings (as he saw them) were a result of the region's history rather than some innate Polish stupidity linked to their biology. The obvious political implication was, of course, that any modification of the prewar status quo in Russian Poland would have to be guided by a strong, paternalistic (German) hand.[45] The idea that an inferior civilization had to be guided (or pushed, if necessary) into modernity by a more sophisticated civilization also smacks of colonialism and the idea of a "civilizing mission." There is a strong family resemblance between the ideas, but "immaturity" and like words were also employed in a more general sense during this period to describe the growing pains associated with major political transitions. Treitschke, for example, in an address to the University of Berlin commemorating Germany's 1871 victory over France, used similar language when talking about Germany's metamorphosis into a unified empire. After 1918, Józef Piłsudski would use similar terminology to describe the antics of the newly founded Polish government; in the same period, the extension of the suffrage to German women led to worries about their political "immaturity" and their need for "education."[46] In addition, to conflate the language of a "civilizing mission" with colonialism itself is to elide the difference between the actual acquisition and rule of colonial territories with the language used to justify such rule. Paternalistic ideology of a sort similar to that which shaped Beseler's ambitions in Poland was certainly an *aspect* of European colonialism, but it was hardly its essence.

The Governor-General's views on the Poles and Poland evolved and changed during his time in office, but he seems to have remained mostly immune to biological racism. His Gymnasium education may have played a role. It certainly nurtured his sharp, inquisitive mind, as did his time at the War Academy. Surely one of the most unusual colleges for officers that has ever existed, its curriculum devoted more time to conventional subjects, both humanistic and scientific, than to more obviously military skills and knowledge.[47] As Governor-General, Beseler continued to enrich and cultivate his intellect, somehow finding the time to read widely and absorb himself in the study of various subjects ranging from statistics to philosophy. (After the war, his impressive store of books, left behind after the occupation collapsed, was added to the collections of Warsaw University Library.[48]) His knowledge of history, personal acquaintance with so many historians, and coming of age at a time and in a place when history exercised a powerful, perhaps unequaled hold on the collective imagination, also shaped his views of Poland and the Poles. In an impassioned 1917 defense of his actions, Beseler answered some of the critics of his policies in Poland by arguing that explanations of German-Polish hostility that drew on biology were foolish and founded on ignorance. Expressing his contempt for what he called the "issue of race" *(Rassenfrage)*, Beseler drew on history to explain this hostility and downplay its importance. "One must consider," Beseler wrote, in the unmistakable voice of the northern German elite,

> that actually the German inhabitants of eastern Germany, are, according to race, quite closely related to the Poles. The irreconcilable antagonism between Germans and Poles is due to history rather than nature, and even our historical antagonism is more legend than historical truth. The German tribes have beat on each other's skulls more than Germans and Poles have. There is therefore no reason why this antagonism should not be able to develop into a peaceful coexistence over the course of time.

If Prussia and Austria could learn to coexist, Beseler seems to be suggesting, then there was no reason why Germany should be unable to come to terms with Poland. Again showing that he had become accustomed to thinking in terms of long-term processes, Beseler admitted in this memorandum that "peaceful coexistence" between Germany and Poland lay some distance in the future. But by the time he wrote this, he had already taken what he believed to be the first steps toward this future, and it remained only to follow through. The Germans and Poles shared a confluence of interests that would, eventually, bind them together, and it was on this belief, he said, that he acted.[49]

As for his initial distrust of and hostility to the Poles, they never fully disappeared, but Beseler's immersion in Polish cultural life played a role in tempering it. The Governor-General appeared regularly at operas, dances, and musical performances in Warsaw. In January 1916, following a ballet, Beseler formally received a deputation of dancers as well as the conductor and the ballet master. He chatted with the artists and presented them with gifts, while the "ballet master—a cultivated man, by the way—read aloud a spirited letter of thanks in exquisite German in which a salad of Mozart, Kant, politics, hope and admiration had been prepared." Beseler called this a "sweet little experience that could have come straight out of a novella."[50] Such moments seem to have made a lasting impression on him. Beseler may have referred to the Poles as "children," but he is also said to have exclaimed, in fits of exasperation, "you're a bunch of poets!" The engineer probably intended this as a kind of insult, implying that the Polish political and cultural elite had their collective head in the clouds and couldn't be entrusted with the responsibilities of government.[51] But it is also a compliment (and one sure to flatter the sensibilities of the nation of Mickiewicz) that acknowledges the rich and vibrant intellectual life that had been nurtured in partition-era Poland.

A Polish Question and a German Answer

These perceptions of the Poles and Poland became solidified into the foundation stone of the long-term political policy of state building that Beseler came to pursue in the Congress Kingdom. Beseler was nudged in this direction by his observation very early on in the occupation that political life in Russian Poland had been electrified by the outbreak of the war. Beseler perceived that the variety of Polish political organizations and parties over which he now had to rule contained within them many different ideological strains and variations, often at odds with each other; but he also perceived that behind the bitter fractiousness of Polish politics was a shared desire to reestablish some kind of distinctly Polish political and cultural entity.[52] The term "nationalism," while vague, is probably best for describing this general desire that something called *Poland* be returned to the map of Europe after the war, even if views varied widely on where Poland might be, or whether it would be sovereign, or who might be permitted to live there and call himself (or herself) a Pole.[53] The intensity and vehemence with which some members of the Polish elite demanded immediate and sweeping changes in the prewar political order were a source of recurring irritation to Beseler. "They are acting," he wrote to Clara in September 1915, "as if *they* had liberated Poland, and need only call 'let there be light'" to re-create some variation on the vanished Polish state.[54] Even if this was not reflective of popular opinion in Congress Poland as a whole, the repeated demands made by Polish elites for self-rule made a deep impression on the Governor-General, who would ultimately conclude that Germany, if it wished for security and stability in the east, could not afford to ignore them. In the fall of 1915, in his private reflections on a memorandum issued by the Eastern Marches Association, Beseler rejected its recommendation that the conquered Polish territories be repartitioned. "That won't solve the Polish Question!" was his reaction. "To the Poles it is the most loathsome solution." Beseler also rejected both the possibility of simply handing it back to Russia as well as the annexation and absorption by Germany of the entire province, though he hoped for annexations along the German-Polish frontier.[55] Then, in a report to the Emperor written at about the same time, Beseler informed the Kaiser that the civilians of the Government-General had been working "to improve [Poland] economically, hygienically, and morally" with the aim of making it "well-ordered and flourishing." It was a task Beseler pledged to embrace, as he saw within it a glimmer of opportunity; his final remark was that bestowing on postwar Poland a "political future that is as favorable to Germany as possible will prove to be one of the most important tasks of German statecraft."[56] This did not mark Beseler's conversion to the cause of Polish autonomy, but the seeds of his long-term ambitions in Poland can be seen germinating here, as can the core characteristics of what became his view of his mission in Poland: combining a "civilizing mission" with the securing of German interests in central Europe. By 1916 at the latest, these intellectual seeds had developed into a conviction that Germany could and should act to determine the shape of postwar Poland. Early that year, Beseler suggested to the Emperor that Germany should set itself two long-term political goals in occupied Poland. The first and most important was securing Germany against future Russian invasions. The second was that Germany should seize the opportunity (or, alternately, necessity) created by the war to find a "satisfactory solution to the Polish Question." At this time, Beseler argued that the easiest, if not most ideal, way to blend all of these ambitions together was to create a Polish state by unifying Russian Poland with Austrian Galicia and annexing territory along the new border. This state would be placed under Austrian sovereignty but would be militarily subordinate to both Central Powers. In its essence, this policy—border annexations combined with a state-building project in Poland that aimed at domestic autonomy and foreign dependence—remained at the heart of Beseler's Polish policy during the war.[57]

Beseler's beliefs finally crystallized into an extensive set of specific policy recommendations that he formally submitted to the Emperor in July 1916. This document, along with subsequent reports and numerous private letters, elaborates on several key themes of Beseler's policy and is powerfully revealing of the means and ends Beseler envisioned for the Germans in Poland. In the July report, he reemphasizes the enduring strength of Polish nationalism, which can be ignored, he argues, only at the peril of those who wish for long-term stability and security in central Europe. Beseler acknowledges that Polish nationalism is not a single, coherent force, but he suggests to Berlin (either disingenuously or naively) that the political form assumed by any new Polish state would not be particularly important, so long as its content was genuinely and unmistakably Polish. The only solution suggested by reasonable "statesmanship" *(Staatsklugheit),* Beseler concludes, is to find a way to meet some Polish demands without working contrary to Austrian and German interests, a solution best achieved by creating a satellite state. The general outlines of this state as envisioned by Beseler highlight the overwhelming importance of national security concerns in his thinking: in matters of education, culture, domestic administration, and law, Poland was to be independent. Economically, Beseler believed that Polish trade and industry should be linked to Germany or to a central European economic federation (in the classic tradition of *Mitteleuropa* ideology) through treaties. Polish trade would also be allowed privileged passage through Germany and German ports. Direct German control over Polish affairs would be tightest in all aspects of administration that touched on diplomacy and war: the Polish postal service, train system, and telegraph network were to be tied directly to existing German infrastructure, Poland would be forbidden from conducting an independent foreign policy, and its army would be (mostly) under German control (an aspect of the Germans' state-building project that will be discussed in detail in Chapter 2).[58]

Military security was to be further strengthened by annexing portions of the future German-Polish borderlands (or, less anachronistically in 1916, the German-*Russian* borderlands). The goal of border annexations sat uneasily with the desire to win Polish support for Germany and its ambitions in the Congress Kingdom. To Beseler, however, the annexations were "of such enormous military importance that all political considerations had to be set aside."[59] Beseler's annexationism is easily misunderstood in light of what the

Germans were to inflict on Poland under another Governor-General a little more than two decades later. Yet neither Nazi ideas of racial supremacy and conquest nor strange reveries about Teutonic knights warring for Kultur in barbarian Slavic lands (such as were entertained by Ludendorff) had anything to do with Beseler's plans for the borderlands. His military engineer's strategic imagination was rather more prosaic, shaped by a lifetime spent thinking about the relationship between geography and military operations. To Beseler, the rivers of northeastern Poland, particularly the Bobr (Biebrza)[60] and the Narew, created an "excellent flank and attack position."[61] (The strategic value of water had been brought home to Beseler in the campaigns of 1914. He had fought at the Battle of the Yser, when Belgian troops flooded their own territory to stall the German offensive. "If it hadn't been for the water," Beseler wrote to Clara in 1917, "the whole war in the west might have been different."[62]) Further German control over key sections of the Vistula and Warthe, as well as the Modlin fortress at the confluence of the Narew and Vistula (which Beseler himself had conquered), would, Beseler believed, render a Russian invasion into Germany nearly impossible. (This generally was the reason why the idea of border annexations in the east enjoyed broad military support, especially after the successful Russian incursions into East Prussia in 1914.[63]) In addition, the ability to station German troops within easy striking distance of Poland would help ensure Poland's reliability in the event of war, should gratitude, affection, common interests, or fear fail to keep Poland on Germany's side. Beseler's border corrections were thus intended mainly to make Germany more easily defensible against foreign invasion, though he didn't ignore, at least in official correspondence, the possibility that economic benefits would accrue as well.[64] Beseler's insistence on these annexations, which were deeply unpopular in Poland, never wavered. In Kries's opinion, this helped undermine his other, more sweeping political goals.[65]

While the fear of a future war with Russia was ever present in Beseler's thoughts about military security in the east, it was not the only power whose influence in Poland he wanted to minimize or exclude altogether. The Austrians were a prime target of Beseler's hostility, and his policies were directed as much against them as the Russians. From the very beginning of the occupation, the need to coordinate Polish policy with the Austrians was a constant source of irritation to Beseler, an irritation increased by his sense of the woeful inadequacy of the Austrians' war effort. ("It's awful to have to fight a war alongside a corpse," he remarked in 1916.[66]) This irritation only increased as Beseler's plans for the occupied territory grew more ambitious. To him, Austrian refusals to simply do as he thought best in Poland were the main obstacle in the way of the realization of his ambitions, especially since they refused to turn their occupation zone over to the Germans, which Beseler thought was essential to his project's success. In addition, Beseler noted that, if the new Polish state were to have any hope of long-term viability, it would have to be "well organized, strong, and reliable," all of which would be precluded by Austrian participation.[67] "Now I am firmly convinced," Beseler wrote to Clara in May 1916, "that we would create something really good here, something beneficial for us and Poland, if the damned Austrians weren't around."[68] By the spring of 1916, Beseler was rejecting outright the possibility of bringing Russian Poland under the sovereignty of the Habsburg crown, declaring that such an Austro-Polish union was "of course unacceptable."[69]

This antipathy to the Habsburg Empire was more than simply the irritation of an ambitious military commander chafing at the restraints imposed by his allies, or the disdain of an officer of the world's finest army for the shortcomings of a force he regarded as inferior. "As individuals they [i.e., the Austrians] are quite nice, but their state, their army and their system are horrible," Beseler wrote to Clara in November 1916.[70] The more deep-seated loathing for the Habsburg Empire revealed in this letter suggests the continuing influence on Beseler of the anti-Austrian animus that was such a central characteristic of the Prussian-centered, Protestant German nationalism that exercised such a powerful allure on so many elite Germans during the era of Unification.[71] The view of Austria as the central enemy of Prusso-German greatness lingering from those days does not seem to have been tempered by the fact that, when Beseler became Governor-General, they were fighting a war on the same side. In fact, Beseler began to see his Polish policy as merely another battle in the Austro-Prussian competition for German supremacy. His Polish policies marked "one of the last phases of the old struggle, now entering its third century, that we <u>must</u> win," Beseler wrote in November 1916, days before the Central Powers' proclamation on the restoration of Polish statehood (see below).[72] He was even more forceful in a letter to his friend Friedrich von Bernhardi. Referring to his seemingly pro-Polish stance, Beseler told his friend that it was "the only way to break <u>Austria's influence;</u> everything that's going on here has to be understood as the last phase of the clash with Austria; Poland is of minor importance and only a means to an end for us." "Now you have the explanation," he warned his friend three days before the proclamation, "for what's about to happen."[73]

More than just prestige or historical grievances were at stake. Beseler did not believe that peaceful relations with Austria were guaranteed ad infinitum. He worried that, should Austro-German tensions once again rise, Austria would be able to wield influence in internal German affairs through Germany's Polish minority. Moreover, a Polish army under Austrian control on Germany's border would constitute a kind of weapon always ready to be loosed on Germany.[74] Thus, he wrote to Clara in 1917, "we can not and ought not tolerate a disguised Austria on our eastern border! This explains our dogged struggle for an autonomous Poland." Beseler further elaborated that, since outright German annexations would merely create more internal problems for Germany, and a new partition would earn them the undying hatred of all of Polish Europe, his policy was the best way of minimizing the Austrian presence. "Therein lies the key to our Polish policy," he explained, "which we of course can't reveal to the rest of the world."[75] The Austro-German conflict of interest in Poland was intractable; everything the Germans saw at stake if they failed to dominate was mirrored in Austria. "Austria-Hungary," sometime Austrian foreign minister Baron von Burián succinctly summarized, would have to "either lose Galicia or bring Congress Poland into some close relationship with the monarchy."[76]

Thus the creation of a dependent Polish state was to solve for Germany the peculiar mix of foreign and domestic threats posed by the reintroduction of the international Polish Question during the war. Yet Beseler had little to say about how Germany might deal with the disruptive effects the creation of a Polish state, even one under tight German control, might have in its own Polish territories. The potential for domestic upheaval in the Ostmark (up to and including an armed Polish uprising aimed at detaching Germany's Polish provinces and unifying them with the newly created Polish Kingdom) that Beseler's policies contained was a major source of criticism of the Governor-General during—and, as will be shown, after—the war. Conservatives and nationalists in Germany thought that Beseler was far too accommodating toward the Poles and that many of the policies his regime came to pursue were reckless. The baffled leader of the Conservative faction in the Reichstag, Kuno Graf von Westarp, concluded that Beseler must have fallen under the seductive sway of "a circle of Warsaw intellectuals."[77] Criticism of his regime and its actions based on domestic German Polish policy irritated Beseler. In January 1917, he complained in a letter to a friendly correspondent that "the understanding of the circumstances in Poland is in [Germany] strikingly poor," which he blamed on the fact that "everything is seen from the point of view of [Prussia's] internal . . . Polish policies, and there is curiously no understanding at all of the great political tasks that [must] be considered when solving the Polish question."[78] That same year, Beseler bridled at accusations, made by ignorant and "incorrigible" malcontents in the German press, that he harbored a "sentimental . . . but politically unwise . . . fondness for Poland."[79] On another occasion, he lamented that the Conservatives and National Liberals were seeing things "through a pan-Germanist and hakatistic lens, and cannot separate their judgment of events [here] from their views on Prussia's Polish policies."[80] His policy did receive some notable support; writing in the *Preussische Jahrbücher*, for example, Hans Delbrück lauded Germany's tolerant policies in occupied Poland and called for similar concessions to be made in Prussian Poland. Delbrück acknowledged that Polish irredentism would be a threat, but he argued that relaxing Prussia's anti-Polish policies would turn the Poles into loyal, reliable citizens. As an added argument, Delbrück pointed out that geography, combined with the sheer number of Germans living in the Prussian east, meant that Polish nationalists wishing to claim these territories "would first have to destroy the German Empire."[81] (It is not quite clear why this was supposed to be reassuring.) Another supporter was Friedrich Naumann, the publicist and enthusiastic partisan of a German-dominated *Mitteleuropa*. "I don't know of anything better about Poland," Beseler declared of Naumann's pamphlet *Deutsche und Polen* (Germans and Poles). "He devotes quite a bit of favorable attention to me in it," Beseler added, obviously pleased, and recommended to his wife that she pick up a copy for herself.[82] Max Weber also approved of Beseler's policies, though not quite as enthusiastically as Naumann.[83] Like Delbrück, Weber thought that Germany would have to relax its domestic Polish policies if Beseler's schemes stood any chance of success. Otherwise, Germany ran the risk of "creating a Serbia before our gates." (Weber was keenly aware of the fundamental problem at the heart of Germany's wartime Polish policies: "A resolution of Germany's and Poland's numerous and difficult conflicts of interest, fully acceptable to both," he observed during the war, "is—unfortunately—not possible."[84]) Despite these eminent supporters, the criticism of the nationalists and pan-Germanists weighed on Beseler. In 1917, he observed to Clara that when it came to judging things "through the lenses of partisanship and prejudice," Poland and Germany were not very different.[85]

To Beseler, the opportunity to answer the Polish Question to Germany's advantage and thereby ensure German security in the east greatly outweighed the dangers—real or imagined—this posed to Prussia's troubled relationship between the state and its Polish subjects. This does not, of course, mean that Beseler did not think at all about such disruptions or about how they might be dealt with. Beseler's preferred solution was an expansion of Polish territory eastward, which would allow Prussian Poles who wanted to leave Germany ample room to resettle in the new Polish Kingdom.[86] In other words, Beseler seemed to count on a kind of voluntary ethnic cleansing through emigration to solve Prussia's Polish problem. This was not an unusual idea. At the beginning of the war, for example, the Silesian National Democrat Wojciech Korfanty had suggested to a representative of the Imperial Office of the Interior that Germany should support Polish expansion eastward. "Prussia's Polish question," he argued (almost certainly insincerely, given his National Democratic political leanings), "would thereby be . . . settled, since in Grodno and Minsk large [and] fertile rural regions await settlement, to which a considerable portion of the Polish population of Prussia could migrate."[87] Voluntary resettlement of Prussian Poles in Poland and Polish Germans in Germany is also mentioned by Weber as a matter in need of serious discussion by Polish and German politicians, though it isn't clear if Weber is endorsing the idea.[88] Beseler had other reasons for wishing to push the border of the new Polish state eastward: it would, he argued, create more distance between Russia and Germany, while the extra territory would give Poland "the possibility to develop" itself as a state.[89] It does seem that there was a colonial-type vision of "the east" at work in Poland during the Great War; however, to Beseler, Poland had the potential to play the role of a colonizing power rather than colonial victim.

By early 1916, all the ideological elements of Beseler's program were thus in place: the desire for border annexations; the strong belief that a workable solution to the Polish Question would have to rest on a foundation of Polish consent; the equally strong belief that Germany would nonetheless have to find a way to maintain unshakable influence over Polish foreign affairs; and, finally, the conviction that the Poles were political "children" who would have to be "educated" in the art of government by those who knew better. In terms of broad historical context and lines of continuity, Beseler and his regime are not the harbingers of the murderous era in German-Polish history that would be inaugurated in 1919, but rather representatives of a rapidly fading earlier era. As Beseler's policy began to be translated into institutions, the subject of the remainder of this book, his actions and beliefs in many way began to resemble those of Count Aleksander Wielopolski, Margrave Gonzaga-Myszkowski, the nineteenth-century nobleman who, under Tsar Alexander II, had liberalized conditions in Russian Poland at the same time that he worked to ensure that Russia retained a steely grip on Poland's affairs.[90] Like Beseler, Wielopolski sought stability in Poland by trying to find the right balance between consent and coercion. It was a historical similarity of which Beseler was fully aware; in December 1916, he quoted to Hutten-Czapski Wielopolski's famous dictum that "one can work for the Poles, but not with them."[91] Beseler certainly must have been aware that Wielopolski's tenure as head of Russia's administration in Poland came to a disastrous end with the outbreak of the January Rising of 1863, a rising arguably caused by Wielopolski's policies, which were coercive enough to stoke resentment and anger and liberal enough to allow the Poles to translate these feelings into action.

In its broad outlines, Beseler's Polish policy also represents the fulfillment of a line of strategic thought that had existed in Germany for decades. Since at least the late nineteenth century, soldiers and civilians less worried about Polish nationalism than about the armies of the Tsar had urged that Germany seriously consider re-creating a Polish state in the east in the event of war. This would potentially win for Germany the support of the Poles, and would also allow Germany to dictate the terms on which a reconstituted Polish state would be created, thereby minimizing, as far as possible, the disadvantages for itself. As noted in the Introduction, even Bismarck had thought that war with Russia would fundamentally alter Germany's long-standing hostility to Polish nationalism and lead it to champion, from sheer strategic self-interest, the cause of Polish autonomy in central Europe.[92] The possibility of acting on this idea had existed in Germany from the very first days of the war. Indeed, Hutten-Czapski claims in his memoirs that Emperor Wilhelm informed him in late July 1914 that a new German-sponsored Polish state was bound to emerge from the war that loomed on the horizon.[93] Until 1916, however, this idea led neither to a firm decision on what direction to take in Poland nor to a set of policies to be implemented in the occupied zone. Beseler would play a key role in guiding Germany policy on both points.

Over the course of the occupation, Beseler would develop his ideas into institutions, sometimes with the support of the German state and sometimes not, and sometimes in harmony with Polish elites and sometimes not. Beseler felt continually thwarted by those who either failed to appreciate the deep wisdom of his plans, like German conservatives, or who stubbornly refused to subordinate their own interests to Germany's, like Austria, or the National Democrats, or the PPS. "You have no idea," he wrote to Clara in 1917, "how awful it is to always be a bound Prometheus."[94] Still, whatever obstacles were placed in Beseler's way, many of his administration's own policies worked at cross-purposes to his ambitions. The harsher aspects of the occupation quickly dissipated whatever goodwill Beseler's conciliatory gestures generated and did much to undermine his credibility in the eyes of the occupied people to whom he liked to think he was bringing light.

Repression, Resistance, and Public Opinion

Beseler's regime began by instituting restrictive measures on associational, political, and cultural life in occupied Poland. These were soon eased, however, as Germany sought first to burnish its public image and then to win the long-term loyalty of the Polish elite. Germany's attempts to influence public opinion in Poland brought, at best, mixed results. German wariness of losing control over the occupied territory, lingering bitterness toward the Germans caused by the Prussian Polish nationality struggle and the attack on Kalisz, and the inescapable burdens and privations caused by total war all conspired to foment widespread antipathy toward Germany in Congress Poland— although it should be borne in mind that generalizations about "Polish perceptions" of the Germans during the war are exceedingly difficult to make. The great events of the war years affected opinion in the occupied zone, making it to some degree contingent. The revolutions in Russia, the Central Powers' proclamation on the restoration of Polish statehood, and the great battlefield victories and losses, among other events, all influenced Polish opinion, both popular and elite.[95] Social caste and class also influenced the way the occupation was perceived. Peasants in Poland, for example—who made up the majority of the population—were generally loyal to the Tsar, despised "their" nobility, and were not interested in nationalism. The patriotic and nationalistic displays that the Germans not only allowed but actively encouraged seemed to them just another display of the power and influence of the hated "gentlemen." Yet the farmers also illustrate the way that the war set in motion changes in the region: by its end, farmers constituted a substantial proportion of fighters in the nationalist, pro-Piłsudski POW.[96] The Archbishop of Warsaw, Aleksander Kakowski, provides another example of how the war was constantly shifting the variables according to which individuals calculated their behavior under the occupation. Kakowski, in the first few years of occupation, had maintained a cool distance from the Germans, since there was still a widespread conviction that the Russians would return someday. But late in November 1917, after the fall of the Tsar and the seizure of power by the Bolsheviks, Kakowski dined with Beseler for the first time. To the Governor-General's surprise, Kakowski adopted a friendly demeanor and led the table in a toast to the Austrian and German emperors.[97]

Still, some of the concessions made by Beseler and his regime did make a positive impression. Many of the most obvious signs of Russian domination were done away with; a German official, Adolf Warschauer, who had visited the city before the war and returned in 1915 to serve as an archivist, was struck upon his arrival at how quickly the city's shop and street signs, which had been written in Russian and Polish, had been completely "Polonized."[98] Statues of Russian heroes were removed, and streets that had been named after Russians were given new Polish names.[99] Polish literature and the arts were also allowed to flourish by the Germans. Censorship had been strict under the Tsars, and anything deemed anti-Russian or too overtly full of Polish patriotism was strictly forbidden. This meant, in practice, an extensive ban on Polish high culture, since much of its literature and art, particularly from the Romantic period, was connected to myths and stories of rebellion and resistance against the Tsar. While the Germans reserved the right to block performances they found objectionable, the departure of the Russians led to a triumphant return to Polish concert houses and theaters of patriotic works that had long been illegal. Thus, while the monument to Ivan Paskewicz, the Russian commander who had crushed the 1830–1831 uprising, was pulled down, Stanisław Wyspiański's drama about the same uprising, *Noc Listopadowa* (November Night), returned to Warsaw's stages. Performances were sometimes accompanied by rousing renditions of Poland's unofficial national anthems, "Jeszcze Polska nie zginęła" (Poland Has Not Yet Perished) and "Boże coś Polskę" (God Save Poland). The patriotic fare on offer, along with light entertainments meant for diversion and relaxation, proved enormously popular. A play about the plight of Polish education under the repressive rule of the Tsars, *Młody las* (Young Forest) by J. A. Hertz, was performed no fewer than seventy-eight times in the 1915/1916 season.[100] Films with an anti-Russian tone also enjoyed great popularity during the war years in Warsaw. Movies such as *The Struggle for Independence (W walce o niepodległość)* and *The Unwanted Guest (Niepożądany gość)* stoked resentments and fed historical grievances. The makers of *The Tsar's Spies in Warsaw and Their Secrets (Ochrana Warszawska i jej tajemnice)* cleverly blended entertainment of the patriotic and more escapist variety by telling the story of a romantic entanglement between a female Polish patriot and a secret policeman.[101]

Włodzimierz Gałecki, the teacher, was the son of actors and a theater enthusiast. He was delighted to have patriotic plays running again in Warsaw's theaters. (He lived through the Nazi occupation as well, and later in life noted that, compared with what happened then, the occupation of the First World War was "like an idyll."[102]) Adolf Warschauer, the German administrator and archivist, experienced firsthand the effect the theatrical performances could have on people. Some time after his arrival, he went to see a performance of a play by Gabriela Zapolska about Warsaw's Russian prison (probably *Tamten* [That Over There]). After waiting several days for a ticket to the popular event, Warschauer was treated to a series of vignettes vividly depicting Russian brutality against Poles. In one scene, for example, a pair of Polish women go to speak to the Russian Governor-General. He receives them with courtesy and speaks to them civilly. When they leave his office, however, his rough Cossack guards fall upon them violently—a scene depicted, in the staging seen by Warschauer, with a great deal of evocative noise. In another scene, Russian troops ransack the rooms of some Warsaw students, looking for subversive materials, which they discover hidden in a young woman's hair. The scenes had precisely the effect the Germans must have wanted, stirring up a strong current of anti-Russian feeling in the room. The man sitting next to Warschauer reassured him over and over again that "nothing in this play is exaggerated, things like this happened all the time." Still, some performances may have gone too far. Warschauer notes that he later saw a staging of living tableaux depicting the Romantic-era art of Artur Grottger. Grottger was known for his lurid, Goya-esque depictions of the suffering and death inflicted on Poland in the wake of its uprisings. In *Po odejściu Wroga* (After the Enemy Has Gone), for example, an image from his series *Polonia*, about the 1863 uprising, a young family, including a baby, is shown slaughtered in its ransacked home. In the background a man in a uniform—a friend, perhaps, or relative returning from the war—covers his face, overwhelmed by grief and horror. The dead man in the bed has managed to expire with his arm balanced on the edge of a nearby chair with his clenched fist thrust upward in a gesture of posthumous defiance. Warschauer found these scenes portrayed live on a stage "repulsive" as, it seems, did many of the Poles in the audience; Warschauer noted that the audience grew steadily smaller as the strange, grotesque performance went on.[103]

The Germans tolerated, and even supported, other displays of Polish national feeling, especially when it aroused memories of Russian oppression. Warschauer, for example, provided a book of photographs for a public exhibition on the 1863 uprising. The public was also invited to attend lectures on Polish history, which were given every day of the week, with multiple lectures taking place on Sunday. The lectures never lacked for attendees, and some of them were repeated several times to accommodate everyone who wanted to hear them. (Warschauer marveled at the ability of the Poles to "use art and scholarship in the service of the national idea."[104]) In the summer of 1916, the Germans allowed for the establishment of a memorial cross at Grochów, where a key battle of the 1830–1831 uprising had taken place and where the Russians had carried out executions of the insurgents.[105]

The high point of this trend was the public celebration of the anniversary of the 3 May 1791 constitution. The constitution, which provided a framework for a monarchical-parliamentary government for Poland and thus would have ended the chaotic rule of the nobles, had been widely admired at the time by liberal and revolutionary reformers throughout Europe. Its adoption, however, provoked Russia and ultimately contributed to the third partition of Poland. The emotional resonance that the constitution continued to evoke within the Polish historical imagination is revealed by the massive

success of a parade held in 1916 to commemorate it. The celebration's organizing committee called on the city's inhabitants to turn out in force to celebrate this public "symbol of [our] inseparable connection with the past and the
announcement of a better future," and Warsaw's denizens responded with enthusiasm. Crowds thronged in the streets, speeches and music lent a sense of
solemnity and celebration, and flags bearing the Polish eagle lined the avenues.
The main event was a massive parade in which thousands of people marched.
Adolf Warschauer was impressed by the cross section of Polish society presented in the parade, each distinguished by a different style of dress; the liberals and the bourgeoisie, for example, in suits, farmers in their traditional cos-
tumes, and Orthodox Jews in their caftans. Schoolgirls danced down the street,
and Archbishop Kakowski strolled along with his clergy.[106] Another observer
was impressed by the show of pan-Varsovian enthusiasm, noting with approval
that the city's Jewish community had circulated copies of "Hebrew hymns
composed 125 years ago in honor of the Polish constitution." The parade itself,
he calculated, took more than three hours to wind its way past the spectators.[107]
It began at Plac Zamkowy and then proceeded south, down the elegant thor-
oughfares of Krakowskie Przedmieście, Nowy Świat, and Aleje Ujazdowskie
before turning west and heading to Plac Unii Lubelskiej. From there it went
north on Marszałkowska, where the marchers dispersed. For all the festive-
ness, old habits proved hard to break. Gałecki, the teacher, watched the parade,
and noted that from time to time a group of marchers would startle suddenly
and run off in a panic, before realizing that they were in no danger and returning to their places. It was simply inconceivable to them that there really
were no Cossacks—or German troops—on their way to break the parade up.[108]

The celebration was undeniably a great success. There was little, if any, display of overt hostility or anger toward the occupiers. Beseler was convinced
that he had managed to create an ample fund of goodwill in Poland on which
he could draw to further his political vision. The time had come, he told Berlin,
to act on his policy recommendations. Any hesitation would mean that the
pro-German sentiment he believed he had created would evaporate.[109]

And yet, for all the success of the 3 May celebrations, it does not seem that
there was much real affection for the Germans in Poland. According to a bit
of wartime Polish popular wisdom, being asked if the Germans were more

agreeable than the Russians was like being asked whether one preferred plague to cholera.[110] Gałecki, who had been so elated to be able to see patriotic plays, nonetheless described the occupation as being marked by "villainy and duplicity."[111] Nor was Alexander Kraushar convinced. Kraushar, from a well-to-do Jewish family, was an assimilationist and a Polish nationalist who had converted to Catholicism in 1903. A veteran of conspiratorial agitation and host to a "salon" dedicated to nurturing Polish culture, Kraushar denounced Germany's attempts to woo Polish opinion as an example of their "characteristic perversity." All of it, he believed, was simply a thin and unconvincing disguise for exploitation and conquest, and in his memoirs Kraushar explicitly warns future historians not to be fooled.[112]

The hostility to Germany in the Kingdom of Poland was not to be so easily overcome for several reasons. For one, the resentments created by Prussia's Germanization policies proved to be deeply rooted. In Lodz, in the years before the war, the Polish press would erupt in anger if Russian military bands played anything German, announcing that "Hakatist hymns" should not be played on "Slavic instruments."[113] The fact that "Hakatism," a byword for virulently hostile anti-Polish sentiment, had become synonymous with Germany itself did not augur well for Beseler's ambitions. Certainly many of the people over whom he ruled during the war did not wish to forgive and forget. In 1916, shortly after Germany officially announced its support for the restoration of Polish statehood, the satirical newspaper *Mucha* published the following poem. The "King Zygmunt" and "Copernicus" conversing here are apparently the statues of each in Warsaw. King Zygmunt's is in Castle Square and Copernicus's is a few blocks south; the two face each other:

King Zygmunt and Copernicus

Late one night
As the arc lamps hissed
King Zygmunt asked
Copernicus this:
—The Germans, they say,
   have promised the sky
   What are your thoughts,
   wise Father Mikołaj?

The great astronomer
was silent for a time
'Til finally he answered
With the following lines:
   —Hakatists! Września!
   Resettlement! Poznań!

And so their conversation ended!
And silence descended.

How well they understood each other.
The Sovereign and
the mighty scholar.[114]

The litany of Prussian aggression against its Polish subjects chanted by Copernicus (Września/Wreschen was a town in Posen famous for a riot by its Polish inhabitants, sparked by the introduction of the German language for religion classes in the schools, and the subsequent trial, which became a media circus) in this weird, unsettling scene suggests that the bitterness caused by the Prussian state's history of hostility to Catholicism and to Polish national identity was thoroughly entrenched in Polish culture. While difficult to calculate its impact with precision, this was certainly one reason why the alliance Beseler came to seek with the Polish elite would prove so elusive.[115]

Some of the actions of the regime and its representatives likewise did little to endear them to the civilians of the Government-General. As noted earlier in the chapter, Beseler's tenure in Poland began with the dissolution of Polish organizations and the institution of restrictions on Polish cultural life. Further organized repression was promised by the establishment of a Central Police Office in Warsaw, created "for conducting counter-espionage and military-political police operations." Agents of the office were detailed to every military district in the Government-General.[116] While some of the harsher aspects of Beseler's early tenure were soon to be relaxed, the regime always remained both willing and able to use force in the name of order and security. In 1916, for example, "42 spies and bandits" met their end "on the old Russ[ian] execution grounds in the Citadel," the hulking Russian fortress and prison in Warsaw's north.[117] Another execution took place in Łuków on 10 July 1916, when the Germans shot one Stanisław Wojnowski for unlawful weapons possession.[118] Some transgressions against the regime brought less lethal but nonetheless unpleasant consequences, as in the case of a political activist named Kronberg, arrested in September 1916 and imprisoned in Germany for calling out in public, "Long live the revolution!"[119] Similarly, two lawyers also found themselves sent to Germany for anti-German activities.[120]

Still, brutish coercion, violence, and terror were not part of the experience of occupation for the vast majority of people living under the rule of the Government-General. The possibility, however, was always there. Gałecki recalled that the head of the school where he taught near Lodz arrived at the building one day to find German soldiers smashing the desks and using them as firewood. The headmaster went to their commanding officer to complain, and was told that, if he was lying, the commander would have him shot. The two went to the school and found that the soldiers had actually grown even more destructive. After putting a stop to it, the German officer asked the headmaster's pardon, explaining that the men were only recently arrived from Belgium ("Poor Belgium!" Gałecki remarks when recounting this story).[121] There was little heat in the German officer's warning, and it is doubtful that he really would have had the director shot. Nonetheless, such threats can leave a lingering sense of fear and anger and are a reminder of the potential for violence that always existed beneath the surface of the occupation, even if it was mostly calm. In addition, it is reasonable to conclude that the sight of rampaging German soldiers was not to be glimpsed only this one time, in a school outside of Lodz. And perhaps not all German commanders were as conscious of their duty as this one obviously was.

Whatever impression the German army may have made, the single greatest source of popular resentment against the German occupiers, and the one most responsible for ensuring that the sought-after alliance would elude them, was the severe material privation that afflicted everyone in Poland during the war. The Great War's voracious appetite for materiel led the Germans to plunder Poland of anything that could be of use to their war effort: wood, horses, metal, leather. The requisitions reached deeply into the private sphere, with doorknobs, cookware, and samovars disappearing from Polish homes, taken to be melted down and put to use in the service of German victory.[122] Requisitions were supposed to be paid for by a complicated process involving a mixed committee of German and Polish authorities as well as

representatives of those directly affected by the confiscations. This committee was to determine a fair price for the goods being requisitioned, with
those affected receiving 10 percent of that amount in cash and the balance
after the war. Of course, the war did not end the way the Germans had
hoped in Poland, meaning that those who had their goods requisitioned lost
a great deal in the transaction. (However, in September 1918 the Germans
did manage to pay off about 30 million marks in outstanding requisition-
related debts.[123]) And bureaucratic niceties were not always followed. A soldier once showed up at Alexander Kraushar's apartment looking for metal
objects to requisition. He took a few things and left a voucher that had been
improperly filled out (and thus was presumably worthless). The same soldier
later returned and ripped the metal door off an oven used to heat one of the
apartment's rooms, this time not even bothering to fill out the paperwork.[124]

The commodity whose disappearance caused the most severe suffering in
wartime Poland was food. Gałecki, who believed the Imperial German occupation to have been a "paradise" compared with the Nazis', nonetheless
thought that, in terms of food supply, the First World War was actually worse
for Polish civilians than the Second.[125] The Germans were relentless in its pursuit and treated Poland as a kind of vast military pantry from which they
could take their fill. One requisitions unit in Kalisz reported having sent no
fewer than 25 million eggs to Germany in the second half of 1916.[126] Warsaw
was essentially blockaded, and all incoming traffic was searched for hidden
food. Soldiers on guard duty would lance bags and sacks being moved into
the city to check their contents. Teams of officials would even board trains
coming into Warsaw, opening traveler's packages to see if there was food in
them.[127] In addition to the well-organized official requisitions, individual soldiers in Poland, in a reversal of the standard route of wartime care packages,
mailed home parcels of food. The sight of these uniformed men in the post
offices with their ill-gotten gains did not endear Germany to the collective
Polish heart.[128] The wholly inadequate supplies left over for Polish consump-
tion were strictly rationed at rates that compared unfavorably with those
allotted to civilians in Germany; the official daily ration of bread in Warsaw
in October 1915, for example, was 160 grams, while in Germany it was 225.
In such conditions, diseases such as typhus, smallpox, measles, and diph-
theria flourished.[129] Riots broke out in Warsaw, fueled by despair, anger,
and hunger.[130]

Several other factors beyond requisitions helped ruin Poland's economy and cause misery among the civilian population. Unemployment was high in occupied Poland, a circumstance linked at least in part to one of the most ruinous economic policies pursued there: the wholesale dismantling of entire factories and the shipping of their equipment to Germany, a policy that virtually destroyed Congress Poland's industry.[131] Workers also suffered under the Germans' short-lived forced labor program. A forced labor drive was begun in the fall of 1916 at the instigation of Ludendorff as part of his attempt to mobilize all available resources in the pursuit of war without limits. (The drive was ended in December as a result of popular hostility.) Those rounded up in forced labor drives were given the chance to accept employment in Germany; refusal brought assignment to a Civil Labor Battalion (ZAB). Most ZABs worked locally on projects of limited duration, though some unfortunates found themselves sent to distant camps where they performed hard labor under terrible conditions (a fate that, for reasons that are not clear, seems to have befallen a disproportionate number of Jews from Warsaw).[132] Finally, even those fortunate enough to have paid work found that severe inflation undermined the purchasing power of their earnings. Between September 1915 and May 1918, for example, the price of meat increased by 477 percent; in the same period, wages for workers in the Warsaw area increased between 147 and 233 percent.[133] As the occupation wore on, Warsaw's streets began to fill with gaunt, unhealthy people in worn-out clothes, shuffling along in cheap wooden shoes. Beggars became ubiquitous while the wealthy in their finery disappeared from the capital's streets.[134]

The Germans' economic policies were a major source of Polish resentment toward the occupiers and occasionally caused unrest and outright resistance. Several strikes took place in Warsaw, for example of the city's tram drivers and of local metalworkers, which led to violent confrontations with the authorities, arrests, and incarceration.[135] Sometimes the violence occasioned by resistance had more serious consequences; in October 1917, a German requisition in Węglowice, in the district of Częstochowa, turned violent when the population refused to cooperate. Troops opened fire, leaving nine people dead.[136] The Germans' policy of seizing the bells from Catholic churches frequently provoked German-Polish clashes as well. The Germans would arrive to perform the requisition only to find that the bells had disappeared; taking the priests and other notable members of the parish hostage usually

caused them to rematerialize.[137] On at least one occasion, the confiscation of
a church's bells led to a violent encounter between occupiers and occupied.
On 12 February 1918, in Włocławek, some intrepid soul alerted parishioners
that the Germans were coming for their cathedral's bells by sounding the
alarm from its tower. Locals hurried to the cathedral and had to be forcibly
dispersed by the Germans. One German soldier was stabbed in the clash, and
a local was shot.[138] Falling afoul of the Germans' rules could bring other kinds
of unpleasant consequences. In 1918, two Polish farmers traveling with a load
of grain from Orły to the village of Korfowe were stopped at a checkpoint.
The guards declared them in violation of a law against illegal transportation
of food and confiscated the load, along with all the money the poor farmers
had on them. They were given a further fine, which, they argued in a written
protest to the authorities, had been unjustly levied on them, for they had done
nothing wrong.[139]

The Wages of Plunder

It is tempting to see Germany's ruthless economic exploitation of Poland as,
at best, a sign of its insincerity regarding Polish autonomy, or, at worst, a clear
harbinger of the horrors of National Socialist rule in Poland. There are, however, other ways of contextualizing Germany's economic policies that, while
not excusing them, suggest that they were mainly a contingent response to
the pressures of total war, rather than part of a German plan to reorganize
central Europe. They were, moreover, responses conceived at a time when reality and norms were parting ways. The formal and informal restraints on
war that had accumulated in Europe before 1914 proved wholly inadequate
to the unimaginable task of coming to grips with a conflict as massive and as
destructive as the First World War. Finally, transnational comparisons suggest
that Germany's responses to the Great War's pressures were not very different
from the responses to similar problems pursued by other belligerents.

In the Second World War, the Nazis plundered Europe in part to shield
German civilians from the burdens of the war. In the First World War, the
German military plundered Germany in much the same way that it was
plundering its occupied territories. Although Reich Germans were certainly
better off than Polish civilians, German tables were also emptying of food,

German churches were losing their bells, and German civilians were reduced to wearing ill-fitting, uncomfortable wooden shoes.[140] This is not to suggest in any way that the German army had the right to plunder Poland; rather, it suggests that the primary cause of the requisitions was the war's voracious appetites (rather than, for example, a colonialist vision of Poland's role in a German-dominated *Mitteleuropa*) and a realization that a prolonged war of industrial attrition was not a kind of war that Germany was well-placed to win. Since German civilians were not spared extensive requisitions, it is difficult to see what could have induced the army to spare Polish civilians. In addition, Russian Poland was already suffering economically when the Germans arrived, owing to Russia's requisitioning of war materiel, requisitions that strongly resembled those carried out by the Germans. Even before their scorched earth retreat had devastated the region, for example, Russia had sent heavy industrial equipment home, contributing to high unemployment in a region whose normal market networks had already been disrupted by the war. Factories that could not be dismantled in time to keep them out of German hands were destroyed as the Russians fled.[141]

It is also difficult to see what could have spared Polish civilians their hunger and the unfavorable rations. Germany's food supplies were severely disrupted by the Allied blockade, since Germany had, before the war, been dependent on imported foodstuffs.[142] The motive behind the blockade was the very same that drove the German requisitions in Poland: the belligerents realized that, in a total war of attrition, civilian morale was a resource that needed to be mustered and managed to keep the war going, and extended periods of severe hunger were a sure path to the collapse of the civilians' commitment to "see it through." Moving food from Poland to Germany was a response to this kind of warfare. Keeping the population fed was part and parcel of the war effort, strategically little different from mounting an attack on the front, or staging a propaganda exhibition at home, or playing on the grievances and resentments of the civilian population of an enemy state.

The question of forced labor, while complex, can also be contextualized in ways that tell us more about the Great War than about the origins of the Nazis. First, it is crucial to note that, in contrast with the Nazi war effort, no laborers were forcibly deported to Germany, though workers were indeed recruited to work in the Reich by a special network of offices in Poland.[143] The entire Nazi war economy, in contrast, was dependent on the millions of slave laborers forced to work for the Reich during the Second World War. Many Polish workers came to Germany willingly in the First World War. It is possible that not all of them felt that they had a rich menu of options from which to choose, and that the line between free and forced labor was not always as clear as it might be.[144] But to fully elide the difference between the two and to treat forced and free labor as essentially the same is to deny Poles any agency and to make them passive objects of German desires. And if the line in Poland between forced and free labor was murky, then so was it also in other places where belligerent countries desperately sought to feed the monstrous need for manpower that the war created. The British, for example, assigned native chiefs in some of its African colonies quotas of laborers to be supplied. It can reasonably be doubted that the men delivered this way had their rights and freedoms carefully guarded. Meanwhile, close scrutiny of the offices set up throughout China by Britain and France would likely reveal that they operated in much the same way as the German labor recruitment offices in Poland.[145]

The drive for Polish labor can also usefully be compared with Ludendorff's ambitions for labor within Germany itself. Ludendorff saw labor as simply one more resource that needed to be placed at the unrestricted disposal of the state as it waged total war. This was the impulse behind the Auxiliary Service Law of 1916, which mandated a civilian draft and regulated the movements of workers between industries. State control over labor was not total after the passage of the law, but not for lack of effort; rather, it was the strength of the German labor movement that prevented the state from treating workers as merely so many potatoes or belt buckles.[146] The impulse in Poland was the same, but without an organized labor movement strong enough to withstand the demands of the German military. (In Germany, the continued support of the Social Democrats was essential to keeping the home front mobilized; workers in Poland had no such card to play with their occupiers.) As Tammy Proctor has shown, most of the European states that were fighting the war found themselves overwhelmed by the demand for manpower it created, most used workers from outside the homeland, and most of them found ways to mobilize labor that blended consent and coercion in different degrees. The main difference, as far as Germany is concerned, is that the Germans, not having much of an empire to draw labor from, ended up treating Europeans the way that the French and British only treated people from Africa and Asia.

A broader context also suggests other ways of interpreting Germany's use of forced labor. First, as far as civilians being sent, or going, to Germany to work are concerned, it has been pointed out that they were not allowed to return home, and this, it has been argued, essentially made them prisoners, and thus forced laborers.[147] If indeed the Poles who signed up to go did not know this was going to happen, this is an outrage. However, it is also important to note that these workers were the subjects of a state—Russia—with which Germany was at war. This made them, in the parlance of societies at war, "enemy aliens." All over the world, enemy aliens had restrictions placed on them, up to and including incarceration in concentration camps. Britain imprisoned 25,000 men on the Isle of Man. (States were particularly interested in keeping track of men of military age, of which at least some of the men who went, or were sent, from Poland to Germany were; hence there was little chance they'd be able to travel freely back into what was, technically, a war zone.[148]) And, in many places, these civilians were forced to work, often under miserable circumstances. Consider the following description of forced laborers tasked with building roads and bridges, describing, not even the work, but the trip to and from work:

> The prisoners and their guards put in exceptionally long days walking to and from the project sites. In some cases they marched from four to six miles each way; according to the inspection report [February 1916], this amounted "practically to a day's work in itself," especially given the snow conditions that winter. To make matters worse, the distance from the camp precluded a warm midday meal and the men had to choke down frozen food.

This is not, as might be expected, a scene from a remote and unfamiliar eastern European location. This is a description of the working conditions of civilian internees in Canada—most likely poor Ukrainians who had immigrated there, with official encouragement, before the war—building a transportation network in Banff.[149]

Finally, there remains the issue of forced labor performed under military supervision within the occupied zone. The laws governing the use of labor in occupied territories were vague at best, drafted as they were in an era when prolonged military occupations had not yet been invented. Section III of the

1907 Laws and Customs of War on Land, "Military Authority over the Territory of the Hostile State," grants full legitimate state power to the occupying army. The laws also state that "requisitions in kind and services shall not be demanded from municipalities or inhabitants *except for the needs of the army of occupation*" (emphasis added). Crucially, the law states that requisitions of goods have to be paid for; but does not say anything about "services."[150] This is not to defend the Germans' actions, but merely to point out that they seem to have been generally in keeping with the norms of warfare in force at the time—norms that were undergoing a wrenching transition from the short "cabinet wars" of the nineteenth century and the long, total wars of the twentieth.[151] In addition, our view of the German use of labor within occupied Poland is analytically distorted by the historical associations we invariably bring to our examination of it. The words "German," "forced labor," and "Poland" conjure up images of hundreds of thousands of skeletal individuals forced to do all manner of horrible work by brutal German overlords who thought them less than human and worked them, quite literally, to death. Yet the use of forced labor on specific projects of limited duration had a long tradition in Europe—the corvée. Thinking of what the Germans instituted in Poland as a corvée, which their forced labor policy much resembled, links it with this more traditional form of state-mandated labor, even if the grim barracks and military guards were a new twist pointing toward the future. In sum, Germany's treatment of labor, in addition to what it tells us about the continuities of German history, also tells us quite a lot about the First World War and its impact—about the blurring lines between soldier and civilian and the shattering of norms and practices wholly inadequate to the struggle at hand.

Such historical subtleties were, of course, of absolutely no concern to those who suffered because of the war and occupation. Germany's economic policies generated misery and outrage, and not all of it was directed against the Germans. Many people in occupied Poland blamed their misfortunes on "speculators," a widely accepted code word for Jews.[152] Speculators were denounced in scathing pamphlets, songs, poems, and jokes. One Varsovian publishing house announced that it would be issuing custom-made medals to recognize the "glory" of the wartime service of speculators and profiteers. The medal would be inscribed with the prices charged during the war, as well as a "portrait of the speculator as well as the image of a historical profiteer" ("ordinary mortals" who bought the medal, the paper continued, would also find it quite suitable for use "as a watch chain").[153] But of course the Germans were also resented, and even hated, because of the requisitions. The plunder of Poland also made for an enduring and glaring contradiction between German promises and the way they treated the people under their authority, sapping the credibility from their pronouncements of friendship and cooperation. "It is the squaring of a circle and a self-contradiction," Administrative Chief Kries noted in November 1916, "when, on the one hand, we call the Poles to fight alongside us as allies, and, on the other, treat them as a conquered people."[154] Even Beseler, who would never have done anything that might have undermined Germany's prospects of victory, admitted to Clara in 1917 that "it's really about time that the awful economic exploitation of the country is eased."[155] But it didn't, and in fact couldn't. Beseler and the Germans were caught in a bind. To impose their vision of a friendly but dependent Polish state on the postwar order, they would first have to win the war; to win the war, they would have to muster everything that could possibly be used to endure a prolonged war of attrition; the longer the entire project hung on the outcome of a war of attrition, the longer the extractions in Poland continued; and the longer they continued, the more embittered the population became. There was no way that these policies would have changed in any meaningful way so long as the war went on, although there is also no reason to think they would have continued in the event of a German victory— another stark contrast with the Second World War, when the end of formal combat merely marked the beginning of new kinds of violence and brutality. In any event, these policies ensured that the Germans stood no chance of winning the sympathy of many people in Poland, and their harshness, along with the suffering they brought, must be borne in mind whenever considering those aspects of the occupation that show Germany in a more favorable light. Polish intellectuals were certainly delighted to have Polish schools reopened. But many of their students had scurvy.

2

Merciless Murderers of the Polish Language

State, Army, and Legitimacy in the Imperial Government-General

On 5 November 1916, it seemed that Beseler's ambitions had finally received the crucial official support that they had lacked during his first year as Governor-General. On that day, a proclamation read out in occupied Russian Poland announced the intention of the Central Powers to support the reestablishment of a Polish state in central Europe when the war was over. The proclamation, often referred to subsequently as the "Act of 5 November," did not result in the immediate creation of an autonomous Polish government. It did, however, continue the destruction of the old political, cultural, and psychological restraints on the Polish Question, making a return to the status quo ante bellum unthinkable. More concretely, the Act accelerated a process of institution building that had begun before the proclamation and would continue until the collapse of the Government-General in the final days of the war. This state-building work, which ranged from the establishment of a university to the creation of elected municipal governments, would ultimately lead, by the end of the occupation, to the emergence of a nascent Polish state. Two of the most visible manifestations of this state-building process were the central Polish government in embryo—for most of 1917, a body known as the Provisional Council of State (Tymczasowa Rada Stanu/ TRS)—and the occupied zone's Polish Military Force (Polnische Wehrmacht/ Polska Siła Zbrojna).

Had Germany's manpower needs not been so dire, Beseler's political vision for postwar central Europe would never have made the existential leap from ideology and memoranda to policy and institutions. The temptation to shore up Germany's forces with Polish recruits played a central role in convincing the German political establishment to back Beseler's plans. Thus the Two Emperors' Proclamation, as the Act was also called, was followed almost immediately by a call for residents of the Congress Kingdom to join up and fight alongside the Central Powers. This made it seem to many observers at the time that Germany's only interest was in Polish cannon fodder; all other concessions were merely a smoke screen behind which innocent Poles would be lured to their deaths. This is certainly true, at least as far as the support of the German political and military establishment is concerned. However, their willingness to grant political and cultural concessions in exchange for soldiers, while crucial to driving Beseler's plans forward past the milestone of 5 November 1916, was short-lived. The attempt to recruit Polish "cannon fodder" was a failure. Yet Beseler continued to build on the concessions made and to move the state-building project forward. This was due in part to the fact that, to Beseler, the purpose of building a Polish army was to serve Germany's *future* political goals, not to throw them immediately into combat. In addition, the Polish army was to him but one of the many institutions meant to further his state-building project. It was important—maybe the most important—but it was an adjunct to his broader political ambitions, not the other way around. There was, however, an immediate wartime purpose the "Polnische Wehrmacht" was meant to fulfill: not to absorb British and French bullets and shrapnel, but to serve as an emblem of legitimate government. In this period of Europe's history, military force and legitimate political authority were synonymous (a connection expressed with brilliant concision by Józef Piłsudski when he observed, in March 1917, that "a soldier needs a legal government in order to be a soldier, and a government needs a legal soldier to be a government"[1]). Commanding Polish soldiers was tantamount to making a claim to sovereign authority over the state.

But if the German occupation regime saw the establishment of a Polish military force as key to its ambitions in Poland, so too did the various Polish political movements that had been mobilized and energized by the war. Each saw in the war the opportunity to advance its own vision of Poland. Part of this story is well known: Piłsudski and the left-wing independence movements organized combat forces in order to establish credibility as liberators and to gain influence with the combatant governments, while Dmowski and the conservatives hoped, as they had in 1905, to gain concessions for Poland through displays of loyalty and service to the Tsar. However, a third side of this story is often left out. There was another rival, Władysław Sikorski, who was backed by the full weight of a Great Power, Austria-Hungary. Sikorski and his patrons saw in the war the opportunity to unify Congress Poland with Galicia under Habsburg authority and organized their military efforts accordingly. Finally, one other important aspect of Polish mobilization during this period is lost by focusing on the Piłsudski-Dmowski rivalry: the way in which competing German and Polish ambitions for Poland intertwined and clashed with one another, resulting in a process of dynamic acceleration that drove Poland's reemergence as a state relentlessly forward. This process at times took on a velocity and trajectory unwanted by those elites, both German and Polish, who clung to the illusory belief that events in wartime central Europe could be kept firmly under their control and guided to a resolution of their choosing.

Poland's War

While the emergence of Polish military units during the First World War was an important development in Polish political history, those who fought in their ranks were not representative of a broader "Polish experience" of the war. To the degree that it is even possible to speak of a "Polish experience," at least among military-aged men, it was one of loyal service in the imperial armies of the partitioning powers. According to one estimate, more than 2 million men from the territories that would comprise the postwar Polish state served in the Prussian, Russian, and Austrian armies.[2] To Polish nationalists, this meant that the Great War was one of Polish fratricide. The emotionally charged despair this caused them was given voice by Edward Słoński in his 1914 poem "That Which Has Not Perished" ("Ta co nie zginęła"):

> We're kept apart, my brother,
> By a fate that we can't deny.
> From our two opposing dug-outs
> We're staring death in the eye.

In the trenches filled with groaning
Alert to the shellfire's whine,
We stand and confront each other
I'm your enemy: and you are mine.

So when you catch me in your sights
I beg you, play your part,
And sink your Muscovite bullet
Deep in my Polish heart.

Now I see the vision clearly,
Caring not that we'll both be dead;
For *that which has not perished*
Shall rise from the blood we shed.[3]

Such overwrought, messianic national feeling, however, does not seem to have been very widely shared. Central Europe in 1914 was still overwhelmingly a world of imperial loyalties. Włodzimierz Gałecki, the teacher who had been stranded in Galicia at the outbreak of the war, reflected on this as he passed through the Congress Poland town of Jędrzejów on his August quest to reach Warsaw. Upon entering Jędrzejów, Gałecki was struck by the sight of a peaceful, orderly mass of townsmen and farmers gathered in the square outside of a government building. They were all army reservists, come to report for mobilization. They waited patiently, but no one came to collect them. The Russian officials had hurriedly cleared out of the town—not because they were afraid of the Austrians, but because they thought a Polish uprising was going to break out. Eventually the reservists started to return home. Gałecki thought the Russian evacuation silly, because "you'd be hard pressed to find people more loyal than [these] . . . peasants and townspeople."[4]

That same month, a little to the south of Jędrzejów, in the town of Skała, a young Polish nationalist named Roman Starzyński learned the hard way about the loyalty of the Tsar's peasants. Starzyński was in many ways typical of the nationalists who had flocked to Piłsudski and his movement in Galicia. A native of the Congress Kingdom, Starzyński had engaged in conspiratorial and nationalistic activities and organizations as a schoolboy. Like many nationalists from the Kingdom, he went to Galicia for his university education, eventually earning a PhD in Kraków. While in Galicia, he had continued

his participation in nationalistic associations and joined the riflemen's movement that trained young men for war with Russia.[5] When war broke out,
Starzyński was "mobilized" by the riflemen's union and participated in the ill-
fated "entrepreneurial" invasion of Kielce by Piłsudski loyalists. Starzyński
and his poorly prepared comrades endured several days of hard marching,
hunger, thirst, and cold, believing, as the Russian officials in Jędrzejów had,
that they would be greeted in Congress Poland by an uprising of their fellow
Poles. As he trudged into the Kingdom, his colleagues falling out left and right
from fatigue and hunger, Starzyński nourished himself with thoughts of
Kościuszko and the glorious traditions of Polish insurrection. On 13 August
1914, Starzyński's unit staggered into the town of Skała, whose inhabitants
taught them a shattering lesson. "It was already midnight," Starzyński writes,

> but despite this, in the town square there was a crowd of curious on-
> lookers gathered to observe the "foreign" army. "Theirs"—had left. No
> one greeted these "foreigners" . . . The curious crowd stared silently. No
> one offered a glass of water or a crumb of bread. This wasn't Kraków,
> this wasn't Polish Galicia, this was Russia, and it was populated by a tribe
> that spoke Polish but felt Russian!
>
> We had had no food since morning, we were exhausted from a fifteen
> hour march, but all of that was nothing compared to the feelings caused
> in us by the hostile silence of the inhabitants of Skała, who on 13 Au-
> gust 1914 gathered in their town square, along with their village priest,
> to look with complete indifference at these madmen, who had not been
> asked to come here.[6]

Despite the fact that he was later wounded, Starzyński calls this moment of
disillusionment in Skała "probably the worst experience of the war." He tried
to comfort himself with the "thought that this godforsaken province and
these half-literate people, with their little priest, didn't represent the opinion
of the whole Kingdom. Onward to Warsaw!" Yet there was much there to dis-
appoint him as well. "I didn't know at the time," he continues laconically in
his memoirs, "that Warsaw had showered the Cossacks in flowers."[7] The loyal
Tsarist subjects of Skała were, despite his reveries, more representative of the
Kingdom than Starzyński and his band of intellectual adventurers were. It is
helpful to bear this in mind when tracing the Germans' failed attempt to

create a Polish military force loyal to the Central Powers. While it may seem puzzling that they ever believed this gambit stood a chance of success, the fact remains that for most of the war, Polish soldiers serving under an imperial banner were the norm, not the exception.

Even if more politically ambitious Poles were less numerous than the peasants, the military organizations they founded were important aspects of the mobilization of central European political life in the Great War. At the outbreak of the war, loyalist-nationalist elites in Russia had requested permission to establish a separate Polish unit within the Imperial Russian army, with distinct uniforms and the use of Polish as the language of command. The Tsarist state refused, though permission was granted to form a group of Polish irregulars, which came to be called the Puławski Legion, after the town where they were organized. The Legion wore Russian uniforms with minor modifications but used the Polish language. It attracted few volunteers, and by early 1915 the units had essentially been dissolved and made regular components of the Russian army. A successor of sorts was the Polish Rifle Brigade, formed in either late 1915 or early the following year. It was composed of ethnic Polish subjects of the Tsar and was commanded mainly by Russian officers, with Russian the language of command. By March 1916, it numbered around 4000 men.[8] Another Polish military force operating in Russian territory was the POW. Formed in Warsaw at the outbreak of the war, the POW was a clandestine network of fighting cells loyal to Piłsudski. Disciplined and experienced, the POW numbered some 13,000 members by early 1917, organized into more than 200 local units throughout Congress Poland.[9] It gave Piłsudski a formidable vehicle for his will within the Government-General, allowing him to pretend cooperation with the Great Powers while directing the POW fighters toward other ends if he wished.

The most important of the Polish military formations created in the first years of the war were the NKN's Polish Legions. The Legions have, since the Great War, been the subject of national mythmaking and popular fascination, as they are seen as the swashbuckling pioneers of Polish independence.[10] In reality, however, the Legions were plagued from the outset by awkward relations with their supposed allies, bitter internal power struggles, and a general haze of uncertainty about their purpose. As detailed in Chapter 1, the

Legions had been established at the outbreak of the war by the NKN to be that committee's military wing and to fight against the Russians.[11] The Austrian military soon took command of the Legions, though the NKN retained a military department headed by Władysław Sikorski that was in charge of matters such as recruiting and training. In August 1914, the fighting strength of the Legions was augmented by the absorption of Piłsudski and his irregulars. The Legions were sent into combat on the eastern front, where they earned renown for their bravery. By 1915, a third brigade had been added. By the middle of that year, the Legions numbered 7,000 men, including six infantry regiments and three cavalry squadrons, as well as their own medical, supply, and communications personnel.[12]

Despite their widely acclaimed bravery, the Legions' reputation was not wholly positive. An Order of the Day *(Tagesbefehl)* of the Austrian 2nd Corps once referred to them as "habitual thieves and robbers."[13] The ranks of the Legions, it was widely suspected among their nominal allies, were filled with an unwholesome and ill-disciplined mix of rogues, idealists, adventurers, charlatans, criminals, and shirkers—a suspicion with more than an adequate basis in reality.[14] Emil Bobrowski, a doctor who gave recruits their enlistment physicals (and, it should be noted, did not support the recruiting effort), lamented the steady stream of "children, cripples, sick people, nutcases—even notorious bandits" sent to him by the recruiters.[15]

The Austrians had other reasons to be wary of the Legions. The semi-regular forces of the Legions, with their disdain for discipline and traditional military formalities, seemed to them shabby amateurs playing at a very serious game for which they were neither suited nor qualified.[16] In addition, the Austrians knew that the loyalty of the Legions could not be counted on, especially after the incorporation of Piłsudski's irregulars as the First Brigade. Despite the perception of the Legions as wholly committed to a vision of independent Poland, the ranks were in fact divided in their allegiances, and each faction struggled for dominance. On the one hand were the rowdy, idealistic nationalists, among them many young people and intellectuals, who were devoted to Piłsudski and complete independence. Among the officers, however, and some enlisted men, loyalty to the Habsburgs and commitment to the "Austro-Polish" solution, the unification of the Kingdom with Galicia under Habsburg sovereignty, was strong. These visions of Poland's future were fundamentally incompatible, making for a pronounced division between the men. There was little hope that the dominant personalities in each camp—Józef Piłsudski and Władysław Sikorski—could be counted on to smooth over their differences and unify the Legions around a common goal, since the two men were deeply divided by both temperament and ideology. Piłsudski had spent his life engaged in insurrectionary and conspiratorial politics against Russia. Possessed by an extraordinary will to power, he expected obedience from his followers, but he himself was not capable of working for or with other people. He enjoyed a near-fanatical following among some nationalistic youths and intellectuals, though he was certainly not universally popular. Maria Lubomirska, the wife of the conservative activist Zdzisław, thought Piłsudski a "dangerous adventurer, a kidnapper who was utterly without scruples and full of ambition, dreaming of establishing . . . a dictatorship of war-socialism."[17] Sikorski represented a very different kind of Polish nationalist, though he and Piłsudski had both been active in the riflemen's movement in Galicia in the years before the war. Sikorski was far more rooted in a stable civil society; he worked as an engineer and was settled into a comfortable private life. He was not a Romantic revolutionary, but a pragmatic Habsburg loyalist (or, in the unkind evaluation of Maria Lubomirska, "Galician, careerist, dull") who nonetheless hoped for an expanded, Austrian-ruled "Poland" to be returned to the map of Europe after the war.[18] Piłsudski and Sikorski had crossed paths before the war and apparently gotten along well, but they had had a falling out after the Legions were established, which, in retrospect, seems inevitable given their deep differences.

The division between the two men and their respective visions of Poland's future had several important effects. For one, the Legions' recruiting efforts were harmed by the rivalry between their respective factions. Two competing recruiting apparatuses were established, one official and one illegal that funneled troops exclusively into Piłsudski's First Brigade.[19] More importantly, the rivalry between the two eventually led to a split in the upper reaches of command and a temporary end to Piłsudski's overt participation in the war. In August 1916, Piłsudski and a handful of other senior commanders, including Józef Haller, commander of the Second Brigade, formally demanded the abolition of the military department of the NKN, the creation of Polish state institutions, the establishment of a new, exclusively Polish command for the Legions, and the transfer of recruiting and training responsibilities away from "Sikorskiite shirkers" and into the hands of line officers. This was a clear threat to the authority of the NKN and the policy of Austro-Polonism it represented. In response, Austria granted a long-standing wish of Sikorski and the NKN and changed the name of the Legions to the Polish Auxiliary Corps (Polnisches Hilfskorps), in order to emphasize their status as component units under Austrian command. His will to power thwarted, Piłsudski submitted his resignation, which was accepted on 26 September 1916.[20] He lived for a time as a civilian in Kraków, until, in the fall of 1916, Germany's desire for Polish troops accelerated the realization of Beseler's political program. This opening of a new phase in the struggle for mastery of the Polish Question would provide Piłsudski with the opportunity to return to the fray in a new, more influential role.

The Lure of Polish Manpower and the Path to 5 November

If Beseler was convinced by the first half of 1916 that a tightly controlled state-building enterprise was Germany's wisest course in Poland, the authorities in Berlin were not. Although the Emperor had supposedly told Hutten-Czapski on 31 July 1914 that if Germany were victorious, it would sponsor a restoration of an autonomous Poland linked to Germany, no decision about what Germany might actually do if the power to answer the Polish Question passed to it had been taken. The closest thing to official guidance about how Beseler should conduct the occupation was a Reichstag speech given by Bethmann Hollweg on 19 August 1915. Delivered in part as a reaction to a Russian rejection of the possibility of a separate peace, Bethmann announced that Germany's administration of Poland would be "just," that it would involve the locals, and that the occupation would hopefully mark the start of a new era of German-Polish cooperation and of a "happy future" for Poland. In a stunning display of political cant, the chancellor also praised the "tenacity" with which the Poles had defended their culture against the Russians.[21] The mildly conciliatory tone of this speech was enough to bring a rebuke from the Eastern Marches Association, which noted in its newspaper that Germany was not fighting for "alien goals."[22] But the Association need not have worried. The speech did not reflect a German commitment to any sort of clear policy in Poland. There were simply too many factors preventing decisive action: the mutually conflicting German and Austrian interests, the reluctance to abandon any hope of a separate peace with Russia, the fears of both German and Polish nationalist reactions within Germany to whatever the Reich did in Poland, and, not least of all, the difficulty of both Bethmann and the Emperor to act decisively.

Neither the Emperor nor the government of Bethmann Hollweg were ready to commit to such a course yet, but there was a powerful force at work that would eventually help to ease official German objections to Beseler's plans. This was the lure of Polish troops. When the Schlieffen Plan failed to bring Germany a quick victory, it became locked into a war of material and human attrition it could not possibly win. In this context, the temptation to try and lure Polish troops to the German colors became hard to resist.[23] In September 1915, Falkenhayn had been willing to consider using the newly conquered Polish territories as a source of Polish manpower, though he was astute enough to realize that it would require concessions to Polish wishes. Falkenhayn further recommended taking advantage of the changed political calculus ushered in by the war to reverse Germany's status as oppressor of the Polish people and instead take up the cause of Polish liberty. Bethmann was less convinced that this was a good idea, and for a time uncertainty about what to do about Poland continued to paralyze the Reich government.[24]

In the summer of 1916, several events conspired to bring a committed German attempt to winning Polish manpower closer to realization. On the battlefield, German troops became enmeshed in intense fighting on both fronts (at the Somme and Verdun in the west and against the Brusilov Offensive in the east, with additional troops directed against Romania after its August declaration of war), placing enormous demands on Germany's resources. Crucially, the summer of 1916 also saw the rise to power of the so-called 3rd OHL, the command team of Paul von Hindenburg and Erich Ludendorff. (Beseler often referred to them in his letters, not with affection, as "the Firm H-L.") Ludendorff was a highly unlikely ally in Beseler's struggle to get the government to act in Poland; in OberOst he was cultivating Lithuanian sympathies at the expense of Polish goodwill, thereby actually working at odds to Beseler's plans. (Wilhelm von Gayl, OberOst's chief political officer, was a veteran of the Prussian-Polish nationality struggle and no friend of the Poles. He once described the relationship between the two occupation regimes as a "state of war" that lasted "until the bitter end."[25]) However,

Ludendorff brought with him to his new post as first quartermaster a dedication to mobilization without limits, fueled by his insatiable desire for the material (including, in his grotesque formulation, the "human material") needed to wage total war. Despite what seems to have been a deep-seated personal loathing for the Poles, this desire for total mobilization translated rather easily into a desire to use Polish troops in the service of German victory.[26] Ludendorff realized that raising these troops would entail a cost in terms of concessions to Polish national demands, but it was a price he was willing to pay.[27]

The idea of raising Polish troops for immediate deployment was coolly received by both Bethmann Hollweg and Beseler, at least initially. In his crucial July 1916 report to the Emperor, Beseler actually spends very little time discussing Polish troops.[28] When he does raise the issue of the Polish army, it is usually done with reference to the *future* defense of Germany's eastern border, noting that a hastily assembled and ill-trained Polish force would be of little use to Germany in the current war. In addition, he points out that raising troops in Poland without first finding a viable political answer to the Polish Question risked creating an army behind Germany's own front lines that was capable of turning on it. Finally, he concludes that work toward building the Polish army could indeed begin immediately, but not without establishing a coherent political framework within which the project could unfold.[29] Beseler does not, in this report, completely rule out the possibility that Polish troops could be used in the present war, but political concerns were paramount. If a Polish army were created by Germany, he tells the Emperor, it would "gain increasing *internal* significance, and, under good political leadership . . . also immediate [*unmittelbar*] war usefulness [*Kriegsbrauchbarkeit*] and importance in central European politics."[30] As for what this Polish army might look like, and how it might be securely anchored within German control, Beseler suggests that Polish would be the language of command, but the troops would be trained in accordance with German methods and to German standards. The Polish army would be formally subordinate to the king of Poland when at peace, though the Emperor of Germany would have the right to conduct inspections. Should war threaten in the east, command authority over the Polish army would pass to the Emperor, who, crucially, would decide when to declare war and mobilize the troops. The deployment of the Polish army elsewhere would require the consent of the king of Poland.[31] Ultimately, Bethmann Hollweg and Emperor Wilhelm began to concede that, by taking a leading role in answering the "Polish Question," they could ensure that Germany's interests predominated in the east. In late July 1916, at a meeting of the Emperor with senior German military commanders at Pless, it was decided to move forward with the Polish Question, with the temptation of Polish recruits playing a decisive, but not exclusive, role in the deliberations.[32]

By the fall, however, word of the government's intentions in Poland had reached the leadership of Germany's political parties, some of whom made their displeasure clear to the chancellor. These critics, drawn primarily from the ranks of the Conservatives and National Liberals, considered it the height of foolishness for Germany to back the restoration of a Polish state. They pressed the chancellor simply to annex a moderate amount of territory in the east and eventually turn the remainder of the territory back over to Russia. Beseler was summoned to Berlin to present the government's case and convince these skeptics. In late September and early October, he and Bethmann Hollweg plunged into a series of meetings with hostile Prussian officials and politicians, trying desperately to convince them of the wisdom of Beseler's plans.[33] On 8 October 1916, the Governor-General was given an opportunity to present his case to the Prussian cabinet (Staatsministerium). At the meeting, Beseler stressed the absolute necessity of permanently securing Germany against future invasions by Russia, whose sheer size ruled out ever achieving this aim by purely military means. Beseler therefore recommended extending Germany's eastern border, repeating his preference for a line bounded by the Biebrza, Narew, and Vistula Rivers. He ruled out the outright annexation of the rest of Poland, citing the stresses that would be placed on Germany's domestic politics by the acquisition of "12 million strict Catholic Slavs and Jews." It would be better, Beseler argued, to create a client Polish state and army to stand between Germany and Russia that, in the event of war, would be commanded by the Kaiser. Beseler thus urged his listeners to back the government in its plan to announce the impending restoration of a Polish state and begin the recruiting of volunteers for the Polish army. Eventually, Beseler told his audience, Poland could perhaps field an army with a peacetime strength of 200,000 men, which would increase to 800,000 upon full mobilization.[34] It would serve as a "vanguard" of the German army in the east and would be commanded by the German Emperor in time of war. Its soldiers would be trained by Germans, not only to impart the necessary skills but also to ensure the "imprinting of the German spirit." As far as Poland's political future was concerned, Beseler suggested the establishment of a constitutional monarchy, linked securely to the Reich "by a number of treaties." Beseler insisted that recruiting for the army could begin only after Germany had proclaimed its commitment to restoring Polish independence. This would allow Germany to realize its ultimate goal, which Beseler expressed in language that unmistakably reveals the concerns at the heart of his vision. "We've got to keep a tight rein on the fortress that is Poland," the career military engineer told his audience. For more immediate use, Beseler suggested that he could have three Polish divisions (about 36,000 soldiers) ready to deploy within eight months. The modesty of this number is emphasized when it is considered against the backdrop of the titanic struggles of the year 1916: by the time Beseler made his pitch to the council, German troops had been through the infernos of Verdun and the Somme, fought off the Brusilov Offensive, and conquered Romania. A force smaller than the premobilization army of Belgium (48,000 men in July 1914) would have been a tiny cog in a vast military machine and of no real consequence to the outcome of the war. Seemingly aware of this, the Governor-General urged his listeners to take the long view, arguing that "a satisfactory army could gradually develop out of" these beginnings.[35] Beseler did suggest that, if the war were to drag on—for how long, he did not say—Polish participation could eventually become "significant." "In any case," he told the politicians, "Polish soldiers will . . . strengthen our armed forces and can perhaps one day occasionally be decisive."[36] Finally, Beseler stated his belief that the Poles "[had] to be trained to run their own government," but he added that the Government-General had already been working toward this end.[37]

It is symptomatic of the peculiar blend of foreign and domestic policy that lay at the heart of Germany's relations with Polish Europe that the greatest skeptic at the meeting was the Prussian Minster of the Interior, Friedrich von Loebell, who protested that proclaiming the restoration of a Polish state would be, for Russia, a "sharp box on the ears," making the conclusion of peace difficult if not impossible. This new state could also be highly threatening to Germany, as it would encourage the ambitions of those Polish nationalists who wanted to "reclaim" Posen for Poland. Proclaiming the intention to create it now would have, Loebell worried, the further adverse consequence of infuriating German nationalists. Loebell went on to make other arguments, but his general irritation and wariness is best summed up by his admonishment to Beseler that Germany must "concern itself with German politics, not Polish."[38] Beseler's efforts garnered mixed results at best. A meeting the following day with leading party representatives produced a split along broad ideological lines. The government managed to win the grudging acceptance of senior National Liberals and Free Conservatives (if not their rank and file), while the Conservatives refused to give way. The Center, Progressives *(Freisinnige),* and Social Democrats readily acquiesced.[39]

This German decision left the problem of Austria's role unresolved. Well before the meeting at Pless, Bethmann Hollweg had decided that the Austro-Polish solution would be contrary to Germany's interests, and had informed Austrian Foreign Minister Burián of this in April 1916, much to the dismay of the latter.[40] Austria's ability to resist Germany's demands, however, was beginning to evaporate, a result of its poor performance on the battlefield—especially during the Brusilov Offensive—and its dire military situation in general. Guided by the maxim "better to lose Galicia than the war," some military commanders—including Conrad—began to concede that allowing Germany to take the political lead in Poland would be an adequate price to pay for raising Polish troops. Such reasoning among highly placed military officials made it difficult for Austro-Polonism's supporters to maintain their ground. In the late summer of 1916, Bethmann Hollweg went to Vienna and secured from the Austrians support for Germany's designs.[41] According to the terms of their agreement, a new Polish state was to be created from the Congress Kingdom, but without Galicia; these intentions would be announced, but the real concessions to Polish ambitions for statehood would follow only after the war; the Germans would play the role of senior partner in the military union between the Polish state and the Central Powers; and, finally, the state's borders would be pushed "as far as possible to the east."[42] Upon learning that the Austrians had given up hope for an Austro-Polish solution, the Austrian Socialist Ignacy Daszyński summed up the reaction of many Austrian Poles, left-wing and right-wing alike, when he pronounced that "the [Austrian] government is led by stupid people."[43]

Against this background of foreign and domestic opposition the Germans proceeded with the plan to announce the impending restoration of the Kingdom of Poland and to begin raising troops. The final decision was taken at an Austro-German meeting held, once again, at Pless on 18 October. Finally, on 5 November, the Two Emperors' Proclamation was read out in both zones of occupation.[44] "Now the main thing," Beseler wrote to Clara, "is to keep a tight rein on these political children, the Poles, and to educate them."[45] Subsequent events suggest that Beseler was a good deal more naive then many of the "children" whom he wished to "educate."

The Act of 5 November

The Act of 5 November 1916 attempted to satisfy both Polish demands for autonomy and Germany's desire to maintain control over the Kingdom. It proclaimed the intention of the Central Powers to create "from [Russian Poland] an autonomous State with a hereditary monarchy and constitutional regime" (thus following the formula preferred by Beseler), but it did not specify who this monarch would be or what his powers were. In exchange for what the Emperors proclaimed would soon become a "free and happy State, enjoying its own national life," the Poles were called to the colors of the two monarchies, though the promise was held out that the soldiers would serve in their "own [Polish] army . . . regulated by mutual agreement." The Act maneuvered around what was likely to be one of the issues of greatest contention—the borders of the new Polish state—by opting to put off a "more precise delimitation of its frontiers" until some unspecified time in the future.[46] The Act was read in Warsaw's Royal Castle, first in German by Beseler, then in Polish by Hutten-Czapski. After Hutten-Czapski finished speaking, the hall erupted into cheers of "Long live independent Poland." "An improvised cheer from a Polish politician for Kaiser Wilhelm," Hutten-Czapski noted, "faded without response." That afternoon, cries of "Long Live Poland" rang out from the balcony of Warsaw's city hall, while German and Polish flags were displayed from government buildings and German army musicians played Polish songs.[47] At a meeting later that day of the Warsaw city council, someone called out "Long live Poznań!" Hutten-Czapski, who was there, "demurely and quietly lowered his eyes."[48]

This awkward moment aside, Hutten-Czapski had been deeply moved by the ceremonial reading of the Act. At one point, a German military band played "Boże coś Polskę," which he termed the "high point of the celebration." Looking around the room, he noted that "the faces of the Poles revealed that they were deeply moved" by what he called "this sublime moment."[49] However, it is possible that not all the emotions he was seeing on the faces of the dignitaries were positive. According to the nationalist Kraushar, the reading of the Act, which was full of promises that the people of Poland neither "could nor wished to believe," was greeted by awkward silence. Kraushar ruminated on historical memories, noting that the throne room of the Royal Castle was where Stanisław Żółkiewski, a Polish military hero of the seventeenth century who had occupied Moscow, had (supposedly) brought the defeated Tsars to make their obeisance to the Polish king. Polish monarchs like Zygmunt Waza and Jan Kazimierz had once ruled from the same chamber, and Napoleon had received visitors there "after the rout [*pogrom*] of the Prussians at Jena." To Kraushar, Beseler in his "pickelhaub" was merely the latest successor to the line of Russian officials who had ruled Poland in the nineteenth century and sullied its historical glories.[50] Another native, Stefan Krzywoszewski, had powerfully mixed feelings:

> A German military band, hidden in a corner of the room, played "Boże coś Polskę" and "Jeszcze Polska nie zginęła." We Poles were powerfully gripped by a strange emotion. We were witnessing an act of enormous significance, the first step in the direction of freedom. A part of our patrimony was being returned to us . . . but under a watchful guardianship that could become the most dangerous of all the yokes yet placed on us. The entire scene—the historic hall, the crowd of Polish notables, the arrogant, teutonic figures of the invaders, the beloved national songs played by German marauders—was this not all a horrible dream?[51]

At his post in the Austrian zone, the idealistic legionary Starzyński attended a ceremonial reading of the Act, which he pronounced "stiff, artificial, and cold." "There was," he noted, "neither enthusiasm nor joy" among the assembled soldiers (despite the presence of a group of local schoolchildren assembled to sing patriotic songs for the occasion).[52]

How the Act was viewed more broadly in Polish Europe is difficult to say. Certainly there were other hostile skeptics, and in general political affiliations determined how the Act was received; Tsarist loyalists and right-wing Polish nationalists were opposed to it, while the pro–Central Powers factions were in favor. But one contemporary, Stanisław Karpiński, noted that "even among decent folks, there are some to be found who believe in the idea of a Poland created by Germany."[53] And Zdzisław Lubomirski, a Tsarist loyalist, declared the occasion "momentous" and told his wife that the "staging [of the ceremony] ... had been a marvel, well calculated to move every Polish heart."[54]

For the Germans, the effects of the Act were mostly disruptive. Beseler received hate mail; a letter arrived, he told Clara, "which accused me of 'joining my glorious name with the most disgraceful deed of the war'!" (His exasperated response—"Father, forgive them"—suggests an evolution in his self-image from persecuted bringer of knowledge to martyred savior.)[55] German administrators in Poland reported that the locals in their districts were refusing to obey the orders of the occupation government, citing the Act as an official announcement of the end of German rule. In December, Beseler was sufficiently troubled by this that he issued a proclamation intended to restore German authority. The proclamation was an odd mixture of threats and pleading. Beseler publicly linked Poland's future as a state with German success in the war, thereby fusing the Poles and the Germans in a common struggle that, Beseler said, was making great demands of both. Beseler also stressed that "the German authorities" were to be seen as "only the temporary place-holders of the Polish authorities," a sentiment unlikely to shore up the legitimacy of the occupation government. Finally, should these arguments fail, Beseler warned of the "severe punishments" that awaited those who continued to disobey the occupiers.[56]

The Act also provoked a display of anger in the Prussian lower house. On 17 November, Conservative and National Liberal members submitted a notice of their reservations about the government's Polish policies.[57] This led to a debate over what the government was doing in occupied Poland and its potential implications for Prussia's domestic Polish policies. The Conservative deputy von Heydebrand launched a lengthy attack on the government's course in occupied Poland and demanded that Prussia not lose sight of its Germanizing mission, "come what may." The unenviable task of defending the Act fell to (of all people) Loebell. He managed to infuriate virtually all present by, on the one hand, insisting that Germans and Poles in the occupied territories shared a common interest and, on the other, stating that Prussia would never seriously tamper with its domestic *Polenpolitik*. The latter argument merely inflamed the anger of the Polish deputies, and the former did little to convince Heydebrand and his allies. In the end, the protest was passed, 181 to 104.[58] The Act also created outrage in the other partitioning powers. In Austrian Galicia, the government tried to offset Polish anger by announcing that preparations were under way to give the region even greater autonomy than it already had. This pleased no one, especially not the Habsburgs' Ukrainian and German subjects, who reacted with dismay to the proposed concessions to the Poles.[59] Finally, the Tsar's government reacted with fury. The Russian press denounced the Act as a "cynical violation of the rights of nations."[60]

The belief that this was a "cynical" grab for troops was widespread. In the wake of the proclamation, the Russian press announced that the winning of Polish troops was the "point and goal of the whole business."[61] *The Times* of London let its readers know that there was "reason to believe that the whole scheme in its present form is merely a device to force the Polish subjects of Russia from the occupied districts into the military service of Germany and her ally." Hindenburg, the paper asserted, was anxious to begin drawing on this "new source of the *Kanonenfutter* he so lavishly consumes."[62] Meanwhile, a cartoon published in the French newspaper *Le Figaro* depicted a corpulent German soldier standing on a gallows platform and placing a spiked German *Pickelhaube* on the head of a stooping figure; next to them waits a menacing noose that appears to be made of barbed wire. Under the noose is a pile of similar helmets, suggesting the numerous victims the well-fed hangman has already dispatched. In the background, a blindfolded man waits, with head bowed in resignation, for his turn. "Le Royaume de Pologne Rétabli" (The Kingdom of Poland Restored) the caption announces.[63] In Poland itself, Aleksander Kraushar denounced the German manipulation of the "chivalrous spirit" of young Polish people in a deliberate attempt to lure them into fighting for the Germans.[64]

This impression was reinforced by the fact that, only days after the proclamation, on 9 November, the Germans issued a call asking for recruits to join up and fight alongside the Central Powers. The recruiting proclamation stressed that the occupation was only temporary, and that the occupiers would be working with the Poles to build a Polish state. The army, which would serve "under the colors and flags of your fatherland, which you love above all else," was simply the first major step in this direction.[65] Given that the German high command *was* primarily interested in Polish cannon fodder, it was probably inevitable that this appeal would follow so quickly after the proclamation. Beseler, too, despite all his caution, advised moving forward quickly with recruitment, since Germany would be able to draw on the amity he hoped would be created by the Act.[66] The recruiting drive, however, was an utter failure and a political disaster for the Germans. Coming so soon after the proclamation, and without the concurrent establishment of any other institutions of government, it provoked hostility and suspicion among many of the Poles it was supposed to entice, since they saw it as confirmation that the Germans were interested only in raising soldiers. The Polish satirical newspaper *Mucha* (publishing from Moscow) depicted on the cover of one of its issues a lurid picture of a young girl, her thin garment slipping down over one shoulder, being held in chains by a guard at each side. (The resemblance to some of the anti-German propaganda that followed their invasion of Belgium, with its strong suggestion of sexual depravity, is marked.) With Warsaw's Vasa Column looming in the background, a burly German in a spiked helmet faces the girl and reads aloud from a piece of paper in his hand. "On behalf of my government," he says, "I cordially thank free Poland for the military support it wishes to provide, of its own free will, to its friends: Germany and Austria."[67]

In the occupied zone itself, the recruiting appeal sparked an act of open defiance by members of the left-wing, pro-independence Central National Committee (Centralny Komitet Narodowy/CKN). On 10 November, the CKN posted a flyer around the city declaring its opposition to the recruiting effort and stating that a "Polish Government . . . alone has the right to expend Polish blood." The Germans had actually heard about the CKN's plans beforehand, leading a high-ranking police official, Erich Schultze, to pay a visit to the head of the CKN, Artur Śliwiński, to ask him not to post the flyer. Śliwiński refused to call the protest off, but invited the Germans to confiscate the flyers instead. Schultze demurred and left. The flyers were put up later that day. For good measure, the phrase "No Polish Army without the Polish Government" was added by protestors to the posted German recruiting appeals. That same evening, Beseler consulted with Śliwiński and other representatives of the CKN and asked them for their cooperation. Using an argument he would return to time and again, Beseler assured them that they would get their Polish state, but it couldn't be rushed, and it was best meanwhile to work to build the first institution of that state, the army.[68] Whatever impression Beseler may have left on the CKN members, public signs of anger at the recruiting drive continued. Two days after the meeting, on 12 November, a street demonstration against the recruiting drive took place in Warsaw. Shouts of "We want to be Polish soldiers, not German mercenaries" mingled with cheers for Piłsudski.[69] Beseler seems to have realized what this disaster meant not only for his ambitions in Poland but also for his credibility. He quickly grasped at what he knew to be the only possible remedy: real political concessions to Polish desires for self-rule. On 12 November, the same day as the street protests against the recruiting drive, the Imperial Government-General issued a decree announcing the creation of a provisional Polish government. Beseler had not consulted the Austrians before issuing this, and they reacted with fury, protesting at the highest levels of the German political and military establishment and demanding Beseler's dismissal. Beseler was not dismissed, but his decree was quietly ignored.[70]

By the end of the year, the recruiting drive had attracted around a hundred potential soldiers.[71] One official in Berlin declared that Germany's Polish policy had produced nothing but a "heap of shattered glass."[72] Beseler was bitterly disappointed and blamed the results partially on Polish fears that the Russians would someday return. However, he also—as he tended to do when the Poles didn't act as he wanted them to—blamed their "childishness." "They are simply overgrown children," he wrote to Clara, "who require the firmest sort of guidance, but reject that which is offered to them."[73] Such condescension aside, Beseler's attempt to move forward with the project of state building shows that he was aware of the true source of the recruiting effort's failure. In a report to the chancellor of 20 December, Beseler noted that the failure to follow up on the promises of 5 November had resulted in "great disappointment."[74] The lesson was clear: if Germany wanted Polish troops to serve under its command, it would have to find Polish elites willing to assist them and create institutions within which these elites could work—even if only, as Ludendorff and the OHL wished, to serve as decent draperies for Germany's cynical exploitation of Polish "Menschenmaterial." This realization led to the establishment of the first proto-state institution in occupied Poland, the Provisional Council of State (TRS).

The Provisional Council of State and the Polish Legions

On 26 November 1916, a decree drafted in consultation with the Austrians announced the formation of the twenty-five-member council. It was expected to serve for the time being primarily as an advisory body and to provide the occupiers with assistance in the continued development of the Polish state. Among such "assistance" was to be full cooperation in the raising of troops for the Central Power's Polish military force.[75] Early in December 1916, Beseler drew up a list of potential members of the TRS he found acceptable, but this met with loud protests from the Polish side, leading Beseler to spend the rest of the month trying to determine a slate of mutually satisfactory candidates. This was no easy task, since Beseler had to find people who were willing to serve in the council, could be relied on to work in accordance with German wishes, *and* carried credibility in Polish opinion.[76]

In general, Polish political activity during the occupation fell within one of three broad groupings. One was the parties of socialist revolution, such as the SDKPiL, the forerunner to the Communist Party of Poland, and the Bund, a party of Jewish socialists. A second broad constellation was referred to as the "Passivists" because they (initially) refused to cooperate with the Germans. The Passivists were generally conservative loyalists or right-wing nationalists and included the Kingdom's most important party, the National Democrats, and their leader Dmowski, as well as the Realists, elites like Lubomirski who had worked to expand Polish autonomy within the framework of the Tsarist empire. The Passivists were represented in occupied Poland by the Inter-Party Political Circle (Międzypartyjne Koło Polityczne/MKP). Opposed to them were the Activists, usually (though not always) left-wing organizations that were willing to work with the Central Powers to reestablish a Polish state of some sort. The most important Activist party was the nationalist wing of the PPS and the most important Activist leader Józef Piłsudski. In occupied Warsaw, an Activist association of left-wing, PPS-influenced parties, the CKN, was founded in February 1916. Center-right Activists groups, usually promoting autonomy under one or the other of the Central Powers, also existed. The Party of Supporters of Polish Statehood (Klub Państwowców Polskich/KPP), led by Władysław Studnicki, promoted German-Polish cooperation along the lines envisioned by Beseler, while Austro-Polish activism found expression in the League of Polish Statehood (Liga Państwowości Polskiej/LPP). This fractious, shifting political landscape promised no easy alliances for Beseler and the Germans. The most important figures in the National Democratic movement had evacuated the country along with the Russians, and, in any event, their ideology made cooperation with the Germans unthinkable. The Austro-Polish orientation of the LPP was inimical to Beseler's vision of the postwar order, while Studnicki and his like were a very small and unimportant minority. That left Piłsudski and his Activists, who were indeed the Germans' most important partners in this phase of Beseler's project. But cooperation with these parties posed their own problems. For one, their view of complete Polish independence was obviously not compatible with Beseler's imperial ambitions. In addition, it must be remembered that each of these political movements, including the left-wing Activists, harbored a vision of Poland that embraced not only domestic politics—*what* Poland would be—but international politics—*where* it would be. Each of these visions clashed in some important way with the prewar political boundaries of central Europe. Even if the National Democrats, for example, had decided to work with the Germans, they would never have abandoned their claim to Poznań. Austro-Polonism, meanwhile, also posed potential problems for the Prussian-Polish conflict at the same time that it advanced sovereign claims to what was, legally, Imperial Russian territory. As for left-wing activists, they were generally not very interested in Poznań, but they did wish to expand their "Poland" into the Baltic lands ruled by OberOst. This, too, meant staking a claim to Russian territory, as well as inevitably clashing with the territorial ambitions of Lithuanian, Estonian, and other Baltic nationalists, whose loyalty Ludendorff was cultivating at Polish expense.[77] This was part of the reason why Germany's pronouncements about the future Polish state were always so vague. It also complicated the search for allies, since backing one meant tacitly backing their territorial ambitions and provoking another state or party. Finally, these territorial claims complicated the attempts to establish an army, since whoever provided the troops and supported the recruiting effort naturally assumed that the new force would become an instrument of their own vision of the world, not just Germany's. The left-wing independence movements, for example, insisted that any army they helped form be used to establish their rule in the Baltic lands controlled by Ludendorff.[78] Piłsudski (who was from the area around Wilno) himself told Beseler that official German proclamations and pronouncements about Poland could not afford to be coquettish in the matter of borders. If he wanted Poles to risk their lives, he would have to assure them that the prize would be a unification of Congress Poland with the northern territories of the erstwhile Rzeczpospolita. He emphasized his point by quoting the opening line of what many would regard as Poland's national epic poem, Mickiewicz's *Pan Tadeusz*: "Litwo Ojczyzno moja!" (Lithuania My Homeland!).[79] The paucity of naturally harmonizing interests between the Germans and the Polish political elite helps explain why Beseler sought alliances in unlikely places.

The failure of the recruiting drive and the announcement of the impending creation of the Provisional Council of State set in motion a wave of politicking in occupied Poland, with the various German and Polish factions seeking allies and trying to build coalitions. Under these circumstances, figures such as Prince Zdzisław Lubomirski became the focus of intense lobbying efforts. Lubomirski does not often figure in accounts of wartime Poland, though he played an important role. This is partly due to the fact that he is not easily classified as a "Passivist" or an "Activist"; nor do the labels "conservative" or "nationalist" fit very well. Lubomirski was a well-known member of one of the most eminent of Poland's great magnate families. His politics most resembled the Realist strain; he was loyal to the Tsar, but before the war he had devoted himself (and his fortune) to promoting Polish cultural and charitable institutions. He also, despite the loyalty that was so deeply ingrained in his caste, kept his distance from the life of the Russian court and its representative in Poland, the Governor-General. This gained him a reputation for independence of thought and action. When the Russians evacuated Warsaw in 1915, the Russian Governor-General advised Lubomirski to leave with them, as many of the other great nobles were doing. "Once we've left, there won't be anyone left here but the riff-raff," Lubomirski was told. "And me," the Prince replied. The two did not part as friends.[80] Once the Germans arrived, Lubomirski generally adhered to the Passivist line and kept his distance from the authorities, but not completely. He continued to serve under the Germans as the Mayor of Warsaw, an important and highly visible position. And, as his reaction to the 5 November ceremony illustrates, he may have been open to having his loyalties won by someone else. To have the backing of such an eminent figure would have been a great prize for whichever faction managed to secure it.

Lubomirski was therefore present at a meeting called by Beseler in December 1916 at the Royal Castle. About fifty Polish notables attended, representing the whole range of Polish political sentiment, staunch Passivists included. In a speech that lasted well over an hour, Beseler made an attempt to convince them all to cooperate in the building of the council and the for-

mation of an army. The Russians, he said, were never coming back. It was time to secure Poland's place where it rightfully belonged—in the west, not the east. It was therefore important to begin building the institutions of a state, the foundation of which had to be an army. The army would also help Poland support its claims to statehood once the war had ended and peace-making began. Beseler further noted that he was not sure why the Poles were not elated to have a military as fine as Germany's there on hand to help them build this all-important institution. He further argued that Poland's place in the society of states would be enhanced by linking its fortunes with Germany. Poland was simply not big enough to be a great power, he said, and therefore needed patrons like the Central Powers. In his memoirs, Hutten-Czapski claims that Beseler's speech was well received and admired all around.[81] The reactions of some Poles in attendance suggests otherwise. Lubomirski thought it was vaguely threatening. His wife added the piercing observation that "everything Beseler [says] always seems very sincere, the mark of a soldier rather than a politician, which means he tends to show Germany's hand."[82] In the end, the judgment of Stanisław Dzierzbicki, a soon-to-be member of the council, is probably most accurate. Beseler's "lecture," he writes, "or sermon, if you will, was unnecessary for the believers and did not convert the doubters."[83]

The Polish factions engaged in their own maneuvering. Piłsudski met with Beseler and urged him to include a wide variety of Polish notables in the TRS, lest it be seen as a German puppet. Piłsudski also met with Lubomirski and urged him to join the council, and to push for full independence for the forthcoming Polish army. It had to be unmistakably Polish, he said, not "slaves to foreigners."[84] Impressed by the sense that forces had been set in motion that could, perhaps, take on a life of their own, the Passivists of the MKP announced that they were willing to abandon their passivism and participate, though they also announced that they would, under no circumstances, support the formation of a Polish army under German auspices, since that would be an act of overt hostility against Russia. This refusal led to the formation of a number of right-wing splinter groups more willing to compromise, such as the National Party, a group of minor nobles led by Count Adam Ronikier. The center and left-wing Activists, linked together in a National Council, were eager to participate in the formation of the army, though they disagreed about the precise terms on which their agreement would be based. Centrists were

willing to work on the simultaneous formation of a representative state body and an army, while the CKN wanted the creation of a representative body first, which would then work on the formation of a Polish army. Finally, on 22 December 1916, the National Council officially declared that the TRS was regarded by them as the foundation of a new Polish government; that they wished to participate in it; and that it had to be given the authority to develop all institutions necessary to a functioning state, including an army.[85]

In January 1917 a new list of members was finally issued by the Government-General, and they were formally installed in their posts. Fifteen delegates represented the German zone of occupation. Of these fifteen, eight were conservatives without formal party affiliations, while three—including the unpopular Studnicki—were drawn from the ranks of the centrist Activists. The left-wing Activists of the CKN were represented by four delegates. The Austrian zone of occupation was represented by ten delegates, including three members of the LPP, three people without party affiliation, and two representatives of the CKN.[86] In terms of social background and occupation, about a third of the council members were magnates, while most of the others were notables of one sort or another, such as bankers, writers, lawyers, and engineers.[87] The occupying forces also sent their own delegates, who were given the title State Commissioners, to the TRS. The Germans, in an unusually astute choice, sent Graf Lerchenfeld-Koefering, a Bavarian Catholic who had worked in the eastern occupation bureaucracy since the early days of the war. His religion and work experience were not the only things that made Koefering a good choice—the Graf had learned Polish, a highly sensible decision not commonly made by German soldiers and administrators sent to the east. The Austrians sent Baron Konopka, a Polish Galician magnate.[88] The Provisional Council was formally inaugurated on 14 January 1917 in a ceremony held in Warsaw's Royal Castle that was attended by both Beseler and the Austrian Governor-General, Karl Kuk. Beseler, Kuk, and the soon-to-be chairman, or Crown Marshall, of the council, Wacław Niemojowski, all gave speeches praising the TRS as the beginning of a Polish government and stressing the importance that an army would have for this new state. The first meeting was held the next day. After attending Mass, the delegates marched through the streets to the Palace of Justice on Krasiński Square.[89]

It is difficult to say if the council could ever have established itself in public opinion as a legitimate governing authority. The fact that Varsovians quickly

nicknamed it "High Treason" (Zdrada Stanu) did not bode well for its future or for Germany's ambitions.[90] A major source of weakness was the lack of any delegates from the MKP and thus from National Democracy, an absence that, given National Democracy's and Dmowski's popularity, seriously undermined its claims to speak as "Poland." On the other hand, Beseler's critics in Germany, like Loebell, considered the creation of the council a reckless mistake. In December 1916, he protested to the chancellor in a memorandum stating that he (Loebell) should have been consulted about the decision to establish the TRS, because everything that occurred in occupied Poland was inextricably linked to domestic Prussian politics. Loebell saw the council's creation as an act "with far-reaching political consequences" for Prussia. In the future, he huffed, he expected to be asked for his judgment on the government's actions in Poland.[91] In many respects, these tensions capture the central problem of Beseler's policy of accommodation in occupied Poland. Whatever concessions the Germans made, they were unlikely to dispel the suspicion, mistrust, and generalized hostility to the Germans that existed in occupied Poland. On the other hand, what was perceived in Poland as half-hearted duplicity was seen in Germany as the very essence of reckless Polonophilia. So long as the war lasted, it could not have been otherwise.

Once the council had been established, they and the occupiers had to decide how to proceed in the matter of the Polish army. The recruiting drive continued to garner meager results. Between November 1916 and May 1917, the various German recruiting efforts attracted a grand total of 2,899 volunteers, of whom 2,132 were accepted for service.[92] As of December 1916, however, there was a body of some 20,000 men in the Government-General who were ready to take on the role of the Polish army: the Legions, who had been transferred in December from Austria to the Imperial Government-General. Beseler had originally expressed wariness about using the Legions in his satellite-building project. He wished to exclude the Austrians from the process of building the Polish army, which he justified to the Emperor on the grounds that the Austrians were not up to the job. Beseler also worried that transferring the Legions would lead to Austrian interference in his plans. He further distrusted the pro-Austrian elements in the Legions themselves, as well as, more generally, its highly politicized nature. Finally, he argued that, as an institution, the Legions were simply not suitable for use as the foundation of the Polish army. Beseler conceded that the troops had potential, but he believed that the entire organizational structure of the Legions would have to be dismantled and built from scratch for any good to come of it.[93] By early November 1916, however, Beseler had changed his mind. That month, the Austrians and Germans agreed to use the Legions as the core of the new Polish army, into which the Legions would eventually be absorbed. In a letter written to Clara from Pless, Beseler suggested that this had been his idea. "My negotiations went quite smoothly," he wrote on 11 November 1916,

> I succeeded in getting our friends to hand over the current Polish Legion[s] to use in the formation of the army. Another good step forward. I hope that now the Poles will come, since they will see that they are to be Polish soldiers, not German. My God these people are mistrustful!—but it's no wonder, after a century of servitude.[94]

In accordance with the terms of the agreement, the formal transfer of the Legions began a few weeks later. On 1 December, the Second Brigade solemnly entered Warsaw. (The First Brigade had not been chosen for this honor because of its close association with Piłsudski.) The locals did not seem particularly excited to see them, though the Uhlans, owing to their special place in the Polish historical imagination, aroused some interest. Maria Lubomirska observed firsthand the entry of the troops she ironically called "our heroes." "First came the cavalry," she noted,

> Szeptycki [their commander] at the head on a pretty horse and with a chrysanthemum bud in his hand. I suddenly recalled the mighty Russian regiments of August (1914), draped with gladiolas by Polish maidens . . . The picturesque red fronting of the Uhlans' coats like some sort of resurrected dream of Napoleon—of glory long past . . . I was seized by a powerful feeling and my eyes clouded up. And so this past was to be resurrected and to glitter, only to fade again; and so these heralds of freedom, who, under a different banner, will condemn us as before.[95]

The troops paraded through the streets to Saxon Square, where Beseler received them. In a speech translated by Graf Szeptycki, Beseler welcomed the fighters to Warsaw, "capital of their Fatherland," praised their bravery, and expressed his hope that they would be the foundation of a Polish army that would fight "shoulder to shoulder" with Austria-Hungary and Germany.[96] The Second Brigade subsequently established its headquarters in Warsaw, while the remainder of the Legions' men were dispatched to garrisons in smaller towns like Łomża, Modlin, and Ostrołęka.[97] Beseler established a training command, meant to be an embryonic general staff, to oversee their instruction. It was commanded by a Saxon, Felix von Barth. A recruiting command, under the charge of Sikorski, was also established.[98] Reflecting the murky legal and political status of the Legions, Szeptycki remained their commander in chief but became a member of Beseler's staff.[99]

Despite their presence in occupied Poland and the agreement to use them in the formation of the Polish army, no one was quite sure what to do with 20,000 rowdy, idealistic, combat-tested Polish Legionaries, most of whom were Austrian or Russian subjects. The first question that had to be answered was: whose orders were they supposed to follow? In other words, whose army *were* they? Given the pressures of war and the welter of competing interests and ideologies coursing through the occupation regime's institutions, these questions would have been difficult to resolve no matter who was conducting the negotiations. Attempts at a mutually bearable compromise, however, were doomed from the outset, because the Provisional Council member charged with organizing the nascent state's military affairs was—incredibly—Józef Piłsudski. Against the wishes of the Austrian high command, who considered him nothing more than a leader of "guerrillas" *(Freischaren)* and was weary of struggling with him for influence in the Legions, Austrian foreign minister Burián backed Piłsudski as a candidate for a seat on the TRS, mainly because he thought Piłsudski could do less harm there than as an independent political actor.[100] Piłsudski had therefore been summoned from conspiratorial obscurity in Kraków and installed on the council. "I don't think the Germans realize who they are dealing with" was Maria Lubomirska's astute judgment.[101] Beseler, for his part, disliked and distrusted Piłsudski—he thought him a "dilettante and a demagogue"—but he believed that Piłsudski's popularity made him a potentially valuable ally as Germany tried to build its Polish army.[102]

In the council, Piłsudski became the head of the "military commission," a de facto war department operating alongside seven ministries in embryo:

finance, foreign affairs, domestic affairs, economics, religion and education, labor, and justice. (Taken together, these departments formed the "executive committee" of the council.[103]) Beseler had made it clear from the beginning that he expected the council's cooperation in the matter of the Polish army. On 22 January 1917, Hutten-Czapski told the council that the Germans wanted them to make a public appeal to the Polish nation to join the fighting force being formed by the occupiers. This was a key German demand of the TRS during its seven-month reign, and one that would cause enormous mutual frustration and bitterness.[104] Germany's immediate insistence on the recruiting appeal reveals what it really wanted from the council at this point: a veneer of legitimacy for its drive for troops. Its military commission and that commission's strong-willed chief, however, had far greater ambitions, thus setting the stage for an irreconcilable clash of interests. In December 1916, Beseler was introduced to Piłsudski's ideas about how the Polish army in the occupied zone should be raised when Piłsudski submitted to him a memorandum detailing his views on the subject. All recruiting, the memorandum argued, should be in Polish hands and conducted through the Legions. In addition, the memo insisted that recruiting could not be conducted in the same bureaucratized manner that a state like Germany or Austria might employ. The Poles, it was argued, owing to their sad history of oppression and exploitation, distrusted any institutions that too closely resembled a state. They were also driven primarily by their emotions. Thus, it was concluded, recruiting had to be informal and rely on the charisma and reputation of individual commanders and the spirit and enthusiasm of serving soldiers.[105]

The memorandum highlights two key reasons why the Germans and Piłsudski were going to spend the next seven months struggling over the Polish army. The most obvious is the question of authority. Piłsudski, and under his influence the Provisional Council of State, would ceaselessly push for full Polish control over the troops the Germans wanted to raise. Obviously this is not what anyone on the German side, even Beseler, had in mind. Another, somewhat more subtle, source of tension was the very different military cultures represented by the Central Powers, on the one hand, and Piłsudski and the Legions, on the other. To Beseler, a career military officer in the service of one of the most powerful and highly professional armies in the world, the idea that recruiting should be organized around charismatic commanders—an idea redolent of a long-vanished age of adventurer-soldiers, private armies, and colonel-proprietors—could only be repellent. This clash between the informal, guerrilla war culture of Piłsudski and his followers and the militaries of the Powers, with their sense of themselves as professional servants of mighty states, and their fittingly elaborate bureaucracies, rules, and traditions, was to be yet another source of friction between occupiers and the occupied.

Open conflict between the Council of State and the Germans on the question of the Polish military surfaced in February 1917, when the council formally adopted a plan, drawn up by Piłsudski, for the raising of an army under its auspices. The nucleus of this army was to be provided by the Polish Legions, who were to be placed under the direct authority of the council. The work of recruiting and organizing the troops would be placed in the hands of Polish officers, and this army was to be deployed only against the Russians. At the same time they approved this plan, the members of the Provisional Council also approved the text of a recruiting appeal. They did not, however, release it, deciding to wait until they had the Germans' reply to their plan.[106]

No reply arrived, and Beseler ignored the council's demands. Thus the attempt to raise a Polish army entered a stall. The TRS, for its part, continued to insist that it be granted control over the troops. Since this concession was not forthcoming, neither was the hoped-for recruiting appeal. Beseler, for his part, simply pressed forward without the council. In March, the Germans issued a set of regulations establishing a new recruiting apparatus, along with requirements for enlistment in the new Polish army. The Provisional Council of State was barely acknowledged in these documents. This provocative act, plus the continued division of the soldiers into "Poles" and "National-Poles" (the former term referring to Poles from outside the Congress Kingdom, the latter to the Kingdom's natives), which offended the national sensibilities of the Polish parties, led to a 19 March protest resolution in which the council threatened to resign. On 10 April 1917, in a major blow to the TRS, Austrian Emperor Karl formally entrusted the Legions to Beseler's command. The council was furious, though Beseler coolly promised to keep it informed as the training and development of the army progressed.[107] (As it often was at such moments, Beseler's pride was given an unneeded boost. "Kaiser Karl has handed over the Polish Legion[s] to me personally," he wrote to Clara, "to be the root of the Polish army I have been charged with setting up. So now I'm to be the constable [*Connetable*] of Poland."[108]) After the transfer, Beseler established new institutions to serve as the army's foundation, the most important of which was a Department of the Polish Military Force (Polnische Wehrmacht), staffed by Germans. (The training command was run, however, by Polish officers.) This further alienated the TRS and its military chief, who continued to demand control over the Legions and the Polish military force to be based on them.[109]

The seemingly intractable question of who would exercise command over the as-yet-nonexistent Polish army was linked with another difficult question, one that, like the dispute over authority, presented no easy solutions and played an important role in stalling the project. When the time came for the soldiers of the new Polish army to complete their training and take their oath of allegiance, to whom, or what, would this oath be sworn?[110] On whose behalf would the soldiers of the military force pledge to fight and, if necessary, die? Multilateral negotiations and arguments over the content of this oath dragged on for months, causing ill will on all sides. The issue was no mere formality: the struggle to formulate an oath acceptable to all concerned parties was a reflection in miniature of the wider political context within which Germany pursued its nation-building project in 1917. The collapse of Russia meant that a simple return to the prewar status quo in Poland, which would have been difficult even before the Tsar fell, was now impossible, lending a sharp new urgency to the question of what would replace it. While the need to answer that question grew increasingly pressing, the advocates of the great multitude of conflicting and mostly irreconcilable views of Poland's place in postwar Europe grew more fractious and strident. Whether Poland was to be an autonomous entity created by the fusion of Galicia with Russian Poland under imperial Habsburg rule; a self-governing region ruled by a liberal Russia and consisting of both Russia's and, someday, Germany's Polish territories; an independent, socialist, sovereign Polish-dominated commonwealth, stretching far to the north and east, into the Baltics and Byelorussia; a German-dominated satellite, whose borders were yet to be determined, but certainly did not include Posen, and may or may not have included Galicia; or perhaps a Bolshevik state that rejected the very idea of borders as a bourgeois fiction and resolved to carry the revolution into Germany; all were visions of Poland's future considered and pursued by the welter of parties, factions, and states vying to assure their supremacy in the struggle to answer the Polish Question. While the war still raged, a decisive resolution of the issue was impossible. And without a clear answer to the question of where Poland was, and who would be ruling it, a soldier's oath was an impossibility. In January 1917, and thus even before the Russian Revolution accelerated the search for an answer to the Polish Question, Beseler was already lamenting "the unfortunate difficulties caused by the matter of the oath."[111] He would have many more opportunities to despair over the oath over the months ahead.

An early draft of an oath drawn up by Beseler was rejected for a reason that never failed to drive him to fury: maintaining good relations with the Austrians. This version of the oath had the soldiers swear allegiance to Emperor Wilhelm as the "Supreme Commander" of the Polish army. No mention was made of the Austrians, which was obviously unacceptable to Germany's ally. An amended version was then rejected by the Polish political parties as being too cold, formal, and legalistic; no Polish soldier, they said, would be inspired by such an oath. (Such was the reason they gave; more likely they didn't think it adequately represented Polish interests, at least as defined by the Provisional Council.) Beseler and the Governor-General of the Austrian Zone then came up with a new version, in which allegiance was sworn to "my Fatherland, the Kingdom of Poland, and my future King." The soldiers would also pledge to fight alongside the Germans and Austrians in the current war and to obey the orders of their superiors. A new roadblock, however, was erected by the OHL, who demanded that the German Emperor be specifically named and that Poland's obligation to fight alongside Germany be made indefinite—thereby clearing the path to long-term German military domination over Poland.[112] Eventually, the OHL's objections were overcome and the "Beseler-Kuk Oath," as it came to be known, was adopted with a slight modification: "Kingdom of Poland" (Königreich Polen) became "Polish Kingdom" (Polnisches Königreich). This kept the territorial implications of the oath deliberately ambiguous, since "Kingdom of Poland" was frequently used synonymously with Congress Poland.[113]

The oath-related difficulties were not only political: the presence in the ranks of many Austrian subjects, who had arrived with the Legions, presented a legal problem. As they were still the subjects of the Austrian Emperor, could they swear an oath to someone else? Could they perhaps be transferred, against their wishes, to the sovereignty of another state (assuming that state wished to have them)? These legal issues were at the heart of the distinction introduced by the Germans between "National-Poles" and "Poles."[114] Beseler's own position was clear: whatever solution was found, no Austrian subjects could be permitted to serve in the new Polish army, where they could act as a conduit for Austrian influence.[115] For the same reason, the Austrians wished to keep their Legionaries in Poland. The German high command was, for once, in harmony with Beseler and favored removing all the Austrian subjects from the ranks of the Polnische Wehrmacht. (The Polish Crown Marshall suggested to Beseler that the army could be restocked with thousands of Prussian Poles, surely to Beseler the most nightmarish solution to the manpower problem.) Finally, all parties decided to simply ignore the issue for the time being and leave the question of citizenship to be resolved later.[116]

These long and wearying debates finally resulted in the following text, approved by both Emperors in late June 1917:

> I swear to almighty God, that I will faithfully and honestly serve my Fatherland, [The Polish Kingdom], and my future King, wherever I may be called upon to do so, on land and on water; that in the current war I will be a loyal comrade-in-arms to the forces of Germany, Austria-Hungary, and their allies; that I will obey my superiors and comply with the orders and regulations given to me; and that I wish to conduct myself in such a way that that I am able to live and die as a brave and upright Polish soldier.[117]

It is improbable that this tepid formula, in which a soldier's life is pledged to the defense of a country that does not exist and a king who is not named and has yet to assume his throne, would have inspired many feats of battlefield courage. The political compromises and evasions necessary to arrive at a consensus had produced an absurd parody of a soldierly oath. But it really did not matter; in July 1917, when the Legionaries were assembled to take the oath, many of them refused, precipitating a major political crisis in the Government-General.

The Legions under German Command

The mass refusal of the oath marked the point at which the tensions festering "above," in the realm of high politics, finally intersected with discontent that

Legionary stabbed a German soldier who had slapped him for not
[?]t of his way fast enough.[131] In many cases of such conflict, the Ger-
[?]ed unsure how to proceed, since the Poles were, technically, their
[?] the Legionaries seemed to sense this uncertainty. In one June 1917
[?]xample, one Sergeant Major Hardt was dispatched to a Polish vil-
[?]uisition cows. Upon arriving at the village he was arrested by sev-
[?] Polish Legionaries, who brought him to their commander. Hardt
[?]hat he was not permitted to requisition anything without written
[?]ns signed by Beseler himself and was thrown out of the village. Later
[?] Hardt and his men found some cows hidden in a forest. He or-
[?]erman soldier, Ehrhardt Engelmann, to bring them back to the vil-
[?]wait there. While waiting with the cows, a detachment of armed
[?]ies descended upon Engelmann and ordered him to accompany
[?]ee the same lieutenant who had thrown Hardt out of the town. He
[?]sing-down by the Polish officer while locals looked on and laughed.
[?]enant told Engelmann that what he was doing was a "disgrace" and
[?]ave it up to the farmers themselves to decide if they want to sell or
[?]plaining that, after all, the people got receipts from the Germans,
[?]ey. Another officer told Engelmann that he was in Poland, not Russia
[?]any, and he couldn't do whatever he wanted. When the hapless En-
[?] returned to the spot where he had been guarding the cows, he found
[?]ifle and ammunition had been spirited away by the Legionaries (the
[?]f which Hardt somehow managed to accomplish).[132] In another in-
[?]hat month, a group of four German soldiers went to the site of a
[?]r festival" being staged by a Polish landowner and attended by
[?]ries and civilians. The Germans had been sent there to conduct a
[?] some paperwork. Things got off to a bad start. "When we entered the
[?]e festival," one of the soldiers, Müller, later reported, "we were imme-
[?]sked by [Polish] officers just what it was we thought we were looking
[?] ugly and tense scene ensued. Surrounded by about a hundred Polish
[?] the Germans insisted they had official business to carry out while the
[?]manded that they leave. When the Germans told the Poles that the
[?]hief himself had sent them, the Germans "were laughed at by the sol-
[?] the civilians, who once again demanded that . . . [they] leave." In the
[?] of this argument, a Polish soldier told Müller to shut his "trap"
[?] "I answered him," Müller reported to his superior, that "a German

had been brewing for months "below," in the ranks of the Legionaries. The
Legionaries had traded in their Austrian Schwarzlose machine guns and
Mannlicher rifles for German Mausers and Maxims and begun their training
under the Germans in January 1917.[118] The schedule was rigorous (one Polish
infantry officer wrote that the days moved along at an "American tempo").
Lectures, hands-on weapons instruction, and physical exercise were all part
of the average Legionary's day.[119] This training was directed and overseen by
German soldiers and officers, about whom the Legionaries held mixed views.
One Legionary complained that his German instructors were second-rate
soldiers and uninterested in the task at hand. More generally, the Polish soldiers were dismayed by the poor command of the Polish language displayed
by their teachers. Józef Herzog, a Polish soldier with the First Infantry Regiment, lamented that the instructors "mercilessly murdered" his native tongue.
Roman Starzyński complained that his instructor, a German from Posen,
spoke a "horrible, mutilated pseudo-Polish jargon." On the other hand, many
Legionaries were impressed by the professionalism and skill of their instructors.[120] Their courtesy was also remarked upon; one Polish soldier in the
Second Infantry Regiment noted that "as a result of their excessive courtesy,
they rather resembled bears dancing a minuet, though no one minded that."[121]
Life in the training camps had its discomforts—the barracks were clean but
sparse and very cold, owing to a shortage of heating fuel, and the food was of
poor quality and in short supply—but the recruits initially proved to be eager
students, conscious of the special role they had been chosen to play, while
the instructors took their job seriously and treated their charges with
respect.

This honeymoon period was brief. The earnestness and unity of purpose
that initially kept spirits high in the training camps simultaneously masked
numerous sources of friction and discontent that would become difficult to
ignore as the enthusiasm of the initial training period began to wane. Many
of the Legionaries had served at the front and chafed at the tedious routines
of barracks life. Their casual attitude toward military formalities also clashed
with the Germans' more elevated notions of military discipline and proper
soldierly comportment. The Legionaries grew irritated by the incessant emphasis on observing military courtesies and wearing one's uniform properly.[122] "Saluting with a hand in your pocket and a cigarette in your mouth is
unacceptable," they were reminded by their commander, Szeptycki, in January

1917.[123] In addition, theft, desertion, and unauthorized absences were endemic in the ranks of the Legions. (The behavior of the Legionaries was a source of anxiety to Szeptycki, who worried that they would prove to be unsuitable material for the core of a regular Polish army, rather than an irregular guerrilla force.[124] He told Maria Lubomirska that he was once greeted by a detachment of Legionaries with hearty cheers of "Long live Piłsudski!" "Are you a bunch of idiots, or are you soldiers?" Szeptycki asked them. "Do you even know what military discipline is?"[125]) Some of the Germans' decisions also angered the Legionaries. The Legions' new uniforms, for example, were thought to be too similar to the Germans'. The Legionaries also disliked that the Germans continued to differentiate between "Poles" and "National-Poles."

Still, these were mostly minor issues and probably could have been handled over time. A serious, and perhaps fatal, blow to the Government-General's military training program was dealt by an event that radically altered the political calculations made by both Germans and Poles in the Government-General: the February Revolution in Russia. In the wake of the collapse of the Tsarist regime, the revolutionaries made appeals to the Russian Empire's constituent nationalities, hoping to prevent the disintegration of the Empire along national lines. This led to the Provisional Government's decree of 2 April (20 March old style [OS]), which instituted full legal equality for all nationalities within the Empire.[126] The Polish Question had specifically been addressed in a previous decree of 29 March (16 March OS), according to which Poland was to be given its independence, though a "free military alliance" was to keep it linked to Russia, ensuring it fulfilled its special strategic duty as a "firm bulwark of Slavdom against the pressure of the Central Powers."[127] On the key question of the borders of Poland, the decree was evasive.

Whatever its effect on the everyday lives of Poles living under the German occupation, the revolution had a major impact on Germany's priorities in the war and, therefore, on the training program of the Legions. The German high command (though certainly not Beseler), who had supported concessions to the Poles in order to raise troops to fight against Russia, lost interest in the project. Their commitment to Beseler's vision had already been weakened by the initial recruiting debacle and Beseler's pessimistic report of 20 December 1916. Russia's precarious military and political position now removed what-

ever lingering sense of urgency had rema[...]
a Polish army forward. The focus of the [...]
would, from this point forward, focus m[...]
political outcome in Poland than on recru[...]
in the Legionaries' camps thus grew slac[...]
tainty pervaded the ranks. In addition, m[...]
their primary enemy. That had now chang[...]
the Legionaries in Starzyński's camp lear[...]
Polish units in their army. "Under the[...]
our war with Russia over," he writes. "[...]
approaching in which our front would ha[...]
Central Powers, the current occupiers of a[...]

The revolution only added to the already-c[...]
in the Legions' training camps. The Legio[...]
cally charged places, given the nature of t[...]
more so as the months dragged on. On [...]
Starzyński's camp had staged a celebration [...]
with a celebration of Mass (a reminder that [...]
other European varieties), a parade, speech[...]
to which local civilians had been invited. T[...]
their superiors to attend and to extend their f[...]
Polish officer. The following month, the Legi[...]
Karl had turned command over to Beseler. [...]
"In a helpless rage," Starzyński writes, "we a[...]
who alone had the right to command us." Sta[...]
loyalists formed a secret cell in the camp, co[...]
Illiterates established contact with other ant[...]
of resistance.[129] Around May, Starzyński (wh[...]
a new post) and his compatriots refused to [...]
forms that were supposed to replace their L[...]
self came to the camp to instruct the soldier[...]
effect.[130]

Tensions between the Poles and the Germa[...]
in drunken brawls in the pubs and restauran[...]

had been brewing for months "below," in the ranks of the Legionaries. The Legionaries had traded in their Austrian Schwarzlose machine guns and Mannlicher rifles for German Mausers and Maxims and begun their training under the Germans in January 1917.[118] The schedule was rigorous (one Polish infantry officer wrote that the days moved along at an "American tempo"). Lectures, hands-on weapons instruction, and physical exercise were all part of the average Legionary's day.[119] This training was directed and overseen by German soldiers and officers, about whom the Legionaries held mixed views. One Legionary complained that his German instructors were second-rate soldiers and uninterested in the task at hand. More generally, the Polish soldiers were dismayed by the poor command of the Polish language displayed by their teachers. Józef Herzog, a Polish soldier with the First Infantry Regiment, lamented that the instructors "mercilessly murdered" his native tongue. Roman Starzyński complained that his instructor, a German from Posen, spoke a "horrible, mutilated pseudo-Polish jargon." On the other hand, many Legionaries were impressed by the professionalism and skill of their instructors.[120] Their courtesy was also remarked upon; one Polish soldier in the Second Infantry Regiment noted that "as a result of their excessive courtesy, they rather resembled bears dancing a minuet, though no one minded that."[121] Life in the training camps had its discomforts—the barracks were clean but sparse and very cold, owing to a shortage of heating fuel, and the food was of poor quality and in short supply—but the recruits initially proved to be eager students, conscious of the special role they had been chosen to play, while the instructors took their job seriously and treated their charges with respect.

This honeymoon period was brief. The earnestness and unity of purpose that initially kept spirits high in the training camps simultaneously masked numerous sources of friction and discontent that would become difficult to ignore as the enthusiasm of the initial training period began to wane. Many of the Legionaries had served at the front and chafed at the tedious routines of barracks life. Their casual attitude toward military formalities also clashed with the Germans' more elevated notions of military discipline and proper soldierly comportment. The Legionaries grew irritated by the incessant emphasis on observing military courtesies and wearing one's uniform properly.[122] "Saluting with a hand in your pocket and a cigarette in your mouth is unacceptable," they were reminded by their commander, Szeptycki, in January

1917.[123] In addition, theft, desertion, and unauthorized absences were endemic in the ranks of the Legions. (The behavior of the Legionaries was a source of anxiety to Szeptycki, who worried that they would prove to be unsuitable material for the core of a regular Polish army, rather than an irregular guerrilla force.[124] He told Maria Lubomirska that he was once greeted by a detachment of Legionaries with hearty cheers of "Long live Piłsudski!" "Are you a bunch of idiots, or are you soldiers?" Szeptycki asked them. "Do you even know what military discipline is?"[125]) Some of the Germans' decisions also angered the Legionaries. The Legions' new uniforms, for example, were thought to be too similar to the Germans'. The Legionaries also disliked that the Germans continued to differentiate between "Poles" and "National-Poles."

Still, these were mostly minor issues and probably could have been handled over time. A serious, and perhaps fatal, blow to the Government-General's military training program was dealt by an event that radically altered the political calculations made by both Germans and Poles in the Government-General: the February Revolution in Russia. In the wake of the collapse of the Tsarist regime, the revolutionaries made appeals to the Russian Empire's constituent nationalities, hoping to prevent the disintegration of the Empire along national lines. This led to the Provisional Government's decree of 2 April (20 March old style [OS]), which instituted full legal equality for all nationalities within the Empire.[126] The Polish Question had specifically been addressed in a previous decree of 29 March (16 March OS), according to which Poland was to be given its independence, though a "free military alliance" was to keep it linked to Russia, ensuring it fulfilled its special strategic duty as a "firm bulwark of Slavdom against the pressure of the Central Powers."[127] On the key question of the borders of Poland, the decree was evasive.

Whatever its effect on the everyday lives of Poles living under the German occupation, the revolution had a major impact on Germany's priorities in the war and, therefore, on the training program of the Legions. The German high command (though certainly not Beseler), who had supported concessions to the Poles in order to raise troops to fight against Russia, lost interest in the project. Their commitment to Beseler's vision had already been weakened by the initial recruiting debacle and Beseler's pessimistic report of 20 December 1916. Russia's precarious military and political position now removed whatever lingering sense of urgency had remained to drive the project of creating a Polish army forward. The focus of the Central Powers' policy in Poland would, from this point forward, focus more on shaping a favorable postwar political outcome in Poland than on recruiting soldiers. The training routine in the Legionaries' camps thus grew slack and a sense of futility and uncertainty pervaded the ranks. In addition, many Legionaries had seen Russia as their primary enemy. That had now changed. Sometime in the spring of 1917, the Legionaries in Starzyński's camp learned that the Russians were forming Polish units in their army. "Under these circumstances, we considered our war with Russia over," he writes. "We realized that the moment was approaching in which our front would have to shift to the west, against the Central Powers, the current occupiers of all Polish territory."[128]

The revolution only added to the already-combustible atmosphere gathering in the Legions' training camps. The Legions' barracks had long been politically charged places, given the nature of the recruits, and became steadily more so as the months dragged on. On 19 March, the Polish soldiers in Starzyński's camp had staged a celebration of Piłsudski's name day, complete with a celebration of Mass (a reminder that Polish socialism was unlike many other European varieties), a parade, speeches, and lectures, and, later, a ball to which local civilians had been invited. The Germans had been ordered by their superiors to attend and to extend their formal good wishes to the ranking Polish officer. The following month, the Legionaries received word that Kaiser Karl had turned command over to Beseler. The news did not go over well. "In a helpless rage," Starzyński writes, "we awaited the instructions of He [*sic*] who alone had the right to command us." Starzyński and his fellow Piłsudski loyalists formed a secret cell in the camp, code-named "The Illiterates." The Illiterates established contact with other anti-German cells and plotted acts of resistance.[129] Around May, Starzyński (who had since been transferred to a new post) and his compatriots refused to put on the German-issued uniforms that were supposed to replace their Legionaries' garb. Sikorski himself came to the camp to instruct the soldiers to do as they were told—to no effect.[130]

Tensions between the Poles and the Germans began to manifest themselves in drunken brawls in the pubs and restaurants of the garrison towns. In one instance, a Legionary stabbed a German soldier who had slapped him for not moving out of his way fast enough.[131] In many cases of such conflict, the Germans seemed unsure how to proceed, since the Poles were, technically, their allies. And the Legionaries seemed to sense this uncertainty. In one June 1917 case, for example, one Sergeant Major Hardt was dispatched to a Polish village to requisition cows. Upon arriving at the village he was arrested by several armed Polish Legionaries, who brought him to their commander. Hardt was told that he was not permitted to requisition anything without written instructions signed by Beseler himself and was thrown out of the village. Later in the day Hardt and his men found some cows hidden in a forest. He ordered a German soldier, Ehrhardt Engelmann, to bring them back to the village and wait there. While waiting with the cows, a detachment of armed Legionaries descended upon Engelmann and ordered him to accompany them to see the same lieutenant who had thrown Hardt out of the town. He got a dressing-down by the Polish officer while locals looked on and laughed. The lieutenant told Engelmann that what he was doing was a "disgrace" and should leave it up to the farmers themselves to decide if they want to sell or not, complaining that, after all, the people got receipts from the Germans, not money. Another officer told Engelmann that he was in Poland, not Russia or Germany, and he couldn't do whatever he wanted. When the hapless Engelmann returned to the spot where he had been guarding the cows, he found that his rifle and ammunition had been spirited away by the Legionaries (the return of which Hardt somehow managed to accomplish).[132] In another incident that month, a group of four German soldiers went to the site of a "summer festival" being staged by a Polish landowner and attended by Legionaries and civilians. The Germans had been sent there to conduct a check of some paperwork. Things got off to a bad start. "When we entered the site of the festival," one of the soldiers, Müller, later reported, "we were immediately asked by [Polish] officers just what it was we thought we were looking for." An ugly and tense scene ensued. Surrounded by about a hundred Polish soldiers, the Germans insisted they had official business to carry out while the Poles demanded that they leave. When the Germans told the Poles that the district chief himself had sent them, the Germans "were laughed at by the soldiers and the civilians, who once again demanded that . . . [they] leave." In the course of this argument, a Polish soldier told Müller to shut his "trap" (Maul). "I answered him," Müller reported to his superior, that "a German soldier doesn't have a 'trap.'" Eventually the Germans did in fact leave, and Müller worried that the civilians had been left with the impression that the Germans were weak and foolish.[133]

The administrator in whose district this happened, Kreischef von Imhoff, also worried about what this was doing to the image of the Germans. Toward the end of June, von Imhoff warned his superiors in Warsaw that the local farmers were beginning to see the Legionaries as their protectors (German requisitions, it should be remembered, remained rapacious). He complained that he did not have the manpower required to respond properly to the sorts of provocations the Germans had been subject to, and asked that strict measures be taken immediately. Otherwise, German authority in the region was in serious peril.[134] When the German authorities sent a stern letter to the local Polish commander demanding that he rein his troops in, von Imhoff wrote back: "I consider it my duty to note that, on the basis of my experiences here, I am firmly convinced that such measures will not improve things. Only exemplary punishments and personnel transfers have the best chance of making an impression."[135]

The frustration lurking behind this restrained bureaucratic language suggests just how poisonous the political atmosphere had become by the spring and early summer of 1917. Roman Starzyński even hints darkly that German soldiers who strayed off by themselves and happened to cross paths with Legionaries would never be seen again.[136] And yet, Beseler pressed ahead with the creation of his Polish army. Beseler had so much of his own energy and reputation invested in the project, it is difficult to see how he could simply have abandoned it. But he also knew that by this point the stakes were political, not military. "Not many people here grasp that the state as such needs an army," he wrote on 15 April 1917, shortly after Emperor Karl had given him command of the Legions. He also pushed ahead because he believed that the burst of optimistic activity and energy that had characterized the initial stages of the formation of the Polish military force would dissipate.[137] Yet a semblance of urgency was in fact maintained, because the Provisional Council of State and Piłsudski also recognized the crucial link between legitimate statehood and force. "The Army," Piłsudski announced in a June speech to the council, "should be a Polish army, depending on a Polish political body, as otherwise it will not be a Polish army but coloured colonial troops."[138] The TRS continued to issue a stream of protests over how the Germans were handling the question of the army and the Legions, protests that were mostly ignored. Finally, on 23 April 1917, the council decided that it could not issue a recruiting appeal, as the Germans wanted it to do (indeed, as they had created it to do). In May, another resolution, full of bitter criticism and demanding "radical change" in the Germans' policies was passed, while the PPS's representative on the council was directed by his party to resign. Beseler pushed ahead with recruiting anyway. The results were predictably disastrous: it began on 16 May and produced only a handful of volunteers. Faced with an embarrassing failure, the Germans terminated the recruiting drive less than a month later.[139] On 2 July, Piłsudski and three other left-wing members of the council resigned in protest over the oath that Beseler and Kuk had concocted. With the left wing out of the way, however, the remaining center and right-wing members of the council were able to approve the oath, and set the swearing-in date for 9 July.[140]

The Germans had initially planned a public oath-taking ceremony but, sensing trouble, moved it to a barracks in Warsaw, where members of the Provisional Council would witness the swearing-in. Other ceremonies were to take place in garrisons outside the city.[141] As feared, most of the soldiers refused to take the oath when the moment arrived. Between the First and Third Brigades, eighty officers and close to 2,000 men refused, though a handful took it (including, intriguingly, a solitary soldier in the First Brigade). The numbers for the Second Brigade, which was commanded by Haller and not quite as heavily influenced by Piłsudski, were somewhat better: 267 men and 12 officers refused, leaving 482 men and 12 officers to take the oath.[142] "Quem Deus vult perdere, prius dementat" (Those whom God wishes to destroy he first drives mad), Beseler wrote to Clara on 9 July, the day of the Warsaw ceremony.[143]

A few days later, Beseler sounded a somewhat more optimistic note, declaring the behavior of the TRS "quite reasonable" and telling Clara that he had grounds for hoping that a total political catastrophe could still be avoided.[144] But it could not. The German reaction was swift: the recruits from the Kingdom who had refused the oath were arrested and sent to prison camps in Poland—officers to Benjaminów, enlisted men to Szczypiorno.[145] Piłsudski and his confederate Kazimierz Sosnkowski were also arrested, but they were imprisoned in Magdeburg.[146] Many of the Austrian subjects requested to be transferred back to the Austrian army. Their requests granted, they soon found themselves fighting on the Italian front. Finally, the high commands of the two powers decided, against Beseler's wishes, to transfer many of the remaining troops to the Austrian army. Beseler gave the formal order for their transfer on 24 August, triggering a resignation, en masse, of the Provisional Council of State.[147] It was a humiliating disaster for Beseler, who, Krics later wrote, "gave . . . for a time the impression of being a broken man."[148]

The failed attempt to establish a Polish army under German oversight illustrates many of the reasons why Germany's wider ambitions in Poland were probably doomed from the outset. Whatever Beseler's intentions were, it was impossible for Germany to avoid the impression that its interest was primarily in Polish raw materials—both human and other—that could be put in the service of its war effort. The brutal demands of total war meant that Germany constantly pursued policies that undercut its desire to win Polish sympathies. In addition, fear of losing control over the situation in Poland made the Germans reluctant to relax their iron grip and make meaningful concessions. Finally, and perhaps most importantly, far too many competing political visions of Poland's future were being pursued in the occupied zone: the Germans', whose own vision was far from uniform, with Beseler pushing for genuine political concessions and the OHL demanding troops above all else; the Austrians, and their Galician allies, and those of the Polish political organizations, which were themselves deeply divided. Such visions of postwar Poland could not be easily harmonized even in the best of times, much less amid the violent collapse of a century-old political order, when each side saw this as its chance to mold Poland into its preferred shape. The struggle for Poland's future carried out in and through the institutions of occupation was perceived by all sides as a high-stakes contest ("after all," one Polish historian has astutely noted, "it was a matter of bestowing a new geopolitical shape on east-central Europe") in which the price of failure would be very high.[149]

However, the fate of the Polish Military Force also shows that Beseler remained committed to political victory in Poland even after the debacle of summer 1917. In a pattern that would be repeated with many of the institutions he helped build, Beseler and his subordinates simply picked up the pieces of their failed policy and began again. A nucleus of troops and training institutions was retained in order to provide a more solid foundation for the

force that was to be built on the ruins of the first attempt. By early 1918, the
Polnische Wehrmacht numbered around 4,000 men, quite a few of whom
were former refuseniks.[150] In October, a joint German-Polish delegation had
gone to Szczypiorno to see if anyone had reconsidered their position. Around
a thousand men declared themselves ready to serve, which sparked a massive brawl in the camp between those who wished to return to the ranks and
those who wished to stay. The Germans had not originally intended to take
all the willing soldiers with them, but as the officials tried to leave, those who
wanted to return crashed through the camp's gates to get away from the "radical elements" who wanted to force them to stay. The Germans ended up
taking all the willing soldiers with them.[151] As will be shown in Chapter 6,
the struggle to exercise authority over Polish soldiers continued to be an en-
gine of German-Polish, German-Austrian, Russo-German, and intra-Polish
hostility until the very end of the occupation. As central Europe continued
its decent into chaos and fragmentation, attempts to establish political legitimacy through the control of Poland's soldiers became more, not less,
intense. The drive to create a government to which these soldiers would be
subordinate also restarted after the resignation of the TRS. In September 1917,
the Central Powers created a three-person Polish Regency Council (Rada
Regencyjna), which was to rule in the place of a monarch to be chosen later.
The Regency Council was theoretically invested with "supreme State power"
and was supposed to serve as a nucleus around which a new state apparatus
of ministers and a legislative council would be formed. It could not act, however, without the approval of a Minister President, who would be selected
with the approval of the Central Powers. In late October, the three Regents
took office. Two of them were highly prominent former Russian loyalists
whom the revolution had left without a Tsar to be loyal to: the Archbishop of
Warsaw, Aleksander Kakowski, and the Polish head of the local government,
Prince Zdzisław Lubomirksi. The third was a less well-known landowner,
Józef Ostrowski. Jan Kucharzewski became Minister President in November.[152]
The argument that "states make war, and vice versa" has probably never been
truer than it was in Polish-speaking Europe from 1914 to the end of the war—
and well beyond.[153]

As Germany—and Poland—headed into the last year of the war, however,
Germany was losing control over many of the institutions it had created to
further its own interests. Among these were the local administrative bodies

created to "train" the Poles in the art of governing themselves. Like the Polnische Wehrmacht, these institutions had become, over the course of the occupation, sites of German-Polish conflict. Unlike the military force, however, the antagonism between occupier and occupied that unfolded in these local administrative bodies was not confined to the level of elite politics. Instead, they functioned as conduits linking the occupation regime to tensions and resentments much more deeply rooted in Polish society—in particular between Poles, whether urban or rural, wealthy or poor, and the minorities who lived among them. And, as in the case of the army, these tensions became sharper as the war dragged on, making it ever clearer that the old order was never returning.

3

Practicing Politics

Self-Administration and Self-Determination

The Provisional Council of State and the soldiers assembled to form the Polish Military Force represented the superstructure of the new polity Beseler wished to call into being in occupied Poland, and, consequently, the most visible institutional expressions of Germany's state-building policy there. This made them frequent objects of criticism and derision within Poland, Germany, and elsewhere, as well as pressing matters to be discussed and argued over at the highest levels of the German and Austrian political and military establishments. For those Poles living under German occupation, meanwhile, especially the political elite who had not fled the country, these institutions were the sites within which the political battle for control over Poland's future was waged in a high-stakes (but generally nonviolent) struggle with both their Polish political rivals and the German occupiers.

But German institution building during the war was far more extensive, and reached far more deeply into Polish society, than an exclusive focus on these institutions would suggest. Beneath the political superstructure of the Provisional Council and the military, the Germans labored to build an institutional base on which its postwar Polish satellite state would rest. Among these foundational bodies was the administrative apparatus established by the occupiers at the level of both municipal and district governance. After the war, erstwhile Administrative Chief von Kries looked back and credited German policy in this very area as being directly responsible for Poland's political resurrection after the war, since it had given the Poles the political "education" *(Schulung)* they needed.[1] While Kries's claims may be safely dismissed, the institutions of local government established by the Government-General are crucially important for what they reveal about the nature and aims of German rule in occupied Poland. In particular, three key characteristics of the occupation are illuminated by a close examination. First, they provide strong evidence against the claim that colonialism provided the political models on which Germany drew in establishing its rule in Poland. Instead, the Germans looked much closer to home for institutional precedents. In particular, the Germans drew extensively on the German tradition of *Selbstverwaltung.* Literally "self-administration," in theory and in practice the term denoted a particular form of elected local government developed in Germany in the wake of the Napoleonic wars. Second, they show that the Germans' attempt to strike the right balance between consent and coercion was carried out at the local as well as the national level, and that it remained just as elusive there. Finally, and most importantly, the institutions of district and city administration linked the Germans much more closely to social and political tensions native to the Congress Kingdom than did the Provisional Council of State and the Polnische Wehrmacht. The Congress Kingdom on the eve of the war had been in the throes of a wrenching transition from a rural and agrarian territory, divided into orders and dominated by a traditional noble elite, to a modern, industrial region in which identities based on social class and nationality were taking both a broader and a deeper hold on the population—with all the associated transformations and dislocations that this shift brought everywhere in Europe.[2] Cities—especially Warsaw and Lodz—filled up with hundreds of thousands of people looking for work, creating a swelling urban proletariat who inhabited the sprawling, overcrowded, and ramshackle tenements and houses that were such a pronounced feature of industrialized cities in this period. In the overpopulated countryside, migrant laborers wandered in search of work, frequently following in the footsteps of those who sought better lives for themselves in the cities. Unlike many places in western Europe, however, the struggle to survive in Poland's expanding towns and cities took on the character of a national conflict, with poor Poles and Jews competing for jobs and business opportunities. Overlapping with and reinforcing this socio-national conflict, new political movements were emerging in Poland that challenged the long-standing status quo, offering different visions of a political future in which "the people" would play a greater role in the life of the state and nation. And, just as in the rest of Europe, figuring out precisely which people might be permitted a role in national life was a potentially explosive question whose answer would have serious consequences for those deemed to be outside the legitimate body politic. To the National Democrats, for example—again, it should be emphasized, the most important political movement among urban elites in Poland—the Jews and other minorities were to be kept out of power. In Lodz, the German nationalist activist Adolf Eichler noted that the outbreak of the war had lent new vitality and urgency to a question that had haunted nationalists like him for decades: "Where do we belong, and what are we?"[3] The same question was asked, mutatis mutandis, by organizations and individuals throughout the eastern front, with increasing urgency, as the old order collapsed. By establishing institutions that allowed for more popular participation in the occupied territory, the Germans were linking themselves to these currents and forces, which flowed through the city and district assemblies and pulled the German administrative apparatus into treacherous waters it had not intended, and did not wish, to navigate.

Initial Measures

Germany's administrative reorganization of Russian Poland began in June 1915, with the promulgation of a decree that reordered Poland's institutions of urban government. The Hindenburg City Order (Hindenburgische Städteordnung), as it was known, officially went into effect on 1 July, subsequently becoming part of the Imperial Government-General's body of administrative codes.[4] The order was based on the great reforming aristocrat Karl Freiherr vom Stein's 1808 Städteordnung, perhaps the most famous formal expression of the ideal of Selbstverwaltung.[5] Like Stein's Urban Order, the Government-General's created two institutions of city government: an executive body (Magistrat) consisting of a mayor (Bürgermeister), a deputy mayor, several "lay assessors" (Schöffen), and, if required, paid professional administrators and a city council (the Stadtverordnetenversammlung). The council, to be elected by the citizenry, would then pick the members of the Magistrat, except for the mayor, who would be installed by the Germans. The Germans also reserved the right to choose the chairman of the council (which, of course, they could dissolve when they wished). To ensure the order's success, it threatened harsh penalties for anyone appointed or elected to participate in the city government who refused to take up his post: a crushing fine of 100,000 marks or a jail sentence of six months, "provided that a more severe punishment according to the laws of war and . . . the Russian penal code is not incurred."[6] The reorganization of the cities was driven mainly by the desire to make the administration of the occupied territories easier for the Germans by delegating numerous tasks to the city governments. The order made the cities formally responsible for drawing up and maintaining a budget, for example, seeing to public health and safety, attending to the upkeep of local infrastructure, and providing social services to the poor. The cities were also required to extract from the population the funds they needed for their activities—a truly wretched obligation for officials ruling over a poor country suffering the privations of war.[7] The order also eased the path of German rule by beginning the process of dissolving and replacing the Polish Civic Committees (see Chapter 1). The Germans grudgingly conceded that the committees were doing a good job given the difficulty of the task. They were dominated, however, by Russian loyalists, which helps explain the vague "political" reasons cited as a reason for their dissolution.[8] On 12 September, Beseler formally dissolved the Central Civic Committee and its related organizations.[9]

The City Order was slowly implemented, without its electoral provisions, as the German armies rolled east in 1915. A major exception was made for Warsaw, whose Civic Committee, headed by Prince Zdzisław Lubomirski, was left in place.[10] Hutten-Czapski's recommendations may have played a role in its preservation.[11] Political and linguistic concerns also intertwined to give Warsaw special status. In other cities where the order had been put into effect, German and Polish had been declared equally valid languages for official business. Given the large number of German speakers in some of Poland's urban areas, Kries claimed, such an approach to language was both necessary and just. In Warsaw, however, "the spiritual center of Polish thought," giving German and Polish official public equality would be viewed as "a political program," an impression that had to be avoided. At the end of the year, Kries reported to his superiors that, where it had been implemented, the City Order had been a great success, bringing stability to the Government-General and getting locals involved in its administration without seriously weakening German control.[12]

Kries, a disciplined and hardworking jurist, bureaucrat, and Conservative member of the Prussian lower house, was to play a central role in implementing German policy at the local level as it evolved through the war. It was not always a duty happily fulfilled, for the Government-General's Administrative Chief was a self-described "son of the Prussian Ostmark," bringing with him to his job a distinct aversion to carrying out political experiments in Polish territory. Kries was a native of the West Prussian district of Marienwerder. In 1903, he had been appointed Landrat in Filehne, a town northwest of Posen with a substantial Polish population; his service in the Prussian house had begun in 1908, the year of the Expropriation Law and the peaking of Polish-German hostility under von Bülow.[13] Kries had thus been on the very front lines of the Polish-Prussian conflict's most bitter struggles.

In the summer of 1915, Kries produced a memorandum for Bethmann Hollweg in which he laid out his thoughts on what Germany should do with the Polish territory it had wrested from Russia. Kries thought that economic reasons argued for a partial Prussian annexation and absorption of parts of Russian Poland. A revival of Polish statehood, however, was to be avoided. His argument on this point was in line with what would be expected from a son of the Ostmark. "I regard the establishment of a Polish protectorate [Schutzstaates]," Kries wrote, "at which our German Poles would always be peering out of the corners of their eyes and which . . . would cultivate its connection with the Prussian parts [of Poland] with all its power while greedily eyeing the mouth of the Vistula, as extremely dangerous."[14] Kries's annexationist ardor cooled considerably over the following year. Trying to absorb large chunks of Polish territory now appeared to him to be too risky, so he recommended to Beseler that moderation based on a prudent concern for German domestic politics inform any decisions about the location of the future German-Polish frontier.[15] Kries managed to carry out his duties in a professional manner, but his reservations about the policies pursued by the Government-General would eventually compel him to leave his position.

The next step in the development of local administrative institutions in occupied Poland was the promulgation, in January 1916, of the District Order (Kreisordnung). This order too was drawn from Prussian models, though it was not based quite as consciously on a specific historical precedent as the

Urban Order was. The District Order was intended to provide a much more comprehensive administrative network for occupied Poland, which was overwhelmingly rural in character (thus limiting the impact of the Urban Order). It delegated to the districts many of the same tasks that had been given to the cities: the administration of social assistance (with the important difference that the districts were charged with the care and support of the families of those serving in the Russian army), contributing to the upkeep of the district's infrastructure, and implementing public health measures (such as opening hospitals and paying for inoculations). The districts were also supposed to ensure that rural communities (whose cooperation in carrying out district business they could compel) maintained a certain standard of public health and safety. Finally, the districts were also given the unenviable task of raising the funds they needed to carry out their duties.[16]

The District Order created district assemblies *(Kreisversammlungen)*, varying in size from twelve to twenty-four members, to carry out its provisions under the leadership of the imperial German district chiefs. The same harsh penalties that attended the refusal of a position in the city government also applied at the district level, though the reference to the laws of war and the Russian penal code was dropped. Special ad hoc commissions could also be formed to carry out district business.[17] Elections for the district assembly were postponed, but the order did inaugurate a period of district "presentation elections." Candidates for the district assemblies, as well as for other administrative positions within the district, were elected by the natives into a "presentation group." The Germans then chose to accept or reject the candidates presented to them. Kries claimed that the practice (which also had nineteenth-century German precedents in the way the mayors of large cities were chosen) was quite popular among the landowners and in the urban areas, though the peasants disliked it.

As with the City Order, the primary aim of the District Order was to make the administration of the occupied lands easier for the Germans. Kries especially hoped that it would help lure the landowners into German service, since qualified rural administrators were in short supply. Kries also hoped that the order would foster social peace and harmony in the countryside, not only between the peasants and estate owners but between town and country as well, by bringing all together for the purpose of "communal work." In addition, friction between the occupier and the occupied was to be mitigated by the presentation elections, which would identify native intermediaries who enjoyed some esteem among their co-nationals.

As if these goals were not ambitious enough, Kries invested the district-level reforms with yet a more lofty purpose: providing the Poles with experience in self-government. "It is to be hoped," according to the Civilian Administration's official report to Berlin (which was signed by Kries), "that the intense antagonism between magnates and peasants, which the Russians artificially cultivated, will gradually disappear through peaceful cooperation in the district assemblies and district commissions and [that] the rural population will become accustomed to effective self-administration."[18] This idea was repeated in a subsequent report that made the supposedly educational aspects of the German reforms at the district level even more explicit. "It can be hoped," the report states, "that further service in an expanded autonomous administration [*in einer größeren Selbstverwaltung*] will gradually train the rural population to participate, with genuine proficiency, in public life."[19]

Again, the telling verb *erziehen* is used to describe what the Germans think they are doing: training an "immature" mass and inculcating in it a certain set of values, habits, and skills. This focus on the "educational" aspects of the District Order further reveals the degree to which the Germans' administrative measures at the local level continued to be animated by the spirit of Stein. In his 1807 "Nassau Memorandum," Stein had argued that introducing Selbstverwaltung at the local level could benefit the state. It would inculcate in an apathetic *Volk*, long shut out of public life, a vigorous ethic of public service. At the same time, this *Volk* would be trained to carry out the business of administration, resulting in more effective local government. In other words, Selbstverwaltung would marry the mission of political training with more efficient government.[20] The actual institutions of the District Order may not have had their historical roots in the Freiherr's political imagination, but Kries's explanation of what he hoped it would achieve could have been taken directly from the text of the 1808 City Order, which stated that its administrative reforms aimed "to arouse and maintain public spirit [*Gemeinsinn*]."[21]

A brief glance at the district of Sokołów shows that this patronizing desire to "educate" the Poles in the business of local public life extended well into the ranks of the Government-General's administrators. It also illustrates how the district reforms unfolded in a rural setting. The district of Sokołów was located to the east of Warsaw and had a population of about 150,000, including several thousand refugees.[22] In the spring of 1916, the district chief informed Warsaw that he was considering allowing the establishment of a local council *(Gemeinderat)*. In addition to the potential such a council had to improve the efficiency of the local administration by providing an alternative to the corrupt rural mayors who were still active in the district, the chief saw in the formation of such an institution a necessary first step toward the more ambitious reorganization being undertaken by the central authorities in Warsaw:

> The District Order . . . includes plans for the future establishment of a district assembly. Such activity . . . requires of the representatives, if indeed it is to be fruitful, an understanding of the interests and needs of the general public [*Allgemeinheit*], of political affairs in general and especially of the demands of the current difficult time of war. In order to rouse and deepen this understanding, a preparatory school [*Vorschule*] in a smaller sphere of activity and with reduced responsibility can be but useful.

The supposed tendency of the locals under his authority to put their private interests above the public good—a tendency spread equally among social, religious, and linguistic groups—was particularly irksome to the district chief. This had inspired him, he informed Warsaw, to establish a "preparatory school" by convening local meetings to discuss economic issues.[23]

The district-level "elections" in Sokołów were held in June 1916. Seventy-two locals were chosen for positions by their coresidents. Twenty-four were then chosen by the Germans to serve in the District Assembly *(Kreistag)*. Reflecting the rural character of the district, ten of the new members represented landowners with large-scale holdings, ten represented peasants, and four represented the district's more urban areas, such as they were. The district chief reported to his superiors in Warsaw that the experiment had been a great success and that he was highly pleased with the work the assembly had been doing.[24]

Up to this point, the Germans had been creating new institutions mainly to make their administrative burden easier to bear. The foundations for something much more substantial, however, had been laid. As the occupation progressed, genuine institutions of self-government began to evolve out of the twin foundations of the City and District Orders. The Germans' views of the institutions' importance evolved along with them: the Poles were now to be given a sound political "education" as part of Germany's state-building policy. Yet the further development of the institutions created several problems for the occupiers. One was the expanded platform they provided for those Poles who wished to challenge the occupation regime. Another was the degree to which national conflict worked its way into local administrative institutions. This was particularly true when the occupation government introduced curial elections into occupied Poland. The first such elections were held in Warsaw in the summer of 1916, and entangled the Germans in the complicated relationship between the Poles and the Kingdom's largest minority: the Jews.

Germans, Poles, and Jews in the Imperial Government General

More than 4 million Jews lived in the territories of the Congress Kingdom and the Pale of Settlement. In many of Poland's cities and towns, they constituted a sizable minority, and in some cases a majority. About one-third of the residents of Warsaw and Lodz, for example, were Jewish, while in smaller cities the numbers were even higher: the Jewish population of Suwałki, for example, was more than 50 percent, while that of Łomża was about 44 percent. The percentages in many small towns were even higher. (Beseler's letters and reports were often elegantly composed, but the profound impression made on him by the pronounced Jewish presence in Poland's towns was crudely expressed in a letter he wrote to his wife after one of his initial tours through the lands under his command. "In the [Polish] cities," he wrote to Clara on 29 September 1915, "Jews, Jews, and Jews!"[25]) The vast majority of central European Jews were what might be called "Orthodox," though they themselves would not have used that term.[26] They were religiously observant and adhered to the myriad rules that governed everything from what they ate to how they interacted with outsiders and with each other. They were also both bound together and marked off from the Gentiles around them by their languages, Hebrew for worship and Yiddish for everyday communication with each attention, save from historians of Zionism, some of whom see in German policy an abandonment of the Jews to the mercies of the emerging Polish state.[37]) A range of negative emotions, from suspicion to outright hatred, was deeply entrenched in the political culture of Polish towns and cities by the eve of the Great War. After decades of increasing nationalist hostility toward Jews, who were widely seen as cultivating separate, "foreign" nations within the body of the Polish nation, the years 1905 and 1912 marked key points in the descent of Polish-Jewish relations toward a nadir. After the failure of the 1905 uprising to secure for Poland many of the concessions it had sought from the Russians, blame fixed, as it often seems to, on the Jews. In the years after 1905, the modest liberalization of political and cultural life in the Kingdom led to new prominence and visibility for Jewish voices advocating various kinds of secular and religious Jewish nationalism, further inflaming Polish suspicions. Then, in 1912, the National Democrats lost the Warsaw elections for the fourth Duma to a Socialist, which they blamed on the Jews. This led to an outpouring of particularly vicious anti-Jewish rhetoric and a boycott of Jewish shops and businesses. While the economic impact of the boycott is debatable, by the outbreak of the war Jews and Gentiles in Poland generally regarded themselves as being divided into two mutually hostile camps, with each feeling suspicious of, and threatened by, the other.[38] It is significant that in 1911, and hence before the Duma elections, a onetime liberal publication, *Tygodnik Ilustrowany,* was serializing Ignacy Grabowski's story "Ungrateful Guests," which railed against the Jewish threat from within. The perennially standoffish Jews had rejected and exploited the Poles among whom they lived, and it was time for the Poles, according to Grabowski, to take radical action. Passive resistance was not enough; if the Polish nation were to be defended from the Jewish threat, Poland would have to be "de-judaized."[39]

The war and occupation accelerated these forces, just as it accelerated all attempts to answer the question "where do we belong, and what are we?" The end of Russian rule in the region meant that the various Jewish political movements had unprecedented freedom to organize and propagate their vision of what it meant to be Jewish (and where that Jewishness should be lived). Cultural and political organizations, publications, and cultural life all flourished, with consequences for both internal Jewish cohesion and Jewish-Polish relations. Within Jewish politics, the assimilationists were shunted aside once

other. Within Poland, a branch of orthodoxy known as Hasidism enjoyed particular popularity. The movement emphasized individual spiritual and emotional experiences over the legalistic formalism of traditional Judaism, and its adherents were distinguished by their particular dress (the men wore tall fur hats, for example) and their long forelocks.[27] While most of Poland's Jews would have lived their lives within these traditionalist or Hasidic frameworks, in the decades before the war small numbers of Jewish elites in central and eastern European cities were increasingly asking the question that haunted Adolf Eichler: "Where do we belong, and what are we?" Amid the general political, cultural, and social ferment that marked this period in European history, Jews were offering new answers to these questions. Some Jewish elites believed that they were merely part of a religious minority that should cast off its atavistic beliefs and assimilate fully into the Gentile nations who dominated the elite culture in central Europe. To others, the Jews *were* a nation, bound together by language, tradition (of which religion was a part), and history, and as such deserved to advance its own claims to national self-determination, whether as an autonomous minority somewhere within Europe or in a new homeland in Palestine. Other Jewish political movements combined socialism, nationalism, and Zionism in various permutations, sometimes including religion and sometimes not. Still others saw the Jews' best hope in adopting German-style orthodoxy, which emphasized deep piety with the assumption of the manners and customs of the Gentile nations within which they lived. One thing bound these movements together: all of them saw in the great mass of millions of traditional Jews an undeveloped, backward people who could be molded in the image of, and according to the aspirations of, the elite political imagination, and won over for Zionism, or socialism, or Zionist socialism, for example.[28] The widespread official and unofficial discrimination against the Jews practiced by the Tsarist regime, however, kept these movements from engaging in active politicization efforts (with some relaxation introduced after 1905).

These movements would be given a new chance to advance their agendas with unprecedented freedom after the war broke out, though it initially brought only misery and suffering to Jews. Many Jews, of course, loyally served in the armies of their respective kings and emperors, marking an important part of the Jewish "experience" of the war that was shared with millions of men, Jewish and non-Jewish, throughout Europe. In an interesting mirror image of the Polish perception of the war, some Jews lamented the war in the east as an outbreak of Jewish fratricide. According to one story that circulated, a German soldier dying on the battlefield cried out, in his last moments, "Hear, O Israel!," the first words of the Shema, one of Judaism's most fundamental prayers. The words reached the ears of the Russian soldier who had shot him—also, it turns out, a Jew, who realizes he has just killed one of his coreligionists and rushes over to comfort the dying man.[29] One aspect of the war's first years in central Europe was, however, distinctively Jewish: the vicious abuse heaped upon the Jews by the Russian army. The Russian state was thoroughly permeated with hostility to Jews, which in the upper ranks of the army metastasized into outright hatred. This hatred was apt to manifest itself in regular abuse, including beatings, murders, and mass deportations, of Jewish civilians. This treatment reached its nadir during the Great Retreat of 1915. A description of these mass deportations, recorded by Maurice Paléologue a few days after the fall of Warsaw, cannot but conjure up vivid associations with future horrors:

> With each new retreat of the Russian armies the police carry the expulsion of the Jews a stage further. As usual, the operation is everywhere carried out in great haste and with equal clumsiness and brutality. Those affected are only notified at the last moment; they have no opportunity or means of taking anything with them. They are hastily crowded into trains, driven like sheep along the roads and not even told their destination, which anyhow changes twenty times during the exodus. Almost everywhere, too, the orthodox [Christian] population rushes out to loot the Ghetto the moment the order of expulsion is known in a town.[30]

This brutality was driven by a deep belief in the treasonous activities of the Jews, who were, in the Russian high command's collective imagination, actively undermining the Russian war effort. Wild and implausible rumors about Jewish treason, such as a tale about Russian Jews secretly sending gold to the Germans concealed in coffins and barrels of vodka, circulated among the Russian armies.[31] It is true that all of Russia's national minorities, including the Germans, were treated with suspicion and brutality and were, both before and during Russia's 1915 retreat, deported in large num-

bers into Russia's interior. But the Jews were on the receiving end o worst of it.[32]

Given these horrors, many of the Congress Kingdom's Jews initially comed the German armies as liberators. (It is one of the great dramatic nies of the central European Great War that the arrival of German ar usually marked both the termination of ethnic cleansing operations an end of wholesale brutalities against civilians.) The war-era legend o "Rabbi of Sochaczewo" captures something of the complex emotional t of Jewish life in central Europe in this transitional period. According t legend, the Russians caught the rabbi helping the Germans. As punishn they sentenced him to die, but they killed his daughter first in order to ment him. Before he died, the rabbi cursed the Russians, condemning t to failure against the Germans. The rabbi's ghost, it was said, had sinc peared on the battlefield at the head of German forces, chasing away the] soldiers, who fled in panic.[33] The relief the Jews of Poland felt when the sians were finally driven away in the offensives of 1915 would sometimes them to welcome the Germans as liberators. In the fall of 1915, Besele: heartily cheered by the Jewish community of Ciechanów as he passed thr (an experience he described as "peculiar" [*ulkig*]).[34] Any initial warm ings between the occupiers and the Jews did not, however, last long numerous reasons. On a very general level, the burdens of the war an cupation, with their attendant economic hardships and military intru: into a daily life that grew increasingly difficult, helped alienate the Jews the occupying power. Profound cultural differences also created a deep of fear and hostility," as one historian has judged it, between the Gerr and the Jews.[35] In the spring of 1917, Beseler informed Berlin that "the are no longer pro-German," mentioning in his report economic hardsh well as rigid German insistence on "discipline, order, and cleanlines factors driving the occupiers and the Jews apart. He also mentioned ano crucially important reason: namely, that the Jews did not want to li the Polish state the Germans were now helping to build.[36]

The Jews may have suffered under Russian rule, but this did not mean they (except for the few remaining assimilationists) were particularly h about exchanging Russian rulers for Polish ones, an understandable fear g the intensity of Polish anti-Semitism. (This important factor in the sou of German-Jewish relations during the occupation rarely receives its other. Within Poland, a branch of orthodoxy known as Hasidism enjoyed particular popularity. The movement emphasized individual spiritual and emotional experiences over the legalistic formalism of traditional Judaism, and its adherents were distinguished by their particular dress (the men wore tall fur hats, for example) and their long forelocks.[27] While most of Poland's Jews would have lived their lives within these traditionalist or Hasidic frameworks, in the decades before the war small numbers of Jewish elites in central and eastern European cities were increasingly asking the question that haunted Adolf Eichler: "Where do we belong, and what are we?" Amid the general political, cultural, and social ferment that marked this period in European history, Jews were offering new answers to these questions. Some Jewish elites believed that they were merely part of a religious minority that should cast off its atavistic beliefs and assimilate fully into the Gentile nations who dominated the elite culture in central Europe. To others, the Jews *were* a nation, bound together by language, tradition (of which religion was a part), and history, and as such deserved to advance its own claims to national self-determination, whether as an autonomous minority somewhere within Europe or in a new homeland in Palestine. Other Jewish political movements combined socialism, nationalism, and Zionism in various permutations, sometimes including religion and sometimes not. Still others saw the Jews' best hope in adopting German-style orthodoxy, which emphasized deep piety with the assumption of the manners and customs of the Gentile nations within which they lived. One thing bound these movements together: all of them saw in the great mass of millions of traditional Jews an undeveloped, backward people who could be molded in the image of, and according to the aspirations of, the elite political imagination, and won over for Zionism, or socialism, or Zionist socialism, for example.[28] The widespread official and unofficial discrimination against the Jews practiced by the Tsarist regime, however, kept these movements from engaging in active politicization efforts (with some relaxation introduced after 1905).

These movements would be given a new chance to advance their agendas with unprecedented freedom after the war broke out, though it initially brought only misery and suffering to Jews. Many Jews, of course, loyally served in the armies of their respective kings and emperors, marking an important part of the Jewish "experience" of the war that was shared with millions of men, Jewish and non-Jewish, throughout Europe. In an interesting mirror image of the Polish perception of the war, some Jews lamented the war in the east as an outbreak of Jewish fratricide. According to one story that circulated, a German soldier dying on the battlefield cried out, in his last moments, "Hear, O Israel!," the first words of the Shema, one of Judaism's most fundamental prayers. The words reached the ears of the Russian soldier who had shot him—also, it turns out, a Jew, who realizes he has just killed one of his coreligionists and rushes over to comfort the dying man.[29] One aspect of the war's first years in central Europe was, however, distinctively Jewish: the vicious abuse heaped upon the Jews by the Russian army. The Russian state was thoroughly permeated with hostility to Jews, which in the upper ranks of the army metastasized into outright hatred. This hatred was apt to manifest itself in regular abuse, including beatings, murders, and mass deportations, of Jewish civilians. This treatment reached its nadir during the Great Retreat of 1915. A description of these mass deportations, recorded by Maurice Paléologue a few days after the fall of Warsaw, cannot but conjure up vivid associations with future horrors:

> With each new retreat of the Russian armies the police carry the expulsion of the Jews a stage further. As usual, the operation is everywhere carried out in great haste and with equal clumsiness and brutality. Those affected are only notified at the last moment; they have no opportunity or means of taking anything with them. They are hastily crowded into trains, driven like sheep along the roads and not even told their destination, which anyhow changes twenty times during the exodus. Almost everywhere, too, the orthodox [Christian] population rushes out to loot the Ghetto the moment the order of expulsion is known in a town.[30]

This brutality was driven by a deep belief in the treasonous activities of the Jews, who were, in the Russian high command's collective imagination, actively undermining the Russian war effort. Wild and implausible rumors about Jewish treason, such as a tale about Russian Jews secretly sending gold to the Germans concealed in coffins and barrels of vodka, circulated among the Russian armies.[31] It is true that all of Russia's national minorities, including the Germans, were treated with suspicion and brutality and were, both before and during Russia's 1915 retreat, deported in large numbers into Russia's interior. But the Jews were on the receiving end of the worst of it.[32]

Given these horrors, many of the Congress Kingdom's Jews initially welcomed the German armies as liberators. (It is one of the great dramatic ironies of the central European Great War that the arrival of German armies usually marked both the termination of ethnic cleansing operations and the end of wholesale brutalities against civilians.) The war-era legend of the "Rabbi of Sochaczewo" captures something of the complex emotional tenor of Jewish life in central Europe in this transitional period. According to the legend, the Russians caught the rabbi helping the Germans. As punishment, they sentenced him to die, but they killed his daughter first in order to torment him. Before he died, the rabbi cursed the Russians, condemning them to failure against the Germans. The rabbi's ghost, it was said, had since appeared on the battlefield at the head of German forces, chasing away the Tsar's soldiers, who fled in panic.[33] The relief the Jews of Poland felt when the Russians were finally driven away in the offensives of 1915 would sometimes lead them to welcome the Germans as liberators. In the fall of 1915, Beseler was heartily cheered by the Jewish community of Ciechanów as he passed through (an experience he described as "peculiar" [*ulkig*]).[34] Any initial warm feelings between the occupiers and the Jews did not, however, last long, for numerous reasons. On a very general level, the burdens of the war and occupation, with their attendant economic hardships and military intrusions into a daily life that grew increasingly difficult, helped alienate the Jews from the occupying power. Profound cultural differences also created a deep "gulf of fear and hostility," as one historian has judged it, between the Germans and the Jews.[35] In the spring of 1917, Beseler informed Berlin that "the Jews are no longer pro-German," mentioning in his report economic hardship as well as rigid German insistence on "discipline, order, and cleanliness" as factors driving the occupiers and the Jews apart. He also mentioned another, crucially important reason: namely, that the Jews did not want to live in the Polish state the Germans were now helping to build.[36]

The Jews may have suffered under Russian rule, but this did not mean that they (except for the few remaining assimilationists) were particularly happy about exchanging Russian rulers for Polish ones, an understandable fear given the intensity of Polish anti-Semitism. (This important factor in the souring of German-Jewish relations during the occupation rarely receives its due attention, save from historians of Zionism, some of whom see in German policy an abandonment of the Jews to the mercies of the emerging Polish state.[37]) A range of negative emotions, from suspicion to outright hatred, was deeply entrenched in the political culture of Polish towns and cities by the eve of the Great War. After decades of increasing nationalist hostility toward Jews, who were widely seen as cultivating separate, "foreign" nations within the body of the Polish nation, the years 1905 and 1912 marked key points in the descent of Polish-Jewish relations toward a nadir. After the failure of the 1905 uprising to secure for Poland many of the concessions it had sought from the Russians, blame fixed, as it often seems to, on the Jews. In the years after 1905, the modest liberalization of political and cultural life in the Kingdom led to new prominence and visibility for Jewish voices advocating various kinds of secular and religious Jewish nationalism, further inflaming Polish suspicions. Then, in 1912, the National Democrats lost the Warsaw elections for the fourth Duma to a Socialist, which they blamed on the Jews. This led to an outpouring of particularly vicious anti-Jewish rhetoric and a boycott of Jewish shops and businesses. While the economic impact of the boycott is debatable, by the outbreak of the war Jews and Gentiles in Poland generally regarded themselves as being divided into two mutually hostile camps, with each feeling suspicious of, and threatened by, the other.[38] It is significant that in 1911, and hence before the Duma elections, a onetime liberal publication, *Tygodnik Ilustrowany,* was serializing Ignacy Grabowski's story "Ungrateful Guests," which railed against the Jewish threat from within. The perennially standoffish Jews had rejected and exploited the Poles among whom they lived, and it was time for the Poles, according to Grabowski, to take radical action. Passive resistance was not enough; if the Polish nation were to be defended from the Jewish threat, Poland would have to be "de-judaized."[39]

The war and occupation accelerated these forces, just as it accelerated all attempts to answer the question "where do we belong, and what are we?" The end of Russian rule in the region meant that the various Jewish political movements had unprecedented freedom to organize and propagate their vision of what it meant to be Jewish (and where that Jewishness should be lived). Cultural and political organizations, publications, and cultural life all flourished, with consequences for both internal Jewish cohesion and Jewish-Polish relations. Within Jewish politics, the assimilationists were shunted aside once and for all. At the same time, the latent divisions between the various Jewish political movements—between Hebrew-promoting Zionists, for example, and Yiddish-promoting nationalists—hardened, transforming from diffuse trends to fully fledged, fully mobilized political movements pursuing goals at odds with each other.[40] As noted above, these movements were animated in part by the increasingly undeniable fact that a new Polish state was on the horizon. At the same time, Polish political elites eyed Jewish mobilization with wariness, and, just as they had since the turn of the century, fretted that the Jews would somehow ruin it all for them (the Poles) just as it seemed that many of their desires were on the cusp of realization. This was made worse still by the general perception among Poles under German occupation that the Jews were somehow profiting from the new order and, with the blithe acquiesence of the Germans, were using the occupation to find new ways to exploit the Poles economically. Suspicions were increased by the number of Jewish businesses set up during the war and the number of army contracts given to the Jews. This reinforced the popular association of Jews with "speculation," though it was merely a continuation of the ancient place of Jews in urban commerce in Poland.[41] Such perceptions of connivance and exploitation were not limited to towns, however. In 1918, for example, a group of farmers from a rural area east of the river Narew wrote to the (Polish) minister of the interior to complain that the Germans had sold the state-owned forests in their district to the Jews, and the Polish farmers were now required by the local authorities to provide transport for the wood at fixed rates. The farmers complained that the Jews were cheating them and were also demanding shipment of large amounts of wood for which the farmers did not have the proper equipment. While they wished to protest this injustice, the farmers stressed that they were not trying to get out of doing the work, declaring that "we understand that at the present time we are obligated to perform labor for the Jews."[42] The phrasing is ominous; the exact words used by the farmers to describe their work—musimy odrabiać pańszczyznę żydom—uses the Polish term for the corvée. Thus the farmers saw the Jews not only as their economic exploiters but masters of a larger system in which they were powerless pawns. This lends "at the present time" a threatening quality. The Jews, it suggests, are lording it over the farmers at the moment, but when their chance arrives, the Poles will put them in their place. This widespread hostility to the Jews, and the perception that they were the true beneficiaries of the occupation, may help explain why there was not more outright resistance to the Germans; like a psychological lightning rod, the Jews, in time-honored fashion, attracted the blame for the misfortunes suffered by those around them.

The Government-General and Poland's Jews

While the Germans did not single out Poland's Jews for special economic treatment, the occupation regime did become deeply involved with Jewish affairs in Poland. The sheer number of Jews there, as well as the difficult political questions that hovered around Polish-Jewish relations—Kries deemed this "one of the most significant and difficult cultural problems in Poland"[43]— meant that, in the interests of a well-run occupation, and, later, the success of their broader political ambitions, the Germans could not avoid entanglement. A recognition of this lay behind the rabbinical conferences periodically convened by the Government-General in order to discuss Jewish matters.[44] It also lay behind the establishment within the Government-General of a network of advisers, both official and unofficial, to help formulate Jewish policies. The senior German official concerned with Jewish issues was Ludwig Haas, head of the department for Jewish affairs, which was a part of the division responsible for educational and religious matters.[45] Haas was a member of the Reichstag, belonging to the left-wing Progressive People's Party, with warm feelings for his Vaterland. "German is our language," he said in a 1913 speech, "German is the land, in which we and our ancestors have lived for a long time; we know no other homeland."[46] At the age of thirty-nine, Haas volunteered for service when the Great War broke out, and he subsequently distinguished himself in some of the most brutal fighting in Flanders. His rather nominal Reform religious tendencies (Haas was notable for many things, his piety not among them) and his ignorance of eastern European Jewish life made him in some respects unsuitable for the job with the Government-General. The Iron Cross First Class with which he emerged from the fighting in the west, however, must have made him an appealing candidate in the eyes of the military establishment.[47]

Haas and the Government-General also had two important advisers on Jewish affairs, Pinchas Kohn from Ansbach and Alexander Carlebach of

Cologne. Both were rabbis; Carlebach was also a school administrator and Kohn an active journalist. In addition, Carlebach brought some knowledge of east European Jewry with him, having served for a time as rabbi in Memel. The two represented the Free Association for the Interests of Orthodox Jews (Freie Vereinigung für die Interessen des orthodoxen Judentums), which hoped to bring German political orthodoxy—combining a commitment to full legal equality for the Jews as citizens of the states in which they lived, a rejection of Zionism and Jewish nationalism, and an emphasis on a deep and profound piety lived and realized within the boundaries of the Jews' home states—to the largely apolitical Jews of Russian Poland, thereby heading off the potential influence of Zionists and Yiddishist nationalists.[48] The Free Association was one of a number of German-Jewish organizations that saw in the occupation an opportunity to import a particular brand of politics to the Jewish masses of the east. One of its main competitors for influence in the occupation zone had been the Committee for the East (Komitee für den Osten/KfdO), founded by the noted German Zionist Max Bodenheimer. The KfdO had advocated organizing the unassimilated Jews of the east into a kind of spearhead of German expansionism in the east, using them as a client nationality that would serve as Germany's reliable vassals against the other eastern nationalities.[49] The Government-General, however, showed little interest in such wild schemes, preferring the cautious conservatism of the Free Association, to which it granted permission to establish a base of operations in Warsaw.[50] The two rabbis, who saw as their goal the establishment of full legal equality for Jews in Poland, became deeply unpopular with Zionists in both Poland and Germany, and were often attacked with striking vehemence in the Zionist press. Beseler was aware of this and troubled by it; however, when German Zionists tried to use their influence to have them brought back to Germany, Beseler and Haas blocked their dismissal.[51] Beyond Beseler, the two advisers had another important ally in Poland, the Gerer Rebbe. The allegiances of the Hasidic Jews were divided among different rebbes, mystical, charismatic figures who wielded tremendous influence within their circles of followers. The Gerer Rebbe was the most important of these figures in Poland, and therefore an invaluable asset for the occupiers.[52]

Carlebach, much like Beseler, wrote a number of detailed and evocative letters to his wife that allow glimpses into the relationship between the regime and Poland's Jews, as well as into the reaction of a German rabbi at work among the Jews of the east. Carlebach was formally an adviser on educational affairs (as will be discussed in Chapter 4, he was involved with the reform of Jewish religious schools, the *chadarim*), but he was besieged during his office hours by visits from Jews from Poland and the Pale seeking his help with all manner of troubles. (Carlebach received these visitors in rooms where signs read, in Hebrew script, PLEASE DO NOT SPIT ON THE FLOOR.) The poor eastern Jews who came to visit Carlebach recited a litany of miseries to him, some ancient and familiar, some new and the products of the war's upheavals. "One, who had lost an eye to a Cossack," Carlebach wrote to his family in January 1916,

> wishes to return to his little town; one asks for the recommendation of his petition for help searching for his children in the forest; one demands that I ask the Governor to approve the request of the Rabbis that civil employees be granted . . . observance of the Sabbath; one asks for permission to become a baker (since everything here is run by monopolies); one files a complaint about a district chief of a nearby town who has threatened to dismiss a Rabbi the next time the Rabbi declares meat "prohibited" that has been approved by a . . . trained meat inspector; this one asks for a job in Germany, that one brings an invitation.[53]

Carlebach's contact with eastern European Jewish life was not confined to official visits during his office hours. He also attended religious services, viewed the Jewish neighborhoods, and attended weddings and Sabbath meals at the homes of many of the Hasidic community's elites. Like many German Jews who went to Poland during the war, his reaction was powerful and deeply conflicted.[54] One the one hand, he found the terrible poverty in which the vast majority of poor Jews lived repulsive. After one visit to a Jewish neighborhood, Carlebach wrote to his wife of the "indescribable misery" he had found there. He had gone into a cellar where many desperately poor and "ill" people were living all crammed together. Wishing to show charity, he tried to hand out some money but was mobbed by the desperate people. (It is indicative of the very different worlds Carlebach navigated that the letter in which he relates this episode is dated simply "Kaisersgeburtstag 1916" and tells of how, a few days later, he enjoyed a meal with other Government-

General school officials in the Germans' officers' mess.[55]) In another letter written shortly thereafter, Carlebach, obviously deeply moved by all he had seen, tells his family that

> of the desperation and the misery and the poverty, the filth and dull res-
> ignation of 300,000 Jewish souls, I shouldn't even try and speak, be-
> cause words are inadequate to the immensity of the suffering. The time
> of the destruction of the Temple, the Crusades, and all the persecu-
> tions of the Middle Ages are child's play compared to this tragedy.[56]

Yet all was not sorrow and pity. In early 1916, Carlebach was invited to a Friday evening Sabbath meal at the house of a relative of the Gerer Rebbe. He recorded an extraordinary experience, a meal filled with joy, prayer, and good cheer. The male family members and guests sat at a table while other male Jews stood around them, singing. (Carlebach caught a fleeting glimpse of the women behind the screen that separated them from the men.) Dinner comprised seven courses and was washed down with, among other things, beer and "schnapps and schnapps and schnapps." Carlebach admired the Hasids' distinctive dress as well as the youthful age at which they married and began families. Carlebach was deeply impressed by the experience and moved to a melancholy reflection:

> Reb Hirsch Henoch [whose house it was] is a marvelous, intelligent man,
> extraordinarily kind and charming, and when I looked across the table
> [and] saw the children, of whom one, recently turned thirteen and al-
> ready engaged, and a fifteen-year-old who is to be married this winter,
> then I had to say to myself, *this* cheder is what you are supposed to help
> destroy, the cheder from which this innocence, this purity comes, [and]
> I got tears in my eyes and was seized by a desire to flee from here and
> leave the job to someone better.[57]

But Carlebach did not flee, and he and the other administrators of the Imperial Government-General worked tirelessly to defend Jewish interests, as they understood them, as best as they could. The Germans' most ambitious official foray into Jewish life in Poland was an ordinance regulating Jewish

affairs issued in November 1916, shortly after the proclamation of 5 November.[58] The ordinance was largely the work of Haas and Kohn; Carlebach
disliked it, thinking it undermined "the old type of *Jüdischkeit* and . . . the
authority of the rabbis."[59] The ordinance decreed that elected local councils
(along with a central twenty-one-person Supreme Council) were to manage
Jewish affairs, including religious matters and social and charitable work. A
provision in the ordinance also allowed for the possibility of Jewish control
over Jewish schools. The most important element of the ordinance, however,
came at its beginning, where it publicly repudiated the claims of Poland's
Jewish nationalists by declaring the Jews of Poland a religious community,
not a nation ("as in all *Kulturstaaten,*" the German Civil Administration
noted).[60] The reaction of Polish Jews was generally unfavorable. "Assimilationists," Carlebach noted, "are angry about the rule of the Shtreimel [i.e., the
Hasidim—after the name of the fur hats customarily worn by the men],
Zionists and nationalists about the constitution of the Jews as a community defined by religion, and the Hasidim fear that they will be overwhelmed by the
better-organized non-Jewish parties."[61] The ordinance was imperfectly implemented during the war; the Supreme Council, for example, was never established, while elections to the local councils, mostly carried out at the end
of 1917 and early 1918, did not take place in Warsaw and Lodz.[62] In its es-
sentials, however, the ordinance endured to become part of the political structure of the Polish Second Republic, where it remained in force until the Nazi
conquest of Poland in 1939.[63] The Government-General's Jewish advisers
made another lasting impact on Polish-Jewish political life. As part of their
struggle to secure the political interests of traditional Jews in an age of
mass mobilization, Kohn and Carlebach were both involved in the founding
of Poland's first mass-based Orthodox political organization, Agudas
Ho'orthodoxim. Officially established on 14 November 1916, the Agudas, in
addition to serving as the vehicle for organized orthodoxy in Poland, also
established orphanages in Warsaw, Kalisz, Białystok, and Kowno. In addition,
it founded an Orthodox newspaper, *Dos Yiddishe Wort* (The Jewish Word,
later *Der Jid,* The Jew), whose first issue appeared on 1 February 1917. More
important than any specific thing the League did during the occupation,
however, was what it went on to become. The organization was the immediate
forefather of the Orthodox Agudas Yisroel, the most important and influential of the Second Republic's Jewish political parties.[64]

The Warsaw Elections of 1916

The elections held by the Germans in occupied Warsaw, however, brought no such fruitful and creative engagement with Polish Jewry. Instead, the elections brought to the fore the question of Polish-Jewish relations and triggered an attempt on the part of the occupiers to limit Jewish influence while maintaining a facade of strict impartiality. In 1916, the Germans were approached by the Warsaw Civic Committee and asked to approve elections for a city council, which they did.[65] Beseler's support stemmed from the recent success of the 3 May celebrations and his increasing commitment to a state-building policy in Poland. He also reasoned that permitting relatively open political activity would provide the Germans with a reliable sampling of public opinion.[66] Disagreements erupted, however, once the occupiers and the committee sat down to work out a set of election regulations. The central issue seems to have been the extent of the franchise. The Germans preferred a carefully restricted one, while the Poles, "guided by political theories," Kries complained, "wanted to erect a monument in honor of democratic political sentiments" (a false impression, as detailed below). The Germans ultimately ignored the committee and simply issued the election rules they themselves wanted.[67] The voting regulations issued by the Germans blended a curial franchise with proportional elections (*Verhältniswahl*, except in the third curia). The curiae were divided as follows:

1. Property owners.
2. The representatives of heavy industry and large commercial concerns.
3. Intellectuals. This curia was further subdivided as follows: the Catholic clergy would elect one representative, lawyers three, teachers three, with one reserved for the faculty of Warsaw University, physicians three, technical experts *(Techniker)* three, with one reserved for the faculty of the Warsaw technical college. Other intellectuals who did not vote in one of the above were given two representatives.
4. The representatives of craft-based industries, lesser merchants, and small businesses.

5. Those who paid an occupancy tax *(Wohnsteuer)*.

6. All others.

These curiae would each send fifteen representatives to the new city council, for a total of ninety members. Men over the age of twenty-five would be allowed to vote in the elections. Unusually, a provision in the electoral regulations allowed a small number of well-off women to vote through a proxy. Men who were over thirty and fluent in Polish were allowed to run for office.[68]

The reference to "democratic political sentiments" above almost certainly represents a misunderstanding of what the Polish elites of the Warsaw committee were trying to do—figure out a way to limit the Jews' representation within the city council. The question of Jewish participation had complicated earlier prewar attempts to introduce limited representative government in the Kingdom of Poland. In the early twentieth century, the Russians considered introducing into Poland elected city administrations of the sort already in place in Russia proper. The plan stalled for a number of reasons, including disagreements over the place of the Polish language in municipal administration. But a major stumbling block had been the question of whether the Jews would be allowed to participate as equals—a question with important implications, given that the Jews were a majority or a very large minority in many cities and towns and, moreover, often possessed the minimum amount of money and property needed to qualify as voters. The Russians were keen on limiting Jewish participation in some way, though they were outdone by the stridency and vehemence of the anti-Semitism of the Polish elites with whom they were working to devise the regulations. A variety of strategies for limiting Jewish influence, such as requiring fluency in Polish, were discussed by both parties. A draft of a proposal from 1910 shows the direction in which the (ultimately unrealized) reforms were headed. Electoral curiae in Poland were to be based on nationality, with a specific number of seats in the municipal councils designated for the three national curiae—Russians, Jews, and "others." For Warsaw, this would have given the Russians—around 4 percent of the city's population—27 seats, the Jews (about 40 percent of the population) 16 representatives, and the "others" (the 56 percent of the population that was Polish) would have had 127 seats. A special provision of the plan would have further limited Jewish influence: the most seats the Jews would be permitted, regardless of their percentage of a town's population, was 20 percent, with 10 percent the maximum for towns where the Jews made up fewer than half of the inhabitants.[69]

This proposal was still languishing in political limbo when the war broke out, but the announcement of elections in occupied Warsaw restarted this debate, with many of the same themes resurfacing. In April 1916, a meeting of the Warsaw Civic Committee was held to discuss the upcoming elections— in particular, to consider "the question of adequate safeguards of the future city council against the possibility of a majority of representatives of the Jewish population hostile to national-Polish interests." In addition to representatives from the committee, many notables from a variety of cultural, political, and charitable institutions were present, including Samuel Dickstein, a distinguished mathematician and professor and, as a Jew assimilated to elite Polish culture, a representative of a fading identity. Just as before the war, various means were considered for minimizing Jewish representation, with Dickstein scoffing, in vain, at the idea that the Jews were a united block, pointing out that they were riven by deep and often acrimonious political divisions (as he would certainly have known from experience). Among those who favored restrictions, some, such as Piotr Drzewicki, a deputy to Warsaw City President Lubomirski, advocated an outright limit on the number of Jews who could participate in the elections. Others, pointing out that this would create an unfavorable image of Poland abroad, suggested drawing up the electoral districts in a way that would subtly disfavor the Jews. In the end, the committee decided to take the latter approach.[70] This seems to have been the recommendation that Kries rejected and misconstrued as the "monument to democratic sensibilities."

The Polish and German elites, however, unknowingly harbored similar goals with regard to Jewish participation in the election. In the Civil Administration's report on the elections, Kries noted that Warsaw's Jews, whom he believed to be about 40 percent of the population, were entitled to "fair representation." He also, however, wanted to preserve "the Polish character of the capital's" city council. The Chief Administrator believed that the intricacies of the curial system and the proportional elections would help limit Jewish influence without blatantly excluding them. It would not, however, do enough. Kries therefore thought it advisable to institute a fifteen-year residency requirement for voters. "In this way," Kries reasoned, "the Russian Jews . . . will gradually gain, with their advancing assimilation, the right of full participation." At the same time, the institutions "of Selbstverwaltung [would] not be burdened by elements" that were "foreign."[71] Kries's concern about the possibility of "Russian Jews" constituting a too-visible presence in the city's administration indicates that the occupiers were primarily worried about the so-called Litwaks. The term "Litwaks" had once referred to Jews who migrated from Lithuania to the Congress Kingdom in the late nineteenth century. By the eve of the war, however, "Litwaks" was used to refer to recent Jewish arrivals to Poland from the Pale of Settlement. They were distinguished, above all, by the fact that they used Russian, rather than Polish, in their dealings with Gentiles. This made them objects of scorn to Polish nationalists, who saw them as a distinct threat to the Polish nation and possibly even secret agents of Russification. The term "Litwak" also became a kind of catch-all code word for all Jews in the tirades of Polish anti-Semites. More long-established Polish Jews tended to dislike the Litwaks as well, seeing them as "cold, aloof," and impious.[72] When the electoral regulations were issued, the residency requirement meant to keep these "Russian" Jews out was buried in a legalistic maze. The criteria establishing eligibility to participate in the elections dated May 1916 mention only two years in Warsaw as a residency requirement. These same criteria, however, also demand "citizenship *(Staatsangehörigkeit)* in the Kingdom of Poland."[73] This was the means by which the "Litwaks" were to be kept out of the elections: if one did not own property, or had not been born in Poland or to parents living in Poland, then the period of residency required for citizenship was set at fifteen years—precisely the period Kries believed necessary to keep the most recent Jewish arrivals out.[74]

When the Germans announced the impending elections, it set off a period of energetic political mobilization in Warsaw. While the Germans may not have intended to grant the city council any real power, many of the political elites in the occupied zone realized that that did not matter. The dominant personalities and organizers from all the major political orientations— including the Passivists—saw in the liberalization of political life the chance to drum up popular support and solidify their position in Polish society. In addition, they realized that participation in the new institutions gave them the opportunity to work to limit the influence of their ideological rivals.[75] In the run-up to the election, three main electoral committees were formed. The Passivists, including the National Democrats, formed the Central National Election Committee (Centralny Narodowy Komitet Wyborczy/CNKW); the Activists joined forced in the Central Democratic Election Committee (Centralny Demokratyczny Komitet Wyborczy/CDKW); and the representatives of various Jewish parties established the Jewish Election Committee (Wyborczy Komitet Żydowski/WKŻ). In a surprising development, the three committees announced, in the run-up to the elections, that a power-sharing agreement had been reached, splitting the seats for the first five curiae. As an important part of the agreement, the Jewish parties agreed to limit the number of mandates they would receive—apparently in the hope of gaining political capital that could be spent later.[76] The bargain enraged the secular Jewish nationalists (the Folkists), who were led by a lawyer, Noyakh Prilutski. Prilutski and his party were opposed not only to the deal struck between the Jewish coalition and the Polish parties but also to the compromises made within the Jewish coalition (i.e., between nationalists and non-nationalists). The Folkists therefore resolved to beat out the coalition in the still-open sixth curia.[77] Alexander Carlebach, however, saw the grand bargain as a major victory for Poland's Jews. Their very participation, he noted, constituted a recognition that the Jews could not be kept out of public life in Poland. He also saw the coalition as a great triumph against the nationalists and Zionists, who, he wrote to his family, "behave like a band of robbers, and used all of the lies, deception, forgery, and craftiness possible to . . . deny the Orthodox the position due to them." However, Carlebach reassured them that "our tactically sophisticated peace with the Poles . . . safeguards the unity of the antisemitic-democratic-Jewish list."[78]

The elections were held in July 1916. According to Beseler's report, minor unrest (including looting) connected with the election occurred, but he blamed "a group of international Social Democrats."[79] Most election-related activity was more tranquil, such as the meeting of the first curia on 2 July, at which a speaker "compared Warsaw with an elegant lady who conceals dirt and disorder under lace, feathers, and jewelry."[80] The greatest amount of political activity was generated by the elections for the sixth curia. The CNKW, for example, held a rally at the Museum of Industry and Agriculture on Sunday, 9 July, while rallies of the National Workers' Election Committee on the same day were held at the hall of the Union of Christian Artisans and, later, at the hall of the Association of Christian Workers; four more rallies aimed at Christian workers were held at various locations from Monday through Wednesday.[81] According to the *Deutsche Warschauer Zeitung,* on election day voters from sixth curia were frequently harassed and jostled by excited crowds hoping to sway their decision. The paper noted that this was especially true in Jewish neighborhoods, where "many of the voters could be quite happy if their coat sleeves were not torn off by the agitators even before they had entered the polling station."[82]

In the end, the power-sharing agreement held, and the power of the National Democrats was further bolstered by a good showing in the sixth curia. They gained seven mandates based on 14,000 votes, while the PPS got two mandates, with around 6,000 votes, and the Folkists (running as the Jewish Peoples' Committee/ Żydowski Komitet Ludowy) garnered four mandates. In the remaining curiae, the National Committee controlled thirty-three seats, the Democratic Committee twenty-seven, and the Jewish representatives fifteen.[83] Kries, while informed about the power-sharing arrangement and therefore not surprised by the overall outcome, was none the less pleasantly surprised by the elections in the sixth curia. He had been certain that the curia's poor voters would bring "the socialist parties and the radical Jews" into the city council, which did not happen.[84] Carlebach was also pleased. "If," he wrote to his wife,

> we are able to keep the worst and noisiest of the nationalist-yiddishist troublemakers out [of the sixth curia] and the clan Davidson, Farbstein, and Co., who unfortunately have been elected, behave decently in the city council and set aside their so-called ideals (Yiddish and Hebrew schools, Yiddish in city council committees, use of Yiddish in the courts., etc., etc., what *Meschuggas,* and how despicable!) and thereby avoid aggravating the Poles, then a better era for the Klal Jisroel [Community of Israel] can really begin here.[85]

The Warsaw city council was formally inaugurated on 24 July 1916. Its initial meeting was preceded by a Mass in the cathedral followed by a celebration at Warsaw's main synagogue, which was, unusually, attended by a number of Polish Catholic notables.[86] The actual opening of the council was marked by solemn and optimistic speeches, though, as usual, Maria Lubomirska, who was in attendance, was not impressed. "Thunderous applause," she recorded in her diary, "and calls of 'Long Live the Legions,' directed towards a shabby soldier who had intentionally been seated in the balcony—an irresponsible, childish farce."[87] Chief of the Civil Administration Kries was actually somewhat more favorable. Once the council was up and running, Kries informed Berlin that it was doing good work. In addition, he added, "it can't be . . . said that the penchant for making pretty speeches out of the window is greater [here] than in other parliaments."[88] This was almost certainly meant as a compliment.

Expanding the Institutions

In the months following the Warsaw elections, the Germans prepared to introduce more elections for both district and city offices. The impetus for district-level reforms came from below; Kries reported that the Poles had grown dissatisfied with the pseudo-elections held to select the members of the district assemblies and had asked the Germans to make them more genuine. Though Kries had little sympathy for such demands—he thought that the presentation elections were quite democratic enough—it apparently carried the day in higher quarters. In addition, what Kries vaguely referred to as changes in the "general political conditions" drove administrative expansion at the district level forward. At the time Kries wrote it (the beginning of 1917), such a reference could only have meant the German proclamation of 5 November and the Germans' public commitment to state building.

A post-proclamation desire to make a show of goodwill led Beseler to direct the Government-General to issue, in November 1916, new regulations for more genuine elections at the district level. Elections were to be held in three electoral associations: one for rural communities *(Gemeinden)*, which would constitute the electoral association of the peasants, one for estate owners, and one for cities. The total number of representatives would vary from twenty-four to fifty, depending on the size of the electorate. The specific number elected by each electoral association would be divided according to the distribution of the population between urban and rural areas. First the number of the cities' representatives would be calculated based on its population vis-à-vis the rural population. The peasants and the estate owners would then split the remaining seats, though a special provision called for a reduction of the landowners' seats (and a corresponding increase in the peasants') if a certain ratio of voters to mandates was not met. Preparations for the elections were being made at the end of the year, but the Germans held off on implementing the reforms.[89]

Events in the cities moved much more quickly. Once again, the impetus came from below: the success of Warsaw's elections inspired Polish representatives from other cities to ask the Germans to extend urban voting rights throughout the occupied territory.[90] The Government-General began drawing up regulations for voting in such elections in the early fall of 1916. The new election regulations maintained six curiae for larger cities, but towns of fewer than 20,000 people would vote in three. Cities were also to maintain the system of proportional representation introduced in Warsaw. According to Kries, the system was "necessary in this country for the protection of the confessional and national minorities."[91] In smaller cities, election was by majority vote, although the regulations left open the possibility of shifting to proportional elections.[92]

The "national minorities" whose fate weighed so heavily on the mind of Kries do not seem to have included the Jews. The potential for Jewish political domination in local politics was something that continued to trouble Kries. The election of "Jewish majorities" to the assemblies, he informed Berlin, would be "extremely undesirable." The new election regulations therefore contained yet more rules intended to minimize the electoral influence of Polish Jewry; the residency requirement and proportional representation of the Warsaw electoral regulations had apparently not been quite effective enough. Jewish participation in the elections was not limited explicitly, but rather through a manipulation of the curia system. The curia for people engaged in commerce was now ranked first among the curiae, and the regulations stipulated that voters had to vote in the first curia for which they qualified. Kries claimed that this limited the Jews, which was "unavoidable in view of the prevailing conditions in Poland," without officially singling them out. It was, moreover, a restriction that, in Kries's mind, provided a future escape route for those affected by relying on a "Jewish habit [meaning, presumably, trade and commerce] . . . from which . . . every Jew can liberate himself."[93] (Kries does not make this quite clear in his report, but in the election regulations, dated 1 November 1916, the commercial curia comes first only in the three-curiae small-town electoral system.[94])

The urban elections took place during the first three months of 1917. Kries reported to Berlin that they had been rather contentious. Most of the various Polish parties had, remarkably, managed to put their differences behind them, but they did this in order to present a united Polish front against the Jews. In many instances, this produced a Jewish surrender, with the Jewish parties agreeing to limit the number of seats they would take. Kries thought this voluntary limiting of influence quite proper for a "minority party," a judgment in which can be heard the voice of a seasoned political veteran of the Prussian-Polish conflict. In two cities (Siedlce and Będzin) the two sides failed to reach an agreement, which Kries blamed on the "Poles' lack of moderation." The result was Jewish-dominated city governments, the only two sizable urban areas where this happened. Kries judged the conflict between the Jews and the Poles to have been an important experience for the Poles, as it served the cause of their political "education":

> Even if such Jewish [majorities] are undesirable, they also cannot be objected to, especially in the present period of transition, since they have an educational effect on the Poles, and strengthen in them . . . a sense of reality and show them . . . that they must use all their energies if they want to hold their ground in the cities.[95]

The elections in the towns of Sokołów and Węgrów, held in January 1917, provide a brief example of how Polish-Jewish electoral conflict unfolded in a rural setting. In Sokołów, six Jews and five Poles managed to gain seats, while in Węgrów a compromise worked out between the competing parties brought seats to five Jews and four Poles. The district chief's report suggests that the local German authorities had to prevent some of the election's initial winners from assuming office because of their poor Polish (the regulations required fluency, a technique of long standing for preventing unassimilated Jews from holding political power). Though it is not made explicit, it was probably Yiddish-speaking Jews who were disqualified. The Germans also disqualified from office (for reasons not made clear) an Orthodox Jew who was elected to the government of Sokołów. The district chief simply replaced him with another Orthodox Jew of his choice.[96]

No election compromise was reached in the industrial metropolis of Lodz, with the result that the elections generated substantial conflict among the city's nationalities. Unlike the elections in Warsaw or some of Poland's smaller cities, conflict between the Germans and the Poles played as important a role as Polish-Jewish conflict. Germans represented about 20 percent of Lodz's population, making it home to one of the Russian Empire's largest urban concentrations of ethnic Germans.[97] During the war, two broad political groupings could be distinguished among them: the conservative, generally loyalist "Passivists," among whose numbers were found many of the city's wealthy industrialists, and the middle-class German nationalist activists.[98] The nationalists were represented by the German Association for the Greater Lodz Area (Deutscher Verein für Lodz und Umgegend), founded in March 1916 and dedicated to the "rousing and stimulation of German national sentiments, the cultivation of a consciousness of fellowship with ethnic brothers in Germany, and the preservation of German ways and customs." Usually known simply as the German Association, its establishment was made possible by the support of the police chief of occupied Lodz, Matthias von Oppen. At the association's head was a nationalist activist named Adolf Eichler.[99]

Many years after the war was over, Eichler wrote that von Oppen had been transferred out of his post because of the support he had given to the German Association.[100] If it is not true, it is believable. Poland's German nationalists and the Imperial Government-General were not natural allies. The occupation regime was loath to lend any obvious support to German nationalist activities in Poland for fear of antagonizing the Poles. This was resented by the German nationalists, particularly as they began to sense that a robust and distinct German minority might not be particularly welcome in the emerging Polish state.[101] The proclamation of 5 November had made them uneasy, and had been followed by requests from some Germans that Lodz be annexed to Germany.[102] This is best seen as a kind of fanciful and rather desperate attempt to find a third way between the two options the German nationalists wanted to avoid—either fully assimilating to the Polish nation or packing up and leaving their *Heimat* for Germany.[103]

At the end of 1916, the Germans' anxiety was becoming acute; to the worries produced by 5 November were added the stresses and strains of the impending elections. On 10 December 1916, the German nationalists convened a meeting that they hoped all Germans in the Lodz area would attend. Between two and three thousand showed up.[104] The rally, which was led by Eichler and held on the premises of the Lodz Men's Choral Society, was intended to address the question of what was to become of the Germans in Poland. All present were strongly encouraged to vote in the elections in order to help secure the place of the Germans in the emerging political order. A resolution was drawn up to express the Germans' collective fears and hopes. It declared the Germans ready to accept the proclamation of 5 November and the resurrection of a Polish state. Yet they were not pleased about it and demanded assurances "that the Imperial German government [would] protect and secure the vital economic and cultural interests of the native German population of Poland." The resolution made it clear that the Germans did not just mean for the period of the occupation. Promising future trouble both within Poland and between Poland and Germany, the document linked the survival of the Germans as a distinct minority with the foreign policy of Germany itself, declaring that the "motherland" had to take the Germans of Poland into its "powerful arms" to keep them safe and preserve them in their way of life.[105]

The Germans apparently did not count on Beseler to make their demands known, as it was decided at the rally to send a number of telegrams conveying the Germans' worries. Seeking sympathy and support in high places, the nationalists dispatched messages to Emperor Wilhelm, Chancellor Bethmann Hollweg, Hindenburg, and von Mackensen.[106] Of the four, only Bethmann Hollweg did not respond.[107] As a final measure of self-defense, taken as the elections approached, Lodz's Germans overcame their own rivalries and joined forces in a single electoral organization, the United German Electoral Committee.[108] The *Deutsche Lodzer Zeitung* campaigned openly on its behalf. "German voters do your duty!" the newspaper encouraged its readers in boldfaced print during the period of the election. To ensure there was no doubt about what they meant, the paper explained that each voter was "to go punctually to the election and cast his vote for the . . . German Electoral Committees' list."[109]

The Germans were far from alone in their scramble to secure a place in Lodz's city government. Numerous rallies and meetings were held by the city's other electoral committees in the weeks leading up to the election. On 21 December 1916, for example, a preelection meeting was held by the Jewish assimilationists. It turned rowdy, with some speakers shouted down by members of the large crowd and the assimilationists publicly branded as traitors.[110] Several weeks later, on the Friday before the election, Polish socialists staged a rally that, according to the German press, was attended by 3,000 people. The topics of the speeches given ranged from the need for greater women's rights to the history of the Polish Socialist Party. Rallies and meetings for three different Jewish election committees (including the socialist Bund) as well as one staged by industrialists were held the following day.[111] In the local press, the fevered activity was compared with elections in the United States.[112]

All of this competition created unbearable pressure along the city's social and national fault lines. An account of the failed attempt by the city's electoral groups to find common ground before the election, published by the *Deutsche Lodzer Zeitung,* perfectly captures the sense of tension and fragmentation that reigned in Lodz during the election period:

> Negotiations between the various nationalities' electoral committees, which we refrained from discussing in detail, guided by the presumption that only the . . . results of these discussions can be of real significance for the upcoming elections, have already been under way for several days. Now that last night at six o'clock the deadline for submissions of election proposals passed, a picture of the state of affairs can to some extent be gained. As we hear it, the Poles first proposed to the German and the Jewish electoral committee[s] entering into negotiations over [the creation of] a common list for the first five curiae, whereby an election campaign in these five curiae was supposed to have been avoided. After the Germans rather quickly left the negotiations, they were continued with the Jewish committees, especially the Central Jewish Committee . . . then the Central Jewish [Committee] and the Committee of Poles Jews [*Komitee der Polen Juden*] submitted separate lists, after the negotiations, it is said, broke down because the Poles . . . had already submitted their own lists. As of seven o'clock last night no list of candidates had been received from the Orthodox Jews. Thus, in contrast to Warsaw, elections and therefore election campaigns are now to be expected.[113]

Lodz's elections commenced on 15 January 1917. Voting took place in six curiae, as in Warsaw, though the post-Warsaw electoral regulations had changed the curia structure somewhat: the first curia was now composed of the intellectuals, the second of the representatives of heavy industry and big business, the third of the lower tier of merchants as well as craftsmen, and the fourth of property owners (the fifth and sixth remained the same).[114] Turnout was high. The greatest number of individuals voted in the sixth curia, in which about 14,000 people voted, representing around 80 percent of those eligible. In terms of the ratio of eligible voters to actual turnout, the first curia had the most impressive numbers, where 94 percent of voters cast their ballots (though this meant only 732 voters). The rest of the curiae fell somewhere in between: 91 percent of the second curia's voters turned out, 77 percent of the third's, 73 percent of the fourth's, and 75 percent of the fifth's. All in all, between 25,000 and 26,000 people voted.[115] Once again, just as in Warsaw, the sixth curia's elections stood out in observers' eyes as being particularly energetic. Partisans of different lists milled about outside polling stations, trying to sway the opinions of the undecided. "Even women are eagerly at work here," marveled the *Deutsche Lodzer Zeitung*. Campaigners wearing signs walked the city's streets to promote the curia's competing factions.[116]

According to Kries, the ultimate results of the election roughly mirrored the city's ethnic composition. He reported that twenty-five seats went to the Jews, while the Poles took twenty-seven and the Germans eight. Kries judged this result a vindication of the occupation government's electoral policies, as the Germans would now, as a bloc, be able to operate as a swing vote. Their collective position in the local administration was thus secure, so long as they continued to work together.[117] The greatest number of seats taken by a single organization was the twenty-one won by the Main Jewish Election Committee (Centralny Żydowski Komitet Wyborczy/CŻKW). The Committee, which had originated in the Zionist movement, had pledged itself to actively defend and promote Jewish interests, which helps explain their overwhelming popularity. (The Orthodox, it seems, had been caught off guard by the collapse of the negotiations for predetermined lists and hence had not sent their own candidates.[118]) Among the Polish parties, the National Democrats and allied organizations captured fourteen seats. The more traditional "Activist" parties, grouped around the Central Polish Democratic Election Committee (Polski Centralny Demokratyczny Komitet Wyborczy), gained nine.[119] The left-wing parties claiming the loyalties of the working class dissipated much of their energies campaigning bitterly against each other.[120] In any event, they seem to have wasted their time; in Congress Poland's most classic industrial city, its "Manchester," the PPS gained 1,430 votes in the workers' curia, earning one seat, while their factional rivals, the PPS-Left, got 1,834 votes and one seat. By contrast, the National Democratic–aligned Polish Central Workers' Election Committee (Polski Centralny Robotniczy Komitet Wyborczy) earned close to 3,000 votes, for two seats. The left socialist party that made the best showing was the Zionist Poalej-Syjon, which captured more than 2,500 votes and two seats.[121] The election results strongly suggest that, in times of turmoil and uncertainty, class identity and its loyalties counted for little, and did not have the unifying power that nationalism did.

Despite professions of general satisfaction with the way the district and city institutions had developed, the Germans actually managed to cause themselves numerous problems. At the level of the district, where elections still had not taken place, disputes between the occupation government and Polish district administrators led to the temporary dissolution of two district assemblies.[122] In the cities, many locals upon whom the Germans had come to rely lost their positions in the voting of 1917. Kries blamed this on the "inadequate political and municipal schooling of the electorate," who had not realized that it was in their interest to leave these administrators at their posts.[123] The elections in the cities also generated tensions between the occupiers and occupied by bringing to prominence people who were openly hostile to the Germans, as had happened, for example, with the National Democrats in Lodz.[124]

Kries credited a recasting by Beseler of the regulations governing the use of Polish as a language of public affairs with helping to ease these tensions. The biggest source of German-Polish conflict at the local level after the elections was not, however, the respective public roles of the German and Polish languages. Rather, the anomalous presence of German mayors serving at the head of city governments that were now elected began to strain the relationship between the cities and the occupation government. The Poles began to demand that the Germans take the next logical step and remove these officials from their posts. In the fall of 1917, Kries reported to Berlin that he was now beginning the process of dismissing the German mayors. His method of replacing them was marked with characteristic caution: a Pole was to be appointed as a deputy mayor and then moved up in rank once the Germans decided that he could be relied on not to cause too much trouble. According to Kries, the city government of Lodz was scheduled to be entirely in local hands by 1 October, while such a turnover had already occurred in Częstochowa. Kries also advised Berlin that it would be best to move very slowly in turning over the administration of Sosnowice, as it was important not to interrupt the flow of coal from there that was helping fuel the German war effort.[125]

In November, representatives of cities throughout Poland—including, importantly, Lublin, which was still under Austrian occupation—gathered in Warsaw, signaling an important milestone in the centralization of the cities' local administrations. They came together to discuss the challenges of urban administration, plan new ways of working together, and trade advice on how to deal with the problems that beset their respective towns. The conference opened on November 19, after the Mass that nearly always began such events. Lubomirski, now serving on the Regency Council, was in attendance, as was a representative of the occupation government. As part of his welcome, the head of the Warsaw city council, Suligowski, expressed his pleasure at the splendid opportunity presented to those who had gathered there—an opportunity not just to deal with immediate issues and problems but to have a hand in establishing "independent" Polish political life in central Europe.[126]

Some among the Germans, including Kries, were rather less enthused by the way German policy had unfolded up to this point. At about the same time that Kries informed Berlin of the decision to start replacing the German mayors, he allowed himself to express a note of criticism of the situation in Poland in his report to his superiors. The time was the fall of 1917, shortly before the creation of the Regency Council, which Kries thought had enormous potential to cause trouble for the Germans.[127] Their state-building experiment had not gone well thus far, Kries thought, in no small measure because the Germans had been too flexible. "The way things have developed," he concluded in his fall 1917 report, "has strengthened the conviction that Poland is relatively easy to govern with a firm hand and clear will." It was, however, important that one avoided "making deals with the Polish elements," who saw such behavior as evidence of "uncertainty and weakness."[128]

Shortly after writing these pessimistic lines, Kries left his position in the Government-General. The official explanation was that he had been released to attend to pressing political business in the Prussian lower house. Readers of the *Deutsche Warschauer Zeitung* were left with the impression that he would probably be back.[129] In his (unpublished) memoirs, Kries writes that this was merely a story concocted to maintain an appearance of unanimity. The real reason for the departure of this "son of the Prussian Ostmark" had been what Kries, ever the cautious bureaucrat, rather obliquely referred to as "political differences of opinion." The proclamation of 5 November had driven him to ask to be discharged from his post as civilian chief in 1916; in late 1917, he got his wish.[130] Beseler did not have proof, but he suspected that Kries had been motivated by his opposition to the Government-General's Polish policies. In an angry letter to Clara, Beseler said that he was suspicious of the reasons Kries had given for his departure, accusing him of "desertion" and noting that he had been going about his duties "halfheartedly" and behaving like an "administrator," not a "man of policy [*Politiker*]."[131]

Despite the departing Administrative Chief's gloomy assessments of the political situation in Poland, the period of the late fall was actually fairly calm. Beseler, however, who had to remain at his post and salvage what he could of his policy, realized that the Government-General was merely drifting through "the calm before the storm."[132] The storm would indeed come, in 1918, when the occupation regime would struggle to maintain stability while being buffeted by powerful currents of disorder and unrest. Before it finally foundered, however, its leaders would work to create a safe postwar harbor for the Polish Kingdom's German minority. This harbor was to be provided by the new Polish state's schools.

General v. Beseler,
der Sieger von Antwerpen.

PHOTOCHEMIE, BERLIN.
· 2844 ·

Hans Hartwig von Beseler as the "Victor of Antwerp." (© Michael Nicholson/Corbis)

Beseler and his Austrian counterpart, Karl Kuk (center), Lublin, 1916.
(Bundesarchiv, Bild 183-2007-1001-500)

Troops assault a peasant accused of stealing food, 1915. German food
requisitions were extensive, leading to severe privation on the part of Polish
civilians and enduring hostility between occupied and occupier. (Bundesarchiv,
Bild 146-2007-0161)

Polish women harvesting potatoes under the watchful eyes of German soldiers.
(Bundesarchiv, Bild 146-2007-0157)

A political cartoon in the satirical newspaper *Mucha* showing speculation as "Our Lord," May 1916. Many occupied Poles blamed their troubles on "speculators," commonly understood to refer to Jews. (Biblioteka Narodowa)

Contemporary claims that the 3 May 1916 parade generated enormous popular enthusiasm is borne out by photographs of the event. Here schoolchildren march in the parade. (Biblioteka Narodowa)

University students in the May 1916 parade. (Biblioteka Narodowa)

1791 — 3 MAJ — 1916. UROCZYSTY POCHÓD W WARSZAWIE.
Rabinat warszawski ze 105=letnim rabinem Perlmutterem na czele ⟨×⟩.

Fot. Marjan Fuks.

Rabbis taking part in the May 1916 parade. (Biblioteka Narodowa)

This December 1916 political cartoon from *Mucha* is captioned: "At the behest of my government I cordially thank free Poland for the military support which it wishes to provide, of its own free will, to its friends: Germany and Austria." The timing of the recruiting drive reinforced suspicions in Poland and abroad that the Germans were only interested in cannon fodder. (Biblioteka Narodowa)

A boy dressed in a traditional Polish military uniform sells flowers to a German soldier, Warsaw, June 1917. (Bundesarchiv, Bild 104-03712)

Wolfgang von Kries with members of the Civil Administration (Zivilverwaltung). His displeasure with Beseler's policies seems evident in his body language. (*Das Generalgouvernement Warschau: Eine Bilderreihe aus der Zeit des Weltkrieges,* Imperial Government-General of Warsaw, Oldenburg, Gerhard Stalling, 1918)

...hauer with Bogdan Graf von Hutten-Czapski (in uniform).
...nt *Warschau: Eine Bilderreihe aus der Zeit des Weltkrieges*,
...General of Warsaw, Oldenburg, Gerhard Stalling, 1918)

Jews in Lodz. Poland's dive
elected city governments. (
der Zeit des Weltkrieges, Im
Gerhard Stalling, 1918)

Members of the Zi
Germany's policie
activity there. (A

Archivist Adolf Wars
(*Das Generalgouverneme*
Imperial Government–

4

Schools of the Nations

Education and National Conflict

In addition to the program of "political education" linked with the introduction of Selbstverwaltung in Poland, the occupation regime devoted an extraordinary amount of time and energy to formulating and implementing an educational policy of a more literal sort: namely, the resurrection of a functioning system of primary and secondary schools.[1] Directly overseen by Administrative Chief von Kries, the Germans' actions in this field were intended to serve three purposes simultaneously. The first was the preservation of order in the occupied zone. Then, as the occupation wore on, educational concessions to the Poles became a centerpiece of German attempts to give a modicum of meaningful content to their promises of Polish autonomy. Finally, the Government-General made its support for German education one of the chief means by which it meant to secure the existence of the German minority in Poland once the war was over, thereby dragging the occupiers into a bitter and wearying struggle over the rights of national minorities in the emerging Polish state. Much like the institutions of Selbstverwaltung, the interactions between occupier and occupied within the field of education reveal the complexity of the relationship between the two, as well as the extent of German institution building at the local level during the war.

The Quest for Stability

In the first months of the occupation, Germany's educational policies were driven primarily by a desire to maintain order.[2] The eastward flight of Russian officialdom in 1915 had included the public school system's teachers and administrators. To fill the void left by their disappearance, the Germans aimed at getting elementary schools *(Volksschulen)* functioning again as soon as possible. Since elementary schools served the entire population (rather than the smaller numbers served by secondary schools, both academic and vocational), reestablishing these institutions would ensure that most of Poland's children had somewhere to be during the day. Elementary education therefore received the most immediate attention from the occupiers. The Germans managed to open some schools as their armies pushed toward Warsaw in 1915; the goal was to have all of them open again by the fall. Curricular oversight was made a firm part of German policy at this early date, with the German district chiefs charged with ensuring that the schools did not become sources of anti-German sentiment.[3]

The district chiefs were assisted in their duties by an educational bureaucracy that expanded as the occupation regime stabilized. In late 1915, the Government-General created a new department *(Abteilung)* of religious and educational affairs out of formerly discrete units *(Dezernate)*. It also added (German) district school inspectors to its ranks of educational bureaucrats.[4] In some areas, Polish "school committees" were created. These five-member committees, chosen by either the German district chief or the chief of police, were meant to help oversee the Volksschulen. Their primary duty was ensuring that the schools remained in good physical condition.[5] Some of the Poles chosen to serve on the committees, however, tried to use their positions to do a good deal more than keep the school grounds looking presentable; in Warsaw, for example, Kries noted that "the formation of a school deputation . . . failed due to the overly ambitious aspirations of the participants," almost certainly a reference to Polish attempts to keep control over education out of German hands (see below). This was an isolated incident, however, and Kries pronounced himself pleased with the work done by the Polish committees.[6]

The obstacles in the way of a smooth reintroduction of education by the Germans were numerous. One was the terrible poverty of much of Russian

Poland. A report from the administrator of the district of Sokołów vividly captures the often desperate conditions in which classes were held. In the spring of 1916, he reported to Warsaw the results of an inspection made of the two secondary schools under his authority, both of them in the town of Sokołów: one Progymnasium for boys with seventy-eight pupils, and one for girls with forty-six. "The instruments," he reported,

> for physics and chemistry instruction are completely absent. Wall dec-
> oration of any sort is also lacking. The classrooms were in bad shape.
> Broken windowpanes were papered over, the wallpaper hung in s[h]reds,
> rain was coming through the ceiling. The heating ovens were not lit in
> any of the rooms. For the most part these ills have been remedied.[7]

In rural areas, the educational ambitions of the occupiers also clashed with the older rhythms of rural life. In the early summer of 1916, Sokołów's administrator reported that school attendance had been very poor during the preceding months because parents were keeping their children at home in order to work the fields. The district chief further noted that religious instruction had absorbed what little time the students had had for school.[8]

Much of the time, however, the Germans were forced to deal with the opposite problem: finding adequate personnel and facilities for dealing with what they called the population's *Bildungseifer* (educational zeal). The shortage of classroom space was acute. Kries claimed that this was because the fighting had damaged many school buildings and made them unusable. This was certainly true, but the German army had exacerbated the shortage by requisitioning some of the remaining space for its own use. The result was that the occupation government simply did not have enough space to accommodate all the prospective pupils. In one district, for example, there were 850 children of school age, but room for only 45.[9]

The Germans were also faced with a shortage of qualified teachers. After the Russian retreat of 1915, a number of instructors of dubious qualification had taken the place of the departed Russian teachers. According to the chief of the Sokołów district, the elementary school teachers under his authority were not fully literate and did "not have command of the multiplication tables from one to ten."[10] In the above-mentioned secondary schools, the dismal physical condition of the institutions was matched by "many of the habits of the teachers." The buildings were littered with "the remains of cigarettes," while "punctuality was unknown."[11] To raise the quality of the teaching staff, the Germans instituted mandatory teacher-training courses.[12] The courses offered general instruction in pedagogy and psychology, as well as the opportunity to receive specialized language instruction in German, Polish, Hebrew, or Yiddish.[13] The courses proved quite popular with Polish Jews, in keeping with the general trend of the upsurge of Jewish political and cultural activity during the occupation. Kries reported that in early 1916, more than 1,700 "predominantly Jewish male and female teachers" took the teacher education course offered by the Germans in Warsaw. (Even more teachers had applied to attend, but had been turned away owing to a lack of space.[14]) The courses were complemented by other measures intended to increase the pool of teachers. One was the qualifying of people by exam. In June 1916, forty-five aspirants took such a test in the district of Będzin; thirty-seven passed.[15] Another was the convening of "teachers' conferences" by district school officials.[16]

The Government-General planned to match its reorganization of the teaching profession with an ambitious overhaul of the Volksschulen themselves. To the Germans, the predominance of one- and two-class schools was a sign of a distinctly "inadequate" school system.[17] They therefore began the process of replacing them with three- to six-class schools. According to Kries, the addition of new classes would help prevent further harm being done to the pupils' "intellectual and moral development," which, he believed, had suffered under the Russian system.[18] (Such sweeping condemnations of the ill-effects of Russian schooling were not confined to arrogant German bureaucrats. Some Polish educational activists were in full agreement with this sentiment. "It is necessary finally to break with the Russian school[s]," Professor Konrad Chmielewski told a meeting of Polish secondary school teachers in Warsaw in January 1917, "and gradually accustom the . . . crippled character of the teachers and pupils to civic duty and to conscience."[19])

After a year of occupation, the Germans were able to record some progress in the field of educational policy. In the second half of 1916, the occupation government established that about 7,000 confessional elementary schools, both public and private, were holding classes. They were attended by more than 400,000 (mostly Catholic) students, who were taught by about 10,000 teachers.[20] These results are not unimpressive given the prevailing conditions.

(Unfortunately, the total number of private schools went into decline soon after these numbers were recorded, casualties of Poland's poverty. "It appears," the Civil Administration's report uncharitably commented, "as though the enthusiasm and eagerness to make sacrifices with which the 'Polish' school[s] were greeted at first [have] already waned, at least among the so-called intellectuals."[21]) In addition, some schools were used to deliver much-needed social services. In Zgierz, for example, poor children (almost certainly ethnically German) were fed at school, while in Lodz pupils (also probably German) had access to doctors detailed to serve the school system.[22]

The Problem of Secondary Education

Most of the progress that the Germans had made in restarting the school system in 1915 and 1916 had been confined to the Volksschulen. Secondary schools, both vocational and academic (i.e., Gymnasien), had not received the same attention. The reasons for this neglect (particularly regarding the Gymnasien) were political. Under the Tsar, secondary schools had been "run according to Russian wishes and . . . mostly attended by the children of Russian civil servants or . . . [loyalist] subjects."[23] These institutions did not, however, just serve the needs of this elite: they also created it (notwithstanding the fact that some of their sons found their way into radical student groups). As in Germany, the students of public secondary institutions went on to attend university and become members of the ruling class. Just who the ruling class in Poland would be after the war, however, was obviously a question of enormous political import that the Germans were not ready to decide. Kries therefore advocated that the Germans act "with caution" in formulating a secondary-school policy, since the institutions were "of special importance for the cultural and national development of the area under administration." The reestablishment of a system of public secondary education was postponed indefinitely. However, the Germans did allow private secondary schools to conduct classes, since they did not have the deep links to public life that public schools did—at least in normal peacetime circumstances.[24] As Chapter 5 will show, some of these private schools began to assume the role of advanced public institutions, despite the Germans' worries, when the opening of

Warsaw University placed pressure on the school system to produce qualified graduates.

Despite the lack of official support, private secondary schools managed to
survive, if not thrive. At the end of 1916, there were sixty-five private boys'
Gymnasien in German-occupied Poland, an increase from the forty-eight
that had existed in the 1915–1916 school year. Counting other kinds of secondary schools, boys' institutions numbered 108 in the first half of the 1916–
1917 school year. Girls' secondary schools of all kinds also increased from
158 in 1915–1916 to 166 in the 1916–1917 school year. Some vocational secondary schools closed down, but Kries informed Berlin that these institutions
had been overrepresented in the educational landscape of the Congress
Kingdom, a result of a quirk of the Russian educational bureaucracy.[25]
Under the Russian system, commercial schools had been subject to the control of the Ministry of Commerce and Industry, whose oversight of its educational institutions was more lax than the Ministry of Education's. Therefore,
when individuals or associations wished to found a school that circumvented
Russia's educational rules, they frequently established commercial schools
with a more ambitious, rigorously academic curriculum than would be expected in a vocational business institution, essentially creating Gymnasien
out of them.[26]

One innovation in Polish secondary education adopted at this time managed to outlast the rule of the Imperial Government-General as well as its
brutal successor. In 1916, Polish Gymnasia adopted German-style leaving
exams, which consisted of a full day of oral interrogation before a committee.
It was maintained until 1960.[27]

Polish Nationalism and Polish Education

As the regime's school policy stabilized and schools continued to open in the
second year of the occupation, the question of *whose* schools these would be
became acute. In particular, the Germans found themselves unable to ignore
Polish pressure for immediate Polonization of the school system. Such pressure had been inevitable from the moment the occupation regime was created. In the era of the partitions, Polish nationalism and Polish education had
become deeply linked. After the disappearance of the Rzeczpospolita, the sur-

vival of the Poles as a distinct nationality was seen by both Polish nationalists and their enemies to be directly connected to the survival of Polish education. This led, on the one hand, to a passionate attachment to the cause of
Polish education on the part of the Polish elite and, on the other, to frequent
attacks on it by the states in which they lived. By the late nineteenth and early
twentieth centuries, the partitioning powers' respective attitudes toward their
Polish subjects were directly mirrored in their Polish educational policies: in-
tolerance on the part of Russia and Prussia, where schools were predominantly institutions of Russianization and Germanization, respectively, and
permissiveness in Galicia. However, in those areas where public Polish education was limited and generally forbidden, it was always somehow kept alive,
whether in private schools or secret societies. The survival of Polish education remained an emotionally charged cause in Polish Europe, embraced by
nationally conscious Poles with a commitment that increased in direct proportion to Russian and Prussian attacks on it.[28]

Polish educational activists in the Russian partition had been given a fresh
burst of energy by the outbreak of the war, with the Tsarist state promising
educational reforms as part of its attempt to harness Polish loyalty to the Russian war effort. Then, in 1915, Polish political activists moved quickly to fill
the void left in the wake of the retreating Russian army. In the brief interlude
between the departure of the Russians and the creation of the Government-
General, the Warsaw Civic Committee established its own Department
of Education (Wydział Oświecenia), headed by an eminent professor of
agricultural chemistry, Józef Mikułowski-Pomorski. One of the department's members, Bogdan Nawroczyński, remembered it rather romanti-
cally as the "first Polish educational authority in Warsaw since the time of
Wielopolski."[29]

West of Warsaw, Kries and his bureaucrats had grappled with this educational enthusiasm even before the great eastern offensive of 1915 had ended.
In his report from July of that year, Kries noted with concern the issuance of
a pastoral letter, dated 26 June 1915, by a Polish bishop who "[loved] his
fatherland dearly." The bishop announced that the time was ripe to ensure that
"every single village gets a school in which our children, without exception,
can be taught and [also] become acquainted with their past, with their traditions and customs." Kries reported that "many statements of the Polish press
are . . . connected with this pastoral letter, [statements] which encourage the

population to establish schools." Kries recommended the Germans keep a close eye on this surge of enthusiasm and require official permission for the founding of new schools.[30]

In August, an incident occurred that further demonstrated to Kries the need for caution in crafting an educational policy. A priest and journalist in Włocławek named "Zak" started a teacher-training program without consulting the German authorities. After Kries found out about it, he (rather surprisingly) let the course continue. Seeing a chance to fill the classrooms with trained teachers, Kries offered Zak a deal. The course's final examination would be taken under the watchful eye of a German official; its graduates would then be certified as teachers by the Germans and employed as such. Zak and his colleagues agreed.

On 12 August 1915, sixty-eight of the course's students assembled to take an examination. Before it began, two of them handed in a statement "on behalf of the course." The statement quoted the German army's proclamation from early in the war about the Poles' impending "liberation from the Russian yoke," pointing out that a central element of this yoke had been the school system. In a polite and restrained tone, the statement expressed a hope for future Polish "freedom and independence" and declined the offer of German-certified credentials. Though given a chance to do so, the students refused to retract the statement. The enraged Germans disbanded the course, while Zak was threatened with punishment should any more trouble arise.

Kries believed that the disturbance was directly linked to the pastoral letter whose contents he had passed on to Berlin only a short time before. (Kries seems to have been somewhat confused; in the report of the trouble with Zak's course, he refers to the pastoral letter from the bishop of Włocławek; in the original report, however, the letter's author is identified as the bishop of Kujawy-Kalisz.) The unnerved administrator told his superiors that he had informed the bishop that the state, not the church, had to rule in matters of education. He vowed to keep a closer eye on the schools in Poland, making sure that they weren't used as vehicles for "anti-German endeavors."[31]

Despite this episode, the Germans did not keep a particularly close eye on the schools. Włodzimierz Gałecki, who landed a job teaching literature at a well-known private Warsaw school run by the eminent pedagogue Wojciech Górski, notes in his memoirs that from time to time a Polish-speaking German school inspector named Müller would visit. Müller would quietly observe the teachers going about their work, all the while making notes and sometimes speaking (exclusively) to Górski. On one of his visits, Müller told the headmaster that he had observed many intelligent and eloquent people at the school; not one, regrettably, was fit to be called a teacher. According to Gałecki, this harsh judgment was due to the fact that most of the courses were lecture based, which was apparently out of fashion in knowledgeable pedagogical circles. Gałecki did not entirely disagree with Müller's assessment; he once listened with horror as a fellow teacher bragged about the two-hour lecture on the minor poet Stefan Witwicki he had given while Müller was on one of his inspection visits.[32]

Generally left to themselves with little guidance or help available from the fledgling Polish authorities, and lacking, after decades of prohibition, textbooks or a standardized curriculum, the schools in German-occupied Poland nonetheless moved with impressive rapidity toward uniformity in their humanities courses. The curriculum became unmistakably Polonized and was clearly intended to nourish both the minds and the national sentiments of the students. Literature courses were generally dominated by the study of Romanticism in general and of the works of the "Three Bards," Adam Mickiewicz, Juliusz Słowacki, and Zygmunt Krasiński, in particular. Polish history was taught as a series of glorious uprisings beginning with that of the great nationalist hero Kościuszko in 1794, while courses on "Polish Geography" informed students of the sweeping expanse of the once mighty Rzeczpospolita.[33] The Górski school enjoyed a thoroughly Polonized cultural life beyond the classroom as well, with ceremonies and other activities held to mark events of particular importance in Polish culture, such as the anniversary of the death of the playwright Wyspiański.[34]

In this respect, nationalism in Poland proved to be a creative and stabilizing force. With little formal guidance from above, the Polish elite, steeped in a shared high culture, was able to draw on a rich common store of ideas, images, and personalities to create a remarkably coherent curriculum for its schools virtually overnight. Yet the nationalism of the educators also created a great deal of tension within the Government-General, both between the Poles and the military administration, as well as between the Poles and the national minorities who did not wish their children to learn, in Polish, about the glories of Mickiewicz or Kościuszko. Troubles caused by conflicting views on how and for what purpose the schools should be run surfaced early in the occupation, when the occupation regime floundered as it tried to answer a deceptively simple question: in what language would classes be held?

The Problem of Language

On this point, there was at least one answer that was generally accepted by most of Poland's political parties and minority communities: not Russian. Russian had begun to disappear from schools in Poland even before the great eastern offensive of 1915 had completely ended.[35] Once German rule had been stabilized under the Government-General, the question of language proved to be the greatest obstacle to implementing a comprehensive, formal set of educational regulations that would give clear guidance to the regime's administrators. The first attempt at this came with the Government-General's school ordinance of 24 August 1915, which was based on an earlier school ordinance issued by OberOst. The ordinance met with major resistance. The central problem was Section 13, the issuance of which Kries declared after the war to have been "unquestionably an error of judgment."[36] It decreed that in Polish Volksschulen, Polish would be the language of instruction, though German would be taught as a foreign language. In schools attended by German or Jewish students, however, the language of the classroom was to be German.[37]

The intention behind Section 13 was not necessarily—as it certainly seemed at the time—the Germanization of Poland's Jews.[38] Rather, Yiddish was not recognized by the German authorities as a fully fledged language, suitable for the conduct of formal education. It was regarded instead as a distinctly inferior "German dialect." This view was hardly idiosyncratic; even many educated and assimilated European Jews thought that Yiddish was "a shameful jargon."[39] In any event, Kries thought that Yiddish would not be around for long, since it would simply transform over time into standard German.[40] The section's ostensible beneficiaries rejected it nearly unanimously, a remarkable fact given the fractious nature of organized Jewish politics during this period. The Zionists wanted Hebrew schools, while those few elite assimilationists still to be found in Poland wanted Polish. Most of the rest of Polish Jewry, elite Jewish opinion notwithstanding, would have preferred Yiddish.[41]

Those Poles who hoped to build a new Polish school system were, of course, also angered by the language provision, which bluntly rejected their hopes.[42] In September 1915, a group of Polish educators from Lodz submitted a lengthy formal protest against it. The educators drew on numerous arguments to convince the Germans that educating the Jews in German was a grave error. It would, they said, create social fissures and cause tension, not only between Poles and Jews, but also in the Jewish community itself, between "Polish-minded" Jews of long residence in the Congress Kingdom and "foreign, anti-Polish" recent arrivals (meaning, presumably, the so-called Litwaks). It would cause further intra-Jewish tension by creating distance between the Jewish masses and the Jewish elite, which was "Polish through and through" (a statement much less true in 1915 than, for example, 1880). Jewish schools, the authors continued, would also be disadvantaged by the fact that there were not enough teachers who could conduct their classes entirely in German. Finally, those unfortunate Jews who were subjected to the regulation would, sadly, be denied the privilege of Polishness. "Every inhabitant of our land, regardless of faith," the authors piously intoned, "must be granted the freedom to be a Pole and as such to participate in the building of his Polish fatherland."[43]

The educators also protested the mandatory inclusion of German as a foreign language in the Volksschulen. Foreign languages, they asserted, had no place in the curriculum of the Volksschulen; obviously the Germans realized the truth of this, as Section 13 did not require that Polish be taught in German schools. The Germans were urged to avoid the appearance of Germanizing tendencies that could reasonably be inferred from Section 13, as well as the next section of the provision, which held that "the official language is German for the German and Jewish teachers, for Polish teachers Polish or German."[44]

The outcry over the linguistic provisions of the school ordinance eventually led to a retreat on the part of the Germans. In December 1915, Kries reported to Berlin that he and Beseler had decided that "the so-called jargon" could be employed as the language of instruction in Poland's Jewish schools after all, though Kries also recommended that some Polish-language Volksschulen be provided for Jewish students who spoke Polish at home. Kries had certainly not modified his opinion of Yiddish: he still thought it was desirable, possible, and perhaps even inevitable that it would be replaced in the classroom by German. He informed Berlin, however, that the teachers for such an ambitious linguistic program were simply not available. He hoped to use the teacher-training courses begun by the Germans eventually to remedy this situation.[45] (The Germans also planned at this point to make a sweeping program of foreign-language instruction compulsory in the upper levels of the Volksschulen. Specifically, they wanted Polish taught in German and Jewish schools, and German in Polish schools. Kries informed Berlin that this was necessary "to facilitate the mutual understanding of the population as a whole."[46]) Finally, in October 1916, the Germans publicly acknowledged the political miscalculation they had made when formulating the school regulations by publishing a short addendum to the original ordinance, signed by Beseler, that formally abolished Section 13.[47]

National Ambitions and National Institutions

Polish desires for a Polish school system also made it difficult for the Germans to create a centralized educational bureaucracy that would not be deeply resented by the occupied population. In this, however, as with the language ordinance, pressure from below eventually led to a limited German retreat. Section 1 of the 24 August ordinance was quite clear on who exercised ultimate authority over all educational matters in the Government-General: the German Administrative Chief. Like the language provision, this rejection of Polish ambitions attracted attention from the angry authors of the Lodz protest. In the same document, the authors quoted from the August 1915 speech by Bethmann Hollweg in which he promised that cooperation with the locals would be a guiding principle of the German occupation. After a long struggle with the Russians, the Poles continued, it was time to begin building a Polish school system; surely the Germans realized this, for had they not abolished Russian as the language of instruction? Thus the best course of action was immediately to establish a joint Polish-German school authority.[48] Such reasoning carried very little weight with Kries, who believed it the responsibility of an occupying power to take control of the school system. Kries also concluded that the Russians had been in charge for so long that the Poles would merely make a mess of things were they to take over. All concerned parties, he reasoned, were actually quite lucky that the Germans were there to keep an eye on things.[49]

Yet the practical challenges faced by the occupiers in their attempt to maintain a school system led them to make at least a partial peace with Polish educational ambitions. On 26 April 1916, the Polish educational organization Polska Macierz Szkolna (Polish Motherland Schools) was officially recreated with Beseler's blessing. The Macierz Szkolna had been founded during the upheavals of 1905 to coordinate underground Polish education. It went on to establish, oversee, and maintain a network of private Polish schools. It was quite successful for a time, but in 1907 the Russians closed its institutions.[50] In its new incarnation, the Macierz Szkolna made no secret of its ambitions, announcing in its German-approved statutes that its purpose was "spreading and promoting education in the national spirit."[51] By the fall of 1916, it was holding teacher-training programs and assisting in the creation of new schools. Along with a charitable organization, the Main Welfare Council (Haupthilfsausschuß zur Linderung der Not/Rada Główna Opiekuńcza), Kries judged it to be providing "very pleasant help."[52]

That same year, the Germans signaled that they would be willing to accept even greater Polish input on educational matters (under German oversight, of course). On 13 October, Beseler approved a plan to establish a central educational advisory body to be composed of natives.[53] After the 5 November proclamation, however, the Polish elites who had indicated that they would be willing to serve backed out; the proclamation seemed to carry with it the promise of far greater responsibilities and opportunities, and the Poles decided to bide their time and await the creation of a more genuinely Polish institution.[54] Such an institution did indeed follow, when the Provisional Council of State created its own department of educational and religious affairs, headed by Mikułowski-Pomorski. The council hoped to use the department to lay the foundation for a new Polish school system. The Germans did not disapprove of the department's existence, though they sent a delegate to observe it at work.[55]

The Government-General and Minority Education

The limited but public concessions made by the German authorities to Polish wishes heightened the anxieties of Poland's ethnic minorities: would they have a place, they wondered, in a school system that was beginning to look distinctly Polish? With regard to Poland's most numerous minority, the Jews, the occupation regime left this question for the nascent Polish authorities to decide. The Government-General took action, however, to ensure that Poland's German minority would be able to preserve its schools once the war had ended and the occupiers returned to the Reich.

The question of the place of specifically Jewish education within the emerging Polish educational system was not an issue with which the Government-General, while not indifferent, was deeply concerned, although it was, of course, a matter of paramount importance to many of Poland's Jews. "The question of Jewish schools is the question of Jewish national existence," declared the Folkist Noyakh Prilutski in the Warsaw City Council in September 1916.[56] Prilutski was voicing a nationalistic view of the importance of Jewish education, but "cultural" or "religious" or "social" could easily be substituted for "national" to reflect other strains of Jewish opinion. Official German policy regarding Jewish schools was primarily directed at the reform of Polish Jewry's traditional private religious schools, the *chadarim* (singular *cheder*). The chadarim were generally viewed by the occupiers as institutions where terrible poverty and ignorant teachers combined to produce an environment in which no real education could possibly take place. This was not simple snobbery or anti-Semitism, though both may have played a role in forming German opinion. According to one historian's summary description, Poland's chadarim were indeed characterized by "unhealthy classrooms . . . untrained teachers, devoid of all pedagogic knowledge . . . and, above all, [by] the complete exclusion of all secular subjects" from the curriculum.[57] Within Russia, elite Jewish dissatisfaction with the schools dated at least from the nineteenth-century Jewish enlightenment (Haskala). "Our chedorim [*sic*]," according to one nineteenth-century Russian Jewish newspaper, "represent a copy in miniature of the medieval inquisition applied to children."[58] The schools were also looked upon unfavorably by the German Jews of the Free Association, with Carlebach writing to his wife in February 1916 that he "regularly emerge[d] from [his] visits to the cheder schools completely resigned a[nd] full of despair."[59]

In mid-1916, Kries reported that a number of chadarim had been closed for sanitary reasons, being replaced by courses held in "pleasant, well-lit rooms." More than just a change of venue, however, was planned by the Germans: Kries reported that efforts were under way to transform chadarim into

standard elementary schools.[60] Kries claimed that this program of cheder reform was immensely popular with the Jews of Poland, even if their rabbis
were not always so pleased.[61] In addition, the German Jews of the Free Association, especially Carlebach, were involved in the reform of cheder education in Poland. Carlebach did not want to abolish the system altogether,
but hoped rather to introduce modern educational standards (as well as
more suitable physical premises) without sacrificing the religious character
of the schools. In conjunction with officials of the Government-General as
well as some Polish rabbis, Carlebach introduced an entire program of curricular reform and teacher training. His efforts ultimately led to the establishment of some eighty new chadarim outside Warsaw, while in the capital
Carlebach opened a handful of display models intended to publicize his
efforts.[62]

The Government-General's entanglement with German education in Poland was far deeper and more complex. It began as early as March 1916, when
Kries wrote to the Secretaries of the Foreign Office and the Interior recom-
mending German support, primarily of a financial nature, for the reestablishment of a German teacher-training institute in Lodz (the existing institute
had been shut down at the beginning of the war). Kries thought that the Foreign Office could either convince the nationalistic Association for Germans
Abroad (Verein für das Deutschtum im Ausland) to make a donation or
supply the funds itself. The latter was not a particularly unusual request,
since a special office in the Foreign Ministry regularly supplied subsidies to
"Auslandsschulen," German schools outside the Reich.[63] (Such assistance,
however, was generally restricted to Volksschulen, as it was intended to provide German citizens with the basic education they would be entitled to were
they living at home.[64]) Kries thought the move advisable in part because the
quality of the teachers working in German schools was so poor. He was not
merely concerned, however, with ensuring that ethnically German schoolchildren received a proper education. Kries linked the creation of the seminar with the survival of a distinct German minority in Poland. "It is in the
interest of the future preservation of the German element," Kries wrote to
Berlin, "to lay the foundation for the creation of a class of professional
teachers."[65] By the end of that year, Kries was confiding to Berlin that he feared
what was going to happen to the German schools when, in postwar Poland,
they passed under the authority of a Polish government. He wanted to use

his position to help them, but, for the time being, he also wished to avoid the appearance of giving official support to German schools.[66]

The Government-General and the imperial German government therefore confined themselves to providing modest and discreet assistance to German education, giving, for example, the German Volksschule in Warsaw a building to use at no charge. The Luisen-Lyzeum, a German school for girls in Lodz, was also given help obtaining suitable quarters, while 8,000 marks were granted to a German Teacher Education Course in Lodz (though Kries insisted that a comparable Polish institution would have received the same amount).[67] Thanks to Kries, more substantial financial assistance arrived the following year. In January 1917, the Foreign Office gave the German Real-gymnasium in Lodz 15,000 marks, the Luisen-Lyzeum 12,000, and the German school in Warsaw 15,000 as "one-time . . . subsidies."[68] The following June, the Office authorized a total of 59,000 marks in subsidies for the three schools.[69] (Eventually, in March 1918, the Foreign Office sent a sharp note to the Secretary of the Interior declaring that the Office was not in the habit of paying for German schools that were a part of a foreign school system.[70]) A combination of quiet official support and educational activity by the nationalists of Eichler's German Association led to a flowering of German education in Poland. The Luisen-Lyzeum and the German school in Warsaw, for example, were established in 1916. That same year, a new Gymnasium was founded in Pabianice. Two more Gymnasien followed the next year, one in Zgierz and one in Sompolno.[71] By 1918, German Volksschulen in Central Poland numbered in the hundreds, with forty of them in Lodz. When counted together with German Volksschulen in the Austrian zone, their total exceeded the prewar high point in their number, which had been reached in the late nineteenth century.[72]

The ceremony marking the opening of Warsaw's German Volksschule, founded by a local school association "for the purpose of preserving the Germans in Warsaw and creating capable pioneers for German commerce," gave the Government-General an opportunity to make at least one public show of support for German education in 1916.[73] Held on 26 October in a room decorated with a picture of the Kaiser, the ceremony was attended by a number of senior officials from the occupation government, including both Beseler and Kries. After music and a speech by one Herr Korff, an industrialist and the chairman of the school association's board, Beseler addressed the crowd. The message of his speech was decidedly mixed, managing to be both supportive and vaguely cautionary. The Governor-General proclaimed that it was the "mission of the school" to ensure that its pupils preserved their "German character" in the midst of a foreign people. At the same time, Beseler admonished (in language that did not quite match the occasional eloquence of his written prose) that "whoever lives as a foreigner in a foreign land shouldn't be an enemy to that foreign land; to the contrary, he will try in every possible way to get on good an[d] proper terms with his environs."[74] Be good Germans, but don't cause trouble: a problematic formulation that was the essence not only of Beseler's message at the ceremony but of his view of how the Germans of Poland should conduct themselves. (It was a message Beseler had sent before, when, in early 1916, he had received a delegation of Lodz Germans in Warsaw. The Governor-General had assured them that they could rely on the "cooperation" of the German occupation government; at the same time, he warned them to "avoid everything that could lead to conflict with the Poles."[75])

The school went on to attract 416 pupils in 1916, twenty-five of whom were from the German Empire, as were most of the teachers.[76] The German sources do not go into great detail about who these teachers were or how they arrived in Poland. A 1917 request from the German School Association in Warsaw to the Imperial Office of the Interior for help in arranging permission to retain some of the Association's Reichsdeutsche employees mentions only three names: Ernst Piehler, from near Chemnitz, Charlotte Voigt, from Neuwedell, and Dorothea Freiwald, from Düsseldorf. The records of the latter two teachers were included with the request; Voigt, twenty-nine, regularly taught gymnastics and needlework at her school in Neuwedell while Freiwald, twenty-six, had recently obtained an additional qualification as a swimming teacher. (Regrettably, little survives to suggest what drove these two young women to make their way to a distant, dangerous, and utterly foreign city run by a military occupation government.[77]) At least one of the Government-General's bureaucrats was very pleased with the results of the staff's efforts to bring German education to Warsaw. Adolf Warschauer, the archivist, was happy to discover that from his desk he could hear the pupils singing German songs in the garden, providing him with a "moving" diversion while he tended to his work.[78]

The Minority Protection Law and the Transfer
of Education to the Polish Authorities

In 1917, the occupiers began to make a clearer commitment to German education in Poland. This was driven by the simultaneous increase in the
momentum of their Polish state-building efforts. In the year following
the 5 November proclamation, the German government decided to make a
demonstration of its intention to meet at least some Polish demands for national self-determination (while simultaneously lightening the burdens of its
rule in the occupied zone) by turning over some administrative responsibilities to Polish authorities. The first limited transfer of powers came on 1 September 1917, when the occupation regime ostensibly turned the legal system
in Poland over to the Provisional Council of State's Department of Justice.
The Department had its own bureaucracy as well as courts that thereafter operated in the name of the Polish crown. Yet Polish authority was seriously
restricted. Beseler remained the head of the whole of the occupied zone's legal
system, while the occupation regime maintained its own separate system of
courts, over which the Polish institutions had no authority.[79] In the event of
a jurisdictional dispute between the Polish and occupation courts, matters
were to be submitted for resolution to a mixed court. The composition of the
court provides an excellent example of the occupation regime's uncertain wa-
vering between the desire to make genuine concessions and an unwilling-
ness to relinquish real control. In solemn legal language, the Germans stipulated that the court would be composed of five members, two of which would
be chosen by the head of the Provisional Council's Justice Department, two
by the Administrative Chief of the Government-General, and one—as though
he truly represented a third distinct institution—by the Governor-General.
And yet it is equally significant that the Germans began to dissolve parts of
their legal apparatus after the turnover. In the course of September, for example, the German public prosecutors' offices were done away with, as were
a number of district courts.[80]

More important and far more complicated was control over education,
which the Germans scheduled for transfer in October 1917. To the Germans,
this transfer represented a major concession to Polish wishes for self-
determination. At the same time, however, Beseler and Kries resolved to

fortify the place of German schools in the educational landscape, since they saw this as the key to guaranteeing the minority's existence when a Polish state was established after the war. The conflicted nature of this policy of simultaneously supporting both Polish and local German educational ambitions was captured in a fall 1917 letter from Beseler to Clara. He felt it necessary, he told her,

> to give the Germans here [in Poland] some proper moral support at this particular moment, when, due to higher reasons of state, we must give a number of things to the Poles . . . In the homeland people are demanding all kinds of unreasonable things in this regard, demands that one cannot make of a state, if it is to bear this name at all . . . In any case I have decided in the matter of the schools . . . to make the protection of the minorities, especially the Germans, a *conditio sine qua non*.[81]

Beseler was especially keen to lend assistance because he distrusted the Protestant clergy, who he dismissed as "Polonized [*verpolt*]."[82] In April 1917, the Government-General helped establish two institutions that were supposed to play a central role in safeguarding German education in postwar Poland: the German-Protestant *(Evangelisch)* National School Association and the German-Catholic National School Association.[83] On the fourth of that month, the Government-General ordered its district school inspectors to begin forming German school districts. Several hundred Protestant districts were formed, as were ten Catholic districts. The two associations were then established to link their respective districts together and give them a collective identity, the Protestant on 23 July 1917 in Lodz, the Catholic on 10 September in Zduńska Wola. The two received Beseler's official approval of their statutes on 12 September.[84] The associations were charged with representing their member schools' interests vis-à-vis the state as well as disbursing the public funds due to them (see below).[85] Kries called the founding of the Protestant Association "an essential component of the measures taken by me for the protection of the German minorities in the field of education." He did not think, however, that it would survive without a bit of extra help, particularly of a financial nature, and he pleaded once again with Berlin for money.[86] In the fall, the Foreign Office granted both associations a "one-time . . . subsidy" of 50,000 marks.[87] (To give some sense of what this sum represented, a highly skilled worker, employed in a war-related industry in Berlin, could take home about 7,500 marks a year; poorer workers in Germany, a little over 1,000.[88])

By that June, difficult and contentious discussions regarding at least a partial turnover of education to the Provisional Council of State were well under way. Little progress was made, owing primarily to Polish reluctance to guarantee minority school rights. This, in turn, made the occupation regime, which insisted on special guarantees for German education, unwilling to delegate too much authority to the council.[89] (The Germans' willingness to turn over powers to the Poles was certainly not increased by claims occasionally heard from the Polish side that "so-called national minorities" were essentially foreigners who had no right to make demands on a Polish school system.[90]) Kries, fretting about the survival of German schools "in a Polish state," hoped for a three-part solution to the problem of the long-term security of German education in Poland: the granting of tax exemptions by the Poles to the German minority; guaranteed access to public educational funds; and the official recognition of some of the secondary schools as "Auslandsschulen" by the Foreign Office.[91]

This latter recommendation was one Kries had made before, in December of 1916, although he had then ruled out the possibility for the Warsaw Volksschule and for the Lodz teacher-training institute. This was apparently decided on legal grounds, as Kries judged that not enough of the students were citizens of the Empire to qualify the institutions as Auslandsschulen.[92] This apparently minor legal detail is in fact crucial for an understanding of what the German occupiers thought they were doing in Poland. Whatever plans for an annexation of Polish border territory may have existed, and however much control the Germans intended to exercise over postwar Poland's security and foreign affairs, they nonetheless acknowledged that the subjects of that kingdom—including the ethnic Germans—would be *foreigners,* to be dealt with much as foreigners in any other state would be. To be formally subordinate to imperial German sovereignty did not automatically translate to being subject to the unrestricted control of the imperial German state.

The difficult negotiations between the Germans and the Poles (who were represented, after the August dissolution of the Provisional Council of State, by the Interim Commission, or Komisja Przejściowa) continued to drag on through the summer of 1917. Finally the Poles gave ground, and the two sides reached an agreement that resulted in the 12 September 1917 "Law Regarding the Consideration of the Minorities' Educational Needs."[93] The law provided rules governing the place of minority education in Poland in three areas: within the public school system, in the sphere of private education, and within special school districts. With regard to public education, formal guarantees were made that, wherever fifty children sharing a common mother tongue lived, they were to be afforded the opportunity to attend a public elementary school in that language. Such a rule would have inevitably laid the foundation for a mass-based Yiddish school system in Poland. The rule, however, carried an important caveat. "This regulation," it stated, "applies for the time being only to the German nationality."[94] That single sentence ensured that, for the Jews of the Government-General, public education would be Polish education.

The law also provided for private schools at all levels (primary and secondary) and in any language to be founded and supported by associations of individuals. This, it seemed, would provide an opportunity for Polish Jews to maintain a private school system. Yet when the Interim Commission issued the emerging Polish polity's educational regulations, they directly violated this provision of the law. A special section of the Commission's school regulations was devoted exclusively to "children of the Mosaic confession." It held that schools could (perhaps) be created that observed the Jewish Sabbath, but the language in all Jewish schools—including private ones—was to be Polish.[95] In defending the Government-General's decision not to do more to support Jewish education in Poland, Ludwig Haas explained to the *Neue Jüdische Monatshefte* that the Poles would "rather have refused to take over educational affairs than . . . allow[ed] a Jewish school system that was separate from the general school system." The Germans simply could not afford to sacrifice their strategic ambitions in Poland over the issue, he added. It was also, Haas told the publication, in the best interests of Poland's Jews if the Germans did not push the matter; if state-building progress were brought to a halt over it, the Poles would simply blame the Jews for getting in the way of Poland's political rebirth.[96]

On neither of these options, however, did the German authorities place their greatest hopes for the preservation of German education: that was to be accomplished by the rules governing the third option held open for minority schools, the special school districts. According to the regulation,

Poland's minorities could found their own school districts to support schools. These latter were to be paid for, in line with Kries's earlier vision, by a rather complicated system of tax refunds. The districts did not have to pay any special taxes or fees for educational purposes. Wherever education was paid for by a local general tax, the districts were to get a rebate. Finally, the districts were to be entitled to educational funds supplied by the federal government. The key to making the system work was to be the system of the school associations, which would disburse the federal funds due to the schools as well as answer to the authorities regarding the proper expenditure of the money. The 12 September law explicitly stated that any associations already existing when the law went into effect did not need the permission of any other authority to stay in business; hence the reason why the two German school associations received their official sanction from the German authorities on 12 September 1917.[97]

Just over two weeks later, on 28 September 1917, Beseler made an official visit to the Lodz Germans. With the rules governing the schools officially in place, the Governor-General could make such a trip without fear of agitating Polish opinion. While in Lodz, Beseler attended a rally staged by Eichler's German Association, where he was praised for doing what he could to help the Germans of Poland, including preserving German education. Beseler then made some remarks that one attendee later claimed were extraordinarily well received; yet the message he delivered was decidedly mixed. On the one hand, Beseler acknowledged that he had worked to insulate and protect German life in Poland from "despotism" *(Willkür)*. But his speech also contained a not very thinly veiled warning. The Governor-General told the crowd to

> depend not only on the care of the authorities, on the imposition of will and protection from above, but above all to use and to summon up [your] own power . . . That is, after all, the high aim of your Association. I will endeavor to give and to preserve the place to which the Germans here are entitled. In this spirit I call out a sincere good luck to your Association and wish that it flourishes happily . . . In the future may you win the high appreciation and also the affection and love [*sic*] of the nation in whose midst you work.

That this speech was really met by a "storm of applause," as was later asserted, seems doubtful, given the clarity of its message: soon you will be on your own. Farewell and don't make trouble.[98]

The German occupation government had now done what it could to balance the preservation of the German minority with the political necessity to make concessions to the Polish authorities. With the road thus cleared, control over education was formally entrusted to the Poles on 1 October 1917. Authority was assumed by a special department of the Interim Commission that was headed by the ubiquitous Mikułowski-Pomorski (who also, it so happened, headed the Commission itself).[99] Despite all his work Kries was not completely convinced that the Germans would fare so well under the new regime, a lack of conviction perhaps not entirely rooted in a fear of aggressive Polish nationalism. "To what extent the Germans here . . . will be capable of building up a real school system on the foundation, completely adequate in itself, of the . . . law" regarding minority schools, he reflected, "only time will tell."[100] The implication could be drawn from this statement that Kries had little faith in the organizational ability of the Polish Germans. In Germany itself, the nationalists of the Association for Germans Abroad also feared for the fate of the German schools, though they disagreed strongly about how "adequate" the laws protecting them were. The Association demanded that more robust measures be undertaken by the Germans to safeguard the schools, a demand rejected by Kries's successor, Otto von Steinmeister. In light of the profoundly difficult negotiations that had led to the creation of the law on minority schools, Steinmeister declared that any German attempts to force its modification might antagonize the Poles and should be seen as "absolutely out of the question."[101] Chancellor Hertling subsequently notified the Association that, for the time being, the German government did not intend to push for a change in the law. It was a product of bilateral negotiations, he argued; thus there was a chance the Poles would continue to respect it when the war and occupation were over.[102]

In the months that followed the turnover, the German authorities began the process of dissolving their educational bureaucracy. The Polish authorities proceeded to fill the vacuum by appointing administrators and teachers of their own, though this was a process over which the Germans kept a close watch. The Polish authorities were not yet sovereign masters in their own house, and the Germans reserved the right to block Polish appointments that they thought carried the potential to make trouble. The Germans also maintained formal authority over the Government-General's five German secondary schools, the Realgymnasium and the Luisen-Lyzeum in Lodz and the Realgymnasien in Pabianice, Sompolno, and Zgierz. These reservations, however, were relatively minor, and the date of 1 October 1917 marked a genuine shift of some of the Government-General's authority into Polish hands. According to Steinmeister, the Poles were already making use of their newfound power to undermine the agreements made regarding German schools. The new Administrative Chief informed Berlin that "the German National School Association" (meaning, presumably, the far larger Protestant one) was already hard at work, doing what the Germans had assumed it would be doing—namely, fending off the encroachments of the Polish authorities.[103]

These authorities, meanwhile, had also assumed control over another educational institution established by the Germans: Warsaw University. As Chapter 5 will show, the Government-General had consistently treated the university very differently from the rest of the educational institutions it oversaw. This was the result of the enormous importance the occupiers invested in the school, which was assigned a crucial role in fashioning the postwar order they hoped to create in Poland.

5

Nation Building and *Bildung*

Warsaw University

In the fall of 1915, just a few months after Warsaw had fallen, Polish higher education returned to the center of the city's political and cultural life after a forced hiatus of several decades. That November, the German occupation government opened both a university and a technical college to replace the institutions of higher learning that had been evacuated by the Russians. Unlike the primary and secondary schools established by the Germans, Warsaw's university and technical college—and especially the university—were intended to play a crucial role in building the postwar order that Beseler hoped to coax from the political wreckage of prewar Poland. From these two institutions, the Germans hoped, would flow a new Polish elite that would be nationally conscious yet willing to leave political affairs in the hands of sovereigns chosen by others.

The history of Polish-language higher education in Warsaw was intimately bound with the unhappy cycle of concession, revolution, and reaction that marked the political life of the Russian partition in the nineteenth century. The city's first university was established in 1816, in the atmosphere of relatively liberal tolerance promoted by Imperial Russia in its newly annexed Polish territories after the Congress of Vienna. It was closed a mere fifteen years later, in October 1831, in the wake of the November Uprising's failure. Warsaw remained without a university until 1862, when the Main School (Szkoła Główna) opened. The school was one of the numerous Russian concessions to Polish national aspirations associated with the era of Aleksander

Wielopolski, who had hoped that granting some Polish wishes for autonomy would lead to stability in those provinces. Once again, however, revolution put an end to Polish university life in Warsaw. As part of the harsh repression that followed the collapse of the January Uprising, the Tsarist state began the gradual transformation of the institution into an instrument of "Russification," until, in 1869, it lost even its name, becoming merely the Imperial University of Warsaw. The institution's interwar chronicler, Tadeusz Manteuffel, described it (with some exaggeration) as a "foreign university, filled with lecturers . . . hostile to all things Polish."[1] Polish students continued to attend the school, but only until the Revolution of 1905, when a boycott ended the last vestiges of significant Polish participation in the institution.

Formal Polish higher education in the Russian partition may have ended with the closing of the Szkoła Główna, but Polish scholarship was kept alive and vibrant by Polish educational activists, including the members of the Society for Scientific Courses (Towarzystwo Kursów Naukowych/TKN), an association founded in 1905 that had actively planned for the reestablishment of Polish schools in the Kingdom. When the outbreak of the Great War produced loud promises from Saint Petersburg of a renewed era of Polish-Russian cooperation, the opportunity awaited by Poland's educational activists appeared to have arrived. In Warsaw, a committee of Polish intellectuals, including members of the TKN, convened in early 1915 to begin preparing the groundwork for the restoration of Polish education. When the Russians fled Warsaw that summer, the committee was succeeded by a Higher Education Section (Sekcja Szkół Wyższych), a subdivision of the Warsaw Civic Committee. Fortunately for the Section, the Russian evacuation had included the faculty and students of the university. These made their way, along with some of the university's books and laboratory equipment, to the city of Rostov-on-the-Don, where they tried to carry on their business as a kind of university in exile.[2] Back in Warsaw, the Section embraced the opportunity afforded by this sudden educational vacuum, throwing itself into the work of drawing up budgets and planning for the organization and staffing of departments. By the time the German occupation authorities arrived in the late summer of 1915, plans for the reestablishment of Polish higher education in the city were well advanced.[3]

Kries conveyed these ambitions to the Governor-General at a meeting of senior German officials held in Warsaw on 25 September 1915. He informed

Beseler that the occupation authorities had been approached by local intellectuals and told of the desire to reestablish Polish education in the city. Kries was in favor of the idea; establishing institutions of higher education, he argued, would not only keep young people out of trouble but would do much to burnish the Germans' image as well. According to Hutten-Czapski, however, Kries did not stop at these purely short-term ambitions. "Germany does not intend," he added,

> to keep this land forever, but rather wishes to bind it permanently to itself [*dauernd mit sich zu verbinden*]. It must be well-administered, it must have good civil servants, jurists, physicians, engineers, architects, technicians, indeed even philosophers. It is important that the Poles, when they one day assume the administration of the state [*Landesverwaltung*], have the necessary specialists.

Beseler did not comment on this speech, but he did, to Hutten-Czapski's elation, grant permission for both schools to be opened. Shortly thereafter, Kries secured the assistance of the Prussian Kultusministerium in the project.[4]

Kries's pronouncement on the manner in which higher education in Poland could serve Germany's ambitions was somewhat premature. As Kries apparently recognized, it reflected neither Beseler's nor Berlin's official policy this early in the occupation. The sentiments voiced by Kries are also extraordinarily difficult to reconcile with Kries's self-professed identity as a "son of the Ostmark," a son who would, moreover, eventually resign from the Government-General over its pursuit of a policy much like the one he outlined in his speech. The explanation for Kries's support probably lies in the timing of his pronouncement. September 1915 was the same month in which Clemens von Delbrück, Imperial Secretary of the Interior, and, it will be recalled, Kries's superior, produced a memorandum outlining his thoughts on the Polish Question. In it, he explicitly stated that supporting a revival of Polish statehood should be given serious consideration as a policy in occupied Poland, since it was preferable to many of the alternatives, including Austro-Polonism.[5] Kries's speech may have reflected this policy trend at the highest level of the ministry to which his administrative apparatus was formally subordinated. In any event, Kries's October 1915 report to Berlin on the opening of the schools did not include any of the sentiments contained in his speech, repeating instead his arguments about how they could help the Germans maintain order and improve their standing in the eyes of the locals.[6] His pronouncements on the state-building role of higher education were thus either ill-timed or reflected a policy commitment on the part of the Administrative Chief that was halfhearted and ultimately fleeting.

The immediate short-term benefits that opening higher education in Poland would bring to the Germans were also stressed by Beseler when, in early November 1915, he sent his report to the Kaiser detailing his decision to open the schools. Order would be best secured, Beseler informed Wilhelm, by keeping the youth of "this politically fissured land" from the temptations of "sterile political agitation."[7] Privately, Beseler had some serious reservations about his decision. He expected his policy to draw the ire of nationalistic German circles, writing to Clara shortly after the schools had opened that "Balt[ic Germans] and Pan-Germanists will scold me." Beseler added, however, that his grasp of what was at stake was superior to theirs. As for the Poles, he did not "trust them an inch."[8] Beseler ultimately judged the risks worth the potential rewards, but both were, he believed, still relatively modest. Over the course of the next year, however, as the occupation regime embarked on its state-building enterprise, Beseler would embrace the more idealistic vision of the role of higher education reflected in Kries's speech.[9]

Joint Polish-German preparations for the opening of the schools began shortly after the September meeting. To aid the German occupation regime in the preparations, the Kultusministerium dispatched Geheimrat Ludwig Elster as well as Wilhelm Paszkowski, an administrator and lecturer from Berlin University. The Polish side was represented by the Higher Education Section under the leadership of a physician, Józef Brudziński. Predictably, a number of disputes arose immediately; somewhat less predictably, they were smoothed over in relatively short order, a feat attributed by Hutten-Czapski to Elster's diplomatic skill. The Polish delegates, presumably in the hope of minimizing German influence, wanted to finance the schools themselves. This the Germans rejected out of hand, insisting that the funds be administered by the occupation government. The Poles also lost their bid to have Polish declared the language of official correspondence between the occupation authorities and the schools. The somewhat more delicate matter of the composition of the faculty was decided by compromise. Elster favored staffing the university with a healthy complement of professors from Prussia, in the hope of thereby securing German influence at the very heart of the institution. This plan was unpopular—presumably with the Polish delegates, but possibly with the German authorities as well, who may have been leery of the thought of Prussian Poles mixing in Varsovian political circles. Another point of contention was the number of professors who would be allowed from Austrian universities. Beseler did not want too many of them arriving in the German zone of occupation and refused to let more than a handful be hired. Ultimately, the Poles received a guarantee from the Germans that their wishes regarding the faculty would at least be listened to, and mutually agreeable candidates for faculty positions were eventually settled upon by the two sides. Brudziński was selected for the post of rector of the university.[10]

The Government-General was to be officially represented within the administrative structure of the schools by the curator, who would serve as the official conduit between the regime and the institutions. In late October, Elster advised Beseler to select a Pole for the position. He suggested Hutten-Czapski, whose long experience in the service of the state, in addition to his Polish identity and the supposedly favorable reputation he enjoyed among the local notables, qualified him for the post. Beseler found nothing to object to in this and asked the count if he was interested in taking up what promised to be a "difficult and awkward post." Hutten-Czapski was more than interested: he accepted Beseler's offer with gratitude and relish, promising the Governor-General he would do his utmost to maintain the apolitical nature of the "new institutions for the cultivation [*Pflanzstätten*] of science."[11] Hutten-Czapski would later call his involvement in the project "the most significant" of all of his "public service."[12]

Elster was not alone in thinking that Hutten-Czapski was well suited for the post of curator by virtue of his (putative) Polishness. Adolf Warschauer, the civilian archivist attached to the Government-General, left a memorable description of Hutten-Czapski in his memoirs, where he describes the count as

an enchanting conversationalist . . . of the most obliging amiability . . . he was one of the most talked-about personalities of the army's retinue. Particularly interesting and the most-often discussed was his national outlook. Just as his family name was composed of a German and a Polish half . . . and just as he managed the German and Polish language[s] with equal mastery, so that each could be considered his mother tongue, so he united in himself the views of a Polish patriot with those of an Imperial German official and officer.[13]

As for his own self-image, Hutten-Czapski summarized the defining features of his identity as "noble birth, Polish nationality, Prussian citizenship, [and] Catholic religion." This combination deeply affected how he saw his life's purpose; in his memoirs, Hutten-Czapski would write that the promotion of peaceful church-state relations and "reconciliation between the Germans and the Poles" had been his long life's animating principles.[14]

Yet it is difficult to see what was very "Polish" about Hutten-Czapski. (Maria Lubomirska agreed, calling him a "spineless, Germanized lackey," though also a "decent chap."[15]) He was indeed born in Smogulec, in the province of Posen, but had had the mobile and cosmopolitan youth of the nobility. His childhood was spent not only in the city of Posen but in Berlin, Italy, France, and Switzerland as well; the family vacationed often at fashionable spas, where they mixed with Prussian royalty.[16] He was a student in Vienna, where he became acquainted with the higher nobility of the Habsburg Empire, and Berlin, where he heard Professor Georg Beseler, the Governor-General's father, lecture on the law.[17] Hutten-Czapski went on to spend all of his adult life in the service of the Prussian state, primarily as a career army officer, but also holding a seat in the Prussian House of Lords. In 1901, Emperor Wilhelm added the title of Captain of the Court (*Schlosshauptmann*) of Posen to the list of Hutten-Czapski's offices, an honorific unlikely to endear him to Polish nationalists. He had been on excellent and rather close terms with Wilhelm I, Empress Augusta, Hohenlohe, and Holstein, and cooler but nonetheless familiar ones with Bismarck and Wilhelm II.[18] However "Polish" Hutten-Czapski may have seemed to many of the Germans of the Government-General, Beseler was right to bet that, in times of crisis, Hutten-Czapski would remain *Kaisertreu* and a reliable servant of the German occupation government.

The First Year

When the joint German-Polish commission had finished laying the basic administrative foundations of the schools and secured Beseler's final approval, the institutions were ready to begin operations. They formally opened on 15 November 1915, an "unusually beautiful, warm, sunny day," according to the account later printed in the university's calendar. The day's festivities began with a morning Mass said by Archbishop Kakowski at Saint John's Cathedral, around which large crowds of excited people gathered to watch the arrival of the dignitaries. A place of honor in the cathedral was afforded to the rectors of both schools, as well as to Hutten-Czapski, who represented the German authorities at the event.[19] A more pronounced German presence at the ceremony had been expressly forbidden by Beseler.[20]

The sacred rite was followed by a lengthy speech by the metropolitan canon, Antoni Szlagowski, who invoked more secular themes from the pulpit. Making no mention of the German occupation government, Szlagowski exhorted the assembled students to wisely use the opportunity that had opened to them. "Youth of Poland," he told his listeners,

> your mother, clad in rags and covered in wounds, demands from you at this time not death, but work; not an honorable demise on the field of battle, but persistent labors in [your] chosen profession[s]; she does not want your blood, but your sweat . . . My brothers, we will rebuild the homeland with our work and our faith.[21]

The canon's emotionally charged call for calm, hard work, and order is a striking example of the enduring legacy of "organic work," a nineteenth-century Polish ideology that blended faith in the virtues of work and progress with a rejection of radical political activism. Events would shortly prove, however, that these beliefs were not quite enduring enough to keep the relationship between the authorities and the students as stable as the canon might have wished.

The official opening of the university followed in the main lecture hall. At this ceremony the German occupiers were much better represented. Kries was present, as were Ernst von Glasenapp, head of the police, and Beseler. (It was probably coincidental that the choir assembled to provide music for the occasion began to sing "Veni Creator" at the very moment Beseler made his formal entrance.[22]) Despite this weightier official presence, the authorities took care not to control the ceremony with too heavy a hand. Security for the event was provided not by soldiers, but by uniformed firefighters. The guests were welcomed by excited young students who took care to speak to the attendees in their respective native tongues, either German or Polish, as they arrived.[23]

The centerpiece of the ceremony was a lengthy speech, delivered primarily in Polish, by Brudziński. The bulk of the new rector's speech dwelt (wisely) on the past. He invoked the former glories of Warsaw University, the notable scholars of its earlier incarnations, and the graduates who had gone on to greatness. Brudziński did allow himself to express a cautious optimism about what he saw as the impending return of vigor to "public life" that the opening of the university was sure to mark, but there was little in his speech to unnerve the Germans.[24] The rector ultimately chose a quote from the writer Zygmunt Krasiński to summarize his sense of the proud tradition that scholars in Warsaw now had the opportunity to build on: "We have great memories, thus may we also harbor great hopes."[25] Brudziński's speech was followed by a few brief and unremarkable lines from Beseler, who concluded by pronouncing the university officially open.[26] A similar but "simpler" event was held the same day at the technical college.[27]

Both the institutions were thus inaugurated without major incident and in an atmosphere relatively free of overt hostility. "For whom," asked the official *Deutsche Warschauer Zeitung*, had the day been one "of celebration"? "For the Varsovians? For the Germans . . . ? No, for all of them, for the Varsovians and for the Germans," was the hopeful (and clumsy) answer the newspaper provided to its own question.[28] Not everyone was so effusive. Adolf Warschauer, who had attended the ceremony of inauguration at the university, recalled in his memoirs that the affair had been "devoid of style." He added, with the benefit of hindsight, and full of the bitter animosity of the postwar years, that those who thought they were witnessing the beginning of a new era of Polish-German scholarly cooperation were "thoroughly disappointed." And yet even Warschauer was forced to admit that "one went away in the end conscious of having taken part in an academic celebration beyond national discord."[29] It seemed an auspicious beginning.

More strenuous denunciations of the Germans' decision to open the schools could be found outside occupied Poland. *Die Ostmark,* the newspaper of the Eastern Marches Association, called the decision to open the university "splendid evidence of the cultural sensibilities of the German people." This did not, of course, mean they were pleased about it, and they reminded the administration to bear always in mind that "nations are usually ungrateful."[30] The Russians, who were furious at the opening of the schools, loudly denounced it in the press. Beseler was aware of this anger and surmised, probably correctly, that the Russians realized the potential the Germans' policy had to improve their standing in Polish-speaking Europe at Russia's expense.[31]

The university proved sufficiently popular within the occupied zone to attract more than a thousand students for the first semester. The favored courses of study were medicine and law, followed "at a great distance" by the humanities. At the technical college, close to 600 aspiring engineers, chemists, and architects also took up their studies in the 1915–1916 school year.[32] The official regulations issued by the Germans at this point emphasized that the schools were to be considered provisional institutions, a tentative gesture of magnanimity that could be withdrawn at the first sign of trouble. The schools were formally placed under the authority of the civilian Administrative Chief (i.e., Kries), who was responsible for selecting the faculty members.[33] In addition, the curriculum was subject to the approval of the occupation authorities.[34] The rules issued for the students at this time also placed tight restrictions on what they were permitted to do outside of class. Student groups were to be established only after careful vetting by the curator, while students were banned from holding any kind of gathering outside the university grounds.[35] Finally, the faculty was sternly warned against allowing politics of any sort into the classroom, and the schools were expected to remain "independent of [political] parties." If there was a broader mission contained in the statutes that went beyond these attempts to maintain order, it was in the Germans' instructions to the faculty of both institutions to further the cause not only of knowledge *(Wissenschaft)*, but also of *Bildung* by attending closely to the "development of the mores and the character of the students."[36]

In the report submitted to Berlin by Beseler shortly after the schools began their first semesters, the Governor-General declared that the decision to open them had paid off, as it had been well received in the occupation zone. Beseler also saw an additional propaganda victory in the policy: the message was now broadcast to the Reich's enemies that "Germany considers its rule in Poland sufficiently secure . . . to begin supporting . . . works of peace and culture." The report also contained reassurances by Beseler on two important points: first, that, while the university was a Polish institution, German culture would get its due representation within the curriculum; second and more importantly, that politics would be kept out of the institutions.[37] Nothing was said, officially at least, about what role the schools might play in Germany's still-inchoate and fluid ambitions in the occupied east. Statements of broader ambitions were also absent from Kries's report filed at about the same time.[38]

Escalating Ambitions, Expanding Institutions

The emphasis on the short-term benefits that would accrue to Germany by supporting the schools began to change in 1916, when Beseler's plans for Poland's future started to take firmer shape in his mind. He now reported to Berlin that the institutions were peaceably engaged in what he termed their "essential task." This was no longer the maintenance of order, but the education of Polish professionals and bureaucrats for the "country's future administration."[39] That same year, the Governor-General publicly announced that he was pleased with the results of the policy and granted both of the schools new, more extensive statutes. In a lengthy preamble to the university's, Beseler praised the ability of "pure scholarship" to overcome national divisions, although the students and faculty were simultaneously assured that this academic bridge between peoples was, rather paradoxically, to be built "on the foundation [of the] national language and culture." The new statutes also reminded the faculty that *Bildung* was central to the university's mission. The academic staff members were told that it was their responsibility to mold their students into respectable, solid citizens, which could only be accomplished if politics were kept completely out of the lecture halls and seminar rooms.[40] The preamble to the technical college's new statutes was rather more prosaic. Making no grand proclamations on the sublime mysteries of scholarship, it emphasized instead that "the training of capable engineers, architects and technicians is of the highest importance for the reconstruction and the economic and cultural improvement of Poland."[41]

Beseler's views on the role of the university contain an essential contradiction, beyond even the one contained in its supposed role as a thoroughly national bridge between nations. On the one hand, it was to be an apolitical institution; on the other, it was to perform an eminently public function by providing the new state with the people required to run it. This was not, however, an unusual view for a German of Beseler's age. In the prewar period, university professors supposed themselves to be somehow above the tedious and sometimes rather dirty business of politics. They inhabited the elevated world of intellect and spirit—of *Geist*—where they devoted themselves to the systematic pursuit of knowledge and to the shaping of their charges' minds and characters. And yet public life in Germany was absolutely inseparable from the world of *Geist* tended by the professoriate. The universities played a central role in shaping Germany's political and cultural elite, who passed through its lecture halls on their way to positions of power and influence. "The Universities," Thomas Nipperdey has written, "molded . . . the language of the civil service, of parliaments and parties, of journalism and the intelligentsia."[42] Beseler was merely importing this German paradox and placing it in the service of his policy—for which, in purely ideological terms, it was perfectly suited.

When the Governor-General's public and private statements on the importance of the schools are situated within the context of his increasing commitment to German sponsorship of a new political order in Congress Poland, the institutions' respective roles come sharply into focus. To the technical college was assigned the task of producing the practically inclined professionals who would develop Poland's infrastructure and bring it as a state into the modern age. The university was to serve an even more important function: by some curious and unspecified alchemy, the projects of *Bildung* and nation building were to be fused together there with the aim of making the "immature" Poles "mature," a process that would be carefully monitored and directed by the German occupiers. The end result would be a steady flow of bureaucrats, physicians, lawyers, and scholars who would be culturally Polish but bound by both duty and inclination to refrain from political activity. The university was thus to be not only an "institution for the careful cultivation and nurturing [*Pflanz- und Pflegestätte*] of intellectual life,"[43] but also of a new national elite for a new national—but not sovereign—state.

The schools expanded along with the ambitions the Germans had for them. In the 1915–1916 school year, the university's teaching staff included thirty-six lecturers *(wykładający)*,[44] the highest rank afforded to teaching staff at this time, twenty-three assistants *(asystenci)*, and six foreign-language in-structors *(lektorzy)*. In the 1916–1917 school year, the numbers increased to fifty lecturers and forty-one assistants (though the number of *lektorzy* de-clined to four).[45] The number of students also increased substantially, from 1,039 in 1915–1916 to 1,621 in 1916–1917.[46] (This brought enrollment num-bers up to prewar levels; as of 1 January 1905, Warsaw University had had 1,556 students.[47]) At the same time, the strict control exercised by the Germans began to ease somewhat. The rule forbidding students from congregating off campus, for example, was done away with in 1916.[48] In addition, the new stat-utes also made a gesture to faculty self-government by permitting the uni-versity teaching staff to elect their deans *(Dekane).*[49]

The expansion of higher education in Warsaw also began to change the relationship between the occupation government and the private secondary schools. As shown in Chapter 4, the Germans wanted to avoid any substan-tial engagement with secondary education. Yet students could not pursue higher education without an officially recognized certification of their qual-ifications for advanced study. In April 1916, this led the Government-General to grant students enrolled in private boys' Gymnasien the right to take a school-leaving exam *(Reifeprüfung)*. The actual implementation of the test was to be overseen by a Polish commission observed by a German official. The examination commission's decisions could be overturned by the German Administrative Chief.[50] Three hundred and seventy-seven students subse-quently took the exam, with 293 passing. In addition, 366 "nonstudents" *(Nichtschüler)*, including 203 women, were also permitted to take the test.[51]

The need to supply the university with students also led some secondary schools to change their structure. The completion of an eight-year *(acht-klassig)* course of secondary study was required for entrance to the university. To allow their students to fulfill this prerequisite, some private secondary institutions began to add classes in order to transform themselves into eight-year Gymnasien or *Oberrealschulen* (which were similar to Gymnasien but had a greater curricular emphasis on science and modern languages). Boys' schools with the appropriate course of study were permitted to begin gradu-ating university-bound students as soon as they were able. The Germans, however, decided to proceed differently with girls' schools, which they held to be inferior in quality to the boys'. In cooperation with Polish educational advisers, the occupation government devised a plan of gradual transformation for girls' institutions, according to which the schools would graduate their first university-qualified students in three to four years.[52]

Once they were at the university, Polish students had the opportunity to join a number of organizations, a result of the easing of the more restrictive of the student regulations. At the beginning of its existence under the occupation government, the university had had only two officially sanctioned student organizations (not counting a student magazine, *Pro Arte et Studio*). One was a club for medical students; the other was a more general association named Fraternal Aid (Bratnia Pomoc). The latter doubtfully claimed to be an "apolitical" club devoted only to improving the quality of life of its members.[53] By the following academic year, a welter of student clubs and organizations, most of them founded in the first half of 1916, had emerged to complement these first two organizations. Many, such as the Historians' Club (Koło Historyków), were organized around academic disciplines. Fraternal Aid, taking advantage of the newly relaxed regulations, expanded as well; a newly established social committee organized events for students, such as a boating expedition on the Vistula. Particularly noteworthy among the student organizations was the Lelewel Society (Towarszystwo im. Lelewela), led by Marceli Handelsman, a young member of the history department (and one who would, after the war, go on to a stellar scholarly career). According to the Society's description printed in the German-approved university calendar, it was established to "[engage] in research on native [Polish] civilization and culture and [prepare its] members in this manner for . . . civic-minded public engagement" *(praca obywatelska).*[54] Some clue as to what its members studied to prepare them for this "employment" can be gleaned from the society's name. Joachim Lelewel was an eminent nineteenth-century Polish polymath, political activist, and historian who had taught at Wilno University, where the young Adam Mickiewicz had heard him lecture. Lelewel had been deeply committed to the cause of Polish independence and a staunch republican who had believed that one day Poland would be resurrected as one of the great nations of Europe.[55]

The coursework offered by the university provided the students with an educational experience that was rich in variety yet distinctly Polish, despite the official control over the curriculum exercised by the occupation regime.[56] In the department of law and administrative sciences (Wydział Prawa i Nauk Państwowych), students took Polish-language courses on subjects ranging from economics to the fundamentals of Roman law to the history of church-state relations. In other departments, students studied topics (in Polish) ranging from classical philosophy to the history of Polish literature. In the history department, courses on classical Greece and Rome found a place alongside lectures on Polish national history. General historical surveys were also offered, taught by Marceli Handelsman. In the faculty of philology, a lonely outpost of *Kultur* was maintained by Paszkowski, who lectured on Goethe's *Faust* and on the history of German literature.[57]

A closer look at what was offered by the department of law in 1916–1917 gives some idea of what kind of institution the university was developing into. That year students could elect to take, among others, classes on Polish law and on the "history of the Polish system." A course dedicated exclusively to the famous constitution of 3 May 1791 was also on offer that year.[58] All of these courses were taught by faculty member Józef Siemieński, a "crimson nobleman" *(karmazynowy szlachcic)*, a label used to designate a member of an ancient and venerable magnate family. Siemieński had been something of a firebrand in his youth, when, as a student at the Imperial University of Warsaw, he had violated the Russian institution's rules by submitting a thesis in Polish. A nationalist and scholar who had devoted much of his life to the cause of Polish education, Siemieński believed that Poland's rich past had bequeathed to the present a veneration of "the freedom of individuals and . . . of nationalities."[59] In his lectures and discussions Poland's future "unpolitical" bureaucrats learned what they needed to know in order to administer their state.

The schools—in particular the university—also began to play an important role in the broader cultural life of the occupied city. The citywide festivities held in 1916 to celebrate the constitution of 3 May, for example, began with a pre-parade ceremony organized by the university. The occupation government was represented on this occasion by Hutten-Czapski, who recalled in vivid detail the quiet but emotionally charged event:

In the Botanical Garden, where the ruin of the unfinished . . . Church of the Divine Providence is, erected on the first anniversary of the Constitution according to the wishes of the people, the professors of both the university and the technical college, invited representatives of scientific and cultural associations and institutions, as well as the students with their flags gathered . . . Rector Brudziński unveiled a marble commemorative plaque with a white eagle that had been set into a wall of the church.[60]

Brudziński was also a senior member of the committee that had planned the subsequent parade.[61] The university and its personnel were thus central to the unfolding of that day's events, whose success did so much to convince Beseler that his ambitions had a chance of success.

Later the following year, invitations were once again sent out from the university to Warsaw's cultural elite, this time to participate in a special ceremony held as part of the citywide festivities being celebrated in memory of the Polish national hero Tadeusz Kościuszko. The highlight of the ceremony was to be the public debut of yet another plaque, this one mounted in the wall of one of the university's buildings and dedicated to the memory of that hero of the anti-Russian struggle.[62] Those who accepted the invitation and gathered at the university were subjected to yet another speech by the ever-passionate Szlagowski, who had exhorted Warsaw's students to shed sweat in lieu of blood at the university's opening ceremonies. This time, the canon expressed his hope that Warsaw's students would learn from the example of Kościuszko "that . . . [one's] heart and soul must belong to the fatherland."[63]

This expansion of the university's role as a center of Varsovian cultural life was accompanied by increasingly public displays of the political importance that Beseler had attached to it. In September 1916, as Berlin's and Beseler's visions for Poland's future began to harmonize, Hutten-Czapski was charged by the Foreign Office and the Chancellery with prodding Beseler into sending a deputation of elite Poles to Berlin and Vienna to ask the two governments to proclaim Poland's impending political resurrection. The impression would thereby be fostered that the Germans and Poles were working together toward shared goals. In late October 1916, such a group was duly dispatched by Beseler to the capitals. At its head was Brudziński, who, on 28 October, personally pressed Bethmann Hollweg to take immediate and concrete steps toward establishing Polish statehood. Bethmann Hollweg responded by counseling, much as Beseler usually did, both hope and patience. The group then left for Vienna to press its case there.[64]

When the proclamation followed on 5 November, the important role that both schools were to play in the reestablishment of Polish statehood was on prominent display during the day's events. The podium from which Beseler delivered the proclamation was surrounded by representatives of the institutions, displaying, as always on such occasions, their flags. After Hutten-Czapski had delivered the Polish translation, the official Polish reply to the proclamation was given by Brudziński, who concluded his speech "with a cheer for . . . 'free independent Poland.'" The cries of "long live Poland" that rang out from the balcony of the city hall that day were likewise delivered by Brudziński, whose shouts were echoed by the crowd gathered below.[65]

Not everyone was pleased with the way the university had developed. In 1916, the Polish writer Adolf Nowazcyński, in lyrics composed to accompany a puppet show, or *szopka,* complained about the number of Jews to be found on the university's faculty:

In the Warsaw "Alma Mater"
Handelsman lectures on Polish history, and
Kleiner drills romanticism into students' heads.
Let's hope that even
The new faculty of theology
Will soon become circumcised and Jewified . . .

Then every one of these fine gentlemen
Will advise the Polish people
The simplest way even for a million
To emigrate, in order to leave the country
To Israel with no arrears at all.[66]

As will be shown below, the university's substantial Jewish student population would also attract the angry attention of Poles with anti-Semitic leanings. In 1916, however, such tensions remained mostly beneath the surface and did not complicate the relationship between the university and the occupation government.

The Problem of the Theological Faculty

It was certainly not, however, a relationship without its troubles. In 1916, an education-related dispute arose between the occupiers and the occupied that would drag on without a satisfactory resolution for most of the war. The central issue was the place of religious education at the university. In January 1916, a meeting of Catholic bishops in Warsaw convened to discuss the future of clerical education in Poland. Prior to the outbreak of the war, advanced Catholic theological training had only been available at a special Ecclesiastical Academy in Saint Petersburg. After the Russian retreat in 1915, many clergy saw their opportunity to reestablish Polish clerical training. The bishops' meeting thus culminated in a letter to Pope Benedict XV asking for papal support for a theological faculty at the university (though the missive simultaneously acknowledged that the idea was not universally popular among Warsaw's intellectual elite). A set of preliminary statutes for such a faculty were also sent to Benedict for his approval.[67] In February, Beseler reported the clergy's wishes to Berlin. He declared that he supported the idea but was forced to reject the bishops' statutes because they provided for far too much independence and too little state control. Beseler suggested that the Germans begin work immediately on the drafting of counter-statutes that would better conform to his vision of the proper relationship between the state and clerical education. Beseler also suggested that Berlin immediately begin the process of diplomatically outflanking the Polish bishops at the Vatican.[68]

The clergy may have chafed at Beseler's attempts to keep tight control over the process of establishing their faculty, but it is remarkable that Beseler supported their efforts at all. Beseler's extreme hostility to the Austrians, noted in Chapter 1, was matched by, and almost certainly rooted in, an equally intense dislike of Catholicism. In January 1909, Beseler had told his friend Friedrich von Bernhardi that he found the energetic political activity of the Center Party quite worrisome. Any increase in the influence of the "black peril" could only bode ill for Germany.[69] His campaigning in Belgium at the beginning of the war had certainly done nothing to moderate his view of the pernicious "peril." The Belgians "do not behave like a civilized people, but a band of robbers—a pretty result of the priests' domination," Beseler wrote to Clara in August 1914.[70] Beseler's diagnosis of the source of supposed Belgian misdeeds shows that his views on the church were not simply rooted in theological disagreements over the nature of salvation or the proper relationship between the clergy and the laity. He saw the church as a poison in the body politic, a corrupting influence that undermined social mores and corroded a nation's political culture. Catholic education therefore had enormous potential to disrupt his project of making the "immature" Poles "mature." His willingness to give at least a modicum of support to the clergy's ambitions was a concession that Beseler most likely found not only distasteful but potentially dangerous.

Deeply entrenched suspicions about the dubious nature of Catholic education also played their role in restraining decisive action in Berlin. On 25 March 1916, representatives of the Kultusministerium, the Imperial Office of the Interior, the Foreign Office, and the Reich Office of Justice met in Berlin to discuss the clergy's wishes. Beseler's administration was vigorously represented by Hutten-Czapski, as well as by Paszkowski and Thaer. In the course of the meeting, a Dr. Naumann, attending on behalf of the Kultusministerium, objected to the proposal on the grounds that the students would be put in a highly precarious situation. Cut off from the outside world, they would be placed in the hands of manipulative clergy, who would wield complete control over their charges. The clergy would surely use this power to lead students down dark paths inimical to German interests. It was essential therefore to ensure maximum state oversight over what transpired behind the faculty's doors.[71]

Naumann added a second objection, one that likewise drew on a hostility with a venerable history in Prussia. Since the Kulturkampf, the priesthood in Prussian Poland had been closely associated (in both elite Prussian imagination and, quite often, in reality) with Polish nationalist agitation there. Thus Naumann warned that a Catholic theological faculty at the university would attract Polish aspirants to the priesthood from Prussia's own Polish provinces, sowing the seeds of even greater trouble between the two.[72] This latter argument was also made by Loebell when he voiced his objections to the project. In April, he advised Bethmann Hollweg that the establishment of the faculty could have serious repercussions for Prussia's Polish provinces. Prussia's Poles, he thought, were sure to flock to it, where they would be exposed to unhealthy political influences.[73] In May, the Minister of Religious and Educational Affairs seconded this concern, providing a summary of what Prussian officials regarded as the central danger in mixing the "black peril" with the "Polish peril":

The power of attraction that a theological faculty . . . [at] the Polish University in the old capital of the former Polish Kingdom is apt to exert on the Catholic theology students and prospective clergy in the Polish-speaking areas of Prussia [would be] so great, that a particularly careful treatment of the question seems advisable.[74]

Beseler responded to such criticism by pointing out that Polish theological training had long been available in Kraków without causing Prussia any great amount of trouble. He added—already in the spring of 1916—another reason not to be overly concerned by the prospect: Germany would, in any event, soon be working toward a restoration of Polish statehood, and this would be bound to have greater disruptive effects in Prussian Poland. Within this larger context, the theological faculty would be a very minor threat.[75] Such an argument was not likely to convince skeptics of Beseler's emerging Polish policies that his course was wise.

These traditional Prussian worries were not all that held the project up. Under the best of circumstances, establishing a theological faculty was a complicated affair, requiring cooperation between the local clergy, the university, the Vatican, and the state. Even in peacetime, the interests of all four could not be expected to harmonize easily or naturally, while the pressures of war and occupation added an extra degree of difficulty. The diplomatic wrangling over the faculty began in earnest in March of 1916, when Benedict XV received a representative of the Polish clergy sent to Rome by Archbishop Kakowski. The Pontiff received news of the clergy's plans with a certain reserved warmth. His position was a difficult one. To support the clergy openly could easily have been interpreted by the Russians as a violation of the Holy See's neutrality and an open declaration of hostility to the Tsar. It could also have been seen by the Germans as a usurpation of their rights, enshrined in the laws and customs of war, as the highest legal authority in the occupied territory. With extraordinary diplomatic tact, Benedict ultimately managed to conclude the meeting with the Polish priest without having explicitly encouraged or discouraged the bishops' ambitions. Benedict listened with interest to his proposals but said he would have to give very careful consideration to the rival set of statutes prepared by the Germans before taking any action.[76]

The persistence of the Austro-German conflict over which of them would exercise the greater influence in Poland after the war also played a complicating role in the matter. On 9 June 1916, Hutten-Czapski, Paszkowski, and

Thaer met with the Austrians in Teschen to discuss the faculty with them. The Austrians demanded certain concessions, such as the inclusion of a number of professors from Habsburg territories on the faculty. Hutten-Czapski agreed on behalf of the Germans, though it is doubtful that Beseler either knew about or would have approved of the sweeping promises made by the count.[77] In any event, the question of how the department should be staffed remained moot into 1917, when the project simply stalled, to great irritation on all sides.

The Student Strike of 1917

That same year, the tensions, annoyances, and grievances generated by the conflict over the theological faculty were suddenly eclipsed by a major episode of student unrest. The spring of 1917, it will be recalled, was a generally difficult time in the Government-General, at least from the German point of view. The initial drive to recruit Polish troops had already met with indisputable failure. Relations between the occupation regime and the Provisional Council of State had deteriorated into a state of mutual frustration and irritation. Perhaps most importantly, the February Revolution in Russia had led to renewed attempts to win Polish opinion by the new Provisional Government. In March 1917, the Russian regime issued a public appeal to the Poles that promised the creation of an "independent Polish state comprised of all the lands in which the Polish people constitute the majority of the population" (though this state was to be tied to Russia by a "free military alliance").[78] It is very difficult to gauge what kind of resonance the appeal found within Poland, but it undoubtedly introduced a new element of charged uncertainty into the Polish Question. Against this background unfolded a massive spring strike by Warsaw's students, an event that, even if it did not seriously threaten German rule in Poland, nonetheless provoked in Beseler a serious crisis of confidence.

The relationship between the occupation government and Warsaw's two institutions of higher education during the first years of their existence had been generally stable, in that there had been no large-scale displays of anger or dissatisfaction by the students and faculty. This certainly did not mean, however, that the dispute over the theological faculty had been the only source of tension between the occupiers and the schools. Warsaw's students, who had a robust sense of the rights due to them as citizens of the academic world, had had run-ins with the police throughout the course of the occupation. Trouble was particularly apt to arise on Polish national holidays. One altercation had occurred as early as November 1915—the month the university opened—during a celebration of the November Uprising. This was followed in January by another run-in stemming from a commemoration of the January Uprising. On the latter occasion, German troops had been forced to enter the university's grounds.[79]

These open eruptions of tension and hostility were accompanied (according to a post-strike analysis written by Kries) by more subtle provocations. Beseler had organized regular presentations and lectures in the Government-General, given by German scholars. Sparse to begin with, attendance by Polish faculty members had, over time, dwindled to nothing. According to Kries, this reflected a generalized sense of hostility to the Germans within the faculty. Kries also reported that the only students who could be relied on to attend courses given by German professors were the institutions' Jews. In addition, Kries singled out the schools' student organizations as "places where anti-German convictions were cultivated." Fraternal Aid in particular had neglected its responsibility to remain apolitical, while it had also caused trouble by adopting a hostile attitude toward Jews.[80] This was bound to create a poisonous atmosphere, given the substantial number of Jewish students: in the winter of 1915–1916, Jews accounted for about 49 percent of the university's student body, while in the summer of 1917–1918, they represented about 43 percent.[81] Finally, the more general and universal privations, anxieties, and hostilities that inevitably accompany war and occupation played their role in fostering a general sense of discontent at the university and technical college.

In May 1917, tensions between the German occupiers and the schools finally erupted in a massive student strike. Celebrations were once again held, as they had been the previous year, to celebrate the constitution of 3 May. This time, the celebrations turned rowdy, and two students, Edmund Budrewicz and Boleslaus Skrzypczynski, were arrested.[82] One of them was led away in handcuffs. The students at both the university and the technical college immediately called a strike and demanded the release of the students, while a sign posted on the university's gates publicly denounced the "violence and impudence" of the authorities.[83] Budrewicz was let go, possibly due to Hutten-Czapski's intervention. The students, however, were not mollified, and the strike continued.[84] Some even took to wandering the streets armed with "sticks and riding whips" and became embroiled in "unpleasant clashes with officers and officials."[85] Anti-German sentiment found a convenient target in Paszkowski, who reported that on 6 May the rooms of the Department of German Studies had been "spitefully" vandalized.[86]

As the strike went on, internal fissures began to appear within the mass of unruly students, in particular between Poles and Jews. On 10 May, a meeting at the technical college turned ugly when a speaker began to abuse Jews verbally. This was warmly received by the students present as well as by the rector, who followed with dismissive comments of his own about students who insisted on speaking "jargon" (Yiddish). A protest lodged by an angry Jewish student organization with the academic senate brought in reply only airy platitudes about the equality of all students. Unhappy about this, Jewish student organizations at both institutions demanded another strike, to take place on 4 June, to protest their ill-treatment by the authorities.[87]

Despite this, the striking students managed to maintain a remarkably united front, presenting a very serious challenge to the occupation authorities. In mid-May, the authorities shut down the technical college. At the university, the faculty pleaded with the students to return to their classes to no avail. The students simply escalated their demands: they now wanted the Germans to grant the institutions full autonomy in exchange for the restoration of order. The Germans did not respond by turning the full means of repression available to them on the students, but by attempting to conciliate them. In mid-May, Hutten-Czapski transmitted the message that plans were well under way to turn more power over to the Polish authorities, including control over the schools.[88]

This did not please the students, though the strikers did shift their tactics somewhat toward the end of the month. Some began to return to their classes, but the students now refused to pay their fees and formally enroll. They also refused to have anything to do with German professors at the institutions. The unfortunate Paszkowski continued to serve as a magnet for anti-German resentment, reporting in June that "the new metal sign mounted on the door of the Department of German Studies was covered with filthy expressions, like 'dla swin [sic]—for pigs.'" This was followed shortly thereafter by the appearance of "still more filthy inscriptions . . . whose repetition," Paszkowski reported with regret, "is forbidden by decency."[89] Hutten-Czapski was also targeted for ostracism by the students, with a group calling itself the "General Student Conference" forbidding all students from having contact with the curator. (The strident tone of their declarations suggests that the "sticks and riding whips" were not for exclusive use against the Germans.[90])

The tensions generated by the strike crested not in a violent clash in the streets of Warsaw but in a quietly unpleasant meeting convened by Beseler on 25 May. In attendance were the rectors of the institutions, Hutten-Czapski, and a number of senior occupation officials, such as the head of the police forces, along with administrators from a number of private occupational colleges. Beseler launched into a lengthy harangue that Hutten-Czapski thought "went beyond the limits" of what could be reasonably expected on such an occasion.[91] The Governor-General blasted both the students and the responsible Polish authorities for what he saw as a dereliction of duty by both parties. The students, for their part, had failed to keep away from politics, while the Polish authorities at the schools had not acted with appropriate vigor in containing the disorder.[92] Beseler filled his lengthy speech with vague warnings and threats, speaking in dark terms of the encouragement that trouble in the occupied territories would give to Poland's enemies in Germany.[93] Beseler did not, however, rely entirely on threats to make his point. He also tried, once again, to fuse German and Polish interests; he accused the Poles of undermining their own future by doing so little (in his view) to restrain the excesses of the students. "Gentlemen," he told the rectors,

> I for my part can declare to you, that I not infrequently have the feeling, [that] I would like to leave this land today rather than tomorrow, and many of our German officials certainly feel . . . just the same. But we can't abandon everything, because we are fulfilling here a duty to your country and to our fatherland. If we were simply to give everything now . . . that many of you want, then you would descend into chaos and soon . . . yourselves confess: "Had we only proceeded a bit more carefully."[94]

Hutten-Czapski, who was angered by the speech, sensed that far more was at work than frustration over the intransigence of Warsaw's students.

Beseler, in Hutten-Czapski's perceptive estimation, inadvertently revealed in his diatribe that he now doubted the wisdom of the policy that he had · crafted in occupied Poland.[95]

This harangue by Beseler set off a round of accusations, counteraccusations, and recrimination, with ample frustration and wounded pride displayed by all parties. At the end of May, Hutten-Czapski reported to Kries that the rectors had come to him to declare that they were angry and deeply offended by the speech.[96] The Polish academic authorities' official response was not issued until the end of the following month. The primary problem, the academic senate complained—not without a certain justice—was that they had no real power. How could they possibly be expected, they asked, to exercise control in a volatile situation? The senate also blamed the proclamation of 5 November 1916 for stirring up trouble. The students had not been inclined to political activity, but that day had created such a frenzy in Poland; how could they possibly have remained unaffected? Then the Germans exacerbated the situation by choosing the worst possible path: failing to act. This, combined with the more general hardships caused by the war and the electrifying effects of the upheaval in Russia, had produced a volatile situation that had erupted in the strike. The senate's remedy was simple: transfer complete control of educational affairs into Polish hands immediately.[97] Beseler was not impressed by these arguments, answering that there was ample authority available to them—it was merely being held on to "temporarily" by the Germans, upon whom the rectors should have called.[98]

By the time Beseler wrote this line in July 1917, however, the affair had been decided. In mid-June, Brudziński had tried to convince the students to end their boycott and pay their fees by pointing out that the students were threatening to undo the small but significant gains that had been made in the cause of Polish education. He reminded them that, for all that was lacking, Warsaw was nonetheless the site of a genuinely Polish university, one where "neither in its classes nor in the spirit that prevails within it" could anything be found that was "foreign to the spirit of the nation and its striving for real independence." Brudziński further assured the students that strenuous efforts were under way to establish Polish control, efforts that were beginning to bear fruit.[99] Also in June, Hutten-Czapski turned in desperation to Piłsudski, who (supposedly) agreed to intervene, but to no effect.[100]

The Germans continued to respond with an uncertain mixture of threats and promises. Assurances to the students that the schools were in the process of being granted autonomy brought only a demand that a statement to that effect be immediately issued in writing. In addition, Kries simultaneously extended the enrollment deadline and threatened those who did not meet it with expulsion. As something of an added benefit for the students, Hutten-Czapski, the target of much of their ire, took ill with exquisitely diplomatic timing and had to be replaced, at least for the time being.[101] All of which was to no avail. The extended enrollment period passed with only eight students at the technical college and seventeen students at the university having enrolled. On 23 June, the schools were closed.[102] Beseler ordered that all students who had not enrolled be expelled.[103]

It would not have been surprising if the Germans had chosen to keep the schools closed for the duration of the war. But they did not. Reopening ceremonies for the institutions were held on 7 November 1917. The month before, they had formally passed under Polish control as part of the transfer of authority over educational affairs (see Chapter 4). The theme of this ceremony was therefore somewhat different from that of the ceremonies held in 1915; Józef Mikułowski-Pomorski, head of education under the Provisional Council of State, praised the opening of schools that were under Polish control "for the first time." Shortly thereafter, Antoni Kostanecki was elected rector, an appointment confirmed by the Regency Council. The university authorities and the Polish Department of Religion and Education set about rewriting the university's rules and regulations.[104] The university certainly did not lack for students; more than 2,000 were enrolled in the 1917–1918 school year. They were taught by fifty-three lecturers and forty-six assistants.[105] The blow delivered to the school's development by the strike and the German response was, apparently, a good deal less than fatal, and the university went about its business that year "in more normal circumstances," according to Manteuffel.[106] The Germans abolished the office of curator.[107] They maintained, however, ultimate authority over the institution and still controlled the crucial area of personnel appointments. The occupiers continued to exercise this power to block faculty appointments they found unsuitable.[108]

In his post-strike report to Berlin, Beseler struck a melancholy note when he presented his analysis of the causes of the disorder. He assigned the primary blame to a small number of troublemakers and to the effects of the events in Russia. He added, however, the thought that the project had probably been fatally flawed from its very inception. "It was an unusual enterprise," Beseler wrote, "to want to cultivate as a foreign power this branch of national life, which must spring from the innermost essence of a people." Beseler did not despair entirely; he believed that German educational policy could continue to serve German interests when the war was over by reminding the Poles of the positive (in his view) impact of the German occupation. "It cannot be doubted," he informed Berlin, "that, when tranquil and peaceful times return, the whole land will realize what a great and lasting service the German administration has rendered to it" by assisting with the development of Polish higher education in Warsaw.[109] It could, of course, be doubted, and with ample reason, and the argument was probably intended to convince both author and audience.

In any event, the return of "tranquil and peaceful" times to both Poland and Germany was a very long way off. In the year following the reopening of Warsaw's institutions of higher education, great events and extraordinary upheavals caused their importance to recede somewhat: the descent of Russia into civil war and the related collapse of state authority in much of eastern Europe, the conclusion of a treaty of peace with the Soviets at Brest-Litovsk and the visible stirrings of deep popular discontent in occupied Poland that were matched by similar expressions of public weariness and frustration everywhere. Yet the schools continued their mission, educating their charges under the watchful eye of the occupation authorities until the Government-General was dissolved at the end of the war, not by a foreign army or its own political masters, but by the German soldiers that composed it.

6

Collapse of the Government-General

The Legacy of Failure

At the beginning of 1918, it was difficult to say if the German regime in Poland, along with all its ambitions, stood on the brink of partial success or total disaster. There had been, to be sure, a number of serious setbacks and embarrassments—such as the 1917 mutiny of the soldiers of the Polnische Wehrmacht, or that year's student strike—for the Germans. In addition, the continued economic plunder of Poland kept alive powerful currents of anti-German hostility in the occupied zone. On the other hand, some of the institutions the German regime had created, such as the university, had been well received and were attracting the support and participation of various Polish elites. The February collapse of Russia heightened this sense of being on the brink of two very different outcomes. In some ways, Germany's hand was greatly strengthened; by the spring, it had emerged as the clear victor in the east, having driven the newly created Red Army east and forced the treaty of Brest-Litovsk on Russia's new Bolshevik rulers. The western offensive that began shortly thereafter with Operation Michael also began promisingly, and for a time it seemed that German victory might, after all, be possible. At the political level, Communist rule in Russia, while turning some of Germany's nominal Activists allies against them, also led many longtime Passivists of the monarchical-conservative variety to reconsider their hostility to the Kaiser. All along, however, the occupation regime was buffeted by disturbances both domestic and foreign—and increasingly, as had been the case in Poland for a century, the two were indistinguishable. These pressures were inflamed and intensified by the total disintegration of the central European political order of which the Russian collapse was merely the harbinger—a process to which the Germans had inadvertently linked themselves by means of the institutions of the Government-General.

By the middle of 1918, it was clear to all concerned that Germany was not going to achieve the crushing victory for which it longed, even if the scope of its impending defeat was beyond the imagination of most. As the war headed into its last months, the German regime in Poland was increasingly unwilling and unable to enforce its will, while the various Polish political factions and movements began to actively prepare to implement their own answer to Joachim Lelewel's famous question—"Polska tak, ale jaka?" (Poland yes, but what sort?) In November 1918, the moral collapse of the German regime met the determination of Piłsudski's loyalists to impose their own answer to that question when the former disintegrated from within and the latter mounted a successful insurgency to disarm the Germans and throw them out of their country. The manner in which the occupation ended left a deep and abiding sense of anger and humiliation in Germany, and it helped prepare the path to the horrors that would be inflicted on Poland when the Germans returned twenty years later.

Pressures Domestic and Foreign

From late 1917 into 1918, the occupation regime managed to maintain stability despite the pressures it had to withstand. In Warsaw, anger had continued to simmer over the continued imprisonment of Piłsudski and the rest of the Polish soldiers jailed in the wake of the July 1917 oath crisis. On 9 December, a large student-led demonstration took place to show solidarity with the prisoners. Beseler noted that England was openly cheered and Germany jeered in the streets. The day ended violently, with a German policeman stabbed and twenty demonstrators injured when the Germans broke up the demonstration.[1] More serious unrest occurred the following month, when strikes broke out in Warsaw and in the coal-producing areas around Sosnowice, in the far southwestern corner of the occupied zone.[2] Strikes also occurred in urban centers, such as Lodz and Włocławek. The strikes were rooted partially in the weariness and misery of the working class and the ability of socialist agitators to transform that weariness into organized action. The momentous events in the east, however, also played a role in destabilizing Poland. The Bolshevik seizure of power in November 1917 had completed the destruction of the old order in Russia and its empire, introduced still greater uncertainty about what would replace it, and electrified those who were sympathetic to the ideology and rhetoric of the new Soviet regime. "The Revolution in Russia has had a major impact on hearts and minds here in Poland," a priest, Wacław Bliziński, warned his fellow clerics at a December 1917 meeting. "Already we can hear Bolshevik slogans here and there, and if the present regime in Russia endures, its impact on us will grow more powerful still."[3]

The disintegration of the multiethnic territories of the former Russian Empire into warring Bolshevik and nationalist factions precipitated, in February 1918, a crisis in occupied Poland linked to the question of the place of Ukraine in the new state system being violently carved out in the east. The precipitating event was the signing at Brest-Litovsk of the peace treaty between the Central Powers and the fledgling Ukrainian government known as the Rada (Council).[4] The Rada was a left-wing Ukrainian nationalist government formed in the early stages of the Russian Revolution, and it held its first meeting in Kiev in April 1917. Its aim had initially been the establishment of an autonomous Ukraine within some sort of larger Russian political entity; this had been opposed first by the Provisional Government and then, after the Communist seizure of power, by the Bolshevik regime. In January 1918, the Rada proclaimed its independence, plunging Ukraine into a civil war between pro- and anti-Bolshevik forces, with the former represented by a Soviet-backed regime in Kharkov. The Rada had sent its delegates to the Brest-Litovsk negotiations hoping to secure the support of stronger states in the midst of this violent chaos. Fortunately, it had something the Central Powers wanted: grain.[5] On 9 February, the two sides signed an agreement in which recognition of an independent Ukraine was exchanged for the creation of a trading relationship between the Powers and the Rada.[6] There were several problems with the treaty, including, not least, the Rada's tenuous grip on power. As far as the Polish Question was concerned, however, the central problem of the treaty was that it awarded the Ukraine control over the Chełm (Ukrainian Kholm) region. Much like the question of representation and language in elected city governments in Russian Poland, the Chełm crisis reactivated a long-standing dispute in Russia's western borderlands that had been ushered in by its attempts to simultaneously modernize and fortify the Russian state while minimizing the power of the Polish elites.

The Chełm region, in the southeast of the former Congress Kingdom, west of the river Bug, had a mixed population of Polish Catholic nobles, Jews, and Ukrainian peasants (though each of these categories of course simplifies identities that were often complex, fluid, and ambiguous). The Ukrainian peasants were largely Uniates—eastern-rite Catholics. As Theodore Weeks has helpfully summarized, the region was mostly devoid of "military, economic, or cultural importance." Nonetheless, it had become a matter of intense emotional concern to Polish and Russian nationalists in the course of the late nineteenth century. In the wake of the 1863 uprising, the Russian authorities had moved against the Polish elite by forcibly converting the Uniates to the Orthodox faith and abolishing their church. This fed the martyrological strain of Polish nationalism, whose adherents saw the forced conversion as yet another nail in the flesh of the "Christ among nations." The Russians, meanwhile—especially the Orthodox clergy brought in to tend to the Ukrainian flock—saw Chełm as a front in the politico-religious struggle against the unsavory national and religious heresies of the Polish elite. By the turn of the century, each side was mustering languages of legitimacy both ancient and modern—drawing, for example, on highly mythologized histories as well as dubious population statistics—to make their claims. Much like the rest of the Russian borderlands, the region drifted somewhere between a renewed era of toleration and a return to repression after 1905. Much to the outrage of the Orthodox clergy, those who wished were allowed to return to Catholicism (though not to the Uniate church, which no longer existed in Russia); however, in 1912, the region was formally detached from the administrative structure of Poland and made a province (Gubernia) of Russia. This reignited Polish outrage, as did the series of anti-Polish measures enacted by the new Russian governor, such as a ban on nationalistic Polish songs and limits on the use of the Polish language.[7] This is where the dispute stood when the war broke out; by the time the Germans and Ukrainians met at Brest-Litovsk, the latter's nationalist movement was well organized enough to mount its own claims to the region. Because the Ukraine possessed grain desperately needed by the Central Powers, it was their nationalists' claims to Chełm that were recognized in the treaty. This concession was particularly painful for Austrian Foreign Minister Czernin, yet the Empire's desperate need for food drove him to agree. "I cannot, and dare not, look on," he wrote in his diary, "and see hundreds of thousands starve for the sake of retaining the sympathy of the Poles." He reluctantly agreed, therefore, to the transfer of the Chełm district (which was in the Austrian zone of occupation), as well as to a secret annex to the treaty that promised special rights and privileges—including, perhaps, autonomy—for the Ukrainian regions of the Empire.[8]

The news of the treaty spread throughout elite Polish circles, where it was furiously denounced as the "Fourth Partition." From the point of view of General Max Hoffmann, German Chief of Staff on the eastern front and the military's representative at Brest-Litovsk, it seemed that "the Poles [had] apparently gone quite mad over the question of the Chełm district."[9] While Polish outrage may not have been universal—the great mass of Polish peasants probably cared about it little or not at all—what it lacked in depth was compensated for in breadth and intensity. Throughout the lands of the partitions, Polish intellectuals, politicians, and activists—many of them well placed and influential—found ways to demonstrate their deep displeasure. In Austria, the long-loyal Polish members of the Reichsrat broke with the government, while demonstrations and strikes erupted in Galicia. This was accompanied by the resignation of high-ranking Austro-Polish officials, including two cabinet ministers, as well as the Governor-General of the Austrian occupation zone, Stanisław Szeptycki. Far more worrisomely, several thousand Polish soldiers mutinied and some of them deserted. On 15 February, about 1,500 troops under the command of Colonel Józef Haller fled over the Austrian lines into the chaotic east in search of fellow Polish soldiers. More tried to make the journey, but were stopped by loyal Austrian units.[10] In Germany, a heated debate over the treaty took place in the Reichstag on 20 February 1918, with the Polish deputy Władysław Seyda denouncing it, to cheers from the Polish seats, as a "document of injustice."[11] ("You say that the Poles had not expected Germany to . . . betray Polish interests," Gustav Stresemann, who would soon be responsible for shaping German policy toward a newly independent Polish state, said in reply. "Just what has been done on the Polish side," he asked, "to win an entitlement to German sympathy?"[12]) A few weeks later, on 6 March, the treaty was denounced once again, this time in the Prussian Lower House, where Sigismund (Zygmunt) Seyda, Władysław's nephew, declared that the Poles would "never . . . recognize" the treaty.[13]

In the Imperial Government-General itself, Beseler noted that awarding Chełm to the Ukraine had "had a profound effect on the public opinion of the whole land."[14] In Warsaw, as flyers began to appear denouncing the "Fourth Partition," the University Senate decided on 13 February to suspend lectures for three days to protest the treaty.[15] The Polish Minister President, Jan Kucharzewski, who had been appointed late in 1917, resigned along with his government, explaining in a letter that "in the face of the peace concluded . . . with the Ukraine, a peace causing a new partition of Poland, we consider it impossible to keep our posts any longer."[16] On 14 February, in a daring display of defiance of the German censors, Warsaw newspapers printed the government's letter, as well as a statement by the Regents calling the treaty an "act of violence."[17] The papers also carried a statement by the Warsaw city council, which publicly pledged itself to "parry this blow" and to maintain an active role in the "struggle for an independent, united, [and] democratic Polish state."[18] That same day, a general strike began in the city. Windows in official German and Austrian buildings were smashed, as were those in the offices of newspapers known to be friendly to the Central Powers. An electrical transformer was blown up, and rowdy, angry crowds clashed with police and troops. In the rest of the Government-General, shops and schools closed, more German windows were smashed, and city assemblies publicly protested the treaty. Demonstrations took place in Częstochowa and Sosnowice, while in Lodz, multiple demonstrations took place on 17 and 18 February in which "red flags" and anti-German slogans revealed the combative and provocative mood of the crowds as well as the presence of socialist agitators. The dispersal of one of these demonstrations took a particularly nasty turn when a policeman was stabbed to death.[19] This violence led to further tensions in Lodz when a member of the city assembly and district school inspector named Remiszewski demanded that public funds be used to assist those hurt in clashes with police. While presenting the idea to his colleagues on the council—which passed his resolution—Remiszewski directed a stream of what Administrative Chief von Steinmeister called "gross, untrue abuse" against the Germans. The German reaction was harsh: Remiszewski was arrested and sentenced to four and a half years in prison, while the chairman of the assembly was sentenced to eight months. The latter, however, was allowed by Beseler to pay a fine instead "in view of . . . [his] difficult position."[20] Other punishments handed out in the wake of the disturbances included fines of 2,000 marks each for the Warsaw papers that had ignored the censors to publish the various declarations on 15 February. In addition, the editor of another newspaper, the *Goniec Częstochowski,* was jailed, another staffer fined, and the newspaper's right to publish suspended for three weeks for reporting on local unrest (under the headline "Demonstrations in Copenhagen").[21] The city governments of the Government-General's most prominent cities, Warsaw and Lodz, were also made to suffer: Warsaw was fined 250,000 marks, Lodz 100,000. Other towns' city councils were also fined, and some Polish city assembly members were jailed.[22] The passions aroused by the Ukrainian Treaty began to fade and a measure of stability returned to the Government-General in the wake of these punishments, though in retrospect this appears as merely a lull in the furious storm gathering momentum in the east.

While it was from the east that the most serious challenges to the established order in central Europe would issue, pressures on the Government-General were also mounting from the west. The United States and its president, Woodrow Wilson, were a major source of these pressures. As early as January 1917, Wilson—acting, at least to some degree, under the influence of the famous Polish composer and pianist Ignacy Paderewski—announced in his "Peace without Victory" speech that the postwar map of Europe should include "a united, independent, and autonomous Poland."[23] Wilson's speech marked yet another irrevocable step away from the prewar political arrangement in central Europe and added yet more urgency to the search for a replacement. In addition, the reception of the speech in Warsaw provided a demonstration of the volatility created in an age when high literacy rates and rapid communications made total control over the circulation of information impossible. The US President's remarks, delivered thousands of miles and an ocean away from Poland, caused a scene in Warsaw, with a boisterous crowd of people from the university and technical college gathering outside the residence of the US consul there to express their thanks, even treating him to a concert. (The consul and his deputies later made a follow-up appearance at the university to thank the Poles for thanking him.[24]) One year later, with the United States now in the war on the side of the Entente and Russia in a state of upheaval, Wilson raised the stakes by including in his Fourteen Points Point XIII, which announced that "an independent Polish state should be erected which should include the territories inhabited by indisputably Polish populations, which should be assured a free and secure access to the sea, and whose political and economic independence and territorial integrity should be guaranteed by international covenant."[25] With Russia—the most important restraint on the Entente's deployment of the Polish Question as a political weapon—in a state of advanced decay, the Allies had now succeeded in moving the Polish Question completely out of the realm of the domestic affairs of the partitioning powers and internationalized it. To the Germans, Point XIII could only be taken as a serious threat to its territorial integrity, since National Democracy claimed extensive amounts of land under German sovereignty, especially Posen and West Prussia, as "indisputably Polish." (Nor does Wilson seem to have realized that many territories claimed as "indisputably Polish" were simultaneously and variously claimed as indisputably and inalienably Ukrainian, Lithuanian, German, and Russian, among others.) In any event, the Fourteen Points raised expectations and generated popular enthusiasm in German-occupied Poland.[26] Not everyone in Poland, however, shared in the affection for Wilson that was sweeping parts of exhausted, shattered Europe. Maria Lubomirska, wary of Wilson's populism, provides a memorably contrarian view, calling Wilson the

> most powerful of all autocrats, undermining conceptions of authority and hierarchy in other nations—smashing in an instant, with a brutal hand, the foundations of European existence, oblivious to the dangers of such revolutions. A professor who has won the war and has suddenly become the arbiter of an unknown world, an *enfant terrible*, possessed of unpredictable whims, who has set about overturning Europe.[27]

Finally, one other source of pressure was building in the west. Roman Dmowski, the highly influential leader of National Democracy, had left Russia before the revolution in order to work for western support for his movement's political ambitions. He went first to London and then to Switzerland, where, in August 1917, the National Democratic–allied Polish National Committee was formed. Dmowski and the committee (which Paderewski represented in Washington) thereafter moved to France. While there, he lobbied for the

Allies to declare the Polish regime created by the Germans illegal and to recognize the committee as the legitimate government of Poland. The Allies were not yet ready to take such a step, but events seemed to be moving in that direction; Paderewski, for example, had had his successes in Washington, while France had begun, in the summer of 1917, to assemble its own Polish military force. By the end of 1917, Great Britain, the United States, and France had all given Dmowski official recognition, though not as a state's representative. Dmowski was thus well placed to influence the course of events in the Allied countries as the war ended. Just as importantly, Dmowski's influence extended throughout central Europe, since his National Committee could claim the loyalties and direct the activities of National Democrats throughout the partitioning powers' Polish territories.[28]

Despite these mounting pressures, Germany's strategic position in the east in early 1918 was generally favorable. The crisis caused by the conclusion of the treaty with the Ukraine had actually strengthened Germany's hand. A great deal of Polish anger was certainly directed at Germany, but the real villains were widely accepted to be Austria in general and Czernin in particular, mainly because better had been expected of them. At a 22 February 1918 meeting at Bad Homburg, Emperor Karl informed Wilhelm that he was no longer committed to pursuing an Austro-Polish solution to the Polish Question, due in part to the poisoning of Polish opinion regarding Austria. At the level of Austro-German relations, the way was now open—for the time being, at least—for Germany to act decisively in imposing its will in Poland.[29] At about the same time, the German position in the east was further strengthened by its victory over the new Soviet government of Russia. On 10 February, Leon Trotsky, head of the Soviet delegation at Brest-Litovsk, had broken off negotiations and left the city. In response, the Germans had resumed offensive operations in the east, beginning on 18 February. Germany's overwhelming military superiority on this front quickly compelled the Soviets to sign, on 3 March, the agreement that became known as the Treaty of Brest-Litovsk. In it, Russia formally and publicly renounced its authority over huge stretches of its territory, including the Ukraine, Courland, Lithuania, and, of course, Poland.[30] When the German spring offensives in the west showed early signs of success, the sense became widespread in occupied

Poland that Germany stood on the edge of victory. Many Polish elites began to resign themselves to the seeming necessity of working to answer the Polish Question in conjunction with the Germans, distasteful as many of them found the idea.[31]

Against this background of a renewed sense of fluidity and open possibilities in the east, Beseler was once again given a chance to press his case for vigorous German action in Poland when he appeared, on 13 March 1918, at a Crown Council discussion of the Polish Question. Beseler's arguments to the council revealed that the troubles that had beset his administration had done little, if anything, to dampen his commitment to his vision of a solution to the Polish Question. As he had consistently done throughout his tenure as Governor-General, Beseler argued against large-scale annexations in Poland, noting that it was manifestly not in Germany's interests to create a lasting sense of grievance and hostility among the Poles, a sure result of overly greedy seizures of land. Some annexations, Beseler informed the council, could not, of course, be ruled out. But Germany's interests would best be secured by working out an arrangement by which Germany could dominate Poland's military capabilities and its communications without causing too much popular resentment.[32] Beseler elaborated on his plans in a 23 March message to Chancellor Hertling. The Governor-General informed Hertling that he had been working with the Regency authorities to formulate a mutually agreeable set of guidelines for moving forward politically in Poland. According to Beseler, the Regents had agreed to accept a king from the Catholic German nobility (Beseler recommended installing Herzog Albrecht of Württemberg as a temporary ruler) as well as Poland's inclusion in "the future . . . central European society of states" by means of a "defensive and offensive alliance" with the Central Powers. Germany, however, was to have a more comprehensive military treaty with Poland. Beseler recommended an agreement to both the Poles and the chancellor according to which in time of war (or sufficiently threatening international tensions) the Polish army would pass under German command, with German forces also having right of movement in and through Polish territory. Peacetime arrangements were to be somewhat different: the Polish army would remain under Polish command, while a special German-Polish committee would monitor and oversee defense-related infrastructure and matters of common military interest.[33]

Beseler reaffirmed to Hertling his belief that annexing some Polish border territory would bring Germany certain military advantages, pointing out, as he had consistently done, the desirability of the Biebrza and Narew rivers as boundaries. He also told the chancellor some extensions of the border near Thorn/Toruń and Będzin would be advisable. Beseler rejected once again, however, the more sweeping eastward expansion demanded by the OHL and other radical annexationists, citing the "political disadvantages" broader seizures of Polish territory would bring. He also soundly rejected the idea that creating a territorial buffer zone between Poland and Germany would lessen the danger that Polish nationalist agitation would migrate from Poland and destabilize Polish Prussia, threatening the Prussian state with upheaval and dismemberment. In a summary rejection of the radical annexationists' reasoning, Beseler explained why completely insulating Germany from all potential irredentist troubles was impossible:

A protective [border] strip against irredentist agitation . . . is made worthless by the . . . possibilities of modern transportation; its establishment without the greatest difficulties is scarcely conceivable . . . What, however, the detachment of a renowned Polish region for the Poles, [and] on the other hand the . . . unavoidable absorption of more than a million Poles into the Prussian state for our internal political circumstances would mean, surely requires little discussion.[34]

Unfortunately, Beseler's arguments did little to persuade the German government to follow through on what it had started. Whatever possibilities were still open to Germany in the early spring of 1918 began to slip very quickly from its grasp, as the government, wallowing in indecision, squandered time it did not have. The Reich's failure to act decisively in Poland in the first half of 1918 was due in large part to the complete inability of Austria and Germany to resolve their differences over Poland's future. In April 1918, von Burián was reappointed Austrian Foreign Minister, replacing Czernin, who had fallen from grace in part because of the Ukraine debacle. Burián was adamant about not allowing the Germans to establish a preponderance of influence in Poland, and the Austrians began once again to push for the Austro-Polish solution.[35] Germany was in no mood to bargain with its weaker ally. At a discussion of German war aims headed by the Emperor himself in early July 1918, the Germans decided that the Austro-Polish solution was not in Germany's interests and was to be definitively rejected. It was further decided that the Poles would be free to pick their own ruler (though whether this ruler had to come from Germany is unclear); that Germany had to secure both economic and military domination in Poland; and that the annexation of some Polish border territory was essential. (As usual, the military high command pressed for these annexations to be as sweeping as possible and accompanied by population transfers.[36] At a meeting of Prussian state and Reich officials, however, held by Vice-Chancellor Payer on 9 August, it was resolved to defy the military on both counts; the border annexations were to be moderate, and population transfers were ruled out.[37]) But decisive action did not follow, and events of the late summer of 1918 would transform Germany's primary task in Poland from the imposition of its will and interests to a desperate attempt to salvage what it could from the disintegrating wreckage of its war.

Institutions, January–August 1918

The development of Polish cultural and political life under German rule during the last year of the occupation tended to reflect the uncertainty that reigned at the highest levels of power. On the one hand, the Government-General continued its general pattern of allowing, and even encouraging, Polish educational and administrative institutions to expand. At the very same time, however, the regime restrained their development into genuinely autonomous expressions of Polish authority, causing resentment and exasperation among the elites whose cooperation they sought.

In May 1918, Warsaw University finally opened its theology department, with five lecturers instructing the department's thirty-nine students in the 1918–1919 school year.[38] In addition, the university's professors were given a new opportunity to contribute to the development of Poland's intellectual life when the Regency government established an institute for the training of teachers in July 1918. It was to be linked to the university by its board, which was to include two university faculty members.[39] The occupiers, however, continued to exercise ultimate authority over all faculty appointments. At the broad administrative level, the Polish educational bureaucracy established after the handover of education grew during the last year of the war. Some of this new bureaucracy's officials tried to use their positions to expand the number of Polish schools, but their efforts were blocked by the German district chiefs, who cited financial reasons for their obstructionism.[40]

The institutions of Selbstverwaltung generally languished during the last year of the war, a source of some discontent among the occupied population. The Germans rejected Polish demands—inspired in part by Austria's introduction of district-level elections into its occupation zone—that they hold the elections formally provided for in the 1916 District Order. Steinmeister explained that, in the wake of the uproar over the peace with the Ukraine, the Germans were leery of doing anything that could potentially create more public discord. The occupiers also worried that elections would end the tenure of the now-experienced representatives in the district assemblies, with whom they seem to have been able to work without too much friction. Pressure from below was also mounting on the regime to create Prussian-style *Kreisausschüssen*—governing committees chosen by the district assembly. This was refused on the grounds that the committees would probably clash with the German district chiefs, and possibly even undermine their power.[41]

The urban institutions of Selbstverwaltung developed somewhat more fully than the district institutions, though real progress toward autonomy was once again checked by the occupiers. By early 1918, an increasing number of Polish cities were being given Polish mayors. At the same time, however, the mayors' power was reduced vis-à-vis the authority of the German district chiefs. (Steinmeister claimed that this was seen as most welcome "help" by the Polish urban administrators.[42]) Steinmeister thought that the exchange of German for Polish mayors had had a distinctly negative effect on the quality of urban government, though it had not been completely without benefit: the new appointments, the Administrative Chief informed Berlin, helped keep the cities calm and stable, "because the Pole understandably prefers to be ruled badly by his own countryman than [well] by a foreigner."[43]

At the proto-national level, an entirely new political institution was established in 1918: the State Council *(Staatsrat)*. According to the 9 February 1918 law that created it, the council was to be composed of 110 members. Fifty-five of these members would be chosen by the institutions of Selbstverwaltung, primarily by the district assemblies, but also by the city assemblies of

Warsaw, Lodz, and (Austrian-occupied) Lublin. Forty-three seats would be filled by representatives chosen by the Regency government, and twelve would be held by Polish elites who would be awarded their seats on the basis of their position in Polish society: six Catholic bishops, two Protestant clerics (one Lutheran, one Reformed), the oldest of Warsaw's rabbis, the rectors of each of Warsaw's two institutions of higher education, and the president of Poland's highest court. The council was intended to be a temporary institution, the most important function of which was creating plans for a new parliament that would replace it.[44]

The elections to the council were originally scheduled for February but were postponed because of the disorder over the Chełm question. They were finally held on 9 April 1918, with some parties, such as the Christian Democrats and the left wing of the Polish Socialist Party (PPS-Lewica), abstaining on the grounds that the council was an undemocratic institution.[45] District assemblies from throughout the former Congress Kingdom, including assemblies in the Austrian zone, chose representatives, perhaps the closest the two occupation governments ever came to fulfilling Beseler's wish and unifying the territories. Voting in eight electoral districts, the assemblies of the German zone sent twenty-four representatives to the council, while those in the Austrian zone, voting in six, sent eighteen. The city governments of Warsaw and Lodz sent eight and four, respectively.[46] (The city of Lublin ended up not sending a representative owing to the dissolution of its assembly.[47]) The results were not a spectacular victory for the occupiers, as the National Democrat–dominated Interparty Club made out handsomely, claiming thirty-seven seats. Though still sometimes referred to as "Passivists," the label did not describe them very well any more. Aware that a new order was emerging in Poland, the National Democrats willingly participated in the institutions created by the occupiers, but they did so in part to block the ambitions of the Central Powers and their allies in Poland. More reliable political partners for the Germans among the Activists claimed only twelve seats. The balance, however, was mostly restored when the Regents made their picks, assigning seats to thirty-two Activists and seven members of the Interparty Club, in addition to four Jews and one German farmer.[48]

The council met for the first time on 22 June 1918, with its members taking their oath of office at an inaugural Mass. Like many Catholic Masses in Poland, this one concluded with the singing of one of Poland's unofficial national anthems, "Boże coś Polskę."[49] The council remained in session until 31 July 1918, holding meetings of its commissions as well as thirteen plenary sessions. Hutten-Czapski was detailed by the Government-General to observe the meetings and intervene if the "political or economic interests of the occupation government were touched on."[50] He does not seem to have intervened either often or forcefully, since Beseler noted that "whenever there was criticism of the occupation authorities, especially the German, the chamber's applause was always warm and ample." Voicing dissatisfaction and discontent was not, however, all that the deputies did; such matters as elementary school teachers' pay and, more importantly, the constitution of the future Landtag were also discussed. Beseler reported to Berlin that, despite the sometimes agitated and hostile tone of the proceedings, he was satisfied with "this young political body," though it needed time to rid itself of its "childhood diseases."[51] Overall, however, the primary effect of the State Council was the spread of a general sense of frustration among Polish elites, as it seemed to be yet another institution that combined all the forms of power and responsibility with no meaningful content.[52]

By the spring of 1918, German-occupied Poland also had a new ministerial government to replace that of Kucharzewski. On 23 March, the Regents recommended Jan Steczkowski, a Galician banker, as the new Minister-President. He was approved for the post by both the Germans and the Austrians shortly thereafter. Steczkowski, described by Beseler as a "calm, prudent, practical, and determined man," was willing to accept a German Catholic as king of Poland, though he was also committed to continuing the development of Poland's state institutions, including the army.[53]

The struggle to create a Polish army remained a source of tension between the Germans and the Polish elites with whom they dealt until the very end of the war. The nominal Polish army, the Polnische Wehrmacht, had failed to evolve into a serious fighting force. What men and materiel that it did possess remained, in any event, under Beseler's command, to the chagrin of Polish political activists. By the spring of 1918, however, a promising new source of Polish manpower had arrived on the scene: the Polish units stranded in what remained of the Russian Empire and no longer subordinated to any state. This was the direct result of the Russian revolutions and the descent of Russia into civil war. After the first revolution, in February 1917, Polish soldiers serving in the Tsarist army began to group themselves into "Polish

Soldiers' Alliances" (Związki Wojskowych Polaków). In the early summer, this was followed by creation of "Naczpol," the Supreme Polish Military Committee (Naczelny Polski Komitet Wojskowy). Founded by Polish officers of the Russian army at a meeting in Petrograd, Naczpol's purpose was to create Polish army units that would continue to fight under Russian command on the eastern front. Three corps of Polish soldiers were eventually established.[54] The Bolshevik Revolution, however, left the Polish units in Russia without a state to fight under. The Regency government, sensing an opportunity to assert its independence against the Germans and build up a military force to solidify its position vis-à-vis its internal Polish rivals, tried to claim these soldiers for its own.

The units that figured most prominently in the Regency's bid for armed autonomy were the Polish I Corps and II Corps. The I Corps had been formed in the late summer of 1917 from the Russian Polish Rifle Division and was commanded by General Józef Dowbór-Muśnicki. In February 1918, the Corps managed to capture the well-stocked fortress of Bobruysk (in present-day Byelorussia), providing Polish forces with a secure assembly site.[55] In early March, with the Corps numbering about 20,000 men, the Regency Council sent an oath to be taken by its soldiers, who were to swear loyalty to the "Most Honorable Regency Council as the supreme authority of the Polish state."[56] When the Germans discovered this, they demanded an immediate demobilization of the Corps. Dowbór-Muśnicki refused, citing his obligations to his oath. The tension was partially defused when Lubomirski, in the name of the Regents, informed Dowbór-Muśnicki that he was still subordinate to Beseler's orders, since the Governor-General was the head of Poland's armed forces. Only in May, however, under pressure from Beseler, did the Regency government formally release Dowbór-Muśnicki from his oath and remove itself from command over the Corps.[57] It was later dissolved by German troops in the area.[58]

This was a happy ending compared with the fate of the II Corps. This corps had its origins in Polish forces assembled in Bessarabia toward the end of 1917.[59] Control was then taken by the mutinous Haller, who augmented it with his own troops (its strength eventually reached about 7,000 men) and led it northeast to Kaniov, on the south bank of the Dnieper about 100 kilometers from Kiev.[60] Haller (going by the nom de guerre "Mazowiecki" to escape detection) declared his loyalty to the Regency Council, though he noted that he was "fully convinced that the . . . Regency Council could not demand that Polish troops subordinate themselves to alien influence without being forced by necessity." At the end of April, Haller refused a Regency Council order directing him formally to notify the Central Powers that his troops were under Regency command (such a declaration would have been anathema to Haller, and would have alerted the Austrians to his presence) and resign his position. His intransigence led to the 11 May Battle of Kaniov, in which the unit was attacked and defeated by German troops. Haller himself managed to elude capture, eventually arriving in France, where he assumed command of the Polish army being assembled there.[61]

War's End

The late summer of 1918 marked the beginning of the end of Germany's war. This was made manifestly clear by the events surrounding the British attack against the Germans near Amiens that began on 8 August, which Ludendorff termed the "black day of the German army." The attack resulted in 20,000 German casualties, which they could ill afford; worse, some 30,000 German soldiers surrendered, an unmistakable sign that the great western offensive had failed and that the German army was losing its will to fight.[62] Germany's faltering position in the west fed an atmosphere of uncertainty, anti-German hostility, and simmering unrest in the east. In the last months of the war, erstwhile Legionary and Benjaminów internee Roman Starzyński detected a loss of "self-confidence" on the part of the occupiers in Poland.[63] Continued radical agitation emanating from Russia and the long-thwarted but steadily inflamed ambitions of Polish nationalists also contributed to this sense of festering tension. (The German Police President of Warsaw, Ernst von Glasenapp, singled out Warsaw's students as a major source of trouble and lamented Beseler's decision to open the university.) In the face of Germany's weakening position, the POW began to make death threats against German officials.[64] The threats were serious. On 1 October 1918, a high-ranking German police official, Erich Schultze, was shot dead in a Warsaw street by assassins linked to the PPS. One of the culprits, Antoni Purtal (also known as "Gap"), already wanted for the murder of two German policemen, revealed in a recounting of the deed written after the war that a secret cell had been planning the assassination since April. Schultze, who had been an active opponent of the PPS's underground activities in occupied Poland, had been watched closely by the cell for months, until that fall day when he encountered Gap and his accomplice, Czesław Trojanowski, while leaving his living quarters on Smolna Street. Gap fired first, wounding Schultze, who called for Jesus as he fell. He was then killed by two shots from Trojanowski.[65] While they did not all engage in such open violence, conspiratorial movements throughout Poland began to mobilize and plan for the end of the war and the occupation.[66]

In the last months of the war, Beseler blamed continued Austro-German disagreements over Poland's future for the Regency government's reluctance to fully and openly embrace a future with Germany. He complained that the Polish government was "behaving like a beauty who wants to let herself be showered with gifts and promises by two suitors without giving her consent to either."[67] At the same time, Beseler warned Berlin that the anti-Austrian hostility drummed up by the treaty with the Ukraine was dissipating. In elite Polish opinion, the Austrians had once again gained their favored position over the Germans. Part of the problem, Beseler told Berlin, were the discussions being carried on openly in the German press about annexing large swathes of Polish territory.[68] Indecision and an inability to follow through on its promises were also ruining Germany's name in Poland. Beseler warned Berlin that Germany was in serious danger of losing out to the Austrians in Poland for good, demanding of the politicians "the immediate announcement of an unequivocal program and a policy conducted in this direction with resolution."[69] By the time he wrote this recommendation, however, Beseler seems to have mostly given up hope that his answer to the Polish Question would be adopted by either Germany or Poland. His letters to Clara began to focus less on politics and administration, and his thoughts turned increasingly to the end of the war and his return home. While he was resigned to failure and frustration, he was nonetheless glad to have had the opportunity to serve as Governor-General. "It is very interesting," he wrote to Clara on 31 August 1918, "to look so deeply into the life of a nation, and I am very thankful that I was able to become acquainted with the . . . splendid work of a regent and *Landesvater*."[70]

By October 1918, Beseler's position in Poland had become untenable. On 29 September 1918, Ludendorff, at the head of a battered and exhausted army that was being driven back toward its own borders, informed the German government that the war could not be won. By the end of the first week of October, Prince Max of Baden had been named chancellor and the Germans had requested armistice negotiations on the basis of Wilson's "Fourteen Points." On 7 October, the Regents got a telegram from the new chancellor that spoke in warm tones of his commitment to advancing good German-Polish relations, as well as an acknowledgment that he would "see to the speediest possible removal of the remaining burdens of occupation."[71] All of this released a tide of excitement and energy in occupied Poland that was difficult to stem. It was clear that Beseler represented a faltering regime; it was also clear that some sort of fundamental change in the status of the Polish Question was at hand. On 7 October 1918, a statement published in the official *Monitor Polski* and transmitted to Entente governments repeated Wilson's Thirteenth Point and declared that Poland was on the cusp of total independence. The Regents further announced that they would convene a council of elites to draft an electoral law that would be used to create a Sejm that would, in turn, guide the organization of the Polish state. The Regents, however, knew that its declarations would be meaningless without armed force to back them up and serve as a symbol of their legitimacy. They also knew they had serious competition for the loyalties of Polish soldiers: the pro-Piłsudski POW continued to attract eager and loyal volunteers while it prepared to assert its (or rather its "Commandant's") will, while the Polish army in France—some 17, 000 strong by the end of the war—was recognized by the French government in late September as an Allied force and Dmowski's National Committee as its legitimate political authority.[72] To shore up their shaky position in the middle of what looked like a brewing civil war, the Regents attempted to create a military force of their own by using the remnants of the Polnische Wehrmacht as a nucleus. On 12 October 1918, without informing Beseler beforehand, the Regents declared themselves the sovereign authority over the troops. At the same time, they issued a new oath (which had previously been approved by the Central Powers) in which loyalty was sworn exclusively to them; no mention was made of allied powers. The audacious move caused something of a crisis in the Government-General, but its will to impose its authority was rapidly ebbing. As a sign that the German occupation of Poland was drawing to a close, Beseler, seeing himself with few good options, formally transferred control of the Wehrmacht to the Regents on 23 October.[73] The time for grand and ambitious projects was obviously at an end. Just as they had been in the first days of the occupation, "security and order" were now Beseler's and the regime's first priorities.[74]

The final dissolution of the old order in Poland began in Austria. On 28 October 1918, the Liquidation Committee, a transitional Polish government headed by the Populist Wincenty Witos, was formed in Kraków, and shortly thereafter was able to spread its authority throughout western Galicia. Eastern Galicia descended into civil war; on 18 October, power had been seized in Lwów (claimed, in Wilsonian terminology, as both "indisputably Polish" as well as "indisputably Ukrainian") by the Ukrainian National Committee, which disarmed local Polish combatants. A civil war between Polish and Ukrainian nationalists erupted, which lasted until Polish reinforcements from the west were able to conquer eastern Galicia. Lwów did not fall until 20 November. Serving as a sad bridge between the old world passing away and the new one emerging, the Jews in Lwów were subjected to a pogrom by the victorious Poles, who wanted to punish the Jews for their "disloyalty" in not clearly supporting the Polish side in the Ukrainian-Polish war. Shops and other buildings were destroyed, people were attacked, and many were killed; the exact numbers are impossible to pin down, but reliable estimates place the total deaths at about 150. Disorder also beset the Austrian zone of Congress Poland before the war had officially ended. On the night of 6–7 November 1918, a Provisional Government of the People's Republic of Poland was proclaimed in the city of Lublin, erstwhile seat of the Austrian occupation regime. Headed by the Galician Socialist Ignacy Daszyński (with Edward Rydz-Śmigły as minister of war) and composed of a variety of socialists, radicals, and populists, the Lublin government openly denounced the legitimacy of the Regents.[75]

The ultimate collapse of the German occupation regime, however, was not occasioned by any of these external forces. The Germans themselves cleared the path for the contest for power in postwar Poland when its occupation army collapsed from within. After 9 November, as Germany descended into revolution at home, German soldiers and sailors throughout the east, from Sevastopol to Reval, mutinied and formed councils that claimed to be the sole legitimate authority within the army. This process began in occupied Poland as early as 9 November, when soldiers—mainly reserve (Landsturm) troops—started to form councils. In Warsaw, a Central Committee was established that claimed to be the new central German authority within the Government-General. There were probably some revolutionary elements at work within the councils, but most soldiers simply wanted to go home.[76]

The dissolution of the German occupation force coincided with an organized seizure of power by native paramilitary forces. On 11 November, in an action coordinated by the POW, armed Polish insurgents seized power from the Germans, taking over official buildings and crucial infrastructure, such as bridges and train stations. It is indicative of the uprising's careful preparation and broad ambitions that by the evening the archives had new signs on their doors reading "Archiwum państwa Polskiego" (Polish State Archive).[77] The German soldiers in Warsaw, with few exceptions, allowed themselves to be disarmed by Polish forces without a struggle. (It is one of the ironies of the occupation that students from the university "took a lively role in disarming the occupiers."[78]) "Right on Wareckiej Street," wrote one observer, Mieczysław Jankowski, who had witnessed the Germans' triumphant entry into Warsaw,

> I saw a small 12- or 13-year-old schoolboy run up behind some sort of German serviceman, a strong, sturdy fellow. When [the boy] reached him, he stopped him and ordered him to hand over [his] weapon, and the big German, without a word, undid his belt and surrendered his sword to the boy.[79]

German occupation troops also began to sport foreign insignia and colors. "Around the 12th of November," one German soldier later recalled,

> I went into town dressed in hunting clothes to see for myself how things stood. I met two young German soldiers wearing blue-white-red ribbons. I asked them if they were Dutch . . . They answered: "We are Alsatians, we are French!" At that I smacked them in the face. This short conversation was sufficient enough to draw a crowd, who of course took the side of the soldiers and began to hit me. I was freed from this situation by two armed Polish students, who declared me under arrest, put me in a droshky, and brought me to the Polish headquarters. The students . . . and the Polish officers at headquarters, who recognized me, behaved correctly and tactfully in every way and immediately let me go.[80]

Similarly, Police President von Glasenapp spotted German soldiers driving around in a car decorated with French flags.[81]

Some Germans, however, did resist, and violence ensued. Glasenapp, for example, holed up in a police station with other Germans who did not want to surrender and fought back against a Polish attack. Glasenapp was ultimately taken into custody by Polish authorities, who advised him to leave the country immediately, as they could not guarantee his safety.[82] In Lodz, the disarmament of the Germans and the Polish seizure of power proceeded with a similar mix of uneasy calm and sporadic violence. Roman Starzyński was on hand to play an active role in the longed-for liberation of his country. After his release from captivity in February 1918, Starzyński had returned to Lodz, where he taught courses and gave lectures on Polish history and literature. As a former Legionary and prisoner, he was considered suspect and was required to check in with the authorities at regular intervals. He was also forbidden from leaving the city. None of this hampered his secret political activities in the least. Starzyński regularly met with other conspirators at the apartment of another former Legionary and active member of the POW, Wacław Lipiński, where he discussed politics and helped plan strikes and demonstrations. He also met separately with a handful of other former officers of the Legions. Meeting at a bakery on Piotrkowska Street, Lodz's main thoroughfare, this second group of plotters was small but disciplined, brave, and well placed: the group included Lieutenant Alfred Białyk, a magistrate; Second Lt. Emil Kaliński, who worked in Lodz's power plant; and Second Lt. Feliks Kwiatek, a doctor at the Anna Maria hospital.[83]

The events of 10–11 November in Lodz demonstrate the mix of wholesale improvisation and careful preparation that enabled the POW and allied militias to seize power. On 10 November, after news of the establishment of the Lublin government arrived in the city, Starzyński and his comrades received instructions from Warsaw to organize a demonstration and rally in support of it. His first hint that the hour of liberation had arrived was that the Germans did nothing to interfere. The next day he met his compatriots, as usual, at the bakery. An acquaintance burst in and told them that the Germans had, quite suddenly, disappeared from public view and formed a Soldiers' Council in the Lodz Soldiers' Center (Soldatenheim). Uncertainty and "panic" gripped the city—but not Starzyński and his friends, who sprang into action. Starzyński went home for some uniform items and then reported to the fire station, previously agreed upon by left-wing conspiratorial movements as the assembly point for the city's various clandestine militias. He encountered many enthusiastic young students from his classes there. Command was assumed by Starzyński's comrade Lt. Białyk (the senior Polish officer in the city could not be located), who organized the men into units and sent out patrols. These disarmed the Germans they found, though not all German units were ready to give up without a fight. One commander, for example, set up a pair of machine guns in the windows of the Grand Hotel on Piotrkowska and swept the street with fire. Starzyński could hear sporadic sounds of battle coming from elsewhere in the city, and one of his students was killed in the fighting. Negotiations began with the Soldiers' Council; they wanted to go home, and the insurgents were happy to let them, but on the condition they leave all their weapons. Not unreasonably, the Germans protested that this would render them defenseless on their journey back to the Reich. The Polish units responded that the weapons were legitimate "spoils of war." Finally, a compromise was reached: the Germans could keep some of their weapons and would be escorted by Polish units to the border, at which point they would have to give up the rest of them. By the evening, quiet had returned to the city.[84] The deal struck with the Lodz garrison was replicated in Warsaw in an agreement worked out between the Central Council of German soldiers and the Polish authorities. According to the agreement, all German soldiers throughout Poland would be allowed to go home in peace, but they had to turn all of their armaments over to the Polish government as they left. Both sides abided by these terms, meaning that Poland soon began to empty of German forces, but not German weapons. The evacuation of German troops began on 14 November, and the Central Committee packed up and left four days later.[85]

More than a century after the Congress of Vienna, Polish independence had been restored with extraordinary rapidity and with remarkably little violence and disorder. This must be attributed, at least in part, to the influence of the Polish politician with whom the German Soldiers' Councils struck their deal: Józef Piłsudski. Piłsudski had been released from prison by the Germans and arrived in Warsaw on the morning of 10 November. Not only was he instrumental in arranging for the mostly peaceful evacuation of the Germans; he also began the process of uniting the country's factions. He had been met at the train station by the local commander of the POW and by

Regent Zdzisław Lubomirski. Each invited Piłsudski to breakfast. Perhaps assured of the POW's enduring loyalty, Piłsudski elected to go with Lubomirski. Over tea at the Regent's Warsaw villa, Lubomirski and Piłsudski discussed Poland's future; Lubomirski urged the Socialist leader to use his influence and popularity to bring the country together in this moment of uncertainty and crisis. "I don't trust him," Maria Lubomirska noted of Piłsudski. "I don't believe him, but how I would like to believe! [B]ecause we . . . very much need a leader."[86] The cooperation between the two that began the moment Piłsudski stepped off his train would help stabilize the country as one era of war ended and another began.

Beseler played no part in the negotiations between the Soldiers' Councils and the Poles and did not assist in the German evacuation of the country. Remaining secluded in his offices, Beseler submitted a request to resign on 9 November. On 11 November, Hutten-Czapski went to see him, pleading with him to stay at his post and keep command with the admonishment that "the captain . . . [must] be the last to leave a sinking ship." The discussion was an unpleasant one for both parties. "For the first time in his life he became unfriendly to me," Hutten-Czapski later wrote, "and said in the most official tone that he was the guardian of his own honor and would do what he thought right."[87] It was also fruitless; the next day, Beseler—who had received neither an order to leave nor formal acceptance of his resignation—fled Warsaw by boat to Thorn, and from there made his way to Berlin. This ignominious end to his long and difficult tenure in Poland would become the subject of much of the scathing criticism directed against Beseler after the war.

The Legacy of Failure

The collapse of German rule in the occupied zone was the first in a series of events that provided the final impetus for the event that had been alternately encouraged and restrained throughout the duration of the war: the reestablishment of Polish statehood. In the Congress Kingdom, the Regents on 11 November transferred supreme command of all Polish military formations to Józef Piłsudski. A few days later, they dissolved the Regency Council and transferred full state authority to him, with the understanding that he would use it to provide temporary stability and coherence while Poland built the required institutions it needed for statehood. Elections were scheduled for January 1919 (remarkably, a Sejm was duly elected without much trouble).[88] Some of Germany's Prussian-Polish territories were soon added to the territory of the consolidating state. At the end of December 1918, Ignacy Paderewski arrived in Posen on his way to Warsaw, where he hoped to broker an understanding between Piłsudski and Dmowski. The province was already in an advanced state of dissolution, with power claimed by a "commission" of Prussian Poles that included several former members of the Reichstag, including Wojciech Korfanty. Paderewski's presence in the volatile area touched off an uprising that led to intense fighting between Polish and German soldiers; by February, when an armistice was signed, most of the province was under Polish control.[89] Polish rule there was formalized when the Treaty of Versailles was signed in June 1919, awarding the new Polish state large chunks of prewar German territory in the east, including a sizable portion of West Prussia and almost all of Posen/Poznań.[90] "Signing of the peace treaty," Hutten-Czapski recorded in his diary on 28 June, "through which my estates pass to the Polish Republic, whose citizen I become."[91] It was an extraordinarily laconic recording of the end of an era, and of an identity that had been created and nourished by it.

To some observers in Germany, these events became linked into a seamless narrative in which Germany's attempts to curry loyalty from the Poles had ultimately resulted in a series of calamities for Germany in the east. This story of self-inflicted disaster generated outrage and bitterness in some German circles, bitterness that fastened on a number of the prominent figures associated with Germany's wartime Polish policies. Bethmann Hollweg was a convenient and obvious target. In a pamphlet published in 1919, Dietrich Schäfer, a well-known professor of history at Berlin University, blamed Bethmann for pursuing a policy that had, in Schäfer's mind, ultimately been responsible for Germany's collapse.[92] Similarly, Ernst von Glasenapp decried Bethmann and his "weak policy" in Poland, which had primarily consisted, in Glasenapp's view, of continuously giving in to Polish demands, which only encouraged them to become more ambitious. The end result, Glasenapp writes, was an embarrassing "fiasco."[93] Bethmann Hollweg defended himself and his Polish policy in the (posthumously published) second volume of his war memoirs. The former chancellor argued that the enormous extension of the Austrian-German border that the Austro-Polish solution would have entailed would have been a most unwelcome development, as well as a poor reward for the fighting done by German troops in the east. In addition, domestic political concerns ruled against outright annexation of Russia's Polish provinces. Yet the forces released by the war, Bethmann pointed out, demanded a new answer to the Polish Question. In the end, Bethmann repeated much the same argument that he had made during the war. "The solution that was . . . tolerable for us—a good one didn't exist—was an independent [*selbständiges*] Poland," he writes. This state had to be "bound so tightly to us that with the full development of mutual economic relations no militarily or politically . . . dangerous new neighbor arose."[94] Bethmann's statement of his aims, however self-serving they may be, can nonetheless be taken as a concise and accurate summary of what those who supported Germany's state-building policy during the war were trying to accomplish and why.

Beseler's name was also thoroughly poisoned after the war, with conservatives and nationalists subjecting him to withering verbal attacks for his conciliatory Polish policies as well as his flight from Warsaw.[95] Both Schäfer and Glasenapp blamed him in addition to Bethmann, Schäfer for pushing too hard for Polish troops during the war, Glasenapp for supposedly showing weakness in the face of increasing Polish hostility and ambitiousness during the war. The thoughts on Beseler and the government's wartime Polish policies recorded in the memoirs of Arthur Rhode, a veteran of the nationality conflict in the Prussian east and a Protestant pastor in Posen, suggest what those who had long warned of Polish designs against Germany thought of Beseler. Rhode, who was also a member of both the Pan-German League and the Eastern Marches Association, thought the proclamation of 5 November had been a deeply foolish act. "The Poles themselves," he judged, "saw the proclamation of the Kingdom [of Poland] as proof not only of our weakness, but also of our stupidity."[96] Rhode was highly critical of both the Kaiser and Bethmann Hollweg's Polish policies, while the Governor-General himself, through his conciliatory policies and "his shameful flight in November 1918 [had] ruined his reputation from Antwerp and Nowogeorgiewsk [Modlin]."[97] At least one attack on Beseler's name was humiliatingly public. On 5 March 1919, Beseler was criticized in the National Assembly by Matthias Erzberger. "It is deeply regrettable," Erzberger told the deputies, "that 16,000 German soldiers and officers [ran] away from Warsaw because 800 poorly armed Poles [formed] a mob." The disarmament and the "none-too-brave conduct . . . of the military governor Beseler" had "contributed to the weak-

ening of Germany's reputation in the east."[98] Beseler was sufficiently moved
by the volume and tone of the criticism directed against him to request that
a formal military investigation into his conduct be opened. The investigation,
conducted by the court of the III Corps, cleared his name. It probably gave
a modicum of comfort to the Governor-General, who died on 20 December
1921, an ill, "broken," and "melancholy" man.[99]

Other critics, hitting closer to the mark, saw the mutinous troops as bearing
responsibility for the shambolic way in which the occupation ended. In July
1919, Walther Reinhardt, the last Prussian Minister of War, told the National
Assembly that the real blame for the embarrassing end of the occupation lay
with the mutinous soldiers of the councils. Because of them "highly valuable military equipment was lost, as was an even greater part of Germany's
reputation." Rising to Beseler's defense, Reinhardt informed the deputies that
the Governor-General had received a message on 11 November from the
Supreme Command that made reference to the "former" occupation regime.
Beseler therefore considered his office dissolved and came back to Germany
as a "retired officer" *(Officier außer Dienst).*[100]

Wolfgang von Kries, too, wrote about the treason of the troops. Like many
observers, he connected Germany's defeat to the "stab in the back" supposedly perpetrated by the revolutionaries in Berlin. However, as of the early
1930s, most of his anger about the way the occupation came to an end was
still directed above all at the mutinous troops:

> Only because most of the German occupation troops, neglecting their
> honor and their duty, cast aside their weapons in an enemy land and,
> without the slightest pretence of an excuse, committed the worst treason
> against their Fatherland, was this shameful end brought about, which,
> moreover, seriously jeopardized the return home of the German troops
> further east and carried the Polish uprising, with all its unhappy con-
> sequences, over the border to Prussia.

It was "bitter," he wrote, that so much effort in occupied Poland had merely
led to the "ruin" of Germany.[101]

Several years after writing these words, Kries requested permission from
the Nazi authorities to publish his account of the Imperial Government-
General and its rule in Poland. (Permission was, for reasons not made clear,
denied.) In this account, Kries had discovered a new culprit for the collapse

of the occupation. "That the failure of Germany's Polish policy led to a shameful collapse of the German occupation in Congress Poland," Kries wrote shortly before the outbreak of the Second World War, "is completely due to the Jewish-Communist revolution in the German homeland and its effects on the eastern territories under occupation."[102] Whether Kries really believed this or was merely trying to curry favor with the authorities in order to have his book published is difficult to say. However, the "stab in the back legend" in its anti-Semitic variety had long been blended, by some observers, into a story linking Jewish conspiracies, German defeat in the war, and the collapse of German rule in the east. In one pamphlet, for example, a writer using the pseudonym "Willehalm" blames an international Jewish conspiracy for engineering both the war and Germany's defeat in order to further its own power. With regard to Poland, Willehalm denounces Bethmann as a dupe and a tool of the conspiracy for committing the "crime" of 5 November. The declaration, according to Willehalm, made peace with Russia impossible, thus supposedly fulfilling the conspiracy's interests. In Willehalm's febrile imag-ination, the Jews also figure as the chief architects of the collapse of the oc-cupation regime in Poland and the subsequent transfer of German weapons to the Polish insurgents—weapons that had, Willehalm complains, been turned against Germany ever since.[103] Blame of the Jews also found its way into an analysis of the collapse conducted internally by the army. In one in-stance, a Jewish military doctor, Cohn, supposedly declared, in front of his comrades shortly after the events of 9 November in Berlin, to have known in advance what was going to happen there, thanks to "his party," and been instructed to prepare a revolution among the German troops in Poland.[104] In addition, a Jewish corporal named Himmelreich was singled out for causing particular trouble and radicalizing the troops.[105]

Germany thus entered a new phase in the history of its relations with Po-land burdened by a host of resentments, some lingering from the nineteenth century, others of a more recent vintage. The host of attitudes and ideologies generated by the Prussian-Polish nationality conflict now combined with the bitterly resented loss of Prussian territory to Poland, the failure of Germa-ny's wartime Polish policies to produce the desired results, and the embar-rassing collapse of the German occupation in Poland. When these grievances became intertwined with Nazi racialist ambitions for the east, the ingredi-ents were in place for a vicious war of enslavement, annihilation, and revenge.

The toxic legacy left by the experience of the Great War and its aftermath in Germany helped ensure that Poland and its citizens, both Gentile and Jew, did not stand a chance when the Germans returned in 1939. It is perhaps possible that a war between the two could have been avoided had Poland co-operated with the Germans. But once the war had begun, it would be waged without restraint.[106]

Conclusion

German Occupation Regimes in Poland,
1915–1945

To view the world wars as two eruptions of the same pathological German imperial ambitions is to miss crucial differences between them. As this book has shown, Imperial Germany's occupation of Poland fundamentally differed, in both its means and ends, from that of the National Socialists. The essential difference between the two occupation governments is clearly revealed by their very different attitudes toward education. The Nazis shut down Warsaw University shortly after Poland's conquest. Subject peoples throughout the occupied east, according to Himmler, were to be afforded only four years of elementary instruction, during which they would be taught rudimentary arithmetic, how to sign their names (though students would not be taught to read), and how to be "hardworking." The virtue and necessity of obedience to the Germans were also to be conveyed in the classroom. Parents in the east who wished to send their children to better schools or to university in Germany had to submit an application to the SS, who would make their decisions based on whether the prospective pupil was "racially impeccable" *(rassisch tadellos)*.[1] In Poland, the pursuit of anything beyond what had been deemed permissible was punishable by death. It does not minimize the hardships suffered under the first occupation government to note that this is a very long way from the Imperial Government-General's insistence that it be allowed to block faculty appointments at the university and its delegation of a functionary to observe the Polish examination commission at work when it carried out the 1916 school-leaving process.

The ultimate fates of two beneficiaries of the first Government-General's educational policies, scholars who had taught at the re-Polonized Warsaw University, illustrate in tragic miniature just how different these regimes were. Józef Siemieński, who had lectured Poland's future bureaucrats on the constitution of 3 May and the intricacies of Polish political history under the Imperial Government-General, had a busy postwar professional life. He served for nearly twenty years as the director of the Main Archive in Warsaw, during which time he continued to give lectures and to write prodigiously, authoring a steady stream of works on archival affairs as well as Polish legal and political history. Siemieński joined the resistance when the Nazis invaded and was arrested by the Gestapo in June 1941, while attending a clandestine meeting at a Warsaw museum. He died in Auschwitz—still an unremarkable Austrian town called Oświęcim when Beseler ruled in Poland—that October. Marceli Handelsman, the young Jewish history professor who had led the Lelewel society, became an eminent scholar after the war. He, too, chose to resist the National Socialist occupation, working in the service of the Home Army and teaching in secret under the name "Maciej Targowski." Betrayed by right-wing Poles, Handelsman was arrested in July 1944 and died the following year in the Dora-Nordhausen concentration camp.[2]

How then should Germany's state-building plan in Poland be interpreted, if not as a prelude to the National Socialist conquest of Europe? It was, above all, an attempt to secure Germany's position in a violently chaotic and dangerously unstable international society, full of threats both ancient (foreign invasion) and modern (the intersection of nationalism with international tensions). This experiment in the creation of international order drew, both consciously and unconsciously, on a set of norms—on those usually unspoken and unwritten but generally shared habits, values, and assumptions that might be called the "constitution" of international society.[3] Germany's state-building plans occurred at a time of profound transition in these norms: the values and habits of the prewar world were in the process of being destroyed, though they were still faintly visible and lingered in European political culture, while the norms of the postwar world were still inchoate and had not yet solidified into a set of universally shared, clearly articulated set of ideas and institutions.

The key uncertainty, from which much else flowed, was where sovereignty would reside in the postwar political world. As James J. Sheehan pointed out in his 2005 presidential address to the American Historical Association, the political history of Europe is, properly considered, less the history of states than of the theory and practice of sovereignty.[4] Both were in profound flux from 1915 to 1918; in terms of the history of sovereignty, Germany's project in Poland is best seen as an experimental way station between the ultimate disappearance of imperial sovereignty and the triumph of the sovereign nation-state. A brief glance at other plans for the postwar political order harbored by other belligerents reveals that Germany's experiment in sovereignty was simply one of many. German plans for Poland, for example, found their near mirror image in Russian Foreign Minister Sazonov's desire to create a satellite Polish state augmented with lands seized from Germany and Austria. Germany's less remarkable plans to annex territory on the German-Polish borderlands, meanwhile, also had their counterpart in Russia, in the General Staff's desire to annex East Prussia up to the Vistula.[5] The Russian Provisional Government's intentions for Poland, meanwhile, bore some resemblance to the Germans'. The March appeal to the Poles held out the promise of new freedoms under Russian sovereignty. And yet the Provisional Government's Minister of War, Aleksander Guchkov, wanted to move quickly to establish a Polish army "imbued with Russian influence and Russian schooling." This force was to provide the foundation for Russian "influence within the borders of the newly built Polish state-organism."[6] In Poland itself, Piłsudski, insofar as a coherent and consistent political program can be ascribed to him, seems to have hoped for the emergence of a central European commonwealth of sorts (inspired by the vanished Rzeczpospolita) with Poland in the role of first among equals.[7] Dmowski and the National Democrats, it will be recalled, had long pushed for the establishment of an autonomous Poland under Russian rule, while Poles loyal to the Habsburg monarchy hoped for a similarly autonomous Poland under that emperor's rule. Such experiments, both intended and actualized, were not limited to eastern Europe; at the highest levels of the French political establishment, both civilian and military, plans to detach the left bank of the Rhine from Germany and create a number of semi-sovereign buffer states between the two countries were not only given serious consideration but became a key component of France's view of postwar Europe, shared by both Foch and Clemenceau.[8] Farther abroad, Britain and France engaged in elaborate intrigues in order to carve up the remains of the Ottoman Empire into spheres of influence. Imperial sovereignty was on the wane, but it had not yet disappeared.

Because the rhetoric of "self-determination" played such a crucial role in shaping the postwar settlement (or at least its ideology), and because the prewar empires did in fact collapse into nation-states, it has long been assumed that emergence of the sovereign nation-state from the ruins of the war was a foregone conclusion. This assumption would have surprised many contemporaries—even those most closely associated with the rhetoric of national self-determination. Alfred Cobban long ago pointed out that few in the belligerent nations actually realized what national self-determination would mean in practice. Woodrow Wilson, for example, believed that national self-determination need not—and, in fact, should not, for the sake of peace—disturb the integrity of the Habsburg Empire (not to mention the fact that it should not be extended in any meaningful way to non-Europeans).[9] Rather than emerging from a clear ideology, the postwar division of central Europe into sovereign states staking their legitimacy on their claims to speak on behalf of a nation arose from several factors. One was the strength of organized nationalist movements in central Europe who were well positioned to advance their ambitions as the empires collapsed. A second was a blending at the Paris Peace Conference of three related but not necessarily inextricable norms that were brought to the conference by various negotiating parties who usually subscribed to one or two of them, but rarely to all three: that small states had a right to exist; that they had a right to be recognized as full equals of larger states; and that sovereignty was, in the final instance, located in the state.[10]

Having considered how Germany's state-building project compared with other experiments in creating international order, the process of contextualizing Beseler and his schemes can also be helped by comparing the Imperial Government-General to other German occupation regimes. Certainly its more unsavory aspects were widely shared, in particular the economic policies that amounted to little more than the wholesale plundering of the occupied lands' resources. Yet it is also important to note that wherever occupation regimes ruled over territory in which the Germans hoped to exercise influence after the war, at least *some* concessions to nationalistic demands were made by the occupiers—not necessarily because they found these demands inherently just, but because they felt they had to. This is true in two important cases. The first was in Belgium, where the Germans supported and encouraged the aspirations of the Flemish population (who had been discriminated against by the dominant French-speaking Walloons before the war) for cultural and political autonomy. German support included, notably, the introduction of Flemish as the language of the University of Ghent.[11] Similar trends were observable in the Baltic lands where Ludendorff ruled. Many of the Germans' policies there can be seen as an attempt to win Lithuanian support—at Polish expense—for German ambitions. It is very difficult to say if any of these schemes held a chance of success, given that Germany's defeat rendered the question moot. In Poland, however, it is likely that Beseler's plans would never have found widespread support. Germany was simply too unpopular in Poland, and the opposition there (in the form of National Democracy and the PPS) too well organized, to make it conceivable that a German-dominated Polish state would have been stable and durable.

Nationalism was just one of the many forces threatening to violently undo the imperial order in central Europe before and during the war. The Revolution of 1905 had suggested that the twilight of empires would be troubled; the Balkan Wars of 1912 and 1913 had given conclusive proof that their collapse would be violent; and the Great War had finally shown that it would not be localized. Once the war broke out, the latent tensions in central Europe were not only given free rein, but accelerated. In addition, new tensions would arise, as with, for example, the emergence of the Bolsheviks. In this sense, the Great War acted as both accelerator and generator for the many sources of instability in central Europe in the early twentieth century. Many of the region's most intractable conflicts emerged before the war, became intertwined with Germany's occupation policies during the war, festered and were given new forms after the war, and reached an awful dénouement in the era of the Second World War and its aftermath.[12] The Ukrainians are an example of this. A national movement, even if not yet mass-based, had emerged by the Revolution of 1905 at the latest, and harbored ambitions irreconcilable with those of Polish nationalists (as noted in the introduction, the Polish governor of Galicia was assassinated by a Ukrainian); the Germans, it was shown in Chapter 6, became unhappily entangled in this dispute when the treaty of Brest-Litovsk revealed to them that the Polish and Ukrainian

"Questions" concealed within them an irreconcilable "Chełm Question." After the war, the Polish state's relations with its Ukrainian minority were poor to say the least and involved attempts at forced assimilation along with the internment of Ukrainian rebels in camps. When the Soviets arrived in 1939 to gain their vengeance for their loss of the 1919 Polish Soviet war, they allowed Ukrainians in the east to rise up in a "revolutionary struggle" against their Polish class enemies, resulting in widespread murders.[13] Once the Nazi invasion of the Soviet Union began, the region as a whole descended into violence on a scale scarcely imaginable; this included the Polish and Ukrainian Partisan movements, who killed each other (and each other's civilians) at the same time they fought a host of other ideological and national enemies. This unhappy period of national conflict was brought to a brutal conclusion with Operation Vistula, the 1947 ethnic cleansing of the Ukrainians by the Communist regime in Poland. This is not, incidentally, to say that all people in this period were involved in political movements or became radical nationalists or Bolsheviks. But indifference to politics is a luxury, and one not afforded those who live in collapsing states, particularly when that collapse becomes violent, and when the visions for what should replace them are so fundamentally different and incompatible. Perhaps most people were not interested in politics from 1905 to 1947, but politics, unfortunately, were very interested in them.

Unlike the French and British in the Near East, Germany during the Great War could not watch this "rolling implosion" of empires (to expand upon Jonathan Gumz's evocative description of what happened to Russian sovereignty after mid-1915[14]) from a comfortable distance. Germany's Polish state was meant, in part, to prevent this implosion from rolling into its Polish borderlands. Even the notorious plans to create a Germanized "border strip" are better seen in this historical context, rather than one determined by a view of what was to come under the National Socialists. The ethnic cleansing foreseen by the border strip's champions (including Beseler's combination of voluntary migration and assimilation) was an attempt to deal with the specific problem created in imperial "shatterzones" by the creation of nation-states where they had not existed before and where they could not be created without destroying older states: namely, the fusion of foreign and domestic threats into a mixture of unusual volatility. This was a problem that existed throughout southern and central Europe and was by no means unique to the

German-Polish borderlands. Nor was the potential response to it envisioned by the "border strip's" proponents entirely unique either.[15] Most German views of how and why to create a *Grenzstreifen* bore little resemblance to Nazi visions of racially motivated conquest and murder; they do, however, strongly prefigure the internationally sanctioned transfer of Turks and Greeks under the terms of the 1923 Treaty of Lausanne. Much like sovereignty, the precise moral and intellectual place that ethnic cleansing held in the constitution of international society was uncertain at best; the terrible practice of uprooting and deporting masses of people would remain an acceptable, if unfortunate, instrument of international politics until the final expulsions of the Germans from eastern Europe after the Second World War. "I am not alarmed by the prospect of the disentanglement of populations," Winston Churchill told the House of Commons in December 1944, "nor even by these large transferences, which are more possible in modern conditions than they ever were before. The disentanglement of populations which took place between Greece and Turkey after the last war . . . was in many ways a success."[16] (Whether the horrible expulsions and transfers after the Second World War were also a "success" in that they ended the long, violent twilight of empires—at a very steep price—is a deeply troubling question; but may, nonetheless, be one worth asking.)

Finally, how the German occupation of the First World War affected post-1918 German-Polish relations up to and including the Second World War is perhaps the largest question raised by this book. In a broad political sense, the war's outcome precisely reversed the parameters of the prewar Polish Question for Germany. Germany no longer had a sizable Polish minority whose loyalty it doubted and who, Germany feared, harbored irredentist plans to unite with their co-nationals in other states. Poland, however, did have a sizable German minority whose loyalty it doubted and who, Poland feared, harbored irredentist plans to unite with their co-nationals in other states. Just as the prewar Polish Question was one in which foreign and domestic policy blurred, so the interwar question of the place of the Germans in Poland was a question with both international and domestic dimensions.[17] This was a profound source of international instability throughout the interwar years, and one that helped provide Adolf Hitler with the combustible material he needed to set the continent ablaze.

The occupation and its embarrassing collapse, combined with the award of German territory to the Polish state after the war and the dismal relations between the two countries from 1918 on, generated intense German hatreds for Poland. As Gerhard Weinberg has noted, one of the salient characteristics of Weimar political culture was that everyone—liberal or conservative, radical or moderate—loathed and despised Poland.[18] While earlier hostilities certainly helped nourish these hatreds, it must be borne in mind that one of the Eastern Marches Association's goals had been to spread an awareness of the "Polish peril" among the great mass of Germans, who they believed (correctly) to be mostly indifferent to the Poles and the Polish Question. This was certainly not the case after the war, which accomplished what the Association's pastors and schoolteachers could not: the transformation of general indifference to Poland into generalized hatred. When German armies arrived back in Poland in 1939, they carried with them a toxic combination of long-existent antipathies to Poland, anger generated by the First World War and the Treaty of Versailles, and, maybe most fatally, Nazi racial theories to blend it all together and make the most brutal of all potential "solutions" to the new Polish Question intellectually conceivable as well as generally desirable. Combined with the brutalizing effects of the First World War in general, and the way that war made large-scale violence seem normal, the effects for Poland were catastrophic.[19] "I would . . . prefer it if there were <u>Germans</u> living here," Beseler had once confided in a letter to his wife, "but there are Poles here, and you can't chase them all away or kill them all, so you've got to find a way to live with them somehow."[20] The vast cultural gulf that divides the two occupations, separated by just over twenty years in time but an infinity in terms of what was conceivable, is succinctly summed up in this one sentence.

As for the long-term effects of the occupation on Poland as well as its minorities, a few tentative observations can be offered, with potential promise for future explorations. The German occupation of the Great War was an event with profound consequences for twentieth-century Polish history. With regard to the emergence of the Polish state, the devastation of Germany's economic policies must be weighed against their more positive institutional policies when determining if Germany's occupation ultimately harmed or helped this process. For too long, the emergence of a Polish state after the war has been taken for granted, the just and wholly natural outcome of the collapse of the partitioning powers, from whose grasp some eternal Poland freed itself when the opportunity arose. The extraordinary will to power of Piłsudski is a necessary, but not nearly sufficient explanation for what must be the infinitely more complicated story of how the new Polish polity was welded together from component parts long become disparate. Perhaps the legacy of the occupation may help explain this phenomenon, which was far more improbable than inevitable. Even the Germans' ruinous economic policies had unintended consequences that may have helped this process. To aid in their extraction of resources, for example, the occupiers improved Poland's road and rail network, improvements that served the interests of new masters when the Germans left and Polish sovereignty was restored.[21]

As for the cultural imprint left by the occupiers, a cursory survey of the evidence suggests that the period was recalled very differently in Poland than in Germany. There is a painting that hangs today in Warsaw's army museum, by an obscure Polish artist named Stanisław Bagieński, which celebrates the 11 November disarming of the occupiers. In it, valiant Polish soldiers swarm over a German military compound in Warsaw as its humiliated occupants file out; an elegantly dressed woman watches the action as she hurries by clutching a child's hand. At the painting's center is a German soldier standing with his hands at his sides as a Pole reaches into his coat, probably removing his pistol. The German soldiers have an almost comical look, with their large mustaches, downcast eyes, and dejected faces. Their spiked helmets, no longer objects of reluctant admiration, as they were to Jankowski in 1915, seem faintly ridiculous. The painting is dated 1939. Bagieński had no way of knowing that that very year the fury unleashed by Germany on Poland would make his painting seem as distant as one of Matejko's coronations or battle scenes.

At the level of individual behavior, the post-1939 course of events in central Europe must have been, to some degree, conditioned by the experience of the first occupation, which would have been within living memory for many of the region's inhabitants. There is something of Bagieński's painting's spirit in an underground Polish publication, the *Biuletyn Informacyjny*, issued in 1940, that exhorted the Poles to resist the new occupation; after all, they had been eminently successful in 1918, so there was no reason why they could not be now.[22] This was dangerous advice, based on a deeply flawed comparison between two historical epochs that, though separated by only two decades, were far more dissimilar than alike. Likewise, historians of central European Jews have long been puzzled by the fact that more Jews did not realize what the Nazis had in store for them, despite what seem to have been relatively clear signals emanating from the Nazi regime, and decide to take their chances with the Soviets.[23] But some of these Jews had lived their formative years in a very different Europe, a Europe in which the Russian army had conducted pogroms and the German army had stopped them. Obviously, a great deal had changed, but perhaps these people carefully weighed their life experiences against the hateful rhetoric and policies of the Nazis, and wondered, as German troops once again approached their towns and cities, which of the two was the "real" Germany.

Twenty years after Beseler fled Warsaw, the western Allies discovered that the peace of Europe still depended on the maintenance of stability in Poland, though it was now up to them to preserve that stability. Their reluctance to go to war in 1939 suggests they had learned a painful lesson—one brilliantly articulated, in an earlier era, by Carl von Clausewitz. Writing in the wake of the 1830 Uprising, Clausewitz chided those who supported the Polish rebels, suggesting that they did not quite understand what was at stake. "We can only say flatly," he writes,

> that this moralistic attitude towards the question of Poland's restoration is unjustified . . . People enjoy this sort of enthusiasm, like the sentimental suffering of a melodrama, and they give in to the diversion because they think it costs them nothing; because they only see two players, Russia and Poland, separated from them by the proscenium; and because they do not suspect that they are part of the play, indeed that they will have to pay for the entire performance.[24]

In the late 1930s, the western Allies discovered that they were indeed part of the play. The supposedly precious right of national self-determination of peoples suddenly became, instead, a faraway struggle between peoples about whom, the western Allies decided, they actually knew nothing. The pious denunciations of the Germans' actions in Poland that had been issued by the Allies during the Great War did not, in 1939, translate into an urgent desire to defend that state when it was brutally invaded by the Nazis and Soviets.

With that invasion, the "rolling collapse" of central Europe once again embroiled Britain and the continent in a nightmarish war, the sheer scale of
which rapidly obscured the fact that it had initially been waged over the question of what would become of the "poorly sealed tomb" of Poland. Six years
later, in the wake of unimaginable brutality, millions of deaths and expulsions, the destruction of roadways, bridges, rail lines, and thousands of buildings, the redrawing of its borders, and the establishment of a Soviet-controlled
Communist dictatorship, Poland's tomb seemed, at last, firmly sealed.
Its central role in first challenging and then bringing down Communism in
central Europe, however, revealed that era of foreign domination to be as
temporary and as impossible to maintain as the rest—as well as the enduring
power of the Polish Question to reach far beyond the confines within which
its neighbors have long sought to keep it.

Abbreviations

Notes

Acknowledgments

Index

Abbreviations

AAN	Archiwum Akt Nowych (Archive of Modern Records)
AGAD	Archiwum Główne Akt Dawnych (Central Archive of Historical Records)
APAN	Archiwum Polskiej Akademii Nauk (Archive of the Polish Academy of Sciences)
BAB-L	Bundesarchiv Berlin-Lichterfelde
BAK	Bundesarchiv Koblenz
BA-MA	Bundesarchiv-Militärarchiv, Freiburg-im-Breisgau
CKN	Centralny Komitet Narodowy (Central National Committee)
GStA PK	Geheimes Staatsarchiv Preußischer Kulturbesitz
HIA	Hoover Institution Archives
NKN	Naczelny Komitet Narodowy (Supreme National Committee)
POW	Polska Organizacja Wojskowa (Polish Military Organization)
PPS	Polska Partia Socjalistyczna (Polish Socialist Party)
TNW	Towarzystwo Naukowe Warszawskie (Scientific Society of Warsaw)
TRS	Tymczasowa Rada Stanu (Provisional Council of State)
WWC	Włodzimierz Wiskowski Collection

Notes

Introduction

1. Mieczysław Jankowski, "Pierwsze dni okupacji niemieckiej," in *Warszawa w Pamiętnikach Pierwszej Wojny Światowej*, ed. Krzystof Dunin-Wąsowicz (Warsaw: Państwowy Instytut Wydawniczy, 1971), 135.

2. That is, that part of the former Polish-Lithuanian Commonwealth annexed by Russia after the Napoleonic Wars. It was also known as simply Poland, the Kingdom of Poland, the Congress Kingdom, and, in the latter part of the nineteenth century, the Vistula Territories. Throughout this book it will usually be called either Russian Poland or, on occasion, Congress Poland or just Poland. The terms "Russian Poland" and "Congress Poland" are unfortunate in many ways, but the terms are useful in that they remind us of two key points: (1) that the territories in central Europe that could plausibly be called Polish were located in more than one state and (2) that no independent Polish state existed in Europe in the period between the Congress of Vienna and the Great War.

3. Cologne: Böhlau, 1958. Conze's primary concern is the high politics of the Polish Question during the war. One of the few works on the occupations of the period that gives equal attention to the western and eastern fronts is Reinhold Zilch's *Okkupation und Währung im Ersten Weltkrieg: Die deutsche Besatzungspolitik im Belgien und Russisch-Polen, 1914–1918* (Goldbach: Keip, 1994). A number of recent essays also note the striking lack of attention given to this intriguing chapter of Germany's (and Poland's) wartime experience. The title of Andreas Hofmann's article "Die vergessene Okkupation: Lodz im Ersten Weltkrieg" (in *Deutsche, Juden, Polen: Geschichte einer wechselvollen Beziehung im 20. Jahrhundert*, ed. Andrea Löw, Kerstin Robusch, and Stefanie Walter [Frankfurt: Campus, 2004], 59–77), which briefly explores how the forces of occupation

interacted with local politics and society in that city, is all too accurate. See also the summary overview of German occupations in both the First and Second World Wars by Polish scholar Eugeniusz Cezary Król, "Besatzungsherrschaft in Polen im Ersten und Zweiten Weltkrieg. Charakteristik und Wahrnehmung," in *Erster Weltkrieg, Zweiter Weltkrieg: Ein Vergleich,* ed. Bruno Thoß and Hans-Erich Volkmann (Paderborn: Schöningh, 2002), 577–591. The standard Polish works on the period are Jerzy Holzer and Jan Molenda's *Polska w Pierwszej Wojnie Światowej,* 3rd ed. (Warsaw: Wiedza Powszechna, 1973), and Janusz Pajewski, *Odbudowa państwa polskiego 1914–1918* (Warsaw: Państwowe Wydawnictwo Naukowe, 1978). While limited to Warsaw, Krzystof Dunin-Wąsowicz's *Warszawa w czasie Pierwszej Wojny Światowej* (Warsaw: Państwowy Institut Wydawniczy, 1974) is nonetheless invaluable. Also useful are the series of volumes edited by Marceli Handelsman and produced under the auspices of the Carnegie Endowment for International Peace, especially vol. 1, *La Pologne, sa vie économique et sociale pendant la guerre* (Paris: Les Presses Universitaires de France, 1933). Volumes 2 through 4 are in Polish only and are much harder to find: vol. 2, *Historja [sic] społeczna* (Warsaw: Towarzystwo Badania Zagadnień Międzynarodowych, 1932 [sic]); vol. 3, *Historja ekonomiczna* (1936); vol. 4, *Finanse* (1939). The overview of the Polish historiography of the period in Marta Polsakiewicz, "Spezifika deutscher Besatzungspolitik in Warschau 1914–1916," *Zeitschrift für Ostmitteleuropa-Forschung* 58, no. 4 (2009): 503–504, is exceptionally helpful.

4. Polish scholar Arkadiusz Stempin's postdoctoral dissertation *(Habilitationsschrift)* on the German occupation of Poland during the First World War, which marks an important contribution to the Polish-language scholarship on the period, was published just as I was finalizing this manuscript: *Próba "moralnego podboju" Polski przez Cesarstwo Niemieckie w latach I Wojny Światowej* (Warsaw: Wydawnictwo Neriton, 2013). The same is true of Włodzimierz Borodziej's and Maciej Górny's promising new survey, *Nasza wojna. Tom I: Imperia, 1912–1916* (Warsaw: Foksal, 2014). Recent political and diplomatic histories of the war and occupation by Polish scholars include Damian Szymczak, *Między Habsburgami a Hohenzollernami: Rywalizacja niemiecko—austro-węgierska w okresie I Wojny Światowej a odbudowa państwa polskiego* (Kraków: Avalon, 2009), and Piotr Mikietyński, *Niemiecka droga ku Mitteleuropie* (Kraków: Historia Iagellonica, 2009), though the latter only covers the period up to 1916. Two Polish monographs deserve special mention: Jan Snopko's exhaustively researched and well-written book on the Polish Legions, *Finał epopei Legionów Polskich, 1916–1918* (Białystok: Wydawnictwo Universytetu w Białymstoku, 2008), is perhaps the single best Polish monograph dealing with the period of the Great War, while Konrad Zieliński's work on Poles and Jews during the war, *Stosunko polsko-żydowskie na ziemiach Królestwa Polskiego w czasie Pierwszej Wojny Światowej* (Lublin: Wydawnictwo Universytetu Marii Curie-Skłodowskiej, 2005), is invaluable.

Among German scholars, the economic policies of the occupation regime and their impact have proven to be popular themes. Christian Westerhoff's book on forced labor in the occupied east, *Zwangsarbeit im Ersten Weltkrieg: Deutsche Arbeitskräfte im besetzten Polen und Litauen 1914–1918* (Paderborn: Ferdinand Schöningh, 2012), has rapidly established itself as the standard work on the subject. For a more comprehensive view of the economic policies of both Germany's and Austria's occupation regimes in Poland, see Stephan Lehnstaedt, "Dwie (różne) okupacje? Polityka gospodarcza Niemiec i Austro-Węgier w Królestwie Polskim w latach 1915–1918," *Dzieje Najnowsze* 45 (2013): 17–33. For other aspects of the occupation, see the following articles in vol. 58, no. 4 of *Zeitschrift für Ostmitteleuropa-Forschung* (2009): on Beseler, Robert Spät, "Für eine gemeinsame deutsch-polnische Zukunft? Hans Hartwig von Beseler als Generalgouverneur in Polen, 1915–1918" (469–500); on Warsaw during the first two years of the war, see Marta Polsakiewicz, "Spezifika deutscher Besatzungspolitik in Warschau 1914–1916" (501–537).

5. Hofmann, "Die vergessene Okkupation."

6. An overview of the state of the scholarship on the First World War can be found in John Horne, ed., *A Companion to World War I* (Chichester, West Sussex: Wiley-Blackwell, 2010), as well as in Alan Kramer, "Recent Historiography of the First World War," parts I and II, *Journal of Modern European History* 12 (2014): 5–27, 155–174. In addition, the International Society for First World War Studies brings together scholars from all over the world, from graduate students to the field's most eminent scholars, in an ongoing, transnational, multidisciplinary scholarly conversation on the war. Its journal, *First World War Studies,* publishes articles and essays on all aspects of the war and its history. Its conference publications are also helpful for gaining a sense of the field's current contours: James Kitchen, Alisa Miller, and Laura Rowe, eds., *Other Combatants, Other Fronts: Competing Histories of the First World War* (Newcastle upon Tyne: Cambridge Scholars, 2011), and Jennifer Keene and Michael Neiberg, eds., *Finding Common Ground: New Directions in First World War Studies* (Leiden: Brill, 2011). Examples of recent work and the general trend toward social and cultural history include Alan Kramer, *Dynamic of Destruction: Culture and Mass Killing in the First World War* (Oxford: Oxford University Press, 2007); Alexander Watson, *Enduring the Great War: Combat, Morale and Collapse in the German and British Armies, 1914–1918* (Cambridge: Cambridge University Press, 2008); Michael Neiberg, *Dance of the Furies: Europe and the Outbreak of World War I* (Cambridge, Mass.: Harvard University Press, 2011); Tammy Proctor, *Civilians in a World at War, 1914–1918* (New York: New York University Press, 2010); and Xu Guoqi, *Strangers on the Western Front: Chinese Laborers in the Great War* (Cambridge, Mass.: Harvard University Press, 2011). The question of the origins of the war has been recently revisited in Christopher Clark's brilliant *Sleepwalkers: How Europe Went to War*

in 1914 (London: Allen Lane, 2012). Issues such as memory and commemoration continue to be the center of a lively and vigorous branch of Great War scholarship: see, for example, Benjamin Ziemann, *Contested Commemorations: Republican War Veterans and Weimar Political Culture* (Cambridge: Cambridge University Press, 2013); Leonard V. Smith, *The Embattled Self: French Soldiers' Testimony of the Great War* (Ithaca, N.Y.: Cornell University Press, 2007).

7. Vejas Liulevicius, *War Land on the Eastern Front: Culture, National Identity and German Occupation in World War I* (Cambridge: Cambridge University Press, 2000), 3. There are, however, signs of a shift, and the war beyond the western front has been the subject of several recent books and essay collections. The collection of articles about the eastern front edited by Jochen Böhler, Włodzimierz Borodziej, and Joachim von Puttkamer and produced under the auspices of the Imre Kertész Kolleg in Jena, *Legacies of Violence: Eastern Europe's First World War* (Munich: Oldenbourg Verlag, 2014), is an important contribution to the field. Since the Kolleg is a major intellectual center for the study of German and eastern European history, the appearance of this work may herald a wider shift in attention toward the eastern front. Other works on the war outside France and Belgium include Gerhard Groß, ed., *Der Osten—Die vergessene Front 1914/15* (Paderborn: Schöningh 2006); Christoph Mick, *Kriegserfahrungen in einer multiethnischen Stadt: Lemberg 1914–1947* (Wiesbaden: Harrassowitz, 2010); Mark Thompson, *The White War: Life and Death on the Italian Front, 1915–1919* (New York: Basic Books, 2008); Eric Lohr, *Nationalizing the Russian Empire: The Campaign against Enemy Aliens during World War I* (Cambridge, Mass.: Harvard University Press, 2003); Michael Reynolds, *Shattering Empires: The Clash and Collapse of the Ottoman and Russian Empires, 1908–1918* (Cambridge: Cambridge University Press, 2011); Mustafa Aksakal, *The Ottoman Road to War in 1914* (Cambridge: Cambridge University Press, 2008); and Sean McMeekin, *The Russian Origins of the First World War* (Cambridge, Mass.: Harvard University Press, 2011). A partial exception to the general inattention to the eastern front is the field of operational history, in which a number of new works have appeared recently: Richard Hall, *Balkan Breakthrough: The Battle of Dobro Pole 1918* (Bloomington: Indiana University Press, 2010); Timothy Dowling, *The Brusilov Offensive* (Bloomington: Indiana University Press, 2008); and Richard DiNardo, *Breakthrough: The Gorlice-Tarnow Campaign, 1915* (Santa Barbara, Calif.: Praeger, 2010).

8. Düsseldorf: Droste, 1961; 3rd ed. pub. 1964. English version, New York: W. W. Norton, 1967.

9. Roger Chickering, "Imperial Germany at War, 1914–1918," in *Imperial Germany: A Historiographical Companion,* ed. Roger Chickering (Westport, Conn.: Greenwood Press, 1996), 489–491.

10. James J. Sheehan, "Paradigm Lost? The 'Sonderweg' Revisited," in *Transnationale Geschichte: Themen, Tendenzen und Theorien,* ed. Gunilla Budde,

Sebastian Conrad, and Oliver Janz (Göttingen: Vandenhoeck & Ruprecht, 2006), 152.

11. Wolfgang Mommsen, "The Debate on German War Aims," *Journal of Contemporary History* 1, no. 3 (July 1966): 47–72, which is restrained in tone but unmistakably critical of Fischer, provides an excellent introduction to *Griff nach der Weltmacht*'s main arguments and gives a good sense of the controversy stirred up by the book's publication. For more overviews of the origins of the war and Germany's role in them, see Niall Ferguson, "Germany and the Origins of the First World War: New Perspectives," *Historical Journal* 35, no. 3 (September 1992): 725–752, and Samuel Williamson and Ernest May, "An Identity of Opinion: Historians and July 1914," *Journal of Modern History* 79, no. 2 (June 2007): especially 359–366. McMeekin's *The Russian Origins of the First World War* contains an excellent discussion of Fischer's work and an analysis of its oddly enduring power. Together with Christopher Clark's *Sleepwalkers* and McMeekin's most recent book, *July 1914, The Russian Origins* gives some hope that the era of a deeply held belief in exclusive, or at least preponderant, German war guilt is over, though it may be too deeply entrenched, and too inextricably fused with the emotions raised by the Second World War, to ever wholly disappear.

12. Lübeck: Matthiesen, 1960. Also cited quite often as a solid buttress of the Fischer thesis, at least as far as it concerns eastern Europe, is Werner Basler's *Deutschlands Annexionspolitik in Polen und im Baltikum 1914–1918* (Berlin: Rütten & Loening, 1962).

13. Geiss, *Der polnische Grenzstreifen*, 148–149; quote from 148. For an evaluation of the importance of the Grenzstreifen in German history, see Wolfgang Mommsen, "Der 'polnische Grenzstreifen.' Anfänge der 'völkischen Flurbereinigung' und der Umsiedlungspolitik," in Mommsen, *Der Erste Weltkrieg: Anfang vom Ende des bürgerlichen Zeitalters* (Frankfurt: Fischer, 2004), 118–136. Mommsen is once again skeptical of the attempt to paint the civilian leadership (especially Bethmann) as rabid imperialists, but he accepts that the horrors to come in the Nazi east are clearly visible in the plans for the Grenzstreifen.

14. See, for example, Mark Mazower, *Hitler's Empire: How the Nazis Ruled Europe* (New York: Penguin, 2008), 24.

15. For recent critiques of this view, see Tara Zahra, "Looking East: East Central European Borderlands in German History and Historiography," *History Compass* 3 (2005): 1–25; Winson Chu, Jesse Kauffman, and Michael Meng, "A Sonderweg through Eastern Europe? The Varieties of German Rule in Poland during the Two World Wars," *German History* 31 (September 2013): 318–344.

16. Henry Cord Meyer, *Drang nach Osten: Fortunes of a Slogan-Concept in German Slavic Relations, 1849–1990* (New York: Peter Lang, 1996); Wolfgang Wippermann, *Der "Deutsche Drang nach Osten": Ideologie und Wirklichkeit eines politischen Schlagwortes* (Darmstadt: Wissenschaftliche Buchgesellschaft, 1981).

17. Vejas Liulevicius, *The German Myth of the East: 1800 to the Present* (Oxford: Oxford University Press, 2009); Gregor Thum, ed., *Traumland Osten: Deutsche Bilder vom östlichen Europa im 20. Jahrhundert* (Göttingen: Vandenhoeck & Ruprecht, 2006); and Wolfgang Wippermann, *Die Deutschen und der Osten: Feindbild und Traumland* (Darmstadt: Primus, 2007).

18. Key works include Kristin Kopp, *Germany's Wild East: Constructing Poland as Colonial Space* (Ann Arbor: University of Michigan Press, 2012); Robert L. Nelson, ed., *Germans, Poland, and Colonial Expansion to the East* (New York: Palgrave Macmillan, 2009); David Blackbourn, "Das Kaiserreich transnational. Eine Skizze," in *Das Kaiserreich transnational: Deutschland in der Welt 1871–1914*, ed. Sebastian Conrad and Jürgen Osterhammel (Göttingen: Vandenhoeck & Ruprecht, 2004), 302–324; Philipp Ther, "Deutsche Geschichte als imperiale Geschichte: Polen, slawophone Minderheiten und das Kaiserreich als kontinentales Empire," in Conrad and Osterhammel, *Das Kaiserreich transnational*, 129–148; and Ulrike Jureit, *Das Ordnen von Räumen: Territorium und Lebensraum im 19. und 20. Jahrhundert* (Hamburg: Hamburger Edition, 2012). For a critique, see Chu, Kauffman, and Meng, "A Sonderweg," and Jesse Kauffman, "The Colonial U-Turn; Why Poland Is Not Germany's India," in *Cultural Landscapes: Transatlantische Perspektiven auf Wirkungen und Auswirkungen deutscher Kultur und Geschichte im östlichen Europa*, ed. Andrew Demshuk and Tobias Weger (forthcoming).

19. William Hagen, *Germans, Poles, and Jews: The Nationality Conflict in the Prussian East, 1772–1914* (Chicago: University of Chicago Press, 1980); Martin Broszat, *Zweihundert Jahre deutsche Polenpolitik* (Munich: Ehrenwirt, 1963; rev. ed., Frankfurt am Main: Surkamp, 1972) are exemplary. Richard Blanke, *Prussian Poland in the German Empire* (Boulder, Colo.: East European Monographs, 1981) is more cautious about drawing lines of continuity.

20. As evidenced, not least, by a recent special issue of *First World War Studies* (vol. 4, no. 1, March 2013) devoted entirely to occupations. For an overview of the current state of the field, see Sophie de Schaepdrijver's introductory essay, "Military Occupation, Political Imaginations, and the First World War" (1–5). An important recent work that deals with occupations, though not exclusively, is Proctor, *Civilians in a World at War*.

21. See note 7. Earlier works on OberOst, which has, for some reason, attracted more attention than the Imperial Government-General, are Wiktor Sukiennicki, *Ober Ost Land: Ludendorff's "Another Kingdom," 1915–1918* (Rome: Institutum Historicum Polonicum, 1978), and Abba Strazhas, *Deutsche Ostpolitik im Ersten Weltkrieg: Der Fall Ober Ost, 1915–1917* (Wiesbaden: Harrassowitz, 1993).

22. Liulevicius, *War Land,* 162.

23. Westerhoff, *Zwangsarbeit,* as well as "'A Kind of Siberia': German Labour and Occupation Policies in Poland and Lithuania during the First World War," *First*

World War Studies 4, no. 1 (March 2013): 51–59; on other eastern occupations, see Mark von Hagen, *War in a European Borderland: Occupations and Occupation Plans in Galicia and Ukraine, 1914–1918* (Seattle: University of Washington Press, 2007); Jonathan Gumz, *The Resurrection and Collapse of Empire in Habsburg Serbia, 1914–1918* (Cambridge: Cambridge University Press, 1914–1918); Wolfram Dornik and Peter Lieb, "Misconceived *Realpolitik* in a Failing State: The Political and Economic Fiasco of the Central Powers in the Ukraine, 1918," *First World War Studies* 4, no. 1 (March 2013): 111–124; David Hamlin, "The Fruits of Occupation: Food and Germany's Occupation of Romania in the First World War," *First World War Studies* 4, no. 1 (March 2013): 81–95; and Lisa Mayerhofer, *Zwischen Freund und Feind—Deutsche Besatzung in Rumänien 1916–1918* (Munich: Martin Meidenbauer, 2010).

24. New Haven, Conn.: Yale University Press, 2001.

25. Just how central the continuity thesis is to the book was the subject of a lively debate between a generally well-disposed but not uncritical reviewer and the book's authors. See Margaret Lavinia Anderson, "A German Way of War?," *German History* 22, no. 2 (May 2004): 254–258; John Horne and Alan Kramer, "German Atrocities in the First World War: A Response," *German History* 24, no. 1 (February 2006): 118–121; and Margaret Lavinia Anderson, "How German Is It?," *German History* 24, no. 1 (February 2006): 122–126. I am grateful to Sophie de Schaepdrijver for many things, among them pointing out the fact that Horne and Kramer's book is, properly considered, a book about an invasion, not an occupation.

26. Jeff Lipkes, *Rehearsals: The German Army in Belgium, August 1914* (Leuven: Leuven University Press, 2007); Annette Becker, *Les cicatrices rouges, 14–18: France et Belgique occupées* (Paris: Fayard, 2010); Philippe Nivet, *La France occupée 1914–1918* (Paris: Armand Colin, 2011); Helen McPhail, *The Long Silence: Civilian Life under the German Occupation of Northern France, 1914–1918* (London: I. B. Tauris, 1999). The standard work on the Germans in Belgium, Sophie de Schaepdrijver's *La Belgique et la Première Guerre Mondiale* (Brussels: Archives & Musée de la Littérature, 2004), is less concerned with German "barbarism" than with the central importance of the war in the place of Belgian history. Jens Thiel, "Between Recruitment and Forced Labour: The Radicalization of German Labour Policy in Occupied Belgium and Northern France," *First World War Studies* 4, no. 1 (March 2013): 41–46 is, like Westerhoff (*Zwangsarbeit*, cited above), cautious in his approach to the question of continuities but nonetheless focused—understandably and to good effect—on the harshest aspects of German occupation in the west.

27. Pajewski, *Odbudowa*, 9–14. For classic formulations of the Communist-era interpretation of the Great War, see Holzer and Molenda, *Polska*, 9, and Leon Grosfeld, *Polityka Państw centralnych wobec sprawy polskiej w latach pierwszej wojny światowej* (Warsaw: Państwowe Wydawnictwo Naukowe, 1962), 322.

28. Grosfeld, *Polityka,* 187.

29. See note 4, to which should be added the works of Jerzy Pająk, especially *Od autonomii do niepodległości: Kształtowanie się postaw politycznych i narodowych społeczeństwa Galicji w warunkach Wielkiej Wojny, 1914–1918* (Kielce: Wydawnictwo Universytetu Jana Kochanowskiego, 2012).

30. Robert Blobaum, "Warsaw's Forgotten War," *Remembrance and Solidarity Studies* 2 (2014): 185–207.

31. Other works that posit the Great War and the postwar era as radical turning points are Gregor Thum, "Mythische Landschaften: Das Bild vom 'deutschen Osten' und die Zäsuren des 20. Jahrhunderts," in Thum, *Traumland Osten,* 181–211; and Annemarie Sammartino, *The Impossible Border: Germany and the East, 1914–1922* (Ithaca, N.Y.: Cornell University Press, 2010).

32. Neiberg, *Dance of the Furies,* 8, 202–207, 234–237; Stéphane Audoin-Rouzeau and Annette Becker, *14–18: Understanding the Great War* (New York: Hill and Wang, 2002), 102–103.

33. Michael Geyer, "Zwischen Krieg und Nachkrieg—die deutsche Revolution 1918/19 im Zeichen blockierter Transnationalität," in *Die vergessene Revolution von 1918/19,* ed. Alexander Gallus (Göttingen: Vandenhoeck & Ruprecht, 2009), 187–222.

34. John Horne, introduction to *A Companion to World War I,* xv. Jörn Leonhard has more recently suggested 1908 to 1923; that is, from the Bosnia crisis to the Treaty of Lausanne: "Legacies of Violence: Eastern Europe's First World War—a Commentary from a Comparative Perspective," in Böhler, Borodziej, and von Puttkamer, *Legacies of Violence,* 322.

35. See Alexander Prusin's startling and excellent *The Lands Between: Conflict in the East European Borderlands, 1870–1992* (Oxford: Oxford University Press, 2010), and Werner Benecke, "Die Revolution des Jahres 1905 in der Geschichte Polens," in *Russland 1905: Perspektiven auf die erste Russische Revolution,* ed. Martin Aust and Ludwig Steindorff (Frankfurt: Peter Lang, 2007), 9–21.

36. See the title of Timothy Snyder's influential book on violence in the region: *Bloodlands: Europe between Hitler and Stalin* (New York: Basic Books, 2010).

37. Zahra, "Looking East"; Liulevicius's *War Land* at times comes close to this position.

38. Geyer, "Zwischen Krieg und Nachkrieg," 187–222.

39. Thanks to Ute Planert and James Retallack for allowing me to participate in the conference they convened at the University of Toronto in May 2013, "Decades of Reconstruction: Postwar Societies, Economies, and International Relations from the 18th to the 20th Century," which was invaluable for helping me to think through some of these issues.

40. Geyer, "Zwischen Krieg und Nachkrieg," 194–196.

41. Alfred Cobban, *The Nation-State and National Self-Determination* (London: Collins, 1969).

42. See McMeekin, *Russian Origins*, 175–213.

43. An idea developed throughout Geyer, "Zwischen Krieg und Nachkrieg."

44. "Commonwealth" is commonly used, but Brian Porter-Szűcs makes a strong case for "republic" instead: *Poland in the Modern World: Beyond Martyrdom* (Chichester, West Sussex: Wiley-Blackwell, 2014), 37n1.

45. Excellent recent English-language surveys of Polish history include Jerzy Lukowski and Hubert Zawadzki's *Concise History of Poland*, 2nd ed. (Cambridge: Cambridge University Press, 2006); Porter-Szűcs, *Poland in the Modern World*. Norman Davies's *God's Playground* (New York: Columbia University Press, 1982) is showing its age but still repays reading; the same is true of Piotr Wandycz's *The Lands of Partitioned Poland* (Seattle: University of Washington Press, 1974). For a German-language survey of twentieth-century Polish history by a Polish scholar, see Włodzimierz Borodziej, *Geschichte Polens im 20. Jahrhundert* (Munich: C. H. Beck, 2010).

46. Throughout this book, I use "nationalism" in a much broader sense than is common in Polish scholarship, where the term denotes exclusivist chauvinism and racism. Nationalism, for the purposes of this study, simply means a desire to reestablish a distinctly Polish cultural and political entity in central Europe, whether as a sovereign nation-state, a kingdom, an autonomous unit within an empire, or in some other variant. While perhaps vague, the term is nonetheless necessary in order to avoid generalizations like "the Poles," since many Polish peasants were loyal to their emperors and uninterested in grand political projects. Such a use of "nationalism" also allows for general statements about the political pressures facing the Imperial Government-General, which had to contend with such desires, whatever their specific claims and ambitions may have been.

47. Blanke, *Prussian Poland*, 17–33.

48. Ibid., 41–47.

49. The best introduction is Richard Wonser Tims, *Germanizing Prussian Poland: The H-K-T Society and the Struggle for the Eastern Marches in the German Empire, 1894–1919* (New York: Columbia University Press, 1941).

50. Max Weber, "The Nation-State and Economic Policy (Inaugural Lecture)," in *Weber: Political Writings*, ed. Peter Lassman and Ronald Speirs (Cambridge: Cambridge University Press, 1994), 14.

51. Blanke, *Prussian Poland*, 180–183; Wandycz, *Lands*, 285.

52. John Kulczycki, *School Strikes in Prussian Poland, 1901–1907: The Struggle over Bilingual Education* (Boulder, Colo.: East European Monographs), 1981; Bülow quoted in Hagen, *Germans, Poles, and Jews*, 180–181.

53. Gotthold Rhode, *Geschichte Polens: Ein Überblick* (Darmstadt: Wissenschaftliche Buchgesellschaft, 1980), 434.

54. Conze, *Polnische Nation*, 58–59; quote from 59n38.

55. Eric Weitz, "Germany and the Ottoman Borderlands: The Entwining of Imperial Aspirations, Revolution, and Ethnic Violence," in *Shatterzones of Empires:*

Coexistence and Violence in the German, Habsburg, Russian and Ottoman Borderlands, ed. Omer Bartov and Eric D. Weitz (Bloomington: Indiana University Press, 2013), 154.

56. Quoted in *The Cambridge History of Poland: From Augustus II to Pilsudski (1697–1935),* ed. W. F. Reddaway, J. H. Penson, O. Halecki, and R. Dyboski (Cambridge: Cambridge University Press, 1951), 267–268.

57. Quoted in Titus Komarnicki, *Rebirth of the Polish Republic: A Study in the Diplomatic History of Europe* (London: Heinemann, 1957), 76–77.

58. See Carl von Clausewitz, *Historical and Political Writings,* ed. and trans. Peter Paret and Daniel Moran (Princeton, N.J.: Princeton University Press, 1992), 369–376.

59. Orlando Figes, *The Crimean War: A History* (New York: Henry Holt, 2010), 329.

60. Blanke, *Prussian Poland,* 8–9.

61. Richard Blanke, "An 'Era of Reconciliation' in German-Polish Relations (1890–1894)," *Slavic Review* 36, no. 1 (1977): 39–53.

62. Quoted in Hagen, *Germans, Poles, and Jews,* 170.

63. Conze, *Polnische Nation,* 22–24.

64. M. B. Biskupski, "The Militarization of the Discourse of Polish Politics and the Legion Movement of the First World War," in *Armies in Exile,* ed. David Stefancic (Boulder, Colo.: East European Monographs, 2005), 79–80.

65. Wandycz, *Lands,* 275–303, 320–327.

66. The phrase is Max Weber's, from "Deutschlands äußere und Preußens innere Politik," in Max Weber, *Zur Politik im Weltkrieg: Schriften und Reden, 1914–1918,* ed. Wolfgang Mommsen (Tübingen: Mohr Siebeck, 1984), 197.

1. Prometheus Bound

1. Bogdan Graf von Hutten-Czapski, *Sechzig Jahre Politik und Gesellschaft* (Berlin: E. S. Mittler, 1936), 2:145–150.

2. Werner Conze, *Polnische Nation und deutsche Politik im Ersten Weltkrieg* (Cologne: Böhlau, 1958), 46–49; Marian Marek Drozdowski, *Warszawa w latach 1914–1939* (Warsaw: Państwowe Wydawnictwo Naukowe, 1990), 26; Laura Engelstein, "'A Belgium of Our Own': The Sack of Russian Kalisz, August 1914," *Kritika: Explorations in Russian and Eurasian History* 10, no. 3 (2009): 441–473.

3. Janusz Pajewski, *Odbudowa państwa polskiego 1914–1918* (Warsaw: Państwowe Wydawnictwo Naukowe, 1978), 57–58.

4. Reprinted in Titus Komarnicki, *Rebirth of the Polish Republic: A Study in the Diplomatic History of Europe* (London: Heinemann, 1957), 66n20.

5. "Litanja Pielgrzymska," in Adam Mickiewicz, *Księgi Narodu Polskiego i Pielgrzymstwa Polskiego,* ed. Stanisław Pigoń (Kraków: Nakładem Krakowskiej Spółki Wydawniczej, 1924), 139.

6. Włodzimierz Gałecki, *Jeszcze raz przez życie: wspomnienia* (Kraków: Wydawnictwo Literackie, 1966), 165.

7. Komarnicki, *Rebirth,* 36–37; emphasis in original.

8. Pajewski, *Odbudowa,* 64–66.

9. Drozdowski, *Warszawa,* 26–32.

10. Gałecki, *Jeszcze raz,* 162–167.

11. Norman Davies, *God's Playground* (New York: Columbia University Press, 1982), 2:381.

12. John Keegan, *The First World War* (New York: Vintage, 2000), 229–233.

13. Drozdowksi, *Warszawa,* 32.

14. Ibid.

15. Eric Lohr, *Nationalizing the Russian Empire: The Campaign against Enemy Aliens during World War I* (Cambridge, Mass.: Harvard University Press, 2003), 84–165.

16. Gerhard Ritter, *The Sword and the Scepter: The Problem of Militarism in Germany,* trans. Heinz Norden, vol. 3, *Bethmann Hollweg as War Chancellor* (Coral Gables, Fla.: University of Miami Press, 1972), 67.

17. Ibid., 3:72.

18. Keegan, *The First World War,* 229.

19. Roger Chickering, *Imperial Germany and the Great War, 1914–1918* (Cambridge: Cambridge University Press, 1998), 32–33.

20. Conze, *Polnische Nation,* 102–105.

21. BAK/N1711 Nachlass Wolfgang von Kries/4/2.

22. Bericht über die Entwickelung [*sic*] der Verwaltung des Generalgouvernements Warschau, 23 Oktober 1915, BA-MA/PH30 Kaiserliche Generalgouvernements und Militärverwaltungen/II Generalgouvernement Warschau/5/p. 3. For most archival citations in this book, the final number indicates the item number assigned to a given document or part of a document (e.g., the Blatt [Bl.] number for German archives). In some cases, multipage documents have a single item number; in these cases, the page number of a specific reference *within* the document is given with the preface "p." or "pp." to distinguish it from the source's archival number.

23. See the invaluable map following page 10 of E. Wunderlich, ed., *Handbuch von Polen (Kongress-Polen),* 2nd ed. (Berlin: Dietrich Reimer, 1918).

24. Theodore R. Weeks, *Nation and State in Late Imperial Russia: Nationalism and Russification on the Western Frontier, 1863–1914* (DeKalb: Northern Illinois University Press, 1996), 80–84.

25. Eugeniusz Cezary Król, "Besatzungsherrschaft in Polen im Ersten und Zweiten Weltkrieg. Charakteristik und Wahrnehmung," in *Erster Weltkrieg, Zweiter Weltkrieg: Ein Vergleich,* ed. Bruno Thoß and Hans-Erich Volkmann (Paderborn: Schöningh, 2002), 578.

26. Conze, *Polnische Nation,* 85–86.

27. Alfred Graf von Waldersee, *Denkwürdigkeiten des General-Feldmarschalls Alfred Grafen von Waldersee,* ed. Heinrich Otto Meisner (Stuttgart: Deutsche Verlags-Anstalt, 1923), 3:225.

28. Conze, *Polnische Nation,* 106–107; Erich von Tschischwitz, Obituary of Beseler, BA-MA/N30 Nachlass Hans Hartwig von Beseler/77/pp. 13–17.

29. Alexander Kraushar, *Warszawa podczas okupacji niemieckiej, 1915–1918: Notatki naocznego świadka* (Lwów: Wydawn. zakładu narodowego im. Ossolinskich, 1921), 63.

30. Letter to Clara, 25 August 1915, BA-MA/N30/53/p. 2.

31. Ibid., 4.

32. Quoted in Conze, *Polnische Nation,* 108.

33. Quoted in ibid., 113.

34. Ibid.

35. Ibid., 117.

36. 13 September 1915, BA-MA/N30/53/p. 8.

37. Bericht über die Entwickelung der Verwaltung des Generalgouvernements Warschau, BAB-L/R1501 Reichsamt des Innern/119759/3/p. 8.

38. Conze, *Polnische Nation,* 116–118.

39. Ibid., 113–114. For more on Hutten-Czapski, see Chapter 4.

40. 1 October 1915, BA-MA/N30/53/p. 17; emphasis in original.

41. 17 November 1915, BA-MA/N30/53/p. 30.

42. Quoted in Conze, *Polnische Nation,* 115.

43. Letter to Clara, 30 July 1917, BA-MA/N30/55/p. 82.

44. Sitzung des Staatsministeriums vom 8. Oktober 1916, BAK/N1045 Nachlass Friedrich von Loebell/18/74–76.

45. Conze, *Polnische Nation,* 115.

46. For Treitschke, see "Zum Gedächtnis des großen Krieges," in Heinrich von Treitschke, *Ausgewählte Schriften: Erster Band* (Amazon Kindle edition).

47. Geoffrey Wawro, *Warfare and Society in Europe, 1792–1914* (London: Routledge, 2000), 79.

48. Kraushar, *Warszawa,* 63.

49. BAB-L/N2126 Nachlass Bogdan Graf von Hutten-Czapski/426/2–6. The extended quote is from Blatt 3.

50. Letter to Clara, 29 January 1916, BA-MA/N30/54/p. 8.

51. Kraushar, *Warszawa,* 64.

52. Bericht über die Entwickelung der Verwaltung des Generalgouvernements Warschau, 23 October 1915, BAB-L/R1501/119759/3/p. 8.

53. See my note in the Introduction on the use of "nationalism."

54. 14 September 1915, BA-MA/N30/53/p. 9; emphasis in original.

55. Conze, *Polnische Nation,* 120–121.

56. Bericht über die Entwickelung der Verwaltung des Generalgouvernements Warschau, BAB-L/R1501/119759/3/p. 10.

57. Conze, *Polnische Nation,* 120–124.

58. Geheimes Bericht des Generalgouverneurs vom 23.7.1916, BAB-L/R1501/119782/A/183–185.

59. Letter to Clara, 29 July 1916, BA-MA/N30/54/p. 50.

60. Not to be confused with the Bóbr, a southern river. For clarity's sake, I will use "Biebrza" for following references.

61. Beseler to Chancellor, 12 November 1917, BAB-L/N2126/426/4.

62. Letter to Clara, 23 October 1917, BA-MA/N30/55/p. 82.

63. Ritter, *Sword,* vol. 3, 70.

64. Beseler's 1916 Report, BAB-L/R1501/119782/A/184–185.

65. "Deutsche Polenpolitik im Weltkriege," BAK/N1711/4/54–55.

66. 29 July 1916, BA-MA/N30/54/p. 50.

67. Geheimes Bericht des Generalgouverneurs vom 23.7.1916, BAB-L/R1501/119782/A/184–186.

68. Letter to Clara, 18 May 1916, BA-MA/N30/54/p. 47.

69. Quoted in Imanuel Geiss, *Der polnische Grenzstreifen, 1914–1918: Ein Beitrag zur deutschen Kriegszielpolitik im Ersten Weltkrieg, 1914–1918* (Lübeck: Matthiesen, 1960), 111.

70. 28 November 1916, BA-MA/N30/54/p. 78.

71. Conze, *Polnische Nation,* 279.

72. 3 November 1916, BA-MA/N30/54/p. 68.

73. 2 November 1916, BA-MA/N30/54/p. 67.

74. Beseler, secret report of 12 November 1917, BAB-L/N2126/426/4.

75. 23 September 1917, BA-MA/N30/55/p. 115.

76. Quoted in Wiktor Sukiennicki, *East Central Europe during World War I: From Foreign Domination to National Independence* (Boulder, Colo.: East European Monographs, 1984), 1:249.

77. Kuno Graf von Westarp, *Konservative Politik im letzten Jahrzehnt des Kaiserreiches* (Berlin: Deutsche Verlagsgesellschaft, 1936), 2:66.

78. 16 January 1917, BA-MA/N30/55/p. 4.

79. Beseler to Chancellor, 12 November 1917, BAB-L/N2126/426/2–6.

80. To Geh. Rat Körte, 23. February 1917, BAMA/N30/55/p. 27.

81. Reprinted in *Polnische Blätter* 1, no. 2 (October 1915): 49–50.

82. Letter to Clara, 15 April 1917, BA-MA/N30/55/p. 52.

83. Henry Cord Meyer, *Mitteleuropa in German Thought and Action, 1815–1945* (The Hague: Nijhoff, 1955), 268–269.

84. Max Weber, "Deutschlands äußere und Preußens innere Politik," in Max Weber, *Zur Politik im Weltkrieg: Schriften und Reden, 1914–1918,* ed. Wolfgang Mommsen (Tübingen: Mohr Siebeck, 1984), 197.

85. 23 September 1917, BA-MA/N30/55/p. 115.

86. Conze, *Polnische Nation,* 178–180.

87. Lewald's report of 24 September 1914, BAB-L/R1501/119612/167.

88. Weber, "Deutschlands äußere und Preußens innere Politik," 200.

89. July 1916 Immediatbericht; BAB-L/R1501/119782/A/184.

90. Davies, *God's Playground,* 2:348–352.

91. Hutten-Czapski, *Sechzig Jahre,* 2:314.

92. Richard Blanke, *Prussian Poland in the German Empire* (Boulder, Colo.: East European Monographs, 1981), 121–123; Bismarck quote, Komarnicki, *Rebirth,* 76–77.

93. Hutten-Czapski, *Sechzig Jahre,* 2:145.

94. 2 March 1917, BA-MA/N30/55/p. 31.

95. Pajewski, *Odbudowa,* 191.

96. Włodzimierz Borodziej, *Geschichte Polens im 20. Jahrhundert* (Munich: C. H. Beck, 2010), 80–82.

97. Robert Spät, "Für eine gemeinsame deutsch-polnische Zukunft? Hans Hartwig von Beseler als Generalgouverneur in Polen, 1915–1918," *Zeitschrift für Ostmitteleuropa-Forschung* 58, no. 4 (2009): 488–489.

98. Adolf Warschauer, *Deutsche Kulturarbeit in der Ostmark: Erinnerungen aus vier Jahrzehnten* (Berlin: R. Hobbing, 1926), 270.

99. Marta Polsakiewicz, "Das Gesicht einer Metropole im Krieg. Warschau 1914–1918" (PhD dissertation, Europa-Universität Viadrina, 2012–2013), 110–119.

100. Ibid., 114–117.

101. Ibid., 116.

102. Gałecki, *Jeszcze raz,* 172.

103. Warschauer, *Deutsche Kulturarbeit in der Ostmark,* 278–279.

104. Ibid., 295.

105. Polsakiewicz, "Gesicht," 110.

106. Warschauer, *Deutsche Kulturarbeit in der Ostmark,* 295–296.

107. "Der dritte Mai in Warschau," *Polnische Blätter* 3, no. 23 (May 1916): 149–154.

108. Gałecki, *Jeszcze raz,* 172–173.

109. Conze, *Polnische Nation,* 166–170.

110. Borodziej, *Geschichte,* 80.

111. Gałecki, *Jeszcze raz,* 172.

112. Kraushar, *Warszawa,* 42–44.

113. Adolf Eichler, *Das Deutschtum in Kongreßpolen* (Stuttgart: Ausland und Heimat, 1921), 94.

114. *Mucha* 45, 6/19 November 1916. *Mucha* carried both the Julian or "Old Style" (OS) date and the Gregorian, or "New Style" (NS) date.

115. On the Wreschen riots, see Richard Wonser Tims, *Germanizing Prussian Poland: The H-K-T Society and the Struggle for the Eastern Marches in the German Empire, 1894–1919* (New York: Columbia University Press, 1941), 83–87.

116. Bericht über die Entwicklung der Verwaltung des Generalgouvernements Warschau, 23 October 1915, BA-MA/PH30/II/5/p. 7.

117. Bericht Über Tätigkeit und Zustände im Gouvernementsgebiet für die Zeit vom 1.07.1916 bis 30.09.1916, AGAD/531 Cesarsko-Niemieckie General-Gubernatorstwo Warszawskie/Syg. 2/23.

118. *Deutsche Warschauer Zeitung,* 15 July 1916.

119. Bericht Über Tätigkeit und Zustände im Gouvernementsgebiet für die Zeit vom 1.07.1916 bis 30.09.1916, AGAD/531/Syg. 2/44.

120. 6. Bericht des Generalgouverneurs über die Verwaltung des Generalgouvernements Warschau. Zeitraum: 1. Oktober 1916 bis 31. März 1917, BAB-L/R1501/119761/4/p. 16.

121. Gałecki, *Jeszcze raz,* 166–167.

122. Ibid., 172.

123. Jerzy Holzer and Jan Molenda, *Polska w Pierwszej Wojnie Światowej,* 3rd ed. (Warsaw: Wiedza Powszechna, 1973), 156.

124. Polsakiewicz, "Gesicht," 153.

125. Gałecki, *Jeszcze raz,* 172.

126. Polsakiewicz, "Gesicht," 147.

127. Henryk Janczewski, *Całe życie z Warszawą* (Warsaw: Państwowe Instytut Wydawniczy, 1986), 19.

128. Polsakiewicz, "Gesicht," 142–143.

129. Holzer and Molenda, *Polska w Pierwszej Wojnie Światowej,* 157–158.

130. Robert Blobaum, "Going Barefoot in Warsaw during the First World War," *East European Politics and Societies* 27, no. 2 (2013): 190.

131. Stephan Lehnstaedt is the leading authority on the economic aspects of the occupation. See "Dwie (różne) okupacje? Polityka gospodarcza Niemiec i Austro-Węgier w Królestwie Polskim w latach 1915–1918," *Dzieje Najnowsze* 45 (2013): 17–33 and "Fluctuating between 'Utilisation' and 'Exploitation': Occupied East Central Europe during the First World War," in *Legacies of Violence: Eastern Europe's First World War,* ed. Jochen Böhler, Włodzimierz Borodziej, and Joachim von Puttkamer (Munich: Oldenbourg Verlag, 2014), 89–112. See also Wolfgang von Kries, "Die Wirtschaftliche Ausnutzung des Generalgouvernements Warschau," *Preußische Jahrbücher* 235 (1934): 221–248; Andreas Hoffman, "Die vergessene Okkupation: Lodz im Ersten Weltkrieg," in *Deutsche, Juden, Polen: Geschichte einer wechselvollen Beziehung im 20. Jahrhundert,* ed. Andrea Löw, Kerstin Robusch, and Stefanie Walter (Frankfurt: Campus, 2004), 65–69; Conze, *Polnische Nation,* 129–136; Martin Bemmann, "'... kann von einer schonenden Behandlung keine Rede sein': Zur forst- und landwirtschaftlichen Ausnutzung des Generalgouvernements Warschau durch die deutsche Besatzungsmacht, 1915–1918," *Jahrbücher für Geschichte Osteuropas* 55, no. 1 (2007): 1–33. An excellent (and oft-overlooked) work on the economic aspects of the occupation is Reinhold Zilch's *Okkupation und Währung im Ersten Weltkrieg* (Goldbach: Keip, 1994).

132. Christian Westerhoff, "'A Kind of Siberia': German Labour and Occupation Policies in Poland and Lithuania during the First World War," *First World War Studies* 4, no. 1 (March 2013): 51–59.

133. Holzer and Molenda, *Polska w Pierwszej Wojnie Światowej,* 157–158.

134. Krzystof Dunin-Wąsowicz, ed., *Warszawa w pamiętnikach Pierwszej Wojny Światowej* (Warsaw: Państwowy Instytut Wydawniczy, 1971), 185.

135. Polsakiewicz, "Gesicht," 195–197.

136. 8. Bericht des Generalgouverneurs über die Verwaltung des Generalgouvernements Warschau. Zeitraum: 1. Oktober 1917 bis 31 März 1918, BAB-L/ R1501/119761/64/p. 20.

137. Halbjahrsbericht des Verwaltungschefs bei dem Generalgouvernement Warschau für die Zeit vom 1. April bis 30 September 1918, BAB-L/ R1501/119762/10/p. 76.

138. 8. Bericht des Generalgouverneurs über die Verwaltung des Generalgouvernements Warschau. Zeitraum: 1. Oktober 1917 bis 31 März 1918, BAB-L/ R1501/119761/64/p. 21.

139. AAN/19 Ministerstwo Aprowizacji w Warszawie/Syg. 17/5–6.

140. See Roger Chickering, *The Great War and Urban Life in Germany: Freiburg, 1914–1918* (Cambridge: Cambridge University Press, 2009).

141. Marta Polsakiewicz, "Spezifika deutscher Besatzungspolitik in Warschau 1914–1916," *Zeitschrift für Ostmitteleuropa-Forschung* 58, no. 4 (2009): 512–513.

142. Polsakiewicz, "Gesicht," 137.

143. Westerhoff, "A Kind of Siberia," 53.

144. Ibid., 51–53.

145. Tammy Proctor, *Civilians in a World at War, 1914–1918* (New York: New York University Press, 2010), 46–47.

146. Chickering, *Imperial Germany,* 77–80.

147. Westerhoff, "A Kind of Siberia," 53.

148. Proctor, *World at War,* 204.

149. Ibid., 209.

150. "Laws and Customs of War on Land (Hague IV)," The Avalon Project: Documents in Law, History and Diplomacy, Yale Law School Lillian Goldman Law Library, http://avalon.law.yale.edu/20th_century/hague04.asp.

151. Jonathan Gumz, "Norms of War and the Austro-Hungarian Encounter with Serbia, 1914–1918," *First World War Studies* 4, no. 1 (March 2013): 97–110.

152. Blobaum, "Going Barefoot," 193–194.

153. Janczewski, *Całe życie,* 19–20.

154. Quoted in Conze, *Polnische Nation,* 241.

155. Letter of 15 November 1917, BA-MA/N30/55/p. 141.

2. Merciless Murderers of the Polish Language

1. Quoted in Wiktor Sukiennicki, *East Central Europe during World War I: From Foreign Domination to National Independence* (Boulder, Colo.: East European Monographs, 1984), 1:294.

2. Lesław Dudek, "Polish Military Formations in World War I," in *East Central European Society in World War I*, ed. Béla Király and Nándor Dreisziger (Boulder, Colo.: Social Science Monographs, 1985), 455.

3. Norman Davies, *God's Playground* (New York: Columbia University Press, 1982), 2:380. Translation is Davies's.

4. Włodzimierz Gałecki, *Jeszcze raz przez życie: Wspomnienia* (Kraków: Wydawnictwo Literackie, 1966), 163–164.

5. Roman Starzyński, *Cztery lata wojny w służbie Komendanta: Przeżycia wojenne 1914–1918* (Warsaw: Erica, 2012), 7–9.

6. Ibid., 75–79.

7. Ibid., 79.

8. Dudek, "Polish Military Formations," 463–464.

9. Jerzy Holzer and Jan Molenda, *Polska w Pierwszej Wojnie Światowej*, 3rd ed. (Warsaw: Wiedza Powszechna, 1973), 469–470.

10. For an excellent overview of the place of the Legions in Polish history and historiography, see Jan Snopko, *Finał epopei Legionów Polskich, 1916–1918* (Białystok: Wydawnictwo Uniwersytetu w Białymstoku, 2008), 7–17.

11. Arthur Hausner, *Die Polenpolitik der Mittelmächte und die Österreichisch-Ungarische Militärverwaltung in Polen während des Weltkrieges* (Vienna: Hollinek, 1935), 5.

12. Dudek, "Polish Military Formations," 457–458.

13. Quoted in Hausner, *Polenpolitik*, 79.

14. Snopko, *Finał epopei*, 89.

15. Ibid., 90.

16. Hausner, *Polenpolitik*, 21–22.

17. Maria Lubomirska, *Pamiętnik księżnej Marii Zdzisławowej Lubomirskiej 1914–1918* (Poznań: Wydawnictwo Poznańskie, 2002), 424.

18. Ibid., 439.

19. Hausner, *Polenpolitik*, 41–42.

20. Ibid., 77–78. Somewhat confusingly, the Legions were usually still referred to as such.

21. On the background to the speech, see Gerhard Ritter, *The Sword and the Scepter: The Problem of Militarism in Germany*, trans. Heinz Norden, vol. 3, *Bethmann Hollweg as War Chancellor* (Coral Gables, Fla.: University of Miami Press, 1972), 71–74; text of speech in Stanislas Filasiewicz, *La question polonaise pendant la Guerre Mondiale* (Paris: Section d'études et de publications politiques du Comité national polonaise, 1920), 2:28–29.

22. Richard Wonser Tims, *Germanizing Prussian Poland: The H-K-T Society and the Struggle for the Eastern Marches in the German Empire, 1894–1919* (New York: Columbia University Press, 1941), 274.

23. Ritter, *Sword*, 3:105.

24. André Scherer and Jacques Grunewald, eds., *L'Allemagne et les problèmes de la paix pendant la première guerre mondiale: Documents extraits des archives*

de l'office allemand des affaires étrangères (Paris: Presses universitaires de France, 1966), 172–173.

25. Quoted in Vejas Liulevicius, *War Land on the Eastern Front: Culture, National Identity and German Occupation in World War I* (Cambridge: Cambridge University Press, 2000), 64.

26. Roger Chickering, *Imperial Germany and the Great War, 1914–1918* (Cambridge: Cambridge University Press, 1998), 70–82.

27. Sukiennicki, *East Central Europe*, 1:248–249.

28. The report, analyzed in more detail in Chapter 1, is reprinted in *Jahrbuch für Geschichte der UdSSR und der Volksdemokratischen Länder Europas* 4 (1960): 390–400.

29. Immediatbericht of 23 July 1916, in *Jahrbuch*, 398.

30. Ibid., 394; emphasis in original.

31. Ibid., 397.

32. Sukiennicki, *East Central Europe*, 1:240–249.

33. "Deutsche Polenpolitik im Weltkriege," BAK/N 1711 Nachlass Wolfgang von Kries/5/46; Kuno Graf von Westarp, *Konservative Politik im letzten Jahrzehnt des Kaiserreiches* (Berlin: Deutsche Verlagsgesellschaft, 1936), 2:64–66.

34. Sitzung des Staatsministeriums vom 8. Oktober 1916, BAK/N 1045 Nachlass Friedrich Wilhelm von Loebell /18/74.

35. Ibid., BAK/N 1045/18/75.

36. Ibid., BAK/N 1045/18/74.

37. Ibid., BAK/N 1045/18/74–76.

38. Ibid., BAK/N 1045/18/76–80.

39. "Deutsche Polenpolitik im Weltkriege," BAK/KLE 710/5/47.

40. Werner Conze, *Polnische Nation und deutsche Politik im Ersten Weltkrieg* (Cologne: Böhlau, 1958), 138–149.

41. Ritter, *Sword*, 3:215–216.

42. Sukiennicki, *East Central Europe*, 1:249–252.

43. Ibid., 1:258.

44. Ibid., 1:260–267; Titus Komarnicki, *Rebirth of the Polish Republic: A Study in the Diplomatic History of Europe* (London: Heinemann, 1957), 95–96.

45. Letter of 11 November 1916, quoted in Conze, *Polnische Nation*, 232n24.

46. Text of the Act in translation in Sukiennicki, *East Central Europe*, 1:266–267.

47. Bogdan Graf von Hutten-Czapski, *Sechzig Jahre Politik und Gesellschaft* (Berlin: E. S. Mittler, 1936), 2:303–306.

48. Janusz Pajewski, *Odbudowa państwa polskiego 1914–1918* (Warsaw: Państwowe Wydawnictwo Naukowe, 1978), 127.

49. Hutten-Czapski, *Sechzig Jahre*, 2:306.

50. Alexander Kraushar, *Warszawa podczas okupacji niemieckiej, 1915–1918: Notatki naocznego świadka* (Lwów: Wydawn. zakładu narodowego im. Ossolinskich, 1921), 48–49.

51. Quoted in Pajewski, *Odbudowa*, 126.

52. Starzyński, *Cztery lata*, 327–329.

53. Pajewski, *Odbudowa*, 126–129.

54. Lubomirska, *Pamiętnik*, 423.

55. Letter to Clara, 11 November 1916, BA-MA/N30 Nachlass Hans Hartwig von Beseler/54/p. 70.

56. Bekanntmachung, 30 December 1916, BA-MA/N30/21/p. 302.

57. Haus der Abgeordneten, *Sammlung der Drucksachen des Preußischen Hauses der Abgeordneten, 22. Legislaturperiode, III. Session 1916–1918* (Berlin: PreußischeVerlagsanstalt, 1918), 4:2336 (Drucksache 285).

58. Haus der Abgeordneten, *Stenographische Berichte über die Verhandlungen des Preußischen Hauses der Abgeordneten, 22. Legislaturperiode, III. Session 1916–1918* (Berlin: Preußische Verlagsanstalt, 1917), 3:2391–2423.

59. Sukiennicki, *East Central Europe*, 1:271–273.

60. Maurice Paléologue, *An Ambassador's Memoirs*, trans. F. A. Holt (New York: George H. Doran, 1925), 3:82–87; quotes from 83.

61. Quoted in Matthias Erzberger, *Erlebnisse im Weltkrieg* (Stuttgart: Deutsche Verlagsanstalt, 1920), 178.

62. 6 November 1916.

63. *Le Figaro*, 8 November 1916.

64. Kraushar, *Warszawa*, 47–48.

65. Text of the recruiting notice in Hausner, *Polenpolitik*, 92–93.

66. Spät, "Beseler," 479.

67. *Mucha* 49, 4/17 December.

68. Sukiennicki, *East Central Europe*, 1:267–269.

69. Hausner, *Polenpolitik*, 94–95.

70. Conze, *Polnische Nation*, 239–240; Hausner, *Polenpolitik*, 96–97.

71. Number from Hausner, *Polenpolitik*, 100.

72. Quoted in Erzberger, *Erlebnisse im Weltkrieg*, 178.

73. Letter to Clara, 18 November 1916, BA-MA/N30/54/p. 73.

74. Sukiennicki, *East Central Europe*, 1:289.

75. Conze, *Polnische Nation*, 238–248.

76. Sukiennicki, *East Central Europe*, 1:284.

77. Pajewski, *Odbudowa*, 108–133; Hausner, *Polenpolitik*, is also an invaluable guide to the fractious, shifting world of organized political life in occupied Poland (see, for example, 117–118).

78. Hausner, *Polenpolitik*, 95.

79. Lubomirska, *Pamiętnik*, 444.

80. Hutten-Czapski, *Sechzig Jahre*, 2:229.

81. Ibid., 2:322–324.

82. Lubomirska, *Pamiętnik*, 444–445.

83. Stanisław Dzierzbicki, *Pamiętnik z lat wojny 1915–1918* (Warsaw: Państwowe Instytut Wydawniczy, 1983), 205.

84. Lubomirska, *Pamiętnik*, 444–445.

85. Hausner, *Polenpolitik*, 117–120.

86. Ibid., 126–127.

87. Conze, *Polnische Nation*, 250–251.

88. Ibid., 251–252. See also Hutten-Czapski, *Sechzig Jahre*, 2:324ff.

89. Hutten-Czapski, *Sechzig Jahre*, 2:326–327.

90. Lubomirska, *Pamiętnik*, 459.

91. Loebell to Chancellor, GStA PK/1.HA Rep 77 Ministerium des Innern/1884/6/488–89.

92. Eligiusz Kozłowski, "The Polnische Wehrmacht, 1916–18," in *War and Society in East Central Europe*, vol. 19, *East Central European Society in World War I*, ed. Belá Király and Nándor F. Dreisziger (Boulder, Colo.: Social Science Monographs, 1985), 475.

93. Immediatbericht of 23 July 1916, in *Jahrbuch*, 398.

94. BA-MA/N30/54/p. 71.

95. Lubomirska, *Pamiętnik*, 438.

96. Hutten-Czapski, *Sechzig Jahre*, 2:312–313.

97. Sukiennicki, *East Central Europe*, 1:287.

98. Kozłowski, "Polnische Wehrmacht," 473.

99. Hausner, *Polenpolitik*, 99.

100. Ibid., 116–117.

101. Lubomirska, *Pamiętnik*, 445.

102. Hutten-Czapski, *Sechzig Jahre*, 2:314; quote from Sukiennicki, *East Central Europe*, 1:290. The quote is from Beseler's 20 December report.

103. Sukiennicki, *East Central Europe*, 1:292.

104. Hutten-Czapski, *Sechzig Jahre*, 2:338.

105. Sukiennicki, *East Central Europe*, 1:290–291. According to Sukiennicki, the author of the memorandum was Julian Stachiewicz. It was edited by Piłsudski.

106. Ibid., 1:293.

107. Ibid., 1:295–299.

108. Letter of 14 April 1917, BA-MA/N30/55/p. 49.

109. Kozłowski, "Polnische Wehrmacht," 474–475.

110. Ibid., 473.

111. Beseler to Paul Helfritz, 26 January 1917, BA-MA/N30/55/p. 7.

112. Conze, *Polnische Nation*, 255–256.

113. Ibid., 296n96.

114. Sukiennicki, *East Central Europe*, 1:296–297.

115. Hausner, *Polenpolitik*, 170–171.

116. Ibid., 148–149.

117. Quoted in Conze, *Polnische Nation*, 256n81. I have altered the text to reflect the oath as administered.

118. Snopko, *Finał epopei,* 94.

119. Ibid., 97.

120. Ibid., 95–96; Starzyński, *Cztery lata,* 353.

121. Quoted in Snopko, *Finał epopei,* 117.

122. Ibid., 77–85.

123. Ibid., 90.

124. Ibid., 90–92.

125. Lubomirska, *Pamiętnik,* 424.

126. Sukiennicki, *East Central Europe,* 1:303–307.

127. Ibid., 1:327.

128. Starzyński, *Cztery lata,* 362.

129. Ibid., 357.

130. Ibid., 360–361.

131. Snopko, *Finał epopei,* 102–104.

132. Report of Korpsgendarm und Vizewachtmeister Hardt, BAB-L/ R1501/119831/Bl. 71–72.

133. Report of Korpsgendarm-Vizewachtmeister Müller, 17 June 1917, BAB-L/ R1501/119831/74.

134. 21 June 1917, BAB-L/R1501/119831/68.

135. 25 June 1917, BAB-L/R1501/119831/86.

136. Starzyński, *Cztery lata,* 358.

137. Letter to Clara, 15 April 1917, BA-MA/N30/55/p. 52.

138. Quoted in Komarnicki, *Rebirth,* 116.

139. Sukiennicki, *East Central Europe,* 1:295–300.

140. Hausner, *Polenpolitik,* 172.

141. Ibid., 173.

142. Kozłowski, "Polnische Wehrmacht," 476.

143. BA-MA/N30/55/p. 66.

144. Letter to Clara, 11 July 1917, BA-MA/N30/55/p. 67.

145. Internierung ehemaliger Legionäre, BAB-L/R1501/119831/211. On conditions in Benjaminów, see, in addition to Starzyński, Aleksander Rudkowski, "Za drutami Benjaminowa," *Niepodległość* 2 (1930): 300–336.

146. Hutten-Czapski, *Sechzig Jahre,* 2:374.

147. Ibid., 2:400–401.

148. "Deutsche Polenpolitik im Weltkriege," BAK/N1711/5/179.

149. Damian Szymczak, *Między Habsburgami a Hohenzollernami: Rywalizacja niemiecko—austro-węgierska w okresie I Wojny Światowej a odbudowa państwa polskiego* (Kraków: Avalon, 2009), 6.

150. Kozłowski, "Polnische Wehrmacht," 478.

151. Chief of the General Staff of the Generalgouvernement Warschau to the Reichsamt des Innern, 29 Dezember 1917, BAB-L/R1501/119831/ 213–216.

152. Sukiennicki, *East Central Europe*, 1:393–407. See also Zdzisław J. Winnicki, *Rada Regencyjna Królestwa Polskiego i jej organy 1917–1918* (Wrocław: Wektory, 1991).

153. In the famous formulation of Charles Tilly. Quoted in James J. Sheehan, *Where Have All the Soldiers Gone? The Transformation of Modern Europe* (Boston: Houghton Mifflin, 2008).

3. Practicing Politics

1. Specifically, Kries credited Polish administration at the level of the district. Quoted in Werner Conze, *Polnische Nation und deutsche Politik im Ersten Weltkrieg* (Cologne: Böhlau, 1958), 128–129.

2. One of the best English-language introductions to this period in Polish history is Robert Blobaum, *Rewolucja: Russian Poland, 1904–1907* (Ithaca, N.Y.: Cornell University Press, 1995).

3. Adolf Eichler, *Das Deutschtum in Kongreßpolen* (Stuttgart: Ausland und Heimat, 1921), 114.

4. Conze, *Polnische Nation*, 127–128.

5. 2. (4.) Vierteljahrsbericht des Verwaltungschefs bei dem General-Gouvernement Warschau für die Zeit vom 1. Oktober 1915 bis zum 31. Dezember 1915, BAB-L/R1501 Reichsamt des Innern/119759/136/p. 9; for an explanation of Stein's Städteordnung, as well as an analysis of its place within the history of Selbstverwaltung, see Heinrich Heffter, *Die deutsche Selbstverwaltung im 19. Jahrhundert: Geschichte der Ideen und Institutionen* (Stuttgart: K. F. Koehler, 1950), 92–95.

6. E. Ginschel, ed., *Handbuch für das Generalgouvernement Warschau* (Warsaw: Deutscher Verlag, 1917), 1:38–42. A scaled-down version of the Order, intended for towns with a population of fewer than 20,000 people, was introduced later; ibid., 44–47.

7. Ibid., 36–38.

8. 2. Vierteljahrsbericht der Kaiserlich Deutschen Zivilverwaltung für Polen links der Weichsel für die Zeit vom 26. April bis zum 20. Juli 1915, BAB-L/R1501/119758/204/p. 14; 2. Vierteljahrsbericht der Kaiserlich Deutschen Zivilverwaltung für Polen links der Weichsel, BAB-L/R1501/119758/204/p. 15.

9. Bogdan Graf von Hutten-Czapski, *Sechzig Jahre Politik und Gesellschaft* (Berlin: E. S. Mittler, 1936), 2:250.

10. 1. (3.) Vierteljahrsbericht des Verwaltungschefs bei dem General-Gouvernement Warschau für die Zeit vom 21. Juli 1915 bis zum 1. Oktober 1915, BAB-L/R1501/119759/11.

11. Hutten-Czapski, *Sechzig Jahre*, 2:227.

12. 2. (4.) Vierteljahrsbericht des Verwaltungschefs bei dem General-Gouvernement Warschau für die Zeit vom 1. Oktober 1915 bis zum 31. Dezember 1915, BAB-L/R1501/119759/136/p. 10.

13. "Deutsche Polenpolitik im Weltkriege," BAK/N1711/3/4; Conze, *Polnische Nation*, 71n67; see also Kries's entry in volume 1 of the *Reichshandbuch der deutschen Gesellschaft* (Berlin: Deutscher Wirtschaftsverlag, 1930).

14. Imanuel Geiss, *Der polnische Grenzstreifen 1914–1918* (Lübeck: Matthiesen Verlag, 1960), 94–95; text of the Denkschrift reprinted on 151–158; quote on 157.

15. Conze, *Polnische Nation*, 122n27.

16. *Handbuch*, 26–28.

17. Ibid., 28–30. Neither Warsaw nor Lodz were absorbed into larger districts.

18. 3. (5.) Vierteljahrsbericht des Verwaltungschefs bei dem General-Gouvernement Warschau für die Zeit vom 1. Januar 1916 bis zum 31. März 1916, BAB-L/R1501/119760/6/pp. 5–6. Extended quote is from page 6. For the use of presentation elections in Germany, see Heffter, *Die deutsche Selbstverwaltung*, 96.

19. 4. (6.) Vierteljahrsbericht des Verwaltungschefs bei dem General-Gouvernement Warschau für die Zeit vom 1. April 1916 bis zum 30. Juni 1916, BAB-L/R1501/119760/25/p. 5.

20. James J. Sheehan, *German History, 1770–1866* (Oxford: Clarendon/Oxford University Press, 1989), 298.

21. Quoted in Heffter, *Die deutsche Selbstverwaltung*, 95.

22. Verwaltungsbericht für Sokolow-Wegrow zum 1.IV.16, BAB-L/R1501/119760/36/pp. 1–2. Kreis Sokolow was created by fusing two formerly separate districts into one administrative unit *(Kreiskommunalverband)* in February 1916. Somewhat confusingly, it is sometimes called in the documents "the districts of Sokolow and Wegrow [*sic*]," sometimes "Kreis Sokolow," and sometimes "Sokolow-Wegrow." For simplicity's and consistency's sake, I will refer to it simply as Sokołów.

23. Verwaltungsbericht für Sokolow-Wegrow zum 1.IV.16, BAB-L/R1501/119760/36/pp. 4–6. The quote is from p. 5.

24. Verwaltungsbericht der Kreise Sokolow und Wegrow für die Zeit vom 1. Oktober 1916 bis 31 März 1917, BAB-L/R1501/119761/38/p. 5.

25. BA-MA/N30 Nachlass Hans Hartwig von Beseler /53/ p. 16.

26. My thanks to Andrew Koss for helping me to understand the complexities and ambiguities of the term.

27. Theodore Weeks, *From Assimilation to Antisemitism: The "Jewish Question" in Poland, 1850–1914* (DeKalb: Northern Illinois University Press, 2006), 151 for the population statistics of cities and towns.

28. Aviel Roshwald, "Jewish Cultural Identity in Eastern and Central Europe during the Great War," in *European Culture in the Great War: The Arts, Entertainment and Propaganda,* ed. Aviel Roshwald and Richard Stites (Cambridge: Cambridge University Press, 1999), 90–91.

29. Ibid., 97.

30. Maurice Paléologue, *An Ambassador's Memoirs,* trans. F. A. Holt (New York: George H. Doran, 1925), 2:41.

31. Ibid., 2:42.

32. Eric Lohr, *Nationalizing the Russian Empire: The Campaign against Enemy Aliens during World War I* (Cambridge, Mass.: Harvard University Press, 2003), 137–150.

33. Adolf Warschauer, *Deutsche Kulturarbeit in der Ostmark: Erinnerungen aus vier Jahrzehnten* (Berlin: R. Hobbing, 1926), 280.

34. Letter to Clara, 14 October 1915, BA-MA/N30/53/p. 22.

35. Steven Aschheim, *Brothers and Strangers: The East European Jew in German and German Jewish Consciousness, 1800–1923* (Madison: University of Wisconsin Press, 1982), 180–181.

36. 6. Bericht des Generalgouverneurs über die Verwaltung des Generalgouvernements Warschau. Zeitraum: 1. Oktober bis 31. März 1917, BAB-L/R1501/119761/4/p. 30.

37. Ezra Mendelsohn, *Zionism in Poland: The Formative Years, 1915–1926* (New Haven, Conn.: Yale University Press, 1981), 39–40.

38. Weeks, *From Assimilation to Antisemitism,* 149–169.

39. Ibid., 162–163.

40. Roshwald, "Jewish Cultural Identity," 113–126.

41. Konrad Zieliński, *Stosunki polsko-żydowskie na ziemiach Królestwa Polskiego w czasie Pierwszej Wojny Światowej* (Lublin: Wydawnictwo Uniwersytetu Marii Curie-Skłodowskiej, 2005), 221–222.

42. AAN/Zesp. 19 Ministerstwo Aprowizacji w Warszawie/Syg. 17/#3.

43. "Deutsche Polenpolitik im Weltkriege," BAK/N1711/4/45.

44. Alexander Carlebach, *Adass Yeshurun of Cologne: The Life and Death of a Kehilla* (Belfast: W. Mullan and Sons, 1964), 60–61.

45. Egmont Zechlin, *Die deutsche Politik und die Juden im Ersten Weltkrieg* (Göttingen: Vandenhoeck & Ruprecht, 1969), 160–161.

46. Quoted in Judith Schrag-Haas, "Ludwig Haas: Erinnerungen an meinen Vater," *Bulletin of the Leo Baeck Institute* 4, no. 13 (1962): 77.

47. On Haas's religious leanings, see Carlebach, *Adass Yeshurun,* 55; on his war service, see Ludwig Luckemeyer, "Ludwig Haas als Reichstagsabgeordneter der Fortschrittlichen Volkspartei (FVP) und der Deutschen Demokratischen Partei (DDP)," in *Kritische Solidarität: Betrachtungen zum Deutsch-Jüdischen Selbstverständnis,* ed. Günter Schulz (Bremen: Röver, 1971), 126.

48. Wilhelm Stein, "Die politische Entwicklung im polnischen Judentum während der Zeit der deutschen Okkupation," in Roth, *Die politische Entwicklung,* 158–159. A number of Carlebach's letters home are reprinted in Alexander Carlebach, "A German Rabbi Goes East," *Leo Baeck Yearbook* 6 (1961): 60–121. They represent a fascinating and extraordinarily rich source for those wishing to explore the encounter between German and Polish Jews during the war.

49. Aschheim, *Brothers,* 157.

50. Ibid., 167.

51. Carlebach, *Adass Yeshurun,* 64–66.

52. Carlebach, "A German Rabbi Goes East," 62–64.

53. Letter of 17 January 1916, in ibid., 80–81.

54. Ibid., 67.

55. Letter of 27 January, in ibid., 74–75.

56. Letter of 3 February 1916, in ibid., 77.

57. Letter of 27 January 1916, in ibid., 72–73.

58. The text of the ordinance can be found in *Handbuch,* 384–396.

59. Quoted in Carlebach, *Adass Yeshurun,* 58.

60. Halbjahrsbericht des Verwaltungschefs bei dem Generalgouvernement Warschau für die Zeit vom 1. Oktober 1916 bis zum 31. März 1917, BAB-L/ R1501/119761/no number (nn)/p. 67.

61. Letter of 22 November 1916, in Carlebach, "A German Rabbi Goes East," 103.

62. Frank Schuster, *Zwischen allen Fronten: Osteuropäische Juden während des Ersten Weltkrieges, 1914–1919* (Cologne: Böhlau, 2004), 271, 276–277.

63. Carlebach, *Adass Yeshurun,* 59.

64. Ibid., 62–63, 73.

65. 3. (5.) Vierteljahrsbericht des Verwaltungschefs bei dem General-Gouvernement Warschau für die Zeit vom 1. Januar 1916 bis zum 31. März 1916, BAB-L/ R1501/119760/6/p. 6.

66. 4. Bericht des Generalgouverneurs über die Verwaltung des Generalgouvernements Warschau. Zeitraum: 1.4. bis 30.6.16, BAB-L/R1501/119760/21/pp. 13–14.

67. 4. (6.) Vierteljahrsbericht des Verwaltungschefs bei dem General-Gouvernement Warschau für die Zeit vom 1. April 1916 bis zum 30. Juni 1916, BAB-L/ R1501/119760/25/p. 6.

68. *Handbuch,* 63–64; Krzysztof Dunin-Wąsowicz, *Warszawa w czasie Pierwszej Wojny Światowej* (Warsaw: Państwowy Instytut Wydawniczy, 1974), 144–145.

69. Theodore Weeks, *Nation and State in Late Imperial Russia: Nationalism and Russification on the Western Frontier, 1863–1914* (DeKalb: Northern Illinois University Press, 1996), 156–171.

70. Zieliński, *Stosunki polsko-żydowskie,* 263–266; quote from p. 64.

71. 4. (6.) Vierteljahrsbericht des Verwaltungschefs bei dem General-Gouvernement Warschau für die Zeit vom 1. April 1916 bis zum 30. Juni 1916, BAB-L/R1501/119760/25/pp. 6–7. See also the population figures in Dunin-Wąsowicz, *Warszawa w czasie Pierwszej Wojny Światowej,* 94.

72. Weeks, *From Assimilation to Antisemitism,* 156–157.

73. *Handbuch,* 63.

74. Ibid., 47; *Deutsche Lodzer Zeitung,* 11 December 1916.

75. Roth, *Die politische Entwicklung*, 26–28.

76. Stein, "Die politische Entwicklung im polnischen Judentum," 161–164.

77. Mendelsohn, *Zionism in Poland*, 49–51; Stein, "Die politische Entwicklung im polnischen Judentum,"161–162.

78. Letter of 6 July 1916 in Carlebach, "A German Rabbi Goes East," 96.

79. 4. Bericht des Generalgouverneurs über die Verwaltung des Generalgouvernements Warschau. Zeitraum: 1.4. bis 30.6.16, BAB-L/R1501/119760/21/21/p. 13.

80. *Deutsche Warschauer Zeitung*, 5 July 1916.

81. *Kurjer Warszawski*, 8 July 1916.

82. *Deutsche Warschauer Zeitung*, 15 July 1916.

83. Marian Marek Drozdowski, *Warszawa w latach 1914–1939* (Warsaw: Państwowe Wydawnictwo Naukowe, 1990), 42–43.

84. 5. (7.) Vierteljahrsbericht des Verwaltungschefs bei dem Generalgouvernement Warschau. Für die Zeit vom 1. Juli 1916 bis zum 30. September 1916, BAB-L/R1501/119760/46/pp. 5–6.

85. Letter of 6 July 1916 in Carlebach, "A German Rabbi Goes East," pp. 96–97.

86. Marta Polsakiewicz, "Das Gesicht einer Metropole im Krieg. Warschau 1914–1918," (PhD dissertation, Europa-Universität Viadrina, 2012–2013), 92–93.

87. Maria Lubomirska, *Pamiętnik księżnej Marii Zdzisławowej Lubomirskiej 1914–1918* (Poznań: Wydawnictwo Poznańskie, 2002), 385.

88. 5. (7.) Vierteljahrsbericht des Verwaltungschefs bei dem Generalgouvernement Warschau. Für die Zeit vom 1. Juli 1916 bis zum 30. September 1916, BAB-L/R1501/119760/46/p. 6.

89. *Handbuch*, 31–32; 6. (8.) Vierteljahrsbericht des Verwaltungschefs bei dem General-Gouvernement Warschau für die Zeit vom 1. Oktober 1916 bis zum 31 Dezember 1916, BAB-L/R1501/119760/66/pp. 5–6.

90. 5. (7.) Vierteljahrsbericht des Verwaltungschefs bei dem Generalgouvernement Warschau. Für die Zeit vom 1. Juli 1916 bis zum 30. September 1916, BAB-L/R1501/119760/46/p. 6.

91. 6. (8.) Vierteljahrsbericht des Verwaltungschefs bei dem General-Gouvernement Warschau für die Zeit vom 1. Oktober 1916 bis zum 31. Dezember 1916, BAB-L/ R1501/119760/66/p. 6.

92. *Handbuch*, 50.

93. 6. (8.) Vierteljahrsbericht des Verwaltungschefs bei dem General-Gouvernement Warschau für die Zeit vom 1. Oktober 1916 bis zum 31 Dezember 1916, BAB-L/R1501/119760/66/p. 7.

94. *Handbuch*, 48–49.

95. Halbjahrsbericht des Verwaltungschefs bei dem Generalgouvernement Warschau für die Zeit vom 1. Oktober 1916 bis zum 31. März 1917, BAB-L/R1501/119761/nn/p. 7.

96. Verwaltungsbericht der Kreise Sokolow und Wegrow für die Zeit vom 1. Oktober 1916 bis 31 März 1917, BAB-L/R1501/119761/38/p. 7.

97. Data are for 1897. Andreas Kappeler, *The Russian Empire: A Multiethnic History*, trans. Alfred Clayton (Harlow: Longman, 2001), 401.

98. Adolf Eichler, *Deutschtum im Schatten des Ostens; Ein Lebensbericht* (Dresden: Meinhold, 1942), 253.

99. Eichler, *Das Deutschtum in Kongreßpolen*, 120–121.

100. Eichler, *Deutschtum im Schatten des Ostens*, 225.

101. Werner Conze, "Nationalstaat oder Mitteleuropa? Die Deutschen des Reichs und die Nationalitätenfragen Ostmitteleuropas im Ersten Weltkrieg," in *Deutschland und Europa: Historische Studien zur Völker- und Staatenordnung des Abendlandes*, ed. Werner Conze (Düsseldorf: Droste, 1951), 215. For more on the Government-General and the Germans of Poland, see Chapter 4.

102. Andreas Hofmann, "Die vergessene Okkupation: Lodz im Ersten Weltkrieg," in *Deutsche, Juden, Polen: Geschichte einer wechselvollen Beziehung im 20. Jahrhundert*, ed. Andrea Löw, Kerstin Robusch, and Stefanie Walter (Frankfurt: Campus, 2004), 71.

103. Conze, "Nationalstaat," 215.

104. Eichler, *Das Deutschtum in Kongreßpolen*, 129.

105. *Deutsche Lodzer Zeitung*, 11 December 1916.

106. Ibid. Mackensen is left out of the coverage in that issue, an oversight corrected in the issue of 12 December.

107. Eichler, *Das Deutschtum in Kongreßpolen*, 130–131. "Ich werde das Deutschtum in Polen nicht vergessen" was Hindenburg's breezy answer. *Deutsche Lodzer Zeitung*, 15 December 1916.

108. Eichler, *Das Deutschtum in Kongreßpolen*, 131; Tadeusz Telma, "Pierwsze wybory do Rady Miejskiej m. Łodzi," *Rocznik Łódzki* 11 (1966): 138; *Deutsche Lodzer Zeitung*, 28 December 1916.

109. *Deutsche Lodzer Zeitung*, 16 January 1917.

110. Ibid., 23 December 1916.

111. Ibid., 15 January 1917.

112. Telma, "Pierwsze wybory," 135.

113. *Deutsche Lodzer Zeitung*, 3 January 1917.

114. *Handbuch*, 48–49; reprinted, with lengthy explanations of each curia's qualifications, in the *Deutsche Lodzer Zeitung*, 5 December 1916.

115. Numbers are estimates. *Deutsche Lodzer Zeitung*, 22 January 1917.

116. Ibid., 19 January 1917.

117. Halbjahrsbericht des Verwaltungschefs bei dem Generalgouvernement Warschau für die Zeit vom 1. Oktober 1916 bis zum 31. März 1917, BAB-L/R1501/119761/nn/pp. 7–8.

118. Telma, "Pierwsze wybory," 138–140.

119. Ibid., 148.

120. Ibid., 141.

121. Ibid., 148.

122. Halbjahrsbericht des Verwaltungschefs bei dem Generalgouvernement Warschau für die Zeit vom 1. April 1917 bis zum 30. September 1917, BAB-L/ R1501/119761/47/p. 5.

123. Halbjahrsbericht des Verwaltungschefs bei dem Generalgouvernement Warschau für die Zeit vom 1. Oktober 1916 bis zum 31. März 1917, BAB-L/ R1501/ 119761/nn/p. 8.

124. Telma, "Pierwsze wybory," 135–136.

125. Halbjahrsbericht des Verwaltungschefs bei dem Generalgouvernement Warschau für die Zeit vom 1. April 1917 bis zum 30. September 1917, BAB-L/ R1501/119761/47/p. 6.

126. *Deutsche Warschauer Zeitung,* 21 November 1917 (Erste Ausgabe). The meeting continued for several days thereafter.

127. Halbjahrsbericht des Verwaltungschefs bei dem Generalgouvernement Warschau für die Zeit vom 1. April 1917 bis zum 30. September 1917, BAB-L/ R1501/119761/47/p. 99.

128. Halbjahrsbericht des Verwaltungschefs bei dem Generalgouvernement Warschau für die Zeit vom 1. April 1917 bis zum 30. September 1917, BAB-L/ R1501/ 119761/47/p. 100.

129. *Deutsche Warschauer Zeitung,* 16 November 1917. Coverage includes a re-printed article from the *Norddeutsche Allgemeine Zeitung.*

130. "Deutsche Polenpolitik im Weltkriege," BAK/N1711/3/4. See also Hutten-Czapski, *Sechzig Jahre,* 2:246.

131. Letter to Clara, 5 February 1918, BA-MA/N30/56/p. 17.

132. 7. Bericht des Generalgouverneurs über die Verwaltung des Generalgouvernements Warschau. Zeitraum: 1. April bis 30. September 1917, BAB-L/R1501/ 119761/46/p. 37.

4. Schools of the Nations

1. "Schools" and "education" refer here to primary and secondary education, both public and private; university-level education was treated very differently by the Germans and is the subject of Chapter 5.

2. Egmont Zechlin, *Die deutsche Politik und die Juden im Ersten Weltkrieg* (Göttingen: Vandenhoeck & Ruprecht, 1969), 193.

3. 1. Vierteljahrsbericht der Zivilverwaltung für Russisch-Polen für die Zeit vom 5. Januar bis zum 25. April 1915, BAB-L/R1501 Reichsamt des Innern/119758/159/p. 42.

4. 2. (4.) Vierteljahrsbericht des Verwaltungschefs bei dem General-Gouvernement Warschau für die Zeit vom 1. Oktober 1915 bis zum 31. Dezember 1915, BAB-L/R1501/119759/136/p. 63.

5. See Section 8 of the ordinance, in E. Ginschel, ed., *Handbuch für das Generalgouvernement Warschau* (Warsaw: Deutscher Verlag, 1917), 1:379.

6. 2. (4.) Vierteljahrsbericht des Verwaltungschefs bei dem General-Gouvernement Warschau für die Zeit vom 1. Oktober 1915 bis zum 31 Dezember 1915, BAB-L/R1501/119759/136/p. 66.

7. Verwaltungsbericht für Sokolow-Wegrow zum 1.IV.16, BAB-L/R1501/119760/36/p. 36.

8. Verwaltungsbericht der Kreise Sokolow und Wegrow für die Monate April, Mai, und Juni 1916, BAB-L/R1501/119760/38/p. 26.

9. 2. (4.) Vierteljahrsbericht des Verwaltungschefs bei dem General-Gouvernement Warschau für die Zeit vom 1. Oktober 1915 bis zum 31 Dezember 1915, BAB-L/ R1501/119759/136/pp. 65–66.

10. Verwaltungsbericht für Sokolow-Wegrow zum 1.IV.16, BAB-L/ R1501/119760/36/p. 33.

11. Verwaltungsbericht für Sokolow-Wegrow zum 1.IV.16, BAB-L/ R1501/119760/36/p. 36.

12. 2. (4.) Vierteljahrsbericht des Verwaltungschefs bei dem General-Gouvernement Warschau für die Zeit vom 1. Oktober 1915 bis zum 31 Dezember 1915, BAB-L/ R1501/119759/136/p. 65.

13. *Deutsche Warschauer Zeitung,* 9 June 1916.

14. 3. (5.) Vierteljahrsbericht des Verwaltungschefs bei dem General-Gouvernement Warschau für die Zeit vom 1. Januar 1916 bis zum 31. März 1916, BAB-L/R1501/119760/6/p. 42.

15. 4. (6.) Vierteljahrsbericht des Verwaltungschefs bei dem General-Gouvernement Warschau für die Zeit vom 1. April 1916 bis zum 30. Juni 1916, BAB-L/R1501/119760/25/p. 47.

16. 3. (5.) Vierteljahrsbericht des Verwaltungschefs bei dem General-Gouvernement Warschau für die Zeit vom 1. Januar 1916 bis zum 31. März 1916, BAB-L/R1501/119760/6/p. 42.

17. In this context, "class" as an organizational unit within a Volksschule generally refers to a single group of students completing a multiyear course of instruction under a single teacher. Thomas Darlington, *Education in Russia, Board of Education Special Reports on Educational Subjects 23* (London: H. M. Stationery Office, 1909), 238. The most common type of Polish elementary school, especially in rural areas, was the one-class school. Kazimierz Konarski, *Dzieje szkolnictwa w b. Królestwie Kongresowym 1915–1918* (Kraków: skł. gł. Książnica Polska w Warszawie, 1923), 64–65.

18. 2. (4.) Vierteljahrsbericht des Verwaltungschefs bei dem General-Gouvernement Warschau für die Zeit vom 1. Oktober 1915 bis zum 31 Dezember 1915, BAB-L/ R1501/119759/136/p. 66.

19. *Deutsche Warschauer Zeitung,* 5 January 1917.

20. 5. (7.) Vierteljahrsbericht des Verwaltungschefs bei dem General-Gouvernement Warschau. Für die Zeit vom 1. Juli 1916 bis zum 30. September 1916, BAB-L/R1501/119760/46/p. 37.

21. Halbjahrsbericht des Verwaltungschefs bei dem Generalgouvernement Warschau für die Zeit vom 1. April 1917 bis zum 30. September 1917, BAB-L/R1501/119761/47/p. 86, quote from p. 88.

22. 2. (4.) Vierteljahrsbericht des Verwaltungschefs bei dem General-Gouvernement Warschau für die Zeit vom 1. Oktober 1915 bis zum 31. Dezember 1915, BAB-L/ R1501/119759/136/p. 66. Zgierz and the communities around it were home to thousands of ethnic Germans. Otto Heike, *Das deutsche Schulwesen in Mittelpolen: ein Kapitel mühsamer Abwehr staatlichen Unrechts* (Dortmund: Veröffentlichungen der Ostdeutschen Forschungsstelle im Lande Nordrhein-Westfalen, 1963), 101.

23. 1. Vierteljahrsbericht der Zivilverwaltung für Russisch-Polen für die Zeit vom 5. Januar bis zum 25. April 1915, BAB-L/R1501/119758/159/pp. 42–43. Secondary schools are usually referred to in the German documents as "mittlere (höhere) Schulen."

24. 2. (4.) Vierteljahrsbericht des Verwaltungschefs bei dem General-Gouvernement Warschau für die Zeit vom 1. Oktober 1915 bis zum 31. Dezember 1915, BAB-L/ R1501/119759/136/p. 67.

25. All numbers include schools recorded as being "i.E." ("in development") 6. (8.) Vierteljahrsbericht des Verwaltungschefs bei dem General-Gouvernement Warschau für die Zeit vom 1. Oktober 1916 bis zum 31. Dezember 1916, BAB-L/ R1501/119760/66/p. 48. By the middle of next year, Kries reported that private secondary educational institutions numbered 296, 19 of which were German-language and 65 of which served Jewish pupils. The language of these latter institutions is not clear; some of the German-language and Jewish institutions may have been the same. Kries to Staatssekretär des Innern, 14 June 1917, BAB-L/R1501/119688/9.

26. Dimitry M. Odinetz and Paul Novgorotsev, *Russian Schools and Universities in the World War, Carnegie Endowment for International Peace* (New Haven, Conn.: Yale University Press, 1929), 35–36.

27. Włodzimierz Gałecki, *Jeszcze raz przez życie: Wspomnienia* (Kraków: Wydawnictwo Literackie), 183.

28. Norman Davies, *Heart of Europe: A Short History of Poland* (Oxford: Clarendon/Oxford University Press, 1984), 262–266. See also John Kulczycki, *School Strikes in Prussian Poland, 1901–1907: The Struggle over Bilingual Education* (Boulder, Colo.: East European Monographs, 1981). For the place of Polish educational institutions in the Revolution of 1905, see Robert Blobaum, *Rewolucja: Russian Poland, 1904–1907* (Ithaca, N.Y.: Cornell University Press, 1995), 157–187.

29. Bogdan Nawroczyński, "Wydział Oświecenia miasta st. Warszawy," in *Nasza walka o szkołę polską, 1901–1917,* ed. Bogdan Nawroczyński (Warsaw: Komitet Obchodu 25-Lecia Walki o Szkołę Polską, 1934), 2:209.

30. 2. Vierteljahrsbericht der Kaiserlich Deutschen Zivilverwaltung für Polen links der Weichsel für die Zeit vom 26. April bis zum 20. Juli 1915, BAB-L/ R1501/119758/204/pp. 113–114.

31. Bericht über einen polnischen Lehrerbildungskursus in Wloclawek, 20 August 1915. Kries to Staatssekretär des Innern, BAB-L/R1501/119783/43–46.

32. Gałecki, *Jeszcze raz*, 181.

33. Jan Lasocki and Jan Majdecki, eds., *Wojciech Górski i jego szkoła: praca zbiorowa* (Warsaw: Państwowy Instytut Wydawniczy), 77–78.

34. Gałecki, *Jeszcze raz*, 184.

35. 2. Vierteljahrsbericht der Kaiserlich Deutschen Zivilverwaltung für Polen links der Weichsel für die Zeit vom 26. April bis zum 20. Juli 1915, BAB-L/ R1501/119758/ 204/p. 115.

36. "Deutsche Polenpolitik im Weltkriege," BAK/N 1711 Nachlass Wolfgang von Kries /3/4.

37. Wilhelm Stein, "Die politische Entwicklung im polnischen Judentum während der Zeit der deutschen Okkupation," in *Die politische Entwicklung in Kongreßpolen während der deutschen Okkupation*, ed. Paul Roth (Leipzig: K. F. Koehler, 1919), 153; Stein identifies the month of issuance as September. The text of the ordinance can be found in Ginschel, *Handbuch*, 1:378–381; Section 13 is on 380.

38. "Deutsche Polenpolitik im Weltkriege," BAK/N 1711/4/45.

39. Zosa Szajkowski, "The Struggle for Yiddish during World War I: The Attitude of German Jewry," *Leo Baeck Institute Year Book* 9 (1964): 131.

40. Kries to Staatssekretär des Innern, 1 December 1915, BAB-L/R1501/119783/ pp. 230–231; see also Zechlin, *Die deutsche Politik*, 193.

41. Stein, "Die politische Entwicklung im polnischen Judentum," 154–155.

42. Ibid., 154.

43. "Seiner Exzellenz dem Kaiserlich Deutschen General-Gouverneur General von Beseler in Warschau," 25 September 1915, HIA/Włodzimierz Wiskowski Collection/Box 4/Folder: Polish Education, 1915–1917/n.p. The document bears the names S. von Garlicki and L. Starkiewicz.

44. Ibid. Section 14 can be found on page 380 of Ginschel, *Handbuch*.

45. Kries to Staatssekretär des Innern, 1 December 1915, BAB-L/R1501/119783/ pp. 205–209; see also Zechlin, *Die deutsche Politik*, 193. In light of the time and energy taken by the Germans in dealing with the language issue, Kries's postwar claim that the trouble caused by Section 13 was "of no special importance" is not quite credible.

46. 2. (4.) Vierteljahrsbericht des Verwaltungschefs bei dem General-Gouvernement Warschau für die Zeit vom 1. Oktober 1915 bis zum 31 Dezember 1915, BAB-L/ R1501/119759/136/p. 66.

47. Ginschel, *Handbuch*, 1:381.

48. "Seiner Exzellenz dem Kaiserlich Deutschen General-Gouverneur General von Beseler in Warschau," 25 September 1915, HIA/Włodzimierz Wiskowski

Collection /Box 4/Folder: Polish Education, 1915–1917/n.p. For the section giving the Verwaltungschef authority over the schools, see Ginschel, *Handbuch,* 1:378.

49. Kries to Staatssekretär des Innern, 1 December 1915, BAB-L/ R1501/119783/ pp. 228–229. Regrettably, a second protest from Lodz, penned in a "crudely impertinent manner," has not survived. Kries to Staatssekretär des Innern, 1 December 1915, BAB-L/R1501/119783/p. 233.

50. Blobaum, *Rewolucja,* 178–184. I have taken the translation of the group's name from Blobaum.

51. Ustawa Towarzystwa Polskiej Macierzy Szkolnej, AAN/Polska Macierz Szkolna, Biuro Zarządu Głównego w Warszawie/1/1.

52. On the reestablishment and early activities of the Macierz Szkolna, see 5. (7.) Vierteljahrsbericht des Verwaltungschefs bei dem Generalgouvernement Warschau. Für die Zeit vom 1. Juli 1916 bis zum 30. September 1916, BAB-L/R1501/119 760/46/p. 37; the quote and the information about the Haupthilfsausschuß is from his subsequent report, 119760/66/p. 47. For more on the charitable organization, see Werner Conze, *Polnische Nation und deutsche Politik im Ersten Weltkrieg* (Cologne: Böhlau, 1958), 118.

53. 6. (8.) Vierteljahrsbericht des Verwaltungschefs bei dem General-Gouvernement Warschau für die Zeit vom 1. Oktober 1916 bis zum 31. Dezember 1916, BAB-L/R1501/119760/66/p. 51.

54. Kries to Staatssekretär des Innern, 14 June 1917, BAB-L/R1501/119688/4–5.

55. Halbjahrsbericht des Verwaltungschefs bei dem Generalgouvernement Warschau für die Zeit vom 1. April 1917 bis zum 30. September 1917, BAB-L/ R1501/119761/47/p. 86.

56. Quoted in Zechlin, *Die deutsche Politik,* 186.

57. Alexander Carlebach, *Adass Yeshurun of Cologne: The Life and Death of a Kehilla* (Belfast: W. Mullan & Sons, 1964), 68.

58. Zvi Halevy, *Jewish Schools under Czarism and Communism: A Struggle for Cultural Identity* (New York: Springer, 1976), 48–49; quote p. 49. Halevy's book is a clear and concise introduction to Jewish education in Russia.

59. Quote is from letter reprinted in Alexander Carlebach, "A German Rabbi Goes East," *Leo Baeck Yearbook* 6 (1961): 76.

60. 4. (6.) Vierteljahrsbericht des Verwaltungschefs bei dem General-Gouvernement Warschau für die Zeit vom 1. April 1916 bis zum 30. Juni 1916, BAB-L/ R1501/119760/25/p. 46.

61. 6. (8.) Vierteljahrsbericht des Verwaltungschefs bei dem General-Gouvernement Warschau für die Zeit vom 1. Oktober 1916 bis zum 31. Dezember 1916, BAB-L/ R1501/119760/66/p. 47.

62. Carlebach, *Adass Yeshurun,* 67–69. It may be these new chadarim that Kries has in mind when he reports to Berlin that German was being used in some Jewish schools as the language of instruction. 3. (5.) Vierteljahrsbericht des Verwaltungschefs bei dem General-Gouvernement Warschau für die Zeit vom 1. Januar 1916 bis zum 31. März 1916, BAB-L/R1501/119760/6/p. 43.

63. Karl-Alexander Hampe, *Das Auswärtige Amt in Wilhelminischer Zeit* (Münster: Scriptorium, 2001), 132.

64. Franz Schmidt, "Grundlinien der geschichtlichen Entwicklung der deutschen Bildungsarbeit im Auslande," in *Aus deutscher Bildungsarbeit im Auslande,* ed. Franz Schmidt (Langensalza: Beltz, 1927) 1:26.

65. Kries to Staatssekretär des Auswärtigen Amtes, via the Staatssekretär des Innern, 16 March 1916, BAB-L/R1501/119701/p. 19.

66. Kries to Staatssekretär des Innern, 19 December 1916, BAB-L/ R1501/119701/p. 66. The institute also received funds—thanks to Kries's earlier efforts—from the Association for Germans Abroad (Verein für das Deutschtum im Ausland). Kries to Staatssekretär des Innern, 19 December 1916, BAB-L/ R1501/119701/p. 65.

67. Kries to Staatssekretär des Innern, 19 December 1916, BAB-L/R1501/ 119701/pp. 64–65.

68. Auswärtiges Amt to Staatssekretär des Innern, 12 January 1917, BAB-L/ R1501/119701/p. 81.

69. Auswärtiges Amt to Staatssekretär des Innern, 23 June 1917, BAB-L/ R1501/119701/p. 140. The German School in Warsaw received 15,000 marks, the Realgymnasium in Lodz 19,000 marks, and the Luisen-Lyzeum 25,000 marks.

70. Auswärtiges Amt to Staatssekretär des Innern, 4 March 1918, BAB-L/ R1501/119701/273.

71. Heike, *Das deutsche Schulwesen,* 20. The older German Realgymnasium in Lodz, which had been turned into a hospital by the Russians at the beginning of the war, had been running again since the fall of 1915, as a result, in large part, of the efforts of its head, Hugo von Eltz. Adolf Eichler, *Das Deutschtum in Kongreßpolen* (Stuttgart: Ausland und Heimat, 1921), 119.

72. Winson Chu, "German Political Organizations and Regional Particularisms in Interwar Poland (1918–1939)" (PhD diss., University of California, Berkeley, 2006), 206. Chu's dissertation has since been revised and published as *The German Minority in Interwar Poland* (Cambridge: Cambridge University Press, 2012).

73. "Ew. Hochwohlgeboren!," September 1916, BAB-L/R1501/119701/p. 41.

74. *Deutsche Warschauer Zeitung,* 27 October 1916.

75. Adolf Eichler, *Deutschtum im Schatten des Ostens: Ein Lebensbericht* (Dresden: Meinhold, 1942), 247.

76. 6. (8.) Vierteljahrsbericht des Verwaltungschefs bei dem General-Gouvernement Warschau für die Zeit vom 1. Oktober 1916 bis zum 31. Dezember 1916, BAB-L/R1501/119760/66/pp. 47–48.

77. Request of the board of the Deutscher Schulverein in Warsaw to the Reichsamt des Innern, 5 May 1917, BAB-L/R1501/119701/127; Freiwald's information, 119701/131–133; Voigt's information, 119701/134. The three teachers were not, however, employed at the school when it was first opened; they began working there the following year.

78. Adolf Warschauer, *Deutsche Kulturarbeit in der Ostmark: Erinnerungen aus vier Jahrzehnten* (Berlin: R. Hobbing, 1926), 303.

79. Bogdan Graf von Hutten-Czapski, *Sechzig Jahre Politik und Gesellschaft* (Berlin: E. S. Mittler, 1936), 2:407–408.

80. Halbjahrsbericht des Verwaltungschefs bei dem Generalgouvernement Warschau für die Zeit vom 1. April 1917 bis zum 30. September 1917, BAB-L/R1501/119761/47/pp. 45–48.

81. Letter to Clara, 30 September 1917. Quoted in Werner Conze, "Nationalstaat oder Mitteleuropa? Die Deutschen des Reichs und die Nationalitätenfragen Ostmitteleuropas im Ersten Weltkrieg," in *Deutschland und Europa: Historische Studien zur Völker- und Staatenordnung des Abendlandes,* ed. Werner Conze (Düsseldorf: Droste, 1951), 217n36; emphasis added.

82. Letter to Clara, 24 August 1918, BA-MA/N30/56/p. 83.

83. A note on usage: I translate "evangelisch" here and throughout the manuscript as "Protestant," since "evangelical" carries certain connotations in American English that render it not entirely suitable as a translation.

84. Halbjahrsbericht des Verwaltungschefs bei dem Generalgouvernement Warschau für die Zeit vom 1. April 1917 bis zum 30. September 1917, BAB-L/R1501/119761/47/pp. 87–88; Heike, *Das deutsche Schulwesen,* 17. The role played by the Government-General in the associations' formation does not seem to have been known either to contemporaries or to those who have written on the subject since.

85. See the statutes of the Deutsch-Evangelischer Verband, BAB-L/R1501/119701/p. 158.

86. Kries to Staatssekretär des Innern, 9 September 1917, BAB-L/R1501/119701/p. 155. Kries also asked for a smaller amount for the (far smaller) Catholic Association.

87. Auswärtiges Amt to Staatssekretär des Innern, 19 October 1917, BAB-L/R1501/119701/p. 171.

88. Jürgen Kocka, *Facing Total War: German Society, 1914–1918,* trans. Barbara Weinberger (Cambridge, Mass.: Harvard University Press, 1984), 21.

89. Kries to Staatssekretär des Innern, 14 June 1917, BAB-L/R1501/119688/5–7.

90. Kries's comment on the document: Kries to Staatssekretär des Innern, 14 June 1917, BAB-L/R1501/119688/10. German copy of the document, entitled "Stellungnahme des Departementsrates," BAB-L/R1501/119688/36.

91. Kries to Staatssekretär des Innern, 14 June 1917, BAB-L/R1501/119688/6–7.

92. Kries to Staatssekretär des Innern, 19 December 1916, BAB-L/R1501/119701/p. 67.

93. Halbjahrsbericht des Verwaltungschefs bei dem Generalgouvernement Warschau für die Zeit vom 1. April 1917 bis zum 30. September 1917, BAB-L/R1501/119761/47/p. 86.

94. The law is printed in the 20 September 1917 "Verordnungsblatt für das Generalgouvernement Warschau" (no. 87), BAB-L/R1501/119688/p. 114.

95. See Section 6 of the school regulations issued by the Komisja Przejściowa Tymczasowej Rady Stanu in Verordnungsblatt 87, BAB-L/R1501/119688/p. 113.

96. Quoted in Zechlin, *Die deutsche Politik*, 210. The interests of Poland's Jews were thus formally and publicly severed from the ambitions of the Government-General.

97. Verordnungsblatt 87, BAB-L/R1501/119688/pp. 115–118.

98. Eichler, *Kongreßpolen*, 134–135. The extended quote is from page 135.

99. Zdzisław Winnicki, *Rada Regencyjna Królestwa Polskiego i jej organy, 1917–1918* (Wrocław: Wektory, 1991), 172.

100. Halbjahrsbericht des Verwaltungschefs bei dem Generalgouvernement Warschau für die Zeit vom 1. April 1917 bis zum 30. September 1917, BAB-L/R1501/119761/47/p. 86.

101. From von Steinmeister to Staatssekretär des Innern, 23 April 1918, BAB-L/R1501/119702/p. 20.

102. Reichskanzler to Verein für das Deutschtum im Ausland, 11 May 1918, BAB-L/R1501/119702/21.

103. Halbjahrsbericht des Verwaltungschefs bei dem Generalgouvernement Warschau für die Zeit vom 1. Oktober 1917 bis 31. März 1918, BAB-L/R1501/119761/66/pp. 77–78. Kries's first replacement was actually Max von Sandt, but he died in January 1918, shortly after taking up the office. See the *Deutsche Warschauer Zeitung*, 1 February 1918.

5. Nation Building and *Bildung*

1. Tadeusz Manteuffel, *Uniwersytet Warszawski w latach 1915–6/1934–35* (Warsaw: Nakł. Uniwersytetu Józefa Piłsudskiego, 1936), 1.

2. Marceli Handelsman, *La Pologne, sa vie économique et sociale pendant la guerre* (Paris: Les Presses Universitaires de France, 1933).

3. Manteuffel, *Uniwersytet Warszawski*, 2–5.

4. Bogdan Graf von Hutten-Czapski, *Sechzig Jahre Politik und Gesellschaft* (Berlin: E. S. Mittler, 1936), 2:253–254.

5. Werner Conze, *Polnische Nation und deutsche Politik im Ersten Weltkrieg* (Cologne: Böhlau, 1958), 139.

6. 1. (3.) Vierteljahrsbericht des Verwaltungschefs bei dem General-Gouvernement Warschau für die Zeit vom 21. Juli bis zum 1. Oktober 1915, BAB-L/R1501 Reichsamt des Innern/119759/24/ p. 32.

7. Beseler to Kaiser, 3 November 1915, BAB-L/R1501/119699/5–6.

8. Letter of 21 November 1915, quoted in Conze, *Polnische Nation*, 119–120.

9. Warsaw University during the war has also been addressed by Arkadiusz Stempin, "Die Wiedererrichtung einer polnischen Universität: Warschau unter deutscher Besatzung," in *Kollegen—Kommilitonen—Kämpfer: Europäische Universitäten im Ersten Weltkrieg*, ed. Trude Maurer (Stuttgart: Franz Steiner, 2006), 127–145.

10. Adolf Warschauer, *Deutsche Kulturarbeit in der Ostmark: Erinnerungen aus vier Jahrzehnten* (Berlin: R. Hobbing, 1926), 277; Hutten-Czapski, *Sechzig Jahre*, 2:254–256; Manteuffel, *Uniwersytet Warszawski*, 5–8.

11. Hutten-Czapski, *Sechzig Jahre*, 2:255–256.

12. Ibid., 2:253.

13. Warschauer, *Kulturarbeit*, 272.

14. Hutten-Czapski, *Sechzig Jahre*, 1:xv–xvii.

15. Maria Lubomirska, *Pamiętnik księżnej Marii Zdzisławowej Lubomirskiej 1914–1918* (Poznań: Wydawnictwo Poznańskie, 2002), 279.

16. Hutten-Czapski, *Sechzig Jahre*, 1:1–6.

17. Ibid.,1:23, 35; 2:243–244.

18. The best source of information on Hutten-Czapski's long life is his highly readable two-volume autobiography, *Sechzig Jahre Politik und Gesellschaft*. In addition, see the recent biography by Katarzyna Grysińska-Jarmuła, *Hrabia Bogdan Hutten-Czapski (1851–1937): Żołnierz, polityk i dyplomata* (Toruń: Europejskie Centrum Edukacyjne, 2011). For older evaluations of the Graf and his life, see Maximilian von Hagen, "Hutten-Czapskis Einfluß auf seine Zeit," *Zeitschrift für Politik* 27 (1937): 520–534, 474–494. The journal is continuously paginated throughout the volume, but the publishers made a pagination error. The second half of the article begins on page 474 of the volume following the one in which the first part appears. It should be numbered 574. See also Adalbert Hahn, "Bogdan Graf von Hutten-Czapski," *Jomsburg* 1 (1937): 481–485.

19. Jan Muszkowski, ed., *Kalendarz Uniwersytecki: Semestr Letni 1915/16* (Warsaw: F. Hoesicka, 1916), 22–23.

20. Hutten-Czapski, *Sechzig Jahre*, 2:256–257.

21. Quoted in Muszkowski, *Kalendarz Uniwersytecki: Semestr Letni 1915/16*, 24.

22. Ibid., 25.

23. Warschauer, *Kulturarbeit*, 278.

24. Brudziński's speech in *Otwarcie Uniwersytetu i Politechniki w Warszawie, 1915* (Warsaw: Deutsche Staatsdruckerei, n.d.), n.p.

25. Ibid.

26. *Deutsche Warschauer Zeitung*, 15 November 1915.

27. Hutten-Czapski, *Sechzig Jahre*, 2:257.

28. *Deutsche Warschauer Zeitung*, 15 November 1915.

29. Warschauer, *Kulturarbeit*, 278.

30. *Die Ostmark*, October-December 1915.

31. 3. Bericht des Generalgouverneurs über die Verwaltung des Generalgouvernements Warschau. Zeitraum: 1. 1. 1916 bis 31. 3. 1916, BAB-L/R1501/119760/3/p. 13.

32. Wolfgang von Kries, "Deutsche Staatsverwaltung in Russisch-Polen," *Preußische Jahrbücher* 233 (1933):144; Krzysztof Dunin-Wąsowicz, "Oświata w Warszawie w latach 1914–1918," in *Szkolnictwo i oświata w Warszawie*, ed. Józef Kazimierski (Warsaw: Państwowe Wydawnictwo Naukowe, 1982), 164.

33. E. Ginschel, ed., *Handbuch für das Generalgouvernement Warschau* (Warsaw: Deutscher Verlag, 1917), 1:327–328, 361.

34. Ibid., 330, 364, 367.

35. Generalgouvernement Warschau, *Vorschriften für die Studierenden an der Universität zu Warschau* (Warsaw: Deutsche Staatsdruckerei, n.d.), 9–10.

36. Ginschel, *Handbuch*, 1:326, 360.

37. 2. Bericht des Generalgouverneurs über die Verwaltung des Generalgouvernements Warschau. Zeitraum: 1.10.1915 bis 31.12.1915, BAB-L/R1501/119759/130.

38. 2. (4.) Vierteljahrsbericht des Verwaltungschefs bei dem General-Gouvernement Warschau für die Zeit vom 1. Oktober 1915 bis zum 31. Dezember 1915, BAB-L/R1501/119759/136/pp. 68–69.

39. 5. Bericht des Generalgouverneurs über die Verwaltung des Generalgouvernements Warschau. Zeitraum: 1. Juli bis 30. September 1916, BAB-L/R1501/119760/42/p. 13.

40. Ginschel, *Handbuch*, 1:325–326.

41. Ibid., 1:359.

42. Thomas Nipperdey, *Deutsche Geschichte, 1866–1918*, vol. 1, *Arbeitswelt und Bürgergeist* (Munich: C. H. Beck, 1990), 572.

43. Ginschel, *Handbuch*, 1:325.

44. Due most likely to the provisional status of the university, the teaching staff are never referred to as "professors" in contemporary documents, either German or Polish. The Germans give them the title only of *Dozent*. The Polish designation of "wykładający," translated here as lecturers, appears to have been invented at the time by forming a noun from the participle of the verb "wykładać," to lecture. There is no entry for *wykładając* in the three-volume *Słownik Ilustrowany Języka Polskiego* published in Warsaw in 1916 by M. Arct.

45. Andrzej Garlicki, ed., *Dzieje Uniwersytetu Warszawskiego 1915–1939* (Warsaw: Państwowe Wydawnictwo Naukowe, 1982), 314.

46. Manteuffel, *Uniwersytet Warszawski*, 273–275.

47. Thomas Darlington, *Education in Russia* (London: H. M. Stationery Office, 1909), 185.

48. Manteuffel, *Uniwersytet Warszawski*, 17.

49. 5. Bericht des Generalgouverneurs über die Verwaltung des Generalgouvernements Warschau. Zeitraum: 1. Juli bis 30. September 1916, BAB-L/R1501/119760/42/pp. 12–13.

50. 4. (6.) Vierteljahrsbericht des Verwaltungschefs bei dem General-Gouvernement Warschau für die Zeit vom 1. April 1916 bis zum 30. Juni 1916, BAB-L/R1501/119760/25/ p. 48.

51. 5. (7.) Vierteljahrsbericht des Verwaltungschefs bei dem Generalgouvernement Warschau. Für die Zeit vom 1. Juli 1916 bis zum 30. September 1916, BAB-L/R1501119760/46/p. 38.

52. Ibid.

53. Muszkowski, *Kalendarz Uniwersytecki: Semestr Letni 1915/16,* 130–141.

54. Jan Muszkowski, ed., *Kalendarz Uniwersytecki: Semestr Zimowy 1916/17* (Warsaw: F. Hoesicka, 1917), 105–109.

55. Piotr Wandycz, "The Historiography of the Countries of Eastern Europe: Poland," *American Historical Review* 97, no. 4 (October 1992): 1013–1014.

56. E. Ginschel, *Handbuch,* 1:330, 333.

57. Muszkowski, *Kalendarz Uniwersytecki: Semestr Letni 1915/16,* 91–99.

58. Muszkowski, *Kalendarz Uniwersytecki: Semestr Zimowy 1916/17,* 66.

59. Biographical information is taken from Siemieński's entry in the *Polski Słownik Biograficzny.* Quote from Siemieński, *Ustrój Rzeczypospolitej Polskiej: Wykład syntetyczny* (Lwów: Książnica Polska Towarzystwa Nauczycieli Szkół Wyższych, 1922), 52.

60. Hutten-Czapski, *Sechzig Jahre,* 2:270.

61. Brudziński's name appears on a printed list of the members of the organizing committee's presidium included on a document sent out by the committee in late April 1916, APAN/ Towarzystwo Naukowe Warszawskie (TNW)/70/993.

62. Invitation to TNW, APAN/TNW/70/1075.

63. *Deutsche Warschauer Zeitung,* 17 October 1917.

64. Hutten-Czapski, *Sechzig Jahre,* 2:299–301. Conze claims that Hutten-Czapski was the plan's original author (*Polnische Nation,* 201n109).

65. Hutten-Czapski, *Sechzig Jahre,* 2:304–306.

66. The work was entitled the "Warsaw Puppet Show" (Szopka Warszawska) and was published by Nowaczyński under the name "Halban." Quoted in Harold B. Segel, "Culture in Poland during World War I," in *European Culture in the Great War: The Arts, Entertainment, and Propaganda, 1914–1918,* ed. Aviel Roshwald and Richard Stites (Cambridge: Cambridge University Press, 1999), 80.

67. Heinz Lemke, "Die Haltung der Mittelmächte zur Errichtung einer theologischen Fakultät an der Warschauer Universität," *Wissenschaftliche Zeitschrift der Humboldt-Universität zu Berlin, Gesellschafts- und Sprachwissenschaftliche Reihe* 17, no. 2 (1968): 205.

68. Report of 19 February 1916, BAB-L/R1501/119699/41–42.

69. Friedrich von Bernhardi, *Denkwürdigkeiten aus meinem Leben* (Berlin: E. S. Mittler and Son, 1927), 298.

70. Quoted in John Horne and Alan Kramer's *German Atrocities 1914: A History of Denial* (New Haven, Conn.: Yale University Press, 2001), 104.

71. Aufzeichnung über die Sitzung im Reichsamt des Innern vom 25. März 1916, BAB-L/R1501/119699/140–141.

72. Ibid., 141–142.

73. Loebell to Bethmann Hollweg, 22 April 1916, BAB-L/R1501/119699/174.

74. 3 May 1916, BAB-L/R1501/119699/198.

75. Beseler to Staatssekretär des Innern, 12 April 1916, BAB-L/R1501/119699/162–163.

76. Lemke, "Haltung," 206.

77. Hutten-Czapski, *Sechzig Jahre,* 2:285–287.

78. Wiktor Sukiennicki, *East Central Europe during World War I: From Foreign Domination to National Independence* (Boulder, Colo.: East European Monographs, 1984), 1:327.

79. Manteuffel, *Uniwersytet Warszawski,* 16.

80. Kries to Beseler, 19 June 1917, BAB-L/R1501/119700/42–43, 45–46.

81. Garlicki, *Dzieje,* 55.

82. Such is the (probably inaccurate) spelling of their names in the German sources.

83. Mitteilung der akademischen Jugend, BAB-L/R1501/119700/70.

84. Police report of 17 May 1917, BAB-L/R1501/119700/68; Hutten-Czapski, *Sechzig Jahre,* 2:356–357. See also the official German chronology of the events, BAB-L/R1501/119700/66.

85. Kries to Beseler, 19 June 1917, BAB-L/R1501/119700/52.

86. Paszkowski's report, BAB-L/R1501/119700/71.

87. German summary report of incident, BAB-L/R1501/119700/106–107.

88. Hutten-Czapski, *Sechzig Jahre,* 2:361.

89. Paszkowski's report, BAB-L/R1501/119760/112.

90. BAB-L/R1501/119700/109–110.

91. Hutten-Czapski, *Sechzig Jahre,* 2:358.

92. Ansprache des Herrn Generalgouverneurs an die Rektoren der Warschauer Hochschulen am 25.5.1917, HIA/Włodzimierz Wiskowski Collection (WWC)/Box 2/Folder: German Authorities in Occupation of Poland, 1916–1917/p. 1.

93. Ibid., 8.

94. Ibid., 3.

95. Hutten-Czapski, *Sechzig Jahre,* 2:359–360.

96. Ibid., 2:360–361.

97. "Do Jego Ekscelencji Pana Jenerał Gubernatora Warszawskiego," HIA/WWC/Box 2/Folder: German Authorities in Occupation of Poland, 1916–1917.

98. Beseler to Brudziński, 10 July 1917, HIA/WWC/Box 2/Folder: German Authorities in Occupation of Poland, 1916–1917. See also Manteuffel, *Uniwersytet Warszawski,* 21–22.

99. Aufruf des Rektors, 16 June 1917, BAB-L/R1501/119700/121–122.

100. Hutten-Czapski, *Sechzig Jahre,* 2:362.

101. Kries to Beseler, 13 June 1917, BAB-L/R1501/119700/117; Hutten-Czapski, *Sechzig Jahre,* 2:361. This is not to say for certain that it was a ploy; it is merely to point out that the timing was fortuitous.

102. Hutten-Czapski, *Sechzig Jahre,* 2:363.

103. 23 June 1917, BAB-L/R1501/119700/126.

104. Manteuffel, *Uniwersytet Warszawski,* 24.

105. Ibid., 277.

106. Ibid., 24.

107. "Deutsche Polenpolitik im Weltkriege," BAK/N 1711 Nachlass Wolfgang von Kries/5/221.

108. Manteuffel, *Uniwersytet Warszawski,* 25; Kries, "Deutsche Staatsverwaltung," 145.

109. 7. Bericht des Generalgouverneurs über die Verwaltung des Generalgouvernements Warschau. Zeitraum: 1. April bis 30 September 1917, BAB-L/R1501/119761/46/p. 28.

6. Collapse of the Government-General

1. Bogdan Graf von Hutten-Czapski, *Sechzig Jahre Politik und Gesellschaft* (Berlin: E. S. Mittler, 1936), 2:442; 8. Bericht des Generalgouverneurs über die Verwaltung des Generalgouvernements Warschau. Zeitraum: 1. Oktober 1917 bis 31. März 1918, BAB-L/R1501 Reichsamt des Innern/119761/64/p. 20.

2. 8. Bericht des Generalgouverneurs über die Verwaltung des Generalgouvernements Warschau. Zeitraum: 1. Oktober 1917 bis 31. März 1918, BAB-L/R1501/119761/64/p. 21.

3. Jerzy Holzer and Jan Molenda, *Polska w Pierwszej Wojnie Światowej,* 3rd ed. (Warsaw: Wiedza Powszechna, 1973), 352.

4. See Stephan M. Horak, *The First Treaty of World War I: Ukraine's Treaty with the Central Powers of February 9, 1918* (Boulder, Colo.: East European Monographs, 1988); Wolfram Dornik and Peter Lieb, "Misconceived *Realpolitik* in a Failing State: The Political and Economic Fiasco of the Central Powers in the Ukraine, 1918," *First World War Studies* 4, no. 1 (March 2013): 111–124.

5. David Hamlin, "The Fruits of Occupation: Food and Germany's Occupation of Romania in the First World War," *First World War Studies* 4, no. 1 (March 2013): 81–95.

6. For the terms of the treaty, see Horak, *First Treaty,* 46, 164–172.

7. Theodore R. Weeks, *Nation and State in Late Imperial Russia: Nationalism and Russification on the Western Frontier, 1863–1914* (DeKalb: Northern Illinois University Press, 1996), 172–192; Weeks's quote on page 172.

8. Wiktor Sukiennicki, *East Central Europe during World War I: From Foreign Domination to National Independence* (Boulder, Colo.: East European Monographs, 1984), 1:545.

9. Quoted in ibid., 2:732. It is difficult to say how far knowledge of these promises of autonomy became general knowledge once the treaty was signed, although it was leaked to a number of Hungarian politicians in Vienna (see also 2:729).

10. Ibid., 2:736–737.

11. Reichstag, *Verhandlungen des Reichstages 311* (Berlin: Druck und Verlag der Norddeutschen Buchdruckerei und Verlags-Anstalt, 1918), 4016.

12. Ibid., 4021.

13. Haus der Abgeordneten, *Wörtliche Berichte über die Verhandlungen des Preußischen Abgeordnetenhauses, 22. Legislaturperiode III. Session 1916–1918,* vol. 7 (Berlin: Preußische Verlagsanstalt, 1918), 8181.

14. 8. Bericht des Generalgouverneurs über die Verwaltung des Generalgouvernements Warschau. Zeitraum: 1. Oktober 1917 bis 31. März 1918, BAB-L/R1501/119761/64/p. 43.

15. Tadeusz Manteuffel, *Uniwersytet Warszawski w latach 1915–6/1934–35* (Warsaw: Nakł. Uniwersytetu Józefa Piłsudskiego, 1936), 24.

16. Quoted in Sukiennicki, *East Central Europe,* 2:734.

17. Ibid., 2:736.

18. *Kurjer Warszawski,* 14 February 1918.

19. 8. Bericht des Generalgouverneurs über die Verwaltung des Generalgouvernements Warschau. Zeitraum: 1. Oktober 1917 bis 31. März 1918, BAB-L/R1501/119761/64/pp. 20–21.

20. Halbjahrsbericht des Verwaltungschefs bei dem Generalgouvernement Warschau für die Zeit vom 1. Oktober 1917 bis 31. März 1918, BAB-L/R1501/119761/66/p. 7.

21. 8. Bericht des Generalgouverneurs über die Verwaltung des Generalgouvernements Warschau. Zeitraum: 1. Oktober 1917 bis 31. März 1918, BAB-L/R1501/119761/64/pp. 33–34.

22. Ibid., 21.

23. Titus Komarnicki, *Rebirth of the Polish Republic: A Study in the Diplomatic History of Europe* (London: Heinemann, 1957), 141–150. See also Eugene Kusielewicz, "Woodrow Wilson and the Rebirth of Poland," *Polish American Studies* 12, nos. 1–2 (January–June 1955): 1–10.

24. 6. Bericht des Generalgouverneurs über die Verwaltung des Generalgouvernements Warschau. Zeitraum: 1. Oktober 1916 bis 31. März 1917, BAB-L/R1501/119761/4/p. 31.

25. "President Woodrow Wilson's Fourteen Points," Avalon Project, Yale Law School, http://avalon.law.yale.edu/20th_century/wilson14.asp.

26. Komarnicki, *Rebirth,* 206.

27. Maria Lubomirska, *Pamiętnik księżnej Marii Zdzisławowej Lubomirskiej 1914–1918* (Poznań: Wydawnictwo Poznańskie, 2002), 693.

28. Hans Roos, *A History of Modern Poland,* trans. J. R. Foster (New York: Knopf, 1966), 25; Piotr Wandycz, *The Lands of Partitioned Poland* (Seattle: University of Washington Press, 1974), 360.

29. Fritz Fischer, *Germany's Aims in the First World War* (New York: W. W. Norton, 1967), 525–526.

30. D. Stevenson, *The First World War and International Politics* (Oxford: Oxford University Press, 1988), 198–201.

31. Janusz Pajewski, *Odbudowa państwa polskiego 1914–1918* (Warsaw: Państwowe Wydawnictwo Naukowe, 1978), 264–266.

32. Fischer, *Germany's Aims,* 526.

33. Beseler to Hertling, 23 March 1918, GStA PK/IHA/77 Ministerium des Innern/863a/#26/133–135.

34. Beseler to Hertling, 23 March 1918, GStA PK/IHA/77/863a/#26/135.

35. Fischer, *Germany's Aims,* 529–533.

36. Ibid., 531. Fischer indicates that the ruler selected by the Poles had to be German. But notes from the meeting reprinted in volume 2 of Albrecht Philipp, ed., *Die Ursachen des deutschen Zusammenbruchs im Jahre 1918* (Berlin: Verlagsgesellschaft für Politik und Geschichte, 1925), 346, simply state that "die Polen sollen einen Kandidaten vorschlagen." The notes also indicate that Poland would be required to help pay for the war.

37. Gerhard Ritter, *The Sword and the Scepter: The Problem of Militarism in Germany,* vol. 4, *The Reign of German Militarism and the Disaster of 1918,* trans. Heinz Norden (Coral Gables, Fla.: University of Miami Press, 1973), 242.

38. Manteuffel, *Uniwersytet Warszawski,* 279.

39. Ibid., 25.

40. Halbjahrsbericht des Verwaltungschefs bei dem Generalgouvernement Warschau für die Zeit vom 1. April bis 30. September 1918, BAB-L/R1501/119762/10/ pp. 77–78.

41. Halbjahrsbericht des Verwaltungschefs bei dem Generalgouvernement Warschau für die Zeit vom 1. Oktober 1917 bis 31. März 1918, BAB-L/R1501/119761/66/p. 5.

42. Ibid., 7.

43. Halbjahrsbericht des Verwaltungschefs bei dem Generalgouvernement Warschau für die Zeit vom 1. April bis 30. September 1918, BAB-L/R1501/119762/10/p. 9.

44. Friedrich Purlitz, ed., *Deutscher Geschichtskalender* 34, vol. 1, part 1 (January–March 1918): 378–380.

45. Paul Roth, *Die politische Entwicklung in Kongresspolen während der deutschen Okkupation* (Leipzig: K. F. Koehler, 1919), 110–111.

46. For a detailed explanation of the electoral regulations, see the *Deutsche Warschauer Zeitung,* 8 February 1918 and 10 April 1918.

47. Roth, *Entwicklung,* 111n1.

48. Ibid.; Pajewski, *Odbudowa,* 266–269.

49. *Deutsche Warschauer Zeitung,* 23 June 1918.

50. Hutten-Czapski, *Sechzig Jahre,* 2:487.

51. 9. Bericht des Generalgouverneurs über die Verwaltung des Generalgouvernements Warschau. Zeitraum: 1. April 1918 bis 30. September 1918, BAB-L/ R1501/119762/7/p. 48.

52. Pajewski, *Odbudowa,* 266–269.

53. Sukiennicki, *East Central Europe,* 2:741; Beseler's quote, 8. Bericht des Generalgouverneurs über die Verwaltung des Generalgouvernements Warschau. Zeitraum: 1. Oktober 1917 bis 31. März 1918, BAB-L/R1501/119761/64/p. 44.

54. M. B. Biskupski, "The Militarization of the Discourse of Polish Politics and the Legion Movement of the First World War," in *Armies in Exile*, ed. David Stefancic (Boulder, Colo.: East European Monographs, 2005), 89.

55. Lesław Dudek, "Polish Military Formations in World War I," in *East Central European Society in World War I*, ed. Béla Király and Nándor Dreisziger (Boulder, Colo.: Social Science Monographs, 1985), 464–465.

56. Quoted in Sukiennicki, *East Central Europe*, 2:751; for the unit's strength in the spring of 1918, see the chart in Henryk Bagiński, *Wojsko polskie na wschodzie, 1914–1920*, 2nd ed. (1921; repr., Warsaw: Gryf, 1990), 297.

57. Sukiennicki, *East Central Europe*, 2:751–756.

58. Dudek, "Polish Military Formations," 465.

59. Ibid., 466.

60. See Bagiński, *Wojsko polskie*, 357.

61. Sukiennicki, *East Central Europe*, 2:756–761; quote from Haller's letter, 758.

62. Roger Chickering, *Imperial Germany and the Great War, 1914–1918* (Cambridge: Cambridge University Press, 1998), 186.

63. Roman Starzyński, *Cztery lata wojny w służbie Komendanta: Przeżycia wojenne 1914–1918* (Warsaw: Erica, 2012), 405.

64. "Die November-Revolution in Warschau," article in the *Kreuz-Zeitung*, 30 November 1922, GStA PK/VI.HA/Nachlass von Glasenapp, Ernst Reinhard von/#29.

65. Antoni Purtal ("Szczerba"), "Zamach na naczelnika niemieckiej policji politycznej Dr. Ericha Schultzego w Warszawie," *Niepodległość* 5 (1932): 250–257.

66. Starzyński, *Cztery lata*, 404–406.

67. 9. Bericht des Generalgouverneurs über die Verwaltung des Generalgouvernements Warschau. Zeitraum: 1. April 1918 bis 30. September 1918, BAB-L/R1501/119762/7/p. 50.

68. Ibid., 46.

69. Ibid., 51.

70. Robert Spät, "Für eine gemeinsame deutsch-polnische Zukunft? Hans Hartwig von Beseler als Generalgouverneur in Polen, 1915–1918," *Zeitschrift für Ostmitteleuropa-Forschung* 58, no. 4 (2009): 493.

71. Hutten-Czapski, *Sechzig Jahre*, 2:508.

72. Werner Conze, *Polnische Nation und deutsche Politik im Ersten Weltkrieg* (Cologne: Böhlau, 1958), 387–388; Dudek, "Polish Military Formations," 462.

73. Hutten-Czapski, *Sechzig Jahre*, 2:511–512.

74. Conze, *Polnische Nation*, 392.

75. Andrzej Garlicki, *Drugiej Rzeczypospolitej Początki* (Wrocław: Wydawn. Dolnośląskie, 1996), 33–40.

76. Ulrich Kluge, *Soldatenräte und Revolution: Studien z. Militärpolitik in Deutschland 1918/1919* (Göttingen: Vandenhoeck & Ruprecht, 1975), 94–101.

77. Adolf Warschauer, *Deutsche Kulturarbeit in der Ostmark: Erinnerungen aus vier Jahrzehnten* (Berlin: R. Hobbing, 1926), 316.

78. Manteuffel, *Uniwersytet Warszawski*, 27.

79. Mieczysław Jankowski, "11 Listopada 1918 Roku," in *Warszawa w Pamiętnikach Pierwszej Wojny Światowej*, ed. Krzystof Dunin-Wąsowicz (Warsaw: Państwowy Instytut Wydawniczy, 1971), 486.

80. BA-MA/RH61 Kriegsgeschichtliche Forschungsanstalt des Herres /Vol. 15/ Bl. 5.

81. "Die November-Revolution in Warschau," 30 November 1922, GStA PK/VI. HA/Nachlass von Glasenapp/#29.

82. Ibid.

83. Starzyński, *Cztery lata*, 402–403.

84. Ibid., 406–409.

85. Conze, *Polnische Nation*, 399–400; Kluge, *Soldatenräte*, 97–101.

86. Lubomirska, *Pamiętnik*, 706–708.

87. Hutten-Czapski, *Sechzig Jahre*, 2:523.

88. Roos, *A History of Modern Poland*, 42–45.

89. Ibid., 50–51. Roos points out that the uprising had something of the quality of a civil war to it, as its organizational impetus was provided by the POW and was directed as much against National Democracy as against Prussia.

90. Richard Blanke, *Orphans of Versailles: The Germans in Western Poland, 1918–1939* (Lexington: University Press of Kentucky, 1993), 9–31, is an invaluable guide through this murky and complicated period.

91. BAB-L/N2126/406/261.

92. Dietrich Schäfer, *Die Schuld an der Wiederherstellung Polens* (Munich: Lehmanns, 1919). In Schäfer's telling of the story, one of the main culprits in Beseler's intellectual corruption was Max Sering, a professor of agriculture at Berlin University.

93. "Die November-Revolution in Warschau," 30 November 1922, GStA PK/VI. HA/Nachlass von Glassenapp/#29.

94. Theobald von Bethmann Hollweg, *Betrachtungen zum Weltkriege* (Berlin: R. Hobbing, 1921), 2:89–93. Quote from page 91. Bethmann's defense is candor itself compared with Hindenburg's total postwar rejection of any responsibility for the state's Polenpolitik and his rather petulant assertion that Beseler had not, technically, been part of his chain of command. Paul von Hindenburg, *Aus meinem Leben* (Leipzig: Hirzel, 1934), 162–165.

95. Hutten-Czapski, *Sechzig Jahre*, 2:531.

96. Arthur Rhode, *Erinnerungen an die Kriegszeit 1914–1920 in der Provinz Posen* (Herne: Stiftung Martin-Opitz-Bibliothek, 2003), 116.

97. Ibid., 114.

98. Reichstag, *Stenographische Berichte über die Verhandlungen der Deutschen Nationalversammlung* (Berlin: Druck und Verlag der Norddeutschen Buchdruckerei und Verlags-Anstalt, 1920), 326:509.

99. Hutten-Czapski, *Sechzig Jahre*, 2:531–532.

100. 29 July 1919. Reichstag, *Stenographische Berichte über die Verhandlungen der Deutschen Nationalversammlung* (Berlin: Druck und Verlag der Norddeutschen Buchdruckerei und Verlags-Anstalt, 1920), 328:2056.

101. Kries, "Staatsverwaltung," 157–158.

102. BAK/N 1711 Nachlass Wolfgang von Kries /8/21.

103. Willehalm, *Jüdische Soldaten-Räte in Polen. Verräterische Machenschaften beim deutschen Rückzuge* (Leipzig: Hammer-Verlag, 1922), 5–7.

104. BAMA/RH61/Vol. 13/22–23.

105. BAMA/RH61/Vol. 13/31.

106. Cf. John Connelly, "Nazis and Slavs: From Racial Theory to Racist Practice," *Central European History* 32, no. 1 (1999): 1–33.

Conclusion

1. Heinrich Himmler, "Einige Gedanken über die Behandlung der Fremdvölkischen im Osten," May 1940. Reprinted in *Vierteljahrshefte für Zeitgeschichte* 5, no. 2 (1957): 196–198; here 197.

2. The information on Siemieński and Handelsman is taken from their respective entries in the *Polski Słownik Biograficzny*.

3. Daniel Philpott, *Revolutions in Sovereignty: How Ideas Shaped Modern International Relations* (Princeton, N.J.: Princeton University Press, 2001), 11–15.

4. See http://www.historians.org/info/aha_history/sheehan.cfm.

5. David Stevenson, *The First World War and International Politics* (Oxford: Oxford University Press, 1988), 119–120.

6. Quoted in Wiktor Sukiennicki, *East Central Europe during World War I: From Foreign Domination to National Independence* (Boulder, Colo.: East European Monographs, 1984), 1:328.

7. M. K. Dziewanowski, *Joseph Piłsudski: A European Federalist, 1918–1922* (Stanford, Calif.: Hoover Institution Press, 1969).

8. Stevenson, *The First World War*, 117; David Stevenson, *French War Aims against Germany, 1914–1919* (Oxford: Clarendon Press, 1982), 166–167.

9. Alfred Cobban, *The Nation-State and National Self-Determination* (London: Collins, 1969), 62–65.

10. Ibid., 75–84.

11. See (in addition to de Schaepdrijver, *La Belgique*), Franz Petri, "Zur Flamenpolitik des 1. Weltkrieges," in *Dauer und Wandel der Geschichte*, ed. Rudolf Vierhaus (Münster: Aschendorff, 1966), 513–536.

12. Although cited in the introduction, Alexander Prusin's *The Lands Between: Conflict in the East European Borderlands, 1870–1992* (Oxford: Oxford University Press, 2010) deserves a second mention, as it is the absolutely indispensable guide through these awful political thickets.

13. Ibid., 128–129.

14. Jonathan Gumz, "Norms of War and the Austro-Hungarian Encounter with Serbia, 1914–1918," *First World War Studies* 4, no. 1 (March 2013): 97–110; quote from p. 110.

15. I deal more extensively with the origins and nature of the *Grenzstreifen* in "The Colonial U-Turn: Why Poland Is Not Germany's India," in *Cultural Landscapes: Transatlantische Perspektiven auf Wirkungen und Auswirkungen deutscher Kultur und Geschichte im östlichen Europa,* ed. Andrew Demshuk and Tobias Weger (forthcoming).

16. Quoted in Max Hastings, *Armageddon: The Battle for Germany* (New York: Vintage, 2005) 264. For a stimulating reflection on the place of ethnic cleansing in European history, see Philipp Ther, "Pre-negotiated Violence: Ethnic Cleansing in the 'Long' First World War," in *Legacies of Violence: Eastern Europe's First World War,* ed. Jochen Böhler, Włodzimierz Borodziej, and Joachim von Puttkamer (Munich: Oldenbourg Verlag, 2014), 259–284.

17. Richard Blanke, *Orphans of Versailles: The Germans in Western Poland, 1918–1939* (Lexington: University Press of Kentucky, 1993), 121.

18. Weinberg, *Foreign Policy of Hitler's Germany: A Diplomatic Revolution in Europe 1933–1936* (Atlantic Highlands, N.J.: Humanities Press, 1994) 13–14.

19. As argued in Alan Kramer, *Dynamic of Destruction: Culture and Mass Killing in the First World War* (Oxford: Oxford University Press, 2007).

20. 16 December 1917. Bundesarchiv-Militärarchiv, Freiburg-im-Breisgau/ N30 Nachlass Hans Hartwig von Beseler /55/p. 153.

21. Włodzimierz Borodziej, *Geschichte Polens im 20. Jahrhundert* (Munich: C. H. Beck, 2010). See also Stephan Lehnstaedt, "Dwie (różne) okupacje? Polityka gospodarcza Niemiec i Austro-Węgier w Królestwie Polskim w latach 1915–1918," *Dzieje Najnowsze* 45 (2013): 17–33.

22. Jan Gross, *Polish Society under German Occupation: The Generalgouvernement, 1939–1944* (Princeton, N.J.: Princeton University Press, 1979), 229.

23. Mordechai Altshuler, "Escape and Evacuation of Soviet Jews at the Time of the Nazi Invasion: Policies and Realities," in *The Holocaust in the Soviet Union: Studies and Sources on the Destruction of the Jews in the Nazi-Occupied Territories of the USSR, 1941–1945,* ed. Lucjan Dobroszycki and Jeffrey S. Gurock (Armonk, N.Y.: M. E. Sharpe, 1993), 77–104.

24. Carl von Clausewitz, *Historical and Political Writings,* ed. and trans. Peter Paret and Daniel Moran (Princeton, N.J.: Princeton University Press, 1992), 373.

Acknowledgments

The origins of this book can be traced back to the undergraduate courses I took at UCLA with Robert Wohl, who first kindled and then encouraged my fascination with the Great War as well as my desire to pursue a life in history. I had the extraordinary good fortune to continue my studies at the graduate level at Stanford University, where I worked under the guidance of James J. Sheehan. Jim's generosity of spirit is matched only by his exacting standards and high expectations. Jim was—and is—a *Doktorvater* in the best possible sense of that term. Norman Naimark, Amir Weiner, and Paul Robinson were outstanding teachers and mentors who also played important roles in my intellectual, personal, and professional development at Stanford. I remain deeply grateful to them all.

Roger Chickering, Christopher Clark, Gregor Thum, John Merriman, Michael Meng, and Margaret Lavinia Anderson have all been invaluable sources of insight, criticism, and encouragement. Brian Porter-Szűcs and Robert Blobaum shared freely of their time and expertise. Richard Blanke provided me with a copy of his book *Prussian Poland in the German Empire*. Vejas Liulevicius has been unfailingly kind and helpful since I first met him over a decade ago, even though he has always known that this project is, in part, a response to *War Land*. He is truly a scholar and a gentleman. John Horne, Michael Neiberg, and Oberst Dr. Gerhard P. Groß provided moral and intellectual support at crucial moments in this project's evolution. I have had many rewarding conversations on the topic of occupations during the Great War with Marta Polsakiewicz, Stephan Lehnstaedt, and Jonathan Gumz.

One of the rewards peculiar to academic life is that the bonds of common intellectual interests are sometimes reinforced and strengthened by the bonds of sympathetic friendship. In this respect, I have been fortunate to know James Ward, Ari Sammartino, Eli Rubin, and, primus inter pares, Winson Chu.

The staff members of the Polish Army Museum in Warsaw, especially Emilia Jastrzębka, graciously and enthusiastically provided their assistance. David Brown of the Leo Baeck Institute in New York and Frau Berit Walter of the Bundesarchiv's photo section in Koblenz were friendly, knowledgeable, and extremely helpful—not qualities that can be taken for granted. Jakub Zapała was a first-rate research assistant. Andrzej Kamiński, Andrzej Nowak, and Adam Kożuchowski provided useful insights during the 2014 meeting of the workshop "Recovering Forgotten History: The Image of East-Central Europe in English-Language Textbooks." My participation in the workshop was facilitated by my editor at Harvard, Kathleen McDermott, whose professionalism is beyond compare. I was able to present portions of this work at the Fortieth Congress of the International Commission of Military History at Varna, Bulgaria, in September 2014 thanks to the support of the US Commission on Military History and its president, Dr. Richard Stewart. Kristjan Luts, Toomas Hiio, and Sandra Niinepuu of the Estonian War Museum–General Laidoner Museum arranged for my attendance at their conference devoted to the Great War in Central Europe. The German Academic Exchange Service (DAAD) provided the funding for the initial research for this project. My Polish-language study was enabled by a Foreign Language and Area Studies (FLAS) grant.

I have found a very happy professional home in the History Section at Eastern Michigan University. Steven Ramold, John McCurdy, and Ron Delph have been great colleagues, mentors, and friends. Department Head Richard Nation has done an admirable job of balancing our department's commitment to teaching with support for research. Rachel Schulz provided reliably cheerful secretarial help. Marty Shichtman, head of the Jewish Studies Program, and Art and Mary Schuman supported conference and research travel for this book. Eastern Michigan University provided further support in the form of a one-semester Faculty Research Fellowship as well as a Provost's Research Fund Grant. University Librarian Tara Lynn Fulton and the staff of EMU's Halle Library do an excellent, and often thankless, job of balancing the many competing demands on their resources. I could not have written this book without them—in particular the outstanding interlibrary loan staff, who are second to none. Thank you for all your hard work.

My greatest debts are to my family. My parents, Mary and Curtis Kauffman-Pickelle, are generous beyond compare. My parents-in-law, Tomas Lindahl and Alice Adams, both provided help of various kinds along the way. Above all, my wife, Lena, has been a source of support, solace, and joy. She has had to share in the burdens that go along with building an academic career without being able to share fully in the rewards. In periods of bleak professional frustration, I would sometimes console myself by imagining how it would feel to be able to finally write these acknowledgments. It is entirely thanks to her that I now know.

Index